W9-BAK-051

MYSTERY READER'S WALKING GUIDE:

CHICAGO

Praise for Mystery Reader's Walking Guide: CHICAGO

"What a wonderful way for everybody who loves mysteries to see the greatest city in the world. Even native Chicagoans like me will be astonished to find how many mysteries are acted out on its streets."

—Andrew Greeley

"Every mystery reader should buy this book. Alzina Dale evokes the spirit of Chicago and the very essence of the Chicago mystery."

—Barbara D'Amato

"This is not only an entertaining summary of Chicago-based mystery fiction, but a darned good general guide to my former hometown. I enjoyed it and I feel sure all those interested in Chicago and/or the mystery will enjoy it too."

—Elizabeth Peters

"I was delighted with the book, and not just because it mentions my books—though that certainly didn't hurt. It is a clever, well-informed, witty book full of humor, mystery lore, Chicago legends, urban apocrypha, and just plain gossip....The Urban Jungle won't seem like such a hard place with a guide like Alzina Stone Dale."

—Michael Raleigh

"Alzina Stone Dale demonstrates an insider's knowledge of her city, which she is gratefully willing to share with her readers—and if you take her 'walks' some of it might rub off on you."

—Edward Baumann

MYSTERY READER'S WALKING GUIDE: CHICAGO

ALZINA STONE DALE

Printed on recyclable paper

PASSPORT BOOKS
a division of *NTC Publishing Group*
Lincolnwood, Illinois USA

Dedication

For Chuck,
because Chicago is really his native heath.

M.A.D.

Library of Congress Cataloging-in-Publication Data

Dale, Alzina Stone, 1931–
Mystery reader's walking guide, Chicago / Alzina Stone Dale ; interior maps by Ben Stone.
p. cm.
Includes bibliographical references and index.
ISBN 0-8442-9607-4
1. Literary landmarks—Illinois—Chicago—Guidebooks. 2. Detective and mystery stories, American—Illinois—Chicago—History and criticism. 3. Walking—Illinois—Chicago—Guidebooks. 4. Chicago (Ill.)—In literature. 5. Chicago (Ill.)—Guidebooks. I. Title.
PS144.C4D35 1995
813′.0872093277311—dc20 94-33414
CIP

Cover illustration by John Babcock.

Published by Passport Books, a division of NTC Publishing Group,
4255 West Touhy Avenue,
Lincolnwood (Chicago), Illinois 60646-1975 U.S.A.

Manufactured in the United States of America.

5 6 7 8 9 VP 9 8 7 6 5 4 3 2 1

CONTENTS

MAPS

Acknowledgments

I must begin by thanking Sara Paretsky, who as MWA Midwest's president, asked Barbara Sloan Hendershott and me to prepare a Chicago "scene of the crime" bus tour for our first meeting of the year. (It was while planning that excursion that Sara and my dog April became enthusiastically acquainted.) As a result of the tour, I wrote an armchair walk for the *Chicago Sun-Times' Book Week*, gave a Newberry Library Lyceum course on Mysterious Chicago, repeated the bus tour for the Friends of the Harold Washington Library, and wrote this book.

For the books I needed to read I relied upon Judy Duhl and Susan Hoelschen at Scotland Yard Books, Marilyn Roth at the Bridgman Public Library, and Rebecca Reynolds at Fifty-Seventh Street Books. Countless friends gave me, loaned me, or told me of mysteries I had never known, from mystery experts like Bill Deeck and Mike Nevins and Betty Nicholas, editor of MWA's *Third Degree*, to Ellie Reed Koppe of Boulder and my childhood chum Damaris Hendry Day, who turned out to be Craig Rice's cousin! Ed Baumann not only sent me his true crime books but read the entire typescript to catch my errors.

Chicago mystery writer friends like Marion Markham and Arthur Maling not only encouraged me, but our entire MWA chapter generously showered me with copies of their books in every shape imaginable, from typescripts and page proofs to the loan of a cherished, single remaining hardback copy: among them are Paul Dale Anderson, Eleanor Taylor Bland, Martin Blank, D. C. Brod, Michael Cormany, Barbara D'Amato, Marc Davis, Michael Dymmoch, Paul Engleman, Richard Engling, John Fink, Roslynn Griffith, Robert Goldsborough, Hugh Holton, Richard Hyer, D. J. H. Jones, William F. Love, Thomas McCall, Michael Raleigh, Sam Reaves, William Sherer, Mark Zubro, and the late Mary Craig, president of both our MWA Chapter and the national MWA.

My Chicago family, friends, and neighbors like Harriet Rylaarsdam, Elizabeth Dale, Damaris Day, Louise Howe, and Susan Hoelschen not only read and made notes on mysteries, but also read the walks as well. Others like Lenore Melzer,

Betsey Bobrinskoy, and George Stone checked out the walks for accuracy. The hardiest group of all walked the walks with me; they included April, Charles Dale, Susan Hoelschen, and Louise Howe.

As a native-born Chicagoan and mystery fan, this guide was a delight to write. The only problem was keeping the book down to a handy size that can be carried on a walk.

INTRODUCTION

How to Use This Guide

Chicago is a major character in mysteries set there. As Bill Granger explained in *The Newspaper Murders*, "this is a story set in a real place, in a real time. But it is fiction. Despite this, the names of real streets, public buildings, taverns, restaurants, parks, and neighborhoods are used because to do otherwise would destroy the illusion of reality."

Chicago's writers alternately try to reform the city or try to take advantage of its reputation, so they write few "private" or cozy stories that do not also have a public side. Just as a foreigner always greets a Chicagoan by pointing his finger and shouting "Bang! bang! bang!," so everyone "knows" that the Chicago Machine can still deliver the vote and that the Mob is still "connected" to its police and politicians.

Chicago's mystery writers also use what Barbara D'Amato calls the Chicago style: gritty, straightforward, and aggressive, to describe the "city that works," despite mayoral floods or snows. Although the distinctive ingredients are still gangsters, crooked cops and politicians, or venal sports stars and brash investigative reporters, Chicago writers also cover other beats from hookers to traders. Many fictional Chicagoans, like Sara Paretsky's V.I. Warshawski, grouse that Chicago's weather is either "August or winter," but others like Andrew Greeley's Father Blackie Ryan, celebrate the city on an October day as a "sacrament."

The image of Chicago projected in mysteries persists in being a bit lopsided. Often there is a time warp, suggesting that

Chicago still has steel mills and stockyards and the world's number one gangster: Al Capone. In *The Million Dollar Deposit*, British E. Phillips Oppenheim, writing about a daring London burglary, had to import a Chicago gangster to turn the trick. Harry Stephen Keeler in *The Washington Square Enigma* called Chicago the "London of the West," raw and lively and commercial, the most American of all cities, but no place to be down and out. In "The Mistake of the Machine," G. K. Chesterton put Father Brown in Chicago as a prison chaplain to his co-religionists "when the Irish population displayed a capacity for both crime and penitence. . . ." Chicago reporters Ben Hecht and Charles MacArthur's comedy *The Front Page*—about a real Chicago crime—set the model for the reporters and investigators who populate Chicago mysteries, just as W. R. Burnett's *Little Caesar* forever labeled Chicago as gangland heaven.

Chicago's makeup as a city of ethnic neighborhoods is shown more by the use of real place names, streets, stores and restaurants, churches and bars than by actual sleuths' forays into the hinterlands. In mysteries, the very rich live on the Gold Coast or affluent North Shore, the Near West Side is Little Italy, where you can hire a hood, North Michigan Avenue has replaced State Street as *the* shopping place, and Lincoln Park is the scene of singles action or quiet contemplation by the lake or zoo. You may stray south to Hyde Park, the university community with special ties to intellectual murder, or dump bodies in Wolf Lake, but in mysteries as in real life, all Chicago roads lead to the Loop, which is still Chicago's main "scene of the crime."

As a result, these walks cover the central parts of the city. You can play cops and robbers through the Loop, trace rich gangsters or businessmen to their Gold Coast lairs, stumble on murdered tourists along the lakefront, watch murder done in Streeterville's classy high rises, or meet mayhem shopping on the Magnificent Mile. You can walk through the gentrifying South Loop to see the remains of the First Ward's Levee and the old kingdom of Al Capone, both located cheek by jowls with the city's central "Cop Shop" and its world-famous museums.

Since Chicago is my home town and its mystery writers my friends, I have tried to include at least one story by every Chicagoan working today, as well as one or more "golden oldies" by Chicago's classic writers like Craig Rice, William P. McGivern, Jonathan Latimer, Robert Bloch, James Michael Ullman, Fredric Brown and Howard Browne, and Mignon G. Eberhart. To find their mysteries, I depended upon friends and libraries, especially the Harold Washington Library Center in the Loop. Inevitably, there will be some great ones you have read that I missed. Current Chicago authors generously gave both their time and their books to help me out.

I did not mention real-life crimes unless they also appeared in mystery fiction. This limitation came partly from space considerations: with true crime, the book would be twice as thick and hard to carry on your walks. But it also follows the format of the earlier books in the series, *Mystery Readers' Walking Guides: London, England,* and *New York* (referred to in text as *MRWG: London, England, NY*). I was glad not to give space to the late John Wayne Gacy, convicted of multiple murders. Gacy was long suspected of the murders of three young boys, but a new suspect has been charged, linking them to the Brach murder in a wild tale of horses worthy of Dick Francis himself.

Walking in Chicago is a great visual treat because the city is blessed with many world-class sculptures and buildings, so be sure to stop and stare up every so often. Finding your way around is easy, because very few streets change names in midstream, and the city is designed on a simple grid system. To Chicagoans "Downtown" always means the "Loop" wherever you may be, and they instinctively orient themselves by Lake Michigan, which is always east. The true center of town is at the corner of State Street and Madison, Chicago's version of Times Square where Craig Rice pulled off two murders at Christmastime in *The Wrong Murder*. "West" means west of State, "east" is east of State, and both north and south of Madison Street the street numbers rise. Eight blocks in any direction roughly make a mile.

These walks begin with a brief historical introduction, followed by a list of Places of Interest such as the Art Institute or Marshall Field's, Places to Eat such as the Berghoff, and a map of the walk. Each walk begins in an easy-to-find location, such as the Michigan Avenue Bridge or the Daley Center Picasso, and includes directions on how to reach its starting point. The walks are neighborhood oriented, so if you want to follow only the footsteps of Craig Rice's John J. Malone or Sara Paretsky's V.I. Warshawski, look them up in the walk by walk lists of authors, books, and sleuths or in the index.

Places of Interest are must-see treasures of the city, while the Places to Eat, which range from very expensive to simple fare, are either those mentioned in a mystery or ones you pass on the walk. Spots for pit stops or resting your feet are suggested, too. Unlike those in New York, Chicago's hotel lobbies continue to be hospitable, and there is always a McDonald's about. The length of each walk is indicated; if it is longer than two miles, it is divided into parts which you can do separately or on another day.

For all its criminal reputation, by day—like most big cities—Chicago is a safe place to walk if you remember that there may be panhandlers, pickpockets, and crowds. None of these walks is located in an area where people do not go and everywhere you will find cabs, see police on the streets, in their squads or even on horseback or bicycle. If every Chicagoan seems to have a tale of being on the scene when someone fired a shot on a busy street, remember that it is mostly civic pride; we like to keep our "criminal" legend alive and well. For, as Harold Klawans wrote in *Sins of Commission*, his sleuth, Dr. Paul Richardson had "proposed a tour of Chicago for a group of visiting European neurologists that would include . . . the Art Institute and the University of Chicago with its Henry Moore sculpture on the site of the first sustained atomic reaction. But all they wanted to see were Al Capone's old headquarters in the New Michigan Hotel, the garage where the St. Valentine's Day Massacre occurred, the Biograph Theater where Dillinger had been shot, and the Lone Star Saloon on South State Street where Mickey Finn earned immortal fame." On these walks you will see all the sinister places Klawans mentioned, so come have fun, but watch your step.

MYSTERY READER'S WALKING GUIDE:

CHICAGO

1

LAKEFRONT/ MUSEUMS WALK

BACKGROUND

The lakefront is the jewel in Chicago's crown, setting it apart from other big American cities. This spectacular front yard beside a vast inland sea, which stretches almost uninterrupted from Evanston in the north to the steel mills near Gary, intriguingly gives the lie to the common image of Chicago, the archetypical industrial city or the Dickensian gangster-ridden, greedy commercial den of thieves that mystery writer Harry Stephen Keeler liked to call the "London of the West."

Chicago's watery history began in a swamp of wild onions and sand dunes, where long ago French explorers and missionaries found that a portage of only a few miles separated the tiny Chicago River from the Des Plaines, the Illinois, and the Mississippi, linking the entire continent from Canada to the Gulf of Mexico. Railroads came next, then cars and the airplane, all keeping Chicago the hub of the country's transportation systems.

But Chicago is unique among the cities of the world because it has kept its lakefront "forever open, clear, and free," Ordinary citizens, as well as VIPs and startled visitors from around the world, can walk beside the lake and admire the green lawns that surround it, enjoying a view which Simone de Beauvoir compared to the Côte d'Azur, making it our own real-life Seurat's *Sunday on La Grande Jatte* every day of the year.

Keeping the lakefront open was a prolonged battle which still goes on today, but Chicagoans like fights, reformers versus the pols, temperance against the saloons, cops against criminals, and vice versa. The idea of keeping the lakefront for the public began in 1836 when the city was laying out tracts for development. As Lois Wille wrote later, "they made a promise that this city, hustler from its infancy, would do what no other city had done . . . it would give its most priceless land to its people." More importantly, the promise was written on the map.

This promise was incorporated in architect Daniel Burnham's Chicago Plan of 1909, where he wrote that the lakefront should be Chicago's playground because it "affords their one great unobstructed view, stretching to the horizon, where water and clouds seem to meet."

But the great fighter was one of Chicago's merchant princes, Montgomery Ward, who looked out of his Michigan Avenue office one day in 1890 and saw only garbage, shacks, circus litter, and a derelict armory used for the masquerade balls of the Lords of the Levee. It made Ward mad and he told his lawyers to find a way to preserve the lakefront. They found the words on the map, and twenty years and $50,000 later, they finally won in court. Only the Art Institute–and later the monstrous McCormick Place–permanently block the view east of Michigan Avenue, from Randolph Street on the north to Cermak Road on the south. But people keep trying, so there may yet be gambling boats or a Chicago lakefront Disney World. In the meantime, there are only a group of world renowned museums from Twelfth Street south, enhancing while not destroying the lakefront's magic.

Although most mystery writers admire the lakeshore, invariably they complain about Chicago's weather, which Sara Paretsky's V.I. Warshawski says is either August or winter.

Driving along the Outer Drive, V.I. also mentions the alewife plague, although the smelly little ocean-going fish die off less frequently these days. Other writers talk about fierce winds, especially the Hawk, while Mignon G. Eberhart suggests that a dense London-like fog is the prevailing scene of the crime.

Arthur Maling often sends his characters abroad in lousy weather. In *The Snowman*, merchandising executive Ches Novak took a cab north on Michigan Avenue on a wintry day when snow was snarling traffic. Bill Granger, another native, insists Chicago has great blizzards every year and murders tourists in Grant Park, while in William P. McGivern's *Very Cold for May* Jake Harrison left his club on Michigan Avenue to drive through a terrible snowstorm to meet a new client, war profiteer Dan Riordan.

But it is British Edgar Wallace in *On the Spot*, his one Chicago mystery, who mistakenly assumed that our gangsters freely dump their victims in the lake. He left traitor Victor Vinsetti, shot at close quarters, floating there with eighty soaked $1,000 bills in his pockets. In real life and in mysteries, Chicago bodies are far more likely to turn up in car trunks, dumpsters, Indiana, or Lincoln Park, while the lakefront museums make wonderful places to chase a murderer or corner a cop.

LENGTH OF WALK: 4½ miles

This walk is divided into two parts. Lakefront North is about 2½ miles; Lakefront South is 2 miles. You may easily decide to do half one time and the other half another. See the maps on pages 7 and 34 for the boundaries of this walk and page 335 for a list of the books and detectives mentioned.

PLACES OF INTEREST

Adler Planetarium, 1300 S. Lake Shore Drive. Open daily 9:30 A.M.–5:00 P.M. year-round and 9:00 P.M. on Fridays. Planetarium admission free, fee for Skyshow. Call 322-0300.*

*The area code for Chicago is 312. Other area codes will be noted.

Art Institute of Chicago, 111 S. Michigan Avenue. Open every day except Thanksgiving and Christmas. Open Wed., Thur., Fri. 10:30 A.M.–4:30 P.M., Tues. 10:30 A.M.–8:00 P.M., Sunday and holidays noon–5:00 P.M. Fee. Admission free on Tuesdays. Call 443-3600.

Buckingham Fountain. Grant Park. Daily May 1–Oct. 1 11:00 A.M.–11:00 P.M.

Chicago Cultural Center, 78 E. Washington. Open Mon.–Thur. 9:00 A.M.–5:00 P.M., Fri. 9:00 A.M.–6:00 P.M., Sat. 9:00 A.M.–6:00 P.M., Sun. noon–5:00 P.M. Call 744-6630. Inside is the ***Museum of Broadcast Communications***. Open 10:00 A.M.–4:30 P.M. Mon.–Sat., noon–5:00 P.M. Sun. Closed on all state and national holidays. Call 629-6000.

Columbia College, 600 S. Michigan Avenue. Museum of Contemporary Photography. Call 663-5554.

Field Museum of Natural History, S. Lake Shore Drive and McFetridge. Open daily 9:00 A.M.–5:00 P.M. Admission free on Thursdays. Call 922-9410.

Fine Arts Building (Studebaker Building), 410 S. Michigan Avenue. At street level is **Bookseller's Row**, 408 S. Michigan. Open Sun. noon–10:00 P.M., Mon.–Thur. 10:00 A.M.–10:00 P.M., Fri.–Sat. 10:00 A.M.–10:30 P.M. Call 427-4242.

I Love a Mystery Bookstore, 55 E. Washington, mezzanine, Suite 250 (in the Pittsfield Building). Mostly paperbacks. Open Mon.–Fri. 10:00 A.M.–5:00 P.M. Call 236-1338.

Mayfair Theater, 636 S. Michigan Avenue (in the Blackstone Hotel). *Shear Madness*. Call 786-9120.

Orchestra Hall, 220 S. Michigan Avenue. Home of the Chicago Symphony Orchestra. Subscription season mid-September through mid-June, plus concerts by the Civic Orchestra. Tickets to Civic concerts are free, but by mail order only. Call 435-6666.

Railway Exchange Building (Santa Fe Building), Jackson Boulevard and Michigan Avenue. At street level is the ***Chicago Architecture Foundation*** Shop and Tour Center, 224 S. Michigan. Open Mon.–Fri. 9:00 A.M.–6:00 P.M., Sat.–Sun. 10:00 A.M.–5:00 P.M. Call 922-3432.

Roosevelt University: Auditorium Theater, 50 E. Congress Parkway. Call the Box Office at 559-2900.

The Savvy Traveller, 50 E. Washington Street (at Garland Court), second floor. Open Mon.–Wed., Fri., Sat. 10:00 A.M.–6:00 P.M., Thur. 10:00 A.M.–7:00 P.M. Call 587-0808.

John G. Shedd Aquarium, 1200 S. Lake Shore Drive. Open daily 9:00 A.M.–6:00 P.M. Fees for both Aquarium and Oceanarium. Aquarium admission free on Thursdays. Call 939-2426.

Soldier Field, McFetridge Drive and S. Lake Shore Drive.

Spertus Museum of Judaica, 618 S. Michigan Avenue. Open Sun.–Thur. 10:00 A.M.–5:00 P.M., Fri. 10:00 A.M.–3:00 P.M. Fee. Call 922-9012.

TOURS

Chicago Motor Coach Co., London Red double-decker bus tours starting in front of the Art Institute. Call 929-8919.

Chicago Trolley Co., Various stops downtown and on the Near North Side. Call 738-0900.

PLACES TO EAT

Americana-Congress Hotel, 520 S. Michigan Avenue: Annie's, Buckingham Pub, Gazebo Coffee Shop, Sweet and Simple Eatery, Tavern Tap.

Art Institute, Michigan Avenue at Adams Street: Court Cafeteria, Court Restaurant, Restaurant on the Park.

Bennigan's, People's Gas Building, Adams and Michigan.

Blackstone Hotel, 636 S. Michigan Avenue: Chequers, Jazz Limited.

Chicago Hilton and Towers Hotel, 720 S. Michigan Avenue: Buckingham's; Kitty O'Shea (authentic Irish pub with live music).

Field Museum, S. Lake Shore Drive and McFetridge: McDonald's (in the basement on east side).

George Mitchell's Artists Snack Shop, Fine Arts Building, 410 S. Michigan Avenue.

Hyatt Regency Hotel, 151 E. Wacker Drive: Bigs, the Fountain, Seasons, and Stetson's.

LAKEFRONT NORTH

Begin your walk at Buckingham Fountain, set in the middle of Grant Park between Lake Michigan and the Congress/Eisenhower Expressway. It was meant to accent the broad avenue that Daniel Burnham planned would lead west to major government buildings. Instead, Congress takes you west to join the Eisenhower Expressway. Made of pink marble and lit up on summer nights, the Beaux Arts fountain with its bronze dolphins and computer-programed lights was given to the city by Miss Kate Buckingham in memory of her brother in 1927. Chicagoans insist it is larger than the one outside Louis XIV's palace at Versailles.

You can reach Buckingham Fountain by way of the Metra/South Station at Van Buren and Michigan—a handsomely restored caramel-colored bit of Victoriana—or by bus or car. There is parking in the South Grant Park Underground Garage at Van Buren and Michigan Avenue, with pedestrian exits at Jackson and Adams.

But be sure to lock your car and look inside when you return. In Sara Paretsky's *Indemnity Only*, her private eye V.I. (Victoria Iphigenia) Warshawski parked there to go to her office on Wabash. In the past V.I. hadn't been worried about parking there, but today she didn't want the long walk through that cool, damp, and not too brightly lit tomb of cars. In Stuart Kaminsky's *When the Dark Man Calls*, radio talk-show emcee Jean Kaiser was also jumpy when she parked there en route to her psychiatrist's office in an old building on Wabash. When Kaiser was small her parents were murdered; now she was being followed by their released killer.

Worse yet, in Michael Cormany's *Red Winter*, his '60s-style P.I. Dan Kruger agreed to meet Israel Lipke, one of the Leftist group he had been scouting for rich contractor Nicholas Cheyney, near a pillar in the garage. Cheyney hired Kruger to find out who was trying to blackball him from membership in Chicago's most prestigious club. Kruger found Lipke shot to death in a beat-up old blue car. He searched the body, then told the gum-chewing garage cashier that somebody in a blue Ford looked sick. The cashier said thanks, but didn't look up.

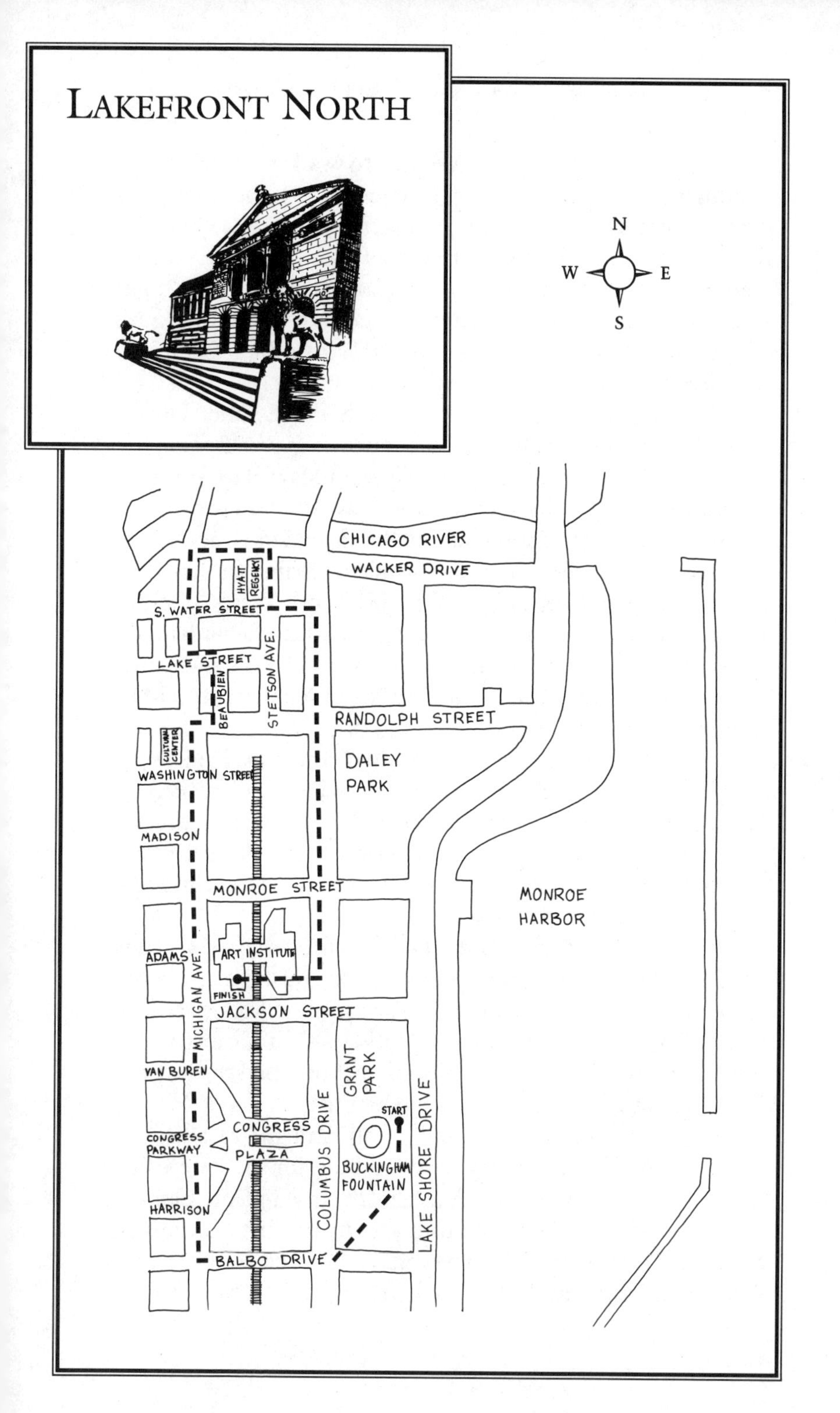
LAKEFRONT NORTH
N
W
E
S
CHICAGO RIVER
WACKER DRIVE
HYATT REGENCY
S. WATER STREET
LAKE STREET
BEAUBIEN
STETSON AVE.
RANDOLPH STREET
CULTURAL CENTER
WASHINGTON STREET
DALEY PARK
MADISON
MONROE STREET
MONROE HARBOR
ADAMS
ART INSTITUTE
FINISH
MICHIGAN AVE.
JACKSON STREET
GRANT PARK
VAN BUREN
LAKE SHORE DRIVE
COLUMBUS DRIVE
START
CONGRESS PARKWAY
CONGRESS
PLAZA
BUCKINGHAM FOUNTAIN
HARRISON
BALBO DRIVE

If you cross Michigan Avenue to walk to Buckingham Fountain, you see the two 1929 equestrian Indian statues by Ivan Mestrovic, recently recoated so they look like chocolate. To your far left in the park is the small (also chocolate-colored) statue of Abraham Lincoln by Augustus St. Gaudens. You are crossing a viaduct over the railroad tracks as did Swedish tourist Maj Kirsten in Bill Granger's *The Public Murders*. Kirsten was murdered near the baseball fields in Grant Park.

Cross Columbus Drive (also known as the Inner Drive)—carefully, the traffic lights are not much help—to Buckingham Fountain. The fountain operates daily from May 30 to September 30 but is boarded up from October to May. In warm weather you will not only see the display but find food vendors all about.

In Sara Paretsky's *Blood Shot*, while searching for her childhood friend's missing father, V.I. had Tenth Ward Alderman Art Jurshak's son Art Jr. set up a wintry rendezvous with his dad at the boarded up fountain. V.I. took a bus down Michigan Avenue and waited, armed, in the rose garden just south of the fountain until she saw Jurshak's limo drive up.

In Mark Zubro's *Sorry Now*, his two detectives Paul Turner and Buck Fenwick were told by Bruce Davidson, a University of Chicago student who was the head of FUCK-EM, that the cops used brutality when they had a demonstration. Turner replied that the demonstrators were camped out in Buckingham Fountain, which upset old ladies.

In John D. MacDonald's *One Fearful Yellow Eye*, Travis McGee came to Chicago to play white knight on a charger for the widow of wealthy Dr. Fortner Geis. Before McGee arrived, Geis's 5-year-old grandson was kidnaped in Evanston and driven to Grant Park, where the kidnaper dumped the boy near Buckingham Fountain to be found by the park police.

After admiring the fountain, walk straight east to Lake Shore Drive. The elegant stairway was built for the state visit of Queen Elizabeth II who sailed here from Windsor, Ontario, and was greeted at Chicago's front yard by the first Mayor Richard Daley. East of the Drive you can see Monroe Harbor, full of sailboats in summer. To your left (north) is the Chicago Yacht

Club, to your right the cluster of museums which occupy the site of the 1933–34 Century of Progress world's fair.

Shipboard murders make superb locked room mysteries. In Barbara D'Amato's *Hard Tack*, free-lancer Catherine ("Cat") Marsala (who hates water) was assigned to take a weekend sail to Michigan in the Honeywells's 62-foot yacht *Easy Girl*. *Chicago Today* (a defunct Chicago newspaper) wanted Cat to get a line on "How the Other Half Lives" the week before the Mackinac Race from Chicago to Mackinac Island. The Honeywells and their family and friends belonged to old Chicago money, but one of their guests was murdered on board during a violent lake storm.

In Michael W. Sherer's *An Option on Death*, writer cum P.I. Emerson Ward met Martha Culbertson at the Chicago Yacht Club (which of the two locations is not specified). Martha turned out to have her own sinister agenda and Ward barely escaped with his life.

In Michael Raleigh's *A Body in Belmont Harbor*, P.I. Paul Whelan talked to Chicago Detective Bauman about the suicide of Philip Fairs, who doused himself and his yacht with kerosene and lit a match. Bauman told him other "richies" on a boat off the Belmont breakwater recognized the Fairs boat, knew the guy, saw it go boom—pieces of boat all over the lake. The body was found about a week later in Monroe Harbor, caught up in the anchor lines of one of the big sailboats.

In Andrew Greeley's *Happy Are Those Who Thirst for Justice*, young Fionna Downs was accused of shooting her grandmother, dictatorial family matriarch Violet Enright. They were aboard Enright's yacht *Violetta*, moored just past the breakwater in Monroe Harbor. Fionna had fantasized about shooting her nasty ancestor but went to pieces when accused of the crime. Fortunately for Fionna, her psychiatrist, Mary Kathleen Ryan Murphy (sister of Monsignor John Blackwood Ryan, aka Father Blackie) was nearby in a sailboat.

Turn right (south) and follow the sidewalk along S. Lake Shore Drive to the place where it takes a diagonal slant to the right through the rose garden back to the corner of Balbo and

Columbus Drive. Cross Columbus Drive and walk west on Balbo to Michigan Avenue.

Cross Michigan Avenue to the Sheraton Blackstone Hotel at 636 S. Michigan Avenue. Just west of the Blackstone Hotel is the old Blackstone Theater, now owned by DePaul University and called the Merle Reskin Theater.

The entrance to the Blackstone Hotel is on Balbo. Go up the steps to its elegant little lobby. In older mysteries, the Blackstone, built in 1911 in French Renaissance style, hosted foreign tourists and presidents, and it was here that Warren Harding was summoned around 2 A.M. to Suite 804–5, the original "smoke-filled room," and asked if he had any secrets that would make him a bad candidate. He did, but he didn't tell.

You can rest here in wood-paneled decor under huge chandeliers, or use the phone or the restrooms on the ground floor. Unlike many New York hotels, Chicago's are still hospitable to strangers. (See *Mystery Reader's Walking Guide: New York*.)

In the lobby Joe Segal's Jazz Showcase is to your left. In D. J. H. Jones's *Murder at the MLA*, assistant professor of English Nancy Cook, who was "assisting the police with their inquiries" into a series of murders at the MLA Convention, made a date with a younger colleague to go to Joe Segal's Jazz Showcase. Cook turned out to be a very knowledgeable tourist who wanted to try all of Chicago's goodies, and got detective Boaz Dixon to escort her to many of them.

The entrance to the Mayfair Theater is on the right where the hotel restaurant was once. The comedy whodunit *Shear Madness* has been running there since 1981, combining audience participation with dinner. There no longer is a separate Blackstone restaurant whose windows look out on Grant Park, but on the ground floor at the south corner of the Blackstone Hotel is the Chequers Grill, a coffee shop with old-fashioned booths.

In Harry Keeler's madcap mystery *Behind That Mask*, Chicago detective Terry O'Rourke went to the Blackstone Hotel to see a publisher, John Macrae of E. P. Dutton, bringing a story David Rand had written about the recent murder of his boss, magazine owner Jack Kenwood. In Keeler's *Thieves' Nights* super jewel thief Bayard DeLancey stayed at the Blackstone, pretending to be East Indian Jagat Singh, a representative of the Maharaja of Bahawalpur. DeLancey was after the rare red fire emerald of tycoon John Atwood.

In British Edgar Wallace's *On the Spot*, young Harvard grad and gangster-in-training Jimmy McGrath claimed he was at a show at the Blackstone when a rival gang leader was shot. In Mignon G. Eberhart's *The Glass Slipper*, Cinderella bride Rue Hatterick and her chief-of-staff husband's handsome assistant Andrew Crittenden lunched at the Blackstone. They ate in a mellowed room overlooking the lake with crimson-shaded lamps on the tables with an ensemble playing softly, making it a safe comfortable world—until angry Dr. Brule Hatterick turned up.

In Ross Thomas's *The Porkchoppers*, Porkchopper union boss Donald Cubbin stayed there in a palatial suite whenever he came to Chicago. He had come to make sure a union election turned out right when he was murdered. In McGivern's *Very Cold for May*, Daniel Riordan, a war profiteer, lived there. When his ex-girlfriend May Duval was murdered after she decided to write her memoirs, Riordan hired Jake Harrison to defend his life and his honor (if any).

Come out of the Blackstone's Michigan Avenue door and turn left to walk up Michigan Avenue to the MBIA Bookstore in the Columbia College building at 624 S. Michigan. Take a look inside. In William Targ's *The Case of Mr. Cassidy*, Hugh Morris, an amateur sleuth cum bibliophile, checked out nearly every bookstore in the Loop, looking for a cheap copy of Poe's first work, *Tamerlane*. Missing Poe manuscripts are popular with mystery writers: a Poe short story was the reason for murder in John Dickson Carr's *The Mad Hatter Mystery*. (See *MRWG: London*.)

Next to the bookstore is the Spertus Museum of Judaica, with exhibits of Jewish history and holidays. Until the opening of a similar room in the Smithsonian museum in Washington, D.C., it had the only permanent room dedicated to the memory of the six million Jews killed in Hitler's Holocaust. Next to Spertus you pass an open space with a statue, then on the corner, the Columbia College building, housing its Museum of Contemporary Photography. Columbia College began as a radio-TV school but has branched out into all the arts. Both Spertus Museum and Columbia College are worth exploring.

Then go on north to Harrison. Cross Harrison Street and keep going north on Michigan Avenue past a closed motel to the Americana Congress Hotel at 520 S. Michigan. It stretches to the Congress Expressway, occupying the rest of this block. Built by Holabird & Root in 1893 in the famous Chicago School style, the hotel has vertical banks of projecting oriel windows, giving maximum light and a sense of movement to the facade. Its handsome lobby has several places where you can sit down, especially at the north end where the Buckingham Pub looks out at Grant Park. There are a number of other restaurants: Annie's, the Tavern Tap, the Sweet and Simple Eatery in the lobby itself, and the Gazebo Coffee Shop.

The Gazebo is probably the best location for the continuous gathering of mystery writers and fans in Max Allan Collins's amusing "faction" about a Bouchercon Convention, *Kill Your Darlings*. (The title is borrowed from the advice given all tyro writers to "kill your darlings," or cut your favorite purple passages.) An aging mystery mentor called Roscoe Kane (Mickey Spillane with a dash of Dashiell Hammett), drunk and down on his luck, was found murdered in his hotel bath. Kane's chief disciple, a young Iowa mystery writer called Mallory, tried to solve the crime. This murder at a mystery convention is like Isaac Asimov's *Murder at the ABA* (in which he featured himself) and Shannon O'Cork's *The Murder of Muriel Lake*. (See *MRWG: NY*.)

Max Allan Collins writes that "Bouchercon, Chicago-Style" was the official title, although the flyers called it "Crime City Capers." Chicago, the fabulous clipjoint, as mystery writer Fredric Brown dubbed it, was the perfect setting for a mystery convention because it was the place where the Outfit was born and John Dillinger died, site of the St. Valentine's Day Massacre, and home of the Untouchables.

Bouchercon was founded in 1970 in honor of *New York Times* critic Anthony Boucher and moves from city to city. In 1984 when the MWA Midwest Chapter was just getting a new lease on life under the vigorous leadership of Mary Craig, she stunned our monthly meeting by announcing casually that we are going to host Bouchercon in Chicago that year. (Few of us had been to one!) With her energy and enthusiasm we did it—at the Congress Hotel.

In Elliott Roosevelt's *The President's Man*, 1932 Democratic candidate FDR stayed at the Congress Hotel and rehearsed his acceptance speech. He was the first candidate to come in person to accept the nomination, and his way was made safe for him by his old school chum Jack ("Blackjack") Endicott, who negotiated a cease fire with the mob who were mad at the inevitable end of Prohibition. Endicott reported to Jim Farley at the Congress Hotel, then went to the FDR suite guarded by Cornelius ("Neely") Vanderbilt.

Cross the Congress Expressway, which west of the Loop becomes the Eisenhower Expressway to the western suburbs. Look left to see the Auditorium Theater parking garage where Cormany's P.I. Kruger parked in *Red Winter* before he went to see the Grant Park Underground to meet Lipke.

The entrance to the Auditorium Theater is on the north side of Congress in the old and famous Auditorium Building, now the home of Roosevelt University. The theater was put up in 1889 as the first major project of Dankmar Adler and Louis Sullivan, with a few touches (the six stained glass windows in the lobby) by the young Frank Lloyd Wright. In Roslynn Griffith's (aka MWA members Patricia Pinianski and Linda Sweeney) *Pretty Birds of Passage*, the firm of O'Rourke and O'Rourke, where Aurelia Kincaid worked as an architect, is meant to be Adler and Sullivan because young braggart Wright appeared as a character.

Walk in and admire the lobby, but you can only see the theater itself if you buy a ticket to an event. The theater is world-famous for its looks and its marvelous acoustics. Once the home of Mary Garden, Marian Anderson, Adelina Patti, and Amelita Galli-Curci, it was restored and reopened in 1967 through the efforts of Mrs. John Spachner and Harry Weese.

In Sara Paretsky's *Guardian Angel*, V.I. Warshawski and her old friend Dr. Lotty Herschel and Lotty's lover (and boss) Max

Loewenthal went there to attend a benefit concert in honor of Max's dead wife Therese. The concert is a benefit for Chicago Settlement, a not-for-profit refugee assistance group. Max's son Michael and Israeli composer Or' Nivitsky were playing in "Louis Sullivan's masterpiece." Their yuppie audience was well-heeled, not very musical, and not well behaved, but they devoured the elegant party food in the lobby.

After looking at the theater, walk around to the Michigan Avenue entrance to Roosevelt University. Go inside to admire the handsome Victorian decor and walk up the sweeping grand staircase that used to lead up to the hotel lobby. Built in 1887–89, it was the first multipurpose building in Chicago, with 136 offices and stores, including a bookstore, a permanent opera house and theater, and a hotel where patrons stayed and dined.

The Chicago Opera Company was here for forty years and it was also the first home of the Chicago Symphony Orchestra under Theodore Thomas. Eleanor Roosevelt came here to dedicate it as Roosevelt University on Nov. 16, 1945, and one of its most famous graduates was the late Mayor Harold Washington.

In Shelby Yastrow's *Undue Influence*, elderly accountant Benjamin Stillman left a huge sum of money to a Chicago synagogue. Young lawyer Phil Ogden had drawn up the will, so Ogden found himself in charge of an $8 million estate with the need to find–and/or fight off–other heirs. Probate Court Judge Verne Lloyd appointed black lawyer Tom Andrews guardian of putative heirs. Andrews and Ogden came to Andrews's alma mater, Roosevelt University, where they had a date with German Professor Otto Wechsler to translate the letter they found in Ben Stillman's strong box. They came in the school entrance with busts of patrons and bulletin boards and walked up the stairs with Professor Wechsler to his office where books and papers were all over.

Come out of Roosevelt University and turn left. Next door is the Chicago Musical College, which is affiliated with Roosevelt. Cross a small alley to Loew's Fine Arts Theaters in the Fine Arts Building at 410 S. Michigan.

Built in 1884 as a showcase for Studebaker carriages, it became a focus for Chicago's artistic life with an inscription over the entrance that reads "All passes—Art alone endures." It's full of artists' and singers' studios and practice rooms, dance companies, music theaters, yoga teachers, hypnotists, and other kinds of culture. Sculptor Lorado Taft had his studio there (he also worked on the Midway; see Walk 9). L. Frank Baum and W. D. Denslow created their highly successful play *The Wizard of Oz* there. *The Little Review*, which published Midwesterners T. S. Eliot and Ernest Hemingway and Irish James Joyce's *Ulysses* was produced there, and it saw the beginnings of Chicago's Little Theater movement, which brought Chicago plays by Strindberg and Shaw, now performed at the Court Theatre in Hyde Park. Now the two Studebaker theaters show the best art films in town. The age of the building is shown by its creaky, manual elevators, and the fact that there is only one woman's restroom in the entire building (on eight).

Outside (and inside) you can get something to eat at George Mitchell's Artists Snack Shop. Max Allan Collins's Iowa mystery writer Mallory did when he came to Bouchercon in *Kill Your Darlings*. Wanting to get away from too many guests, he remembered the Artistic in the Fine Arts Building, "where young actresses and ballerinas, in tights and leg-warmers . . . often wandered in for coffee." The Artistic was a good place to sit and think, but this time Mallory was joined by Kathy Wickman, the editor of *Noir*, a crime magazine, wearing a black deco *Noir* sweatshirt.

In Harry Keeler's Halloween mystery, *Behind That Mask*, Dr. Hippolytus Zing took his brother's advice and falsely confessed to the murder of a magazine editor. (He had an iron-clad alibi so it was purely self-advertisement. It worked so well, Dr. Zing was able to move his offices to the Fine Arts Building, where he had many women clients eager for him to try numerology on them.)

Go inside to look around the lobby. At the north end is the entrance to Booksellers Row at 408 N. Michigan. It sells both new and used books and has many Chicago books and mysteries. Since it is the only general bookstore around here, lawyer Rachel Gold in Michael A. Kahn's *Grave Designs* may have stopped in to find an atlas showing Massachusetts. She was en route to visit call girl Cindi Reynolds in her lakefront condo on Randolph.

Come out of Booksellers Row and go left to the corner of Van Buren. The massive red stone building at 81 E. Van Buren is the exclusive Chicago Club, put up in 1929. You can go under the canopy on Van Buren and see the lobby, but visitors/tourists are not welcome. The lobby has dark wood paneling, lush red carpet and red leather chairs, and a much friendlier gatekeeper than the Harvard Club in New York. This one agrees with me that Chicago might as well give in and capitalize on the Capone legend. (See *MRWG:NY*.)

In Michael Cormany's *Red Winter*, P.I. Kruger—who has a quirky social conscience—was hired to find out why a group of "Reds" was trying to blackmail Nicholas Cheyney, a self-made business executive who wanted to become a member of the "Michigan Avenue Club." Cormany located the most exclusive club in Chicago about six blocks south of the Ritz-Carlton Hotel (about where the Women's Athletic Club is) but he must have meant this club because coming out of the Berghoff, Cheyney and Kruger bumped into a well dressed drunk who told Cheyney he soon hoped to see him at the club. Kruger then shadowed the man east to Michigan where he went into the club under its canopied entrance.

Cross Van Buren and continue north on the west side of Michigan Avenue. The pink granite building at 332 N. Michigan is the old McCormick Building, which could be the Minary Building, built by the Minary family who owned a Great Lakes shipping company in Mignon Eberhart's *Dead Men's Plans*. The Minary family drove from their Gold Coast home across the Michigan Avenue Bridge and past dripping Art Institute lions to the family building. Their corporate offices, on the top floor overlooking Lake Michigan, were decorated with photos of the fleet of ships named for the girls in the family. The only Minary son and heir had just returned home with an unexpected wife when someone tried to kill him.

The showrooms and offices of Baldwin Pianos, who used the works of Chicagoan Adam Schaaf, were once next door but today the building houses offices of the City of Chicago. The old CNA Building with its chimes and its lighted blue beehive on top (a company of busy workers) is at 310 S. Michigan. A combination of the old CNA building and the new red CNA highrise behind it on Wabash are real-life models for Sara Paretsky's Ajax Insurance Company, but their architecture is not quite right. In *Indemnity Only*, V.I. came to Ajax to find out more about murdered University of Chicago student Peter Thayer, whose father was a banker and whose girlfriend's father was a union chief. Paretsky herself once worked for CNA.

The old CNA Building is now the Britannica Center. In Richard Engling's *Body Mortgage*, which takes place in 1999, P.I. Gregory Blake and his sidekick Billy dashed across Michigan Avenue into this building, called the Taos Pinnacle Building, to escape from evil businessman Regore, who was planning to take over Chicago. It was owned by Quiller, an ex-hippie who looked like Fu Manchu and was a chum of P.I. Blake's mother.

Cross Jackson to the Railway Exchange (Santa Fe) Building at 80 E. Jackson. Handsomely trimmed with white terra-cotta, the lobby has been redone and often has architectural exhibits. Daniel Burnham had his offices on the top floor, and in 1909 he and Edward H. Bennett released their "Chicago Plan" here. Burnham is famous for saying "Make no little plans. They have no magic to stir men's blood."

Just beyond the Santa Fe Building is the Chicago Architecture Foundation's store with many books and maps on Chicago. They also sponsor architectural and boat tours of the city. Next door is the Symphony Store, with recordings of the Chicago Symphony, and at 220 S. Michigan is Orchestra Hall itself, home of the symphony which plans to expand behind it and around the Borg-Warner building on the corner of Adams.

In Michael A. Kahn's *Grave Designs*, Rachel Gold's East Rogers Park landlord was John Burns, who played trombone in the symphony. Burns's wife Linda was a social worker who was staying home with their two small kids and also minded Rachel's golden retriever Ozzie, whom the murderer tried to poison.

In Craig Rice's *Knocked for a Loop*, Frank McInnis was a good-looking young gangster. John J. Malone's mobster friend Max Hook assigned McInnis the job of confessing that he killed Lake Forest financier Leonard Estapool, whom Malone found dead in his Loop office. (See Walk 3.) McInnes agreed and told Malone that he once went to an Orchestra Hall concert with the murdered man's niece Jane Estapool. McInnis found Orchestra Hall a little shabby, but still "what I call real nice."

For many years the Cliff Dwellers's Club was located on the top of Orchestra Hall. Chicago newspaperman Emmett Dedmon said it was named for the Indians of the Southwest (that is, Tony Hillerman's turf), but others say it was founded and named by writer Hamlin Garland. The club's original purpose was to increase the status of writers and artists, especially local ones. Garland was one of many American writers like Vachel Lindsay, Theodore Dreiser, Sherwood Anderson, Carl Sandburg, Edgar Lee Masters, Edna Ferber, Willa Cather, and Ben Hecht who came to Chicago in the pre–World War I period. This in-gathering made critic H. L. Mencken call Chicago the literary capital of the United States in 1917. By 1927, however, Mencken had published "Chicago: An Obituary" and declared the "Chicago Renaissance" over.

On the southeast corner at Adams you come to the Borg-Warner Building, a modern steel and glass highrise with a marble lobby, which physically comes the closest to Paretsky's description of the Ajax Insurance Company. In Paretsky's *Deadlock*, V.I. went there to quiz Roger Ferrant from Lloyds of London, who had come to check out the bombing of the Lake Michigan grain ship *Luella* in the Sault Ste. Marie locks with V.I. on board.

Cross Adams. Across Michigan Avenue you see the Art Institute with its famous lions. There is also a pickup for the London-style Red Double Decker Bus Tours. In Max Allan Collins's *Kill Your Darlings*, Iowa mystery writer "Mallory" (shades of G. K. Chesterton's urban knight, Chandler's Marlowe, and Parker's Spenser) took a Crime Tour with his friend Kathy Wickman, editor of *Noir*. She came along because "Chicago is the Disneyland of crime . . . gotta see the sights."

Over a static-ridden intercom the tall, lanky bearded tour guide welcomed them by saying, "Welcome to the Chicago . . . Crime Tour . . . Unfortunately, many of Chicago's most famous–and infamous–buildings have made way for urban renewal and/or blight." (Basically, Collins takes you on the Untouchables Tour.)

Across Adams on the corner, in the old People's Gas Building, is a Bennigan's Restaurant where you can stop and eat or drink. In Thomas McCall's *A Wide and Capable Revenge*, after touching base at Police HQ at 11th and State about the shooting at Holy Name Cathedral, detective Nora Callum parked her car and walked to Adams to Shenanigan's, a big brassy restaurant decorated in turn-of-the-century touches and hung with memorabilia like old Coke bottles and Norman Rockwell posters, and leafy green plants.

After sampling Bennigan's, continue north on Michigan, past the Chicago pizza place with outdoor tables used in the recent movie *The Fugitive*, directed by former Chicagoan Andrew Davis, which also has scenes at City Hall and the Conrad Hilton. (It is only since the death of Mayor Daley I that the city has allowed Hollywood to shoot violent films here.)

As you come to the corner of Monroe Street you pass the former Illinois Athletic Club at 112 N. Michigan, now the School of the Art Institute. Tarzan Johnny Weismuller trained there. Tarzan's creator, Edgar Rice Burroughs was a Chicago native, like L. Frank Baum of Oz fame and Walt Disney. The Illinois Athletic Club is probably the club in William McGivern's *Very Cold for May* where PRman Jake Harrison got a call from his boss that big wartime munitions maker (and profiteer) Daniel Riordan had hired them to handle May Laval's possible leaks in her memoirs. Jake left the Saxon Club to grab a cab and head north to 333 N. Michigan.

Before you cross Monroe Street, look up at the Gothic top of the University Club on the northwest corner of Michigan and Monroe. You can walk inside, but not far unless you're a guest. This club lobby has predictable red carpet and paneling and a founder's portrait on the staircase.

Michael A. Kahn's *Grave Designs* opens there with young

lawyer Rachel Gold lunching with Abbott & Windsor's managing partner Ishmael Richardson. He told her to call him Ishmael and she asked if the chef was named Queequeg, setting the tone for a mystery involving Puritan New England. Richardson wanted Rachel to find out what dead partner Graham Marshall's codicil about the firm minding "Canaan's" grave meant. Rachel found the Cathedral Hall somewhat ludicrous—with stained glass, gray stone walls, columns, and a timbered ceiling—and called it Chicago's cathedral of capitalism.

Continue up Michigan past the University Club to Burger King, a handy, less exclusive place for a snack or pit stop. (In Chicago, most fast food places have open restrooms.) In midblock is the Chicago Athletic Club, which also will not let you inside unless you are a member. It is the headquarters of the first Rotary Club (founded in 1905), which still meets Tuesdays at 12:10.

In Charles Merrill Smith's *Reverend Randollph and the Unholy Bible*, former L.A. Rams player the Reverend "Con" Randollph had a membership at the Chicago Athletic Club paid for by his affluent Loop congregation.

In Harry Keeler's *Thieves' Nights*, "Big Tim" O'Hartigan, the corrupt Governor of Illinois, who was secretly married to a black woman whom he left locked up back East, dropped by the Club for a light lunch. He then went back to his Cleveland Avenue home to meet jewel thief Bayard DeLancey (in disguise) who had come to Chicago to make sure the governor did not pardon his sister's murderer.

Next door to the Chicago Athletic Club is Willoughby Tower at 8 S. Michigan. The former headquarters of the Chicago Press Veterans Association is inside, so there is a brass plaque on the building showing the site is dedicated to Chicago newspapermen from 1818–1968. It has the names of all the Chicago newspapers that once existed, but—a footnote to history—it does not include the city's black paper, the *Chicago Defender*.

Continue along Michigan Avenue past the old John M. Smythe furniture building, which now houses some coffee houses and other boutiques. In Barbara D'Amato's *Hard Tack*, the beautiful people named Honeywell, with whom Cat Marsala sailed to write about their wealthy life-style, had made their "old money" from a family furniture business. As you walk along, look across Michigan Avenue to Grant Park. In good weather, you will see all kinds of lunching workers, tourists, pigeons, and a few bums. The joggers usually head across the park for the lakefront.

In Harry Keeler's *Thieves' Nights* the Man with Gray Eyes (aka wealthy Gold Coaster Algernon van de Puyster) had amnesia. He sat in Grant Park a lot (it was during the Great Depression and there were no jobs), trying to remember his past. He also read newspapers other people left behind and consorted with a group of similarly unemployed men in Washington Square Park (Bughouse Square). (See Walk 4.)

Chicago merchant prince Aaron Montgomery Ward had an office at 6 N. Michigan from which he could see shacks, trash, and freight cars piling up along the lakeshore. It made him angry, so he and his lawyers found a way to keep the lakefront "forever open, clear, and free." In grateful memory of his long legal efforts (1890–1910), Chicago recently renamed Grant Park from Randolph to Monroe the A. Montgomery Ward Gardens.

At the south corner of Washington and Michigan is the 30 North Michigan Building with a bank on the first floor. It is not a branch of First National Bank, but in Richard Engling's futuristic *Body Mortgage*, this was the First National Bank, which held a Human Resource Loan on the body of Jeremy Scott. Scott blew up the bank to try to prevent loan collection, then hired P.I. Gregory Blake to protect him.

Turn left to walk through the lobby of 30 N. Michigan and come out its Washington Street door. Heading west, cross the alley, which is really a continuation of Garland Court, to the Pittsfield Building at 55 E. Washington. A handsome '20s structure, it suffered terrible damage during the so-called Great Chicago Flood of 1992.

Go into the building and turn right to take an elevator to the second floor to reach the I Love a Mystery Bookstore on the mezzanine (stairs are locked). The bookstore—the only one in the Loop specializing in mysteries—is on the far side but well worth a trip. It stocks many paperback mysteries unavailable from American publishers.

Interestingly enough, in Targ's *The Case of Mr. Cassidy* amateur sleuth Hugh Morris, working his way through Loop bookstores, visited Argus Books up one flight of stairs between Madison and Washington, run by Ben Abramson. Coming back down Morris met bearded, jovial Christopher Morley, with Somerset Maugham and Vincent Starrett. He greeted Starrett, a fellow mystery addict and one of Chicago's major Sherlockians, who wrote *The Private Life of Sherlock Holmes*. Then Morris stopped at Max Siegel's bookshop in the Pittsfield Building. The bookseller gave Morris some useful information on cheap modern Parisian editions of Edgar Allan Poe's *Tamerlane*. Siegel's shop also was crowded with visiting authors, of whom the best known today is Phyllis Whitney. Her first mystery *Red Is for Murder* (*The Red Carnelian*) was set in Chicago and dedicated to Max Siegel. (See also Walk 2.)

In Michael Raleigh's *A Body in Belmont Harbor*, P.I. Paul Whelan had an appointment in the Pittsfield Building. Whelan saw the Pittsfield as a relic of a more genteel time when office buildings were expected to have a little brass and marble to tell visitors they were going someplace special. Whelan saw Victor Tabor, whose Reliable Finance Company had business dealings with an outfit called High Pair that Whelan was investigating. Tabor said High Pair was run by a pair of crooks who nearly put him out of business.

After shopping at I Love a Mystery come out of the Pittsfield Building and cross Washington Street at Garland Court. To your left in the Garland Building on the second floor is The Savvy Traveller. They carry everything the traveling mystery fan needs, including all the *Mystery Reader's Walking Guides: London, England* and *New York*.

Recross Garland Court east to the Cultural Center at 78 E. Washington. This was Dearborn Park in 1852 when Abraham Lincoln spoke against slavery. Built in 1887 to be the main Chicago Public Library, the Italian Renaissance building housed a collection of books sent as a gift from the City of London after the Great Chicago Fire of 1871. Although it is one of Chicago's great treasures, the building was barely saved from demolition in 1973 by "Sis" Daley, wife of the mayor.

Inside, the building has gorgeous floors and ceilings of mosaic tile and walls of marble. The marble grand staircase on the Washington side is inlaid with Tiffany-style mosaics and on the third floor is the Preston Bradley Hall, a huge circular reception room with a gigantic Tiffany stained glass dome. The Randolph Street side was built to house the museum of the Grand Army of the Republic and is also elegant, with a dome, a theater, and Memorial Hall, but the GAR exhibits are missing, the subject of a squabble among the library's ruling elite.

Go inside the Washington Street entrance. To your left is the Museum of Broadcast Communications, where, armed with your driver's license and two dollars you may listen to tapes of old radio shows like *I Love a Mystery* and *Inner Sanctum*.

There are marble benches facing the elevators on either side of the grand staircase. In Craig Rice's *The Wrong Murder*, Helene and Jake Justus were told by Helene's father that he took the ransom money for kidnaped Ellen Ogletree to the Chicago Public Library. Following orders, he sat on a bench facing the elevators with the money in a briefcase. A strange little man sat down next to him, took the briefcase, and left. The day after George Brand told this tale, the little man, a petty crook named Gumbel, was shot to death during the Christmas rush at the corner of State and Madison. (See Walk 3.)

In Thomas McCall's *A Wide and Capable Revenge*, Detective Nora Callum went to the downtown public library's first-floor reading room with a long wall of magnificent arched windows looking out on Grant Park. (This is now an art gallery.) Callum was tracing a group of Russian emigres from the Siege of Leningrad. In Harry Keeler's *Thieves' Nights* the Man with Gray Eyes went there to read up on amnesia, discovering it would last until he received another bang on the head.

Walk through the library to the Randolph Street side. Along the left-hand corridor is a photographic exhibit of Chicago landmarks, as well as public restrooms. In the center near Randolph there is a coffee shop and in the Randolph Street lobby there is a City of Chicago Visitors Information Center.

Guided tours of the Cultural Center are given by the friends of the Cultural Center at 1:30 Tuesdays.

Walk out the Randolph Street entrance and stop on the steps to look around. Across the street are a sole remaining 1890s building, some low rises, and then on the corner the strange 1984 skyscraper at 150 N. Michigan with the sliced-off top. Looking right across Michigan Avenue you can see the Doral Plaza rising up in front of One Prudential Plaza.

Before the Doral was built, in Arthur Maling's *Dingdong* has-been actor Mike Wiley was tapped on the shoulder at that corner by his former girlfriend, Holly, who was in town to star in a play. Wiley took Holly to the Stouffer's bar in the Prudential Building with the result that she, too, got mixed up with the blond baby-faced killer Dingdong. The 1955 Prudential Building was not only the first building put up downtown in twenty years, but also the tallest, with an observation deck and Stouffer's Top of the Rock restaurant. This has been turned into a private club.

In John Ashenhurst's *The World's Fair Murders*, a taxi en route to the Randolph Street I.C. (Metra) Station was wrecked on Michigan Avenue by a fire truck. The passenger had a big brown suitcase belonging to Professor Arturo del Grafko of Almania, who was coming to the opening of the World's Fair to tell the world about a new discovery. The Chicago police took possession of the suitcase but five of them died as a result.

Turn right to go down the library steps and walk to the stairs that lead into the Pedway (pedestrian walkway) and the old Illinois Central (now Metra) Railroad's Randolph Street Station. Keep going through the tunnel into the station proper.

Walking through this tunnel on his way to the races, *Chicago Tribune* crime reporter Jake Lingle was gunned down on June 9, 1930. His killer ran out the Michigan Avenue exit and escaped west down Randolph.

Howard Browne tells the story of Jake Lingle in *Pork City*. Like many mystery writers of the '30s and '40s Browne was a reporter and knew the people involved. He quotes Dion O'Banion, leader of Chicago's North Side mob who had been shot earlier across from Holy Name, as saying that "There's two kinds of guys you don't lay a finger on—men of the cloth and newspaper slobs."

In Max Allan Collins's *True Detective*, Chicago cop Nathan (Nate) Heller was on duty at the Randolph/Michigan Avenue corner and saw the blond killer racing west on Randolph. But the mob handed another man over to justice; therefore Heller later saw the murderer again in Florida, where he shot Chicago Mayor Anton Cermak, who was standing next to president-elect FDR.

Bill Granger in *The Newspaper Murders* calls Jake Lingle's murder the prototypical Chicago crime because it turned out that Lingle, whose death caused Colonel Robert McCormick of the *Chicago Tribune* to thunder about freedom of the press and offer a reward, had been on Al Capone's payroll. This embarrassing double life of his reporter led McCormick to appeal directly to President Herbert Hoover for help in shutting down the mob, which, in turn, led to Eliot Ness and the Untouchables.

Inside the Randolph Street Station you can use the restrooms and get a snack or a drink. Then take the staircase to the left near the track exits. It leads to One Prudential Plaza on the east side of Randolph and Michigan Avenue. When you come up in the Prudential lobby, go left out the side door to tiny Beaubien Court, facing the Doral Plaza. Mark Beaubien was a genial early settler who ran the ferry across the Chicago River and owned the Sauganash Tavern.

Doral Plaza is a multiuse building with a restaurant and luxury condos and offices. In Andrew Greeley's *The Patience of a Saint*, Pulitzer-prize winning columnist Red Kane took his wife Eileen Ryan Kane, a trial lawyer and sister of Father Blackie, there for some "extra" marital lovemaking while an aging gangster was gunning for his entire family.

Turn right to walk north along Beaubien Court to Lake Street. On the right you can see the 1990 Two Prudential Plaza one block east on Stetson. It is Chicago's fancy reply to New York's Art Deco Chrysler Building. At Lake Street turn left and go west to Michigan Avenue. Then turn right again to walk to South Water Street. You are walking above the original Chicago market area, which ran from Fort Dearborn along the south bank of the river. It is preserved today in the network of docks and tunnels beneath Michigan Avenue and Wacker Drive.

If you want to detour to explore the Lower Level take the stairs at South Water Street down below and look around. To your right is the entrance to the South Water Street Metra Railroad Station (an extension of the Randolph Street Station). Because the homeless camp below ground level, it is no longer really safe to go there by yourself except at rush hours. The Metra Station is closed on weekends.

In Engling's *Body Mortgage* P.I. Gregory Blake took Lower Wacker Drive to escape his pursuers, remembering that this had been where ships and barges unloaded their wares from the river, dotted with ramshackle warehouses, shops, and wagons. In Barbara D'Amato's short story, "The Lower Wacker Hilton" Police Officer Susannah Maria Figuroa and her partner Norm Bennis got a radio call about someone moaning in a sewer. They drove down into Lower Wacker and found four men living in a cardboard shelter near an air shaft. One of them was dead. The others blamed their large marmalade tomcat for smothering him.

Come back upstairs and cross South Water Street to the Old Republic Building at 307 N. Michigan. It's a lovely example of '20s classical with an arched entrance, terra-cotta trim and a colonnaded top. The next building is 333 N. Michigan, built in 1928 on part of the site of old Fort Dearborn. It was one of the first skyscrapers built in Chicago with Art Deco's vertical lines and stylized geometric trim. The Tavern Club on the top floor has a striking view of the city, making this the most likely candidate for the "new skyscraper" with a supper club in Vera Caspary's *Evvie*. Written in 1960, the story is set in the '20s when Caspary herself was a young Chicago reporter. In it, two "bachelor girls," Louise and Evvie, were taken there, where they could see the new Wrigley Building and Tribune Tower and the dark Chicago River.

Across Michigan Avenue to your left is the 1923 London Guarantee Trust Building, no longer so named, making use of the irregular site where Wacker and Michigan meet. The London House once had a restaurant with a live radio show, and in William McGivern's *Very Cold for May*, PR man Jake Harrison was supposed to meet his girl there at Dave's Radio Bar. It is now a Burger King where you can stop for a snack or use the restrooms.

Turn right to go around the corner to One Illinois Center (111 E. Wacker). Inside, turn off Michigan Mall to Wacker Mall to reach the Hyatt Regency Hotel. (The outdoor staircase takes you between One Illinois Center and Two Illinois Center, both part of the complex designed by Mies van der Rohe over the Illinois Central Railroad's air rights. Three Illinois Center is south of the Hyatt Hotel on Stetson.)

The Hyatt Regency Hotel at 151 E. Wacker Drive has two towers connected by an atrium walkway, but the atrium is not ten stories high. This hotel was the site of the 1990 Modern Language Association annual convention (also known as the slave market) where Catherine Kenney, author of *The Remarkable Case of Dorothy L. Sayers*, ran a Special Session on Dorothy L. Sayers and organized a 100th Birthday party for Lord Peter Wimsey.

This convention clearly was the model for the MLA Convention in D. J. H. Jones's *Murder at the MLA*, which takes place in fictional Hotel Fairfax. There were a series of academic murders with one professor tossed off the tenth floor of the atrium, one poisoned by room service coffee, and another mugged in the alley. To solve these murders, Assistant Professor of English Nancy Cook (who was not up for tenure that year) and Chicago Detective (and former redneck) Boaz Dixon teamed up to explain his/her professional jargon and expertise to each other.

In Kahn's *Grave Designs*, Rachel Gold got acquainted with the call girl Cindi Reynolds in whose apartment Abbott & Windsor senior partner Graham Marshall died. When Cindi's lakefront condo was blown up she hid out at the Hyatt Regency, where she sat with Rachel drinking gin in the lounge on the top floor of the hotel, watching herself be the lead story on TV. There is no such restaurant on the top floor, but you can sit in the Seasons Cafe and look over the city.

In Sam Reaves's *A Long Cold Fall*, P.I. Cooper MacLeish went to the Hyatt Regency after a run-in with Billy Galloway's thugs on the lower-level parking lot at Harbor Point Towers east of the hotel. Cooper went there to see his son Dominic, whose mother Vivian had been murdered.

Go out the Hyatt doorway to Stetson Avenue to left to walk south to South Water Street. On your right you go past Two Illinois Center, which is the home of Chicago's famous classical FM station WFMT. Compass/Second City stars Elaine May and Mike Nichols once worked at WFMT, pop historian Studs Terkel still has his show here, and the station has a long history of spinoffs like the University of Chicago Folk Festival and Flying Fish Records. Like most Hyde Parkers or ex–Hyde Parkers, Paretsky's V.I. Warshawski listens to WFMT on her car radio when not listening to the Cubs lose.

At Stetson and South Water turn left to walk to the pink towered Fairmont Hotel at 200 N. Columbus Drive. Ahead of you is the Parkshore Apartments. Turn right on Columbus Drive and walk south past Edward Durell Stone's 1973 Amoco Building on Randolph. It looks just like one tower of New York's World Trade Center.

To your left on Randolph is another group of condos: Outer Drive East, Harbor Point, and Lakeshore Towers. In Bill Granger's *The Public Murders* a nightclub owner with a taste for very young blonds had an apartment there, making him a suspect in the murder of Swedish tourist Maj Kristen. In Kahn's *Grave Designs*, Cindi Reynold's friend Andi Hebner—a graduate student at the University of Chicago—had a client, so she took him to Cindi's apartment in Harbor Point and got blown up. In Sam Reaves's *A Long Cold Fall,* Cooper parked his old car underneath this complex of new highrises when he went to visit Billy Galloway, a rich man's son with mob connections. When Cooper left, he was chased through the parking area but managed to get away.

Cross Randolph to Daley Park. Walk south along Columbus Drive through Daley Bicentennial Plaza to Monroe Drive. Cross Monroe. The archway of Adler and Sullivan's demolished Chicago Stock Exchange Building is set up at the corner and inside the Art Institute is the old Trading Room. Just past the arch are the entrances to the Goodman Theater and the Art Institute.

To the south in Grant Park you can see the Petrillo Band Shell where Grant Park concerts are held during the summer. In Kahn's *Grave Designs*, Rachel Gold's secretary Mary met her boyfriend to picnic and listen to the concert the same evening Abbott & Windsor held a ritzy cocktail party at the Shedd Aquarium. In McCall's *A Wide and Capable Revenge* Detective Callum kidded her partner when he complained about being tired of the job and the city. She asked him where else he could see the White Sox half the nights of the summer or listen to Mozart while lying on the grass at Grant Park.

Walk past Goodman Theater to the Art Institute and go inside. Since World War II the Art Institute has been remodeled a great deal and four new wings added on, so if a mystery describes a basement with a balcony walk connecting the two sides of the building, you know you are reading a golden oldie.

All the exhibits, permanent and current, are worth seeing. Get a map and plan to stay awhile. You can eat in the Court Cafeteria in the basement or in the outdoor McKinlock Court or the second-floor Restaurant on the Park. There are restrooms on both the Columbus Drive and Michigan Avenue sides of the building.

Among the many gifts of Chicagoans, one of the odd ones is the remains of George Harding's eclectic collection, once housed in a castle on Lake Park Avenue. (See Walk 9.) The armor of the Harding Collection now lines the corridor from Columbus Drive to Michigan Avenue. The museum's most famous collection is its French Impressionists, identified with Mrs. Potter Palmer, a mover and shaker of many talents. In Roslynn Griffith's historical mystery, *Pretty Birds of Passage*, Bertha Palmer spoke at the opening of the Women's Building of the World's Columbian Exposition of 1893. In Amanda Cross's *In the Last Analysis*, amateur detective Professor Kate Fansler was trying to solve the murder of one of her graduate students. The murdered student had left her money to Chicagoan, Dr. Daniel Messinger, and Kate finally flew out to interview him, saying that she always meant to come to Chicago because "They've got Picasso's *Man with the Blue Guitar*" there.

In Harry Keeler's *Thieves' Nights*, jewel thief Bayard DeLancey pretended to be the East Indian representative of a Maharajah who wanted his red emerald, now in John Atwood's jewel collection. (Shades of Wilkie Collins's *The Moonstone*.) Atwood loaned the Art Institute his collection but the day of his funeral, his son agreed to give the emerald back and went to the Art Institute to arrange it with the curator. They went in past the big bronze lions, past several big halls filled with plaster-of-Paris and marble statuary (the old basement below the bridge, filled with Columbian Exposition leftovers) to a tiny office. The fat and balding curator understood only too well how art collections often come from dubious sources.

In Kahn's *Grave Designs* senior lawyer Joe Oliver of Perrini & Oliver, who grew up on the West Side and was known in the trade as the Great White Shark, endowed the Joseph P. Oliver Gallery of Mexican Art, which featured a collection of pre-Columbian figures. He was also another client of call girl Cindi Reynolds.

In Targ's *The Case of Mr. Cassidy* Morris came along when police Lieutenant Withers was told the Fiend was trapped at the Art Institute. (He was caught by a gallery guard in the act of slitting the throat of another young blond.) When Morris and Withers went racing down Michigan Avenue in a police car with sirens screaming they found five hundred people standing on the front steps, the doors closed and guards in front. But as they talked in the main lobby the Fiend ducked out, the cops shot—missed—he ran upstairs, knocking statues off pedestals, leaving plaster casts lying on the floor in pieces and pictures hanging askew. The Fiend ducked back downstairs to the basement into the Egyptian Room. The cops dashed in and out—then the Fiend sneaked out from behind a mummy. Morris saw him brandishing a long gleaming knife, and heading toward the men's restroom. The cops had to bang open each cubicle, but they found him in the last one, snarling like a trapped lion. This chase may make you think twice about using the basement restrooms, but they are usually quite peaceful.

In Charles Merrill Smith's *Reverend Randollph and the Unholy Bible*, Art Institute curator Dr. Joyce Compton was pleased that murdered recluse Johannes Humbrecht left the Art Institute his collection of paintings, but she also tried hard to get his Gutenberg Bible. A direct descendent of Gutenberg, Humbrecht was also a member of Randollph's Church of the Good Shepherd and Con Randollph took the trouble to visit him, so Humbrecht had left him the Bible.

In Paretsky's *Guardian Angel*, V.I. remembered her mother taking her to see the masterpieces of the Italian Renaissance, but V.I. fell for the Buddha, so calm, so unblinking benign. V.I. dreamed that the Buddha grew larger and beckoned her so she let go of Gabriella's hand and climbed onto his lap.

In Richard Himmel's *The Twenty-Third Web*, a thriller about Israelis, Arab terrorists, and Chicago's Jewish community, banker Livingston Stonehill was at an Art Institute gala when he learned that his grandson and heir had been kidnaped.

In Eleanor Taylor Bland's *Slow Burn*, Detective Marti MacAlister visited the expensive new suburban home of Dr. Edwards whose clinic burned down, killing a woman receptionist and a young girl. His place reminded Chicagoan Marti of a class trip to the Art Institute when she was in grade school.

Walk through the Art Institute to Michigan Avenue and go outside. If the weather is good the steps are usually full of students and tourists, very like the New York Public Library with its equally famous lions. In Craig Rice's hilarious put-down of New York, Malone told a cabbie he was allergic to New York lions. (See *MRWG:NY*.)

In Engling's *Body Mortgage* there was a New Age demonstration in front of the Art Institute to celebrate the approaching millennium. Young punks were pouring buckets of red paint over the heads of the lions and self-flagellants with whips surrounded a platform at the base of the steps.

Walk to the right to look into the small garden where you can see Lorado Taft's 1914 *Fountain of the Great Lakes*. The first part of the walk ends here in front of the Art Institute. You can do the second part after taking a break for lunch or you can do it on a second day.

LAKEFRONT SOUTH/MUSEUMS

Begin your walk five blocks south of the Art Institute at the corner of Michigan and Balbo Drive. East of Michigan at Balbo on a small green hill in Grant Park you can see the equestrian statue of Civil War General John Logan. The statues became world-famous as the site of antiwar demonstrations during the 1968 Chicago Democratic Convention. The Conrad Hilton Hotel was the nerve center of the convention, so it was in front of it that most of the demonstrations occurred. Literary lights who covered the fracas included Norman Mailer in *Miami and the Siege of Chicago* and Jean Genet, whose story is republished in *Chicago Stories*.

In Andrew Greeley's *The Patience of a Saint*, pregnant trial lawyer Eileen Ryan Kane, Father Blackie's sister, was teargassed and knocked about by Chicago police during the uproar. In Ross Thomas's *The Porkchoppers*, union boss Daniel Cubbin's son Kelly supported Gene McCarthy and came to the 1968 Democratic Convention. Kelly was gassed in front of the Conrad Hilton near the statue of General Logan and switched his allegiance to Bobby Kennedy; soon after he became a D.C. policeman. In *The Priestly Murders* Bill Granger quoted Mayor Richard J. Daley as saying "Gentleman, get it straight: The policeman is not there to create disorder. The policeman is there to preserve disorder."

Cross Balbo to the Chicago Hilton Hotel and Towers at 720 S. Michigan Avenue. This was once the Stevens Hotel, built by the family of the Supreme Court Justice John Stevens, billed as the biggest hotel in the world. In Sam Reaves's *Fear Will Do It*, cabbie MacLeish dropped off a Personage in a Dark Blue Suit at the Hilton and was flagged by a Lady on a Shopping Spree who wanted to go up Michigan to Water Tower Place, even though she could hardly carry the packages she had.

In Elliott Roosevelt's *The President's Man*, the Democratic Convention of 1932 was being held in Chicago. Nominee Franklin Delano Roosevelt was convinced either he or president Hoover would have to repeal Prohibition, so FDR persuaded his old school chum "Blackjack" John Endicott to tell the underworld it would be pointless to kill FDR. Reporting to campaign headquarters in the Congress Hotel, Endicott saw a brass band playing outside the Stevens. All the musicians were girls wearing red jackets and skirts that barely covered their hips.

Go inside the main entrance. In Keeler's *Behind That Mask*, wax artist Yin Yi told an ancient Chinese customer, Sing Ling, that he had visited the great Shakespearean actor Sir Alfred Leets at the Stevens Hotel to demonstrate his acting ability.

In Howard Browne's *Pork City* he reports that *Chicago Tribune* crime reporter Jake Lingle had an elegant permanent suite on the twenty-seventh floor at a reduced rate (in return for using his influence to keep the hotel out of the papers).

In Mark Zubro's *Sorry Now*, detectives Fenwick and Turner found themselves in massive chaos in the lobby of the Chicago Hilton because archconservative author Arnold Bennett (aka William Buckley?), who wrote one thriller a year, was holding court for media and fans. Eccentric to a fault, Bennett made only one copy of his manuscripts and the current one had been stolen by some fake room service guys who said "Sorry now?"

The Hilton is often the scene of major banquets. In Mortimer Post's *Candidate for Murder*, four faculty members of the fictitious Chatham University constituted themselves an unofficial detective group to solve murders taking place on campus. (Post was really University of Chicago English Professor Walter Blair; see Walk 9.) The annual faculty dinner took place at the Franklin Hotel where a page boy told English Professor Gaylord a man was waiting for him near the telephones, but the call turned out to be a trap. Go up the stairs to the mezzanine if you like, but be very cautious if you are paged.

Walk through the lobby to the south end of the hotel. To your right at the end of the lobby are public phones and restrooms (downstairs) and some chairs to sit in. Then go outside and turn right to cross 8th Street to the Essex Inn at 800 S. Michigan. In *Death in Uptown* Michael Raleigh called it the Estes Motel. Whelan's client, small-town Jean Agee, stayed there while in town trying to find her brother Gerry. (Whelan specialized in finding lost kids.) Whelan went to the motel and took Jean to the Berghoff; then they walked back to Grant Park to see Buckingham Fountain lit at night.

Lakefront South

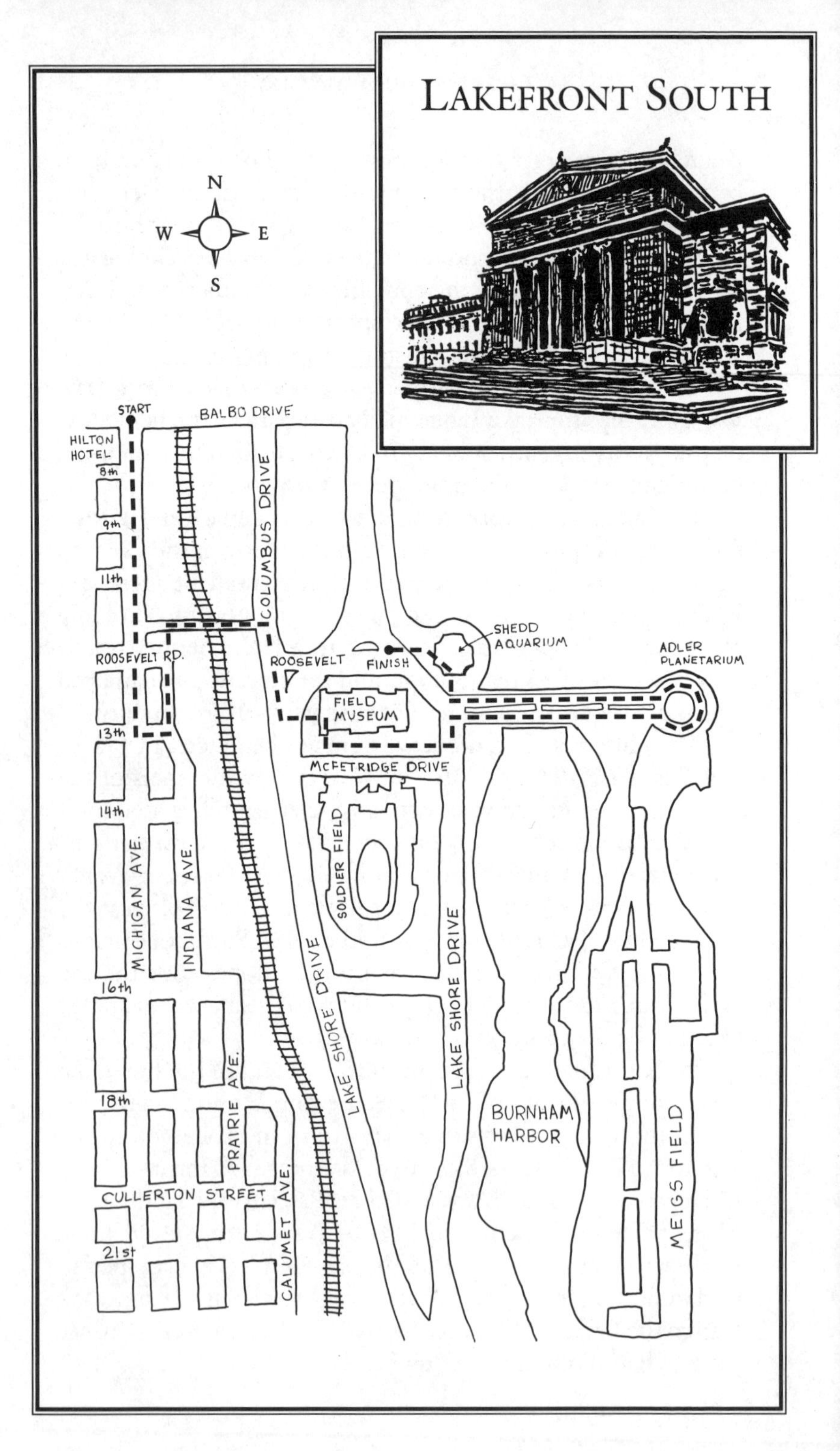

Keep walking south along Michigan Avenue past the gray facade of *Ebony/Jet* and a number of seedy-looking buildings. Cross 9th Street (there is no 10th Street), keep going past 11th Street and on to 12th Street, which is also Roosevelt Road. On the left you are passing the site of the old Illinois Central Railroad Station, a multistoried 1892 Victorian building with a clock tower, known as the Twelfth Street Station. It was the main station for trains from Florida and New Orleans. Now there is only a Metra suburban train station.

In Harry Keeler's *Behind That Mask* "Little Dolly," the incredibly fat love of Yin Yi's life, was supposed to catch the midnight train to New York with her suspicious husband Herman, the sword swallower, on Halloween night.

In Stuart Kaminsky's *You Bet Your Life*, Hollywood P.I. Toby Peters arrived on the City of Miami from his Florida visit with Al Capone. Louis Mayer of Metro-Goldwyn-Mayer had hired Peters to get the Mob to lay off Chico Marx, whom they accused of welshing on a Las Vegas gambling debt. A detective called Kleinhans from the Maxwell Street Station picked Peters up and insisted he check in at the LaSalle Hotel. (See Walk 3.)

In H. E. F. Donohue's *The Higher Animals*, a motley collection of grad students and young professors from the University of Chicago got mixed up in the Steinbeckian saga of three poor Southern whites trying to get back home. They first encountered each other at Lou's place which was near campus (aka Jimmy's), then everyone ended up at the Twelfth Street Station which the police had staked out because the three shot a black cop. But the three were holding some U of C hostages, making it a standoff. When the young wife of one hostage walked out in the middle of the waiting room asking them to let the hostages go, they shot her. Then both groups started shooting, leaving nearly everyone dead. In the parking lot where the station used to be there is now a sign announcing Central Station, the new development where Mayor Richard M. Daley lives, having left Bridgeport.

Walk down Michigan Avenue to 13th Street. In the middle of the next block at 1340 S. Michigan Avenue on the west side of the street is a tall, ornamented gray building with civic flags, commonly known as Greylords Court. It was the scene of a major Chicago scandal involving the court system.

James Touhy and Rob Warden described that scene of the crime in *Greylord Justice, Chicago Style*. It included judicial kickbacks and bribes, handled by a cooperative network of judges, lawyers, bailiffs, and other court personnel. In Barbara D'Amato's *Hardball*, murder victim Louise Sugarman complimented freelancer Cat Marsala on her article about the son of a Greylords judge. Cat had investigated how it felt to have your dad sent to jail.

Turn left to cross Michigan Avenue on 13th Street. On the east side of the street is a firehouse and beyond it the crumbling facade of an old hospital building, originally Wesley Memorial Hospital.

Walk east one block to Indiana Avenue where you will see the front of old St. Luke's Hospital on the east side of Indiana. It is a redbrick highrise building now turned into condos. St. Luke's joined Presbyterian Hospital and is part of the West Side Medical Center. (See Walk 10.) Wesley Memorial Hospital moved to Streeterville and is now part of Northwestern Memorial Hospital. (See Walk 5.)

But in Mignon Eberhart's 1938 mystery *The Glass Slipper*, the Cinderella nurse who married St. Luke's Chief of Staff Dr. Brule Hatterick returned here seeking clues to his first wife's murder. She met Dr. Andy Crittenton, Brule's assistant, and he took her to lunch.

In John Ashenhurst's 1933 *The World's Fair Murders*, St. Luke's Hospital was the one nearest Chicago Police Headquarters at 11th and State, so the five police officers who handled the mysterious suitcase owned by Professor Arturo del Grafko of Almania died there within an hour of each other.

Turn left on Indiana and walk through newly developing Central Station back to 12th Street. It is named for the old I.C. Central Station located here.

Walk north on Indiana until you come to the newly repaired pedestrian (not the railway) bridge over the I.C. Metra tracks that takes you to Columbus Drive. Take it toward the lake, but stop midway to look south where you get a splendid bird's-eye view of the site of the old Twelfth Street Station and the new Central Station houses. Eventually the entire area will be developed.

Continue to Columbus Drive. Turn right on the sidewalk to go south to Roosevelt Road (12th Street) where Columbus Drive ends. The statue of Columbus in the park is waving his sword south toward the site of the 1893 Columbian Exposition held in Hyde Park. (See Walk 9.)

Use the pedestrian push signals to cross Columbus Drive and then walk east on Roosevelt Drive to the Field Museum. Turn right to walk south past the west side of the Field Museum to McFetridge Drive. (William McFetridge was Park District President and a very powerful labor leader. Chicago, in spite of the Haymarket Riots and the Pullman Strike, is a strong "union town.")

Turn left again and walk behind the Field Museum; across the street to your right is the north end of Soldier Field. The huge colonnaded stadium was built in the '20s to honor World War I soldiers, and is used for sports, concerts and even demonstrations. Today it is known as the home of the Chicago Bears.

In Brian Michael's *Illegal Procedure* Soldier Field is called Daley Field (prophetic note?) and the Bears are the Chicago Cougars. In a Cougar's game when quarterback star Deke Campbell caught the ball, it blew up and he died in front of a huge audience. Chicago Police Lieutenant Frank Lesniak had to investigate this media event carried live on WBCC-TV.

In Carolyn Haddad's *Caught in the Shadows*, Bill Townsend took Becky Belski to watch a Bears' game from his brother Alan's skybox. It was a nasty cold day with wind off the lake, but the skyboxes were enclosed. The men talked business, the women were very polished, but Becky found their conversation was genteel oneupmanship that left her out. Wine and beer and hors d'oeuvres were served during the game; at halftime a whole new buffet luncheon appeared, but the Bears still lost.

In Mark Zubro's *Sorry Now*, Chicago detectives Paul Turner and Buck Fenwick questioned televangelist Bruce Mucklewrath's son about his father's Chicago crusade after his sister was shot dead on Oak Street Beach. Donald Mucklewrath insisted his father was looking forward to a successful run in Chicago, where Soldier Field was sold out for a week.

Cross Lake Shore Drive at McFetridge, heading toward Lake Michigan. Turn left to walk to Solidarity Drive, renamed by Mayor Jane Byrne in honor of Lech Walesa and Solidarity. The avenue had already been known as the "Polish corridor" because of the statues of Polish notables at either end.

Standing here and looking south, you are at the northern end of the World's Fair of 1933–34, which celebrated Chicago's Century of Progress. The fair stretched south from Roosevelt Road (12th Street) east of the railroad tracks, to 39th Street along Lake Michigan. It was largely built on landfill. Like the Hollywood sets it resembled, the fair helped to counter Depression "blues." The fair not only created jobs, its paid attendance was 39 million, more than any other fair to date.

The three museums, Meigs Field, and a classic column near the south end of Soldier Field in memory of Italian aviator General Italo Balbo and his flying armada who flew direct from Italy to Chicago, are the only remaining mementos of the fair. There are posters, maps, and souvenirs of the fair at the Chicago Historical Society. (See Walk 7.)

It began with a light beam from Arcturus—a star 225 million miles away—caught by telescope and focused on a photoelectric cell that provided enough power for the entire fair. Many of the buildings had no windows. Its exhibits were mostly of advances in science and technology. The Travel and Transport Building had a dome 206 feet in diameter suspended from cables. The Sky Ride—a trip through air on cable cars 200 feet off the ground—was very popular. A rebuilt Fort Dearborn and a group of other historic Chicago buildings such as a model of the log cabin where Abraham Lincoln was born, ended up at the Chicago Historical Society.

In Max Allan Collins's *True Crime*, P.I. Heller said that Chicagoans, having watched the Art Deco spires rise from the eighty-six acres along the lake, by summer were eager to leave hard times behind and enter the City of Tomorrow.

The fair also created jobs. Ex-cop Nate Heller was hired to

coach the private police force at the fair, where he became intimately acquainted with the fair's star, fan dancer Sally Rand. According to Kenan Heise and Ed Baumann in *Chicago Originals*, Rand got her start playing Lady Godiva, which led to her show at the fair's Streets of Paris. After originally refusing to take them, in 1966 the Chicago Historical Society accepted a pair of her ostrich fans.

Later in Collins's *Dying in the Postwar World*, ex-cop Heller worked on the real-life Wynekoop Case. He was hired by the family of Dr. Alice Wynekoop, accused and convicted of murdering her daughter-in-law, because her son Erle had also worked at the fair and knew Heller. The Wynekoop Case was also covered by crime reporter Craig Rice.

In *Daily News* crime reporter John Ashenhurst's *The World's Fair Murders*, Allison Bennett, a veteran police reporter for a leading evening newspaper, was sent by his editor to cover the arrival of VIP scientist Professor Arturo del Grafko of Almania. Del Grafko was going to reveal his earth-shaking secret invention at the fair. But as the professor was introduced planes zoomed over the rostrum, just clearing the cables of the Sky Ride and leaving behind them a prismatic trail of colored smoke—and the professor, shot dead. There was no clue who shot him or from where, but Allison discovered that the dead professor was an impostor and the real one had been shanghaied from the train in Fort Wayne.

Walk east on Solidarity Drive. In the parkway you first pass an equestrian statue of Kosciuszko, a Polish war hero; midway there is a standing statue of a Bohemian hero, Karel Havlicek; and finally, in front of the Adler Planetarium, a seated figure of Copernicus with a sphere of the heavens in his hand. These statues not only reflect Chicago's deep pride in her ethnic heritage but they also show that on ceremonial occasions ethnic groups prefer to assemble in safe places like the lakefront or the Daley Center.

This is the place to get the best view of Chicago's lakefront. To the north you can see the skyscraper skyline with Burnham Harbor in the foreground, to the south, McCormick Place and the steel mills of South Chicago where Paretsky's V.I. grew up.

On your right is the drive to Meigs Field, located on Northerly Isle which was part of the fairgrounds. In spite of prevailing west winds that make landing very tricky, Meigs is a city airport popular with company and small commercial planes. Its fate, however, is up in the air.

In Richard Himmel's *The Twenty-Third Web*, Chicago banker Livingston Stonehill was at an Art Institute gala when he heard that his grandson had been kidnaped. After a wild chase past the Field Museum, around Adler Planetarium, and a shoot-out near Meigs Field, he rescued the boy, took him home to Astor Street, and returned to the party.

In John Fink's *The Leaf Boats*, ad man Frank Gillespie had driven home from the Loop one stormy night only to have his house collapse, breaking his leg. The next day Gillespie had to drive to Meigs Field to fly to Galena with an obnoxious client called Terry Bennigan who wanted to build a recreational apartment complex near the Mississippi (aka the Galena Territory). Gillespie found that flying with a broken leg is no joke.

In Paul Engleman's *Catch a Fallen Angel*, New York P.I. Mark Renzler flew to Chicago in the private silver jet of *Paradise* magazine (aka Hefner's *Playboy*). In flight Renzler was plied with booze and girls until they landed at Meigs Field. In Paretsky's *Deadlock*, V.I. Warshawski drove to Meigs to try to find out who had been flown in there after the ship explosion in the Sault Ste. Marie locks. V.I. went into the small terminal and pretended to have been a passenger who lost an earring on the same company plane.

Detour to look at Meigs Field or keep walking east on Solidarity Drive until you reach the Max Adler Planetarium at 1300 S. Lake Shore Drive. Built in 1930, it was the first public planetarium in the United States. The twelve-sided granite domed Planetarium with its signs of the zodiac and its Astronomical Museum has different sky shows and exhibits depending upon the season. There are also telescopes available outside.

Circle the planetarium to walk back on Solidarity Drive to the Shedd Aquarium. In Paretsky's *Deadlock*, the fictional Grafalk Maritime Museum, given by the old Chicago family of shipowner Niels Grafalk, was located next to the Shedd Aquarium.

There used to be a maritime museum at North Pier but it has been replaced by a bicycle museum.

The John G. Shedd Aquarium, built in 1929, has the front of a Doric temple and a rear of modern glass housing its new Oceanarium. The interior is dim, as if you were under the ocean itself, even in the Coral Reef display.

In Michael A. Kahn's *Grave Designs*, Abbott & Windsor's law firm held a cocktail party there for partner Bill Williams, who was being made a judge. As sleuth Rachel Gold came in through the Doric columns, she saw the usual white-coated bartenders with the bar to the left of the Coral Reef in the large rotunda and the guest of honor to the right—glad-handing everyone. Rachel came with Professor Paul Mason, a "Young Turk of American literature" who taught Detective Fiction at Northwestern University. Mason had been Rachel's heart throb until she discovered he was playing "conferences" with his students on the side.

As Rachel passed the shark tank she saw a limp hand hanging down. Scared, she went through a forbidden door and upstairs into the fish tank access rooms where she found the murderer. Paul Mason came after her, but cowered under a table, so Rachel was rescued by chubby Benny Goldberg who heaved the murderer into the moray eels' tank.

Feel free to investigate the tanks, coral reef, and Oceanarium to your heart's content, taking care not to fall in, then come outside and take the pedestrian tunnel under the Outer Drive to the Field Museum.

The Field Museum grew out of the Columbian Exposition of 1893. Its backers felt the objects shown at the Palace of Fine Arts should have a permanent home in Chicago, and persuaded merchant prince Marshall Field to contribute a million dollars to keep the Palace of Fine Arts at the fairgrounds (now the home of the [Rosenwald] Museum of Science and Industry). The collection was kept there until 1920 when Field left another $8 million in his will, which allowed the Field Museum to build its present classical marble temple with caryatids (female figures) copied from Athens's famous Erechtheion. Inside, the museum has collections of animals, dinosaur bones, native American and

Egyptian objects and artifacts, a New Zealand Maori house, and Chicago's pet gorilla Bushman and beloved panda Su Lin, stuffed. Currently the museum is overhauling many of its exhibition halls.

In Robert Campbell's *The 600 Pound Gorilla*, the very thought of stuffing Lincoln Park Zoo's gorilla Baby sent shudders through the mayor who wanted to be reelected. In Michael Raleigh's *Death in Uptown*, P.I. Paul Whelan's client Jean Agee told him she had walked through Grant Park to the "museum with the dinosaurs."

When Clyde B. Clason wrote *The Man from Tibet*, Tibet was still independent. Adam Merriweather, a very rich but nasty collector, who lived in a mansion on North Sheridan Road, had a huge private collection on display in his Tibetan Room. Everyone agreed that the only Tibetan collection that matched Merriweather's is the one in the Field Museum, but much of his collection was of questionable provenance. Many items were found by his brother Dr. Jed Merriweather, an explorer, whose expeditions Adam financed. (Marshall Field's brother Stanley also made expeditions for the Field Museum.) Jed Merriweather helped his brother buy a stolen eighth-century sacred Tibetan manuscript, but using a magic ceremony described in the manuscript, Adam Merriweather was killed by lightning inside his "locked" Tibetan Room. His death was investigated by the Chicago police with the help of Theocritus Lucius Westborough, a small, spry 70-year-old scholar of ancient history, who wore gold-rimmed bifocals. He was assisted by Tibetan lama Tsongpun Bonbo who had turned up with $20 thousand to buy back his lamasery's sacred book.

The Field Museum's Tibetan exhibit is located on the balcony above the Great Hall with its fighting elephants and newly created Brachiosaurus. Go look at it, but to be on the safe side, try not to be there if there is a thunderstorm outside on Lake Michigan.

End your walk with a snack in the Field Museum's basement McDonald's, or if the weather is nice, go outside to buy a Chicago hot dog from one of the vendors near the Aquarium. From the Field Museum steps you have another spectacular view of the city.

2

EAST LOOP WALK

State Street

BACKGROUND

As all roads led to ancient Rome, all roads in Chicago lead to the Loop, the city's "downtown." Today, like New York's Wall Street or the "City" of London, the Loop is a workaday world. Mondays through Fridays, nine to five, its streets are jammed with people, and this is the best time to explore Loop shopping, eating, art and architecture. For city politics, law, finance, and trading see Walk 3: Loop West: LaSalle Street.

Shopping is Chicago's middle name. The art of modern merchandising was invented by the city's merchant princes, who founded the giant companies like Sears, Roebuck; Montgomery Ward; Wieboldt's; Goldblatts; and most important Marshall Field's and Carson Pirie Scott. The centerpiece of this walk therefore is State Street, the late "Great Street," now a mall that natives hope will regain its former glory.

From its beginnings in 1837 when land speculation was booming until the Great Chicago Fire in 1871, the Loop area was both residential and commercial because with poor transportation it made sense to live near work. Wabash Avenue was the street of rich Protestant churches; south of Van Buren were elegant houses, while workers' shanties and vice lurked about the edges.

Pioneer trader Gurdon Hubbard, whom the Indians called Swift Walker, had laid out Hubbard Trail from Vincennes to Chicago in 1834. It was renamed State Road when official milestones were placed along it. Then Potter Palmer, one of Chicago's first great developers, in 1866 bought up most of State Street, paved it, built a store to rent to Marshall Field, and in 1871, opened his luxury Palmer House Hotel. His hotel burned to the ground during the Chicago Fire, but Palmer had a new, fireproof one opened by 1873. Mystery writer Mary Craig's historical *The Chicagoans: Dust to Diamonds,* is the post-Fire saga of a fictional Potter Palmer.

The original grid pattern of the Loop was maintained after the Fire and by 1880 it had become a business center encircled by cable cars, which were replaced by the electric elevated trains in 1897. The fact that the Loop numbering system begins at State and Madison—long ballyhooed by civic boosters as "the World's Busiest Corner"—meant that it became Chicago's Times Square when theaters lined Randolph and State Streets and people gathered to celebrate New Year's Eve or VJ Day marking the end of World War II. Its demise came from the decision in 1979 to make State Street a mall—a decision now being reconsidered.

Unlike New York's long-gone "Els," Chicago's Els are still there, and their noisy, dirty presence is often evoked by Chicago writers like Nelson Algren who called them Chicago's "rusty iron heart." Long before cars were so common—and parking such a problem—the El brought Chicagoans downtown to enjoy the sights. Robert Bloch in his introduction to *Murder and Mystery in Chicago* says he and his sister learned the geography of the city through the windows of elevated trains and spent their weekends in the Loop. Their Saturdays began with shopping and ended with a vaudeville show or musical. In *War in Heaven* Andrew Greeley wrote that the El is as important to many of his characters as it was to him growing up when no girl would complain about an El ride to a movie or nightclub.

In Charles Merrill Smith's *Reverend Randollph and the Unholy Bible,* former L.A. Rams quarterback "Con" Randollph, observing the city from his skyscraper church, says that "Downtown Chicago was just another city—busy, grubby streets packed with people rushing to perform duties or complete errands that made little difference in the scheme of things . . . [but] there was a current of vitality running through this city.

He supposed it was generated by the crowds, the traffic, the . . . constant noise of buildings being built or destroyed."

Come see it for yourself. You can observe the changes from the days when Craig Rice let Helene Justus park by Marshall Field's and dash inside to lose a police tail to the present when you can ice skate on the site of Clarence Darrow's office building. The Loop is in transition, but then as now, characters in Chicago mysteries go to the Loop because they work there, stay at its hotels, eat at its restaurants, or shop at its department stores.

LENGTH OF WALK: About 1½ miles

A note about Loop streets and directions: Native Chicagoans instinctively know that Lake Michigan is on the east and use it as the fixed point for getting around. State and Madison is the "center" of the city because north/south street numbers begin at Madison and east/west street numbers begin at State Street. Using the numbering system, east to west, north to south, figure every 400 numbers (or 4 blocks) is half a mile.

See the map on page 49 for the boundaries of this walk and page 338 for a list of the books and detectives mentioned.

PLACES OF INTEREST

Carson Pirie Scott & Company, 1 S. State Street. Cast-iron facade designed by Louis Sullivan. Open Mon.–Fri. 9:45 A.M. to 7:00 P.M., Sat. 9:45 A.M.–6:00 P.M., Sun. noon–5:00 P.M. Call 641-7000.

Chicago Theatre, 175 N. State Street.

Harold Washington Library Center, 400 S. State Street. Public tours Mon. noon and 2:00 P.M., Tue.–Sat. 11:30 A.M., noon, 2:00 P.M. Open Mon. 9:00 A.M.–7:00 P.M., Wed., Fri., Sat. 9:00 A.M.–5:00 P.M., Tues., Thur. 11:00 A.M.–7:00 P.M. Call 747-4200.

Marshall Field & Company, 111 N. State Street. 450 departments based on Field's dictum "Give the lady what she wants." Open Mon.–Fri. 9:45 A.M.–7:00 P.M., Sat. 9:45 A.M.–6:00 P.M., Sun. noon–5:00 P.M. Call 781-1000.

Monadnock Building, 53 W. Jackson Boulevard.

Palmer House, 17 E. Monroe Street. Call 726-7500.

Reliance Building, 32 N. State Street.

PLACES TO EAT

Binyon's, 327 S. Plymouth Court. Midwest Chapter of Mystery Writers of America meets here.

The Ferris Wheel, 182 S. State Street.

Monadnock Building, Jackson Boulevard and Federal Street: Cavanaugh's Restaurant and Bar, Federal Street entrance; Jacobs Bros. Bagels, Jackson Street entrance.

Marshall Field's, 111 N. State Street: Restaurants (including the famed Walnut Room) are on the seventh floor, cafeterias in the basement, ice cream parlor on the third floor.

Miller's Pub, 134 S. Wabash Avenue.

Palmer House, 17 E. Monroe Street: Boca Raton Cafe, French Quarter, Palmer's Steak & Seafood House, Trader Vic's.

— EAST LOOP WALK: STATE STREET —

Begin your walk at the corner of State and Van Buren by the neoclassic red stone Harold Washington Library Center. Van Buren is the southern boundary of the CTA's elevated track that circles the downtown area, familiarly known as the Loop. One block east on Wabash Avenue, the El turns the corner past the new Old Saint Mary's Church, Chicago's first Roman Catholic parish founded in 1833, to head north to Lake Street, go west to Wells, turn south and come back around to Van Buren again.

Until the new library opened in 1991, this part of Van Buren Street—and the South Loop—was a hodgepodge of pawn shops, broken sidewalks, not-for-profits' storefront offices, and funny little restaurants and bars. You still get the feel of old times by going west past Clark Street or by looking up Wabash under the El. Ronny's III a block east at Wabash and Van Buren is the kind of joint Sara Paretsky's private eye, V.I. Warshawski patronized when working late at her office in *Indemnity Only.*

This territory is in transition. It was V.I.'s Loop turf but in *Burn Marks* she realized that the neighborhood was gentrifying as she walked west on Van Buren hunting for a store that sold work clothes. (There used to be a big Army and Navy store where the library is now.) V.I. complained that the systematic mowing down of the Loop to make room for glitzy highrises has driven most of the low-rent business away (panhandlers and homeless, too).

One hundred years ago this was called "Satan's Mile," a vice district, whose most famous businessman was Mickey Finn who ran the Lone Star Saloon on State Street between Van Buren and Jackson. Finn operated a confidence game like the scam pulled off by Robert Redford and Paul Newman in *The Sting,* which is set in gangster-land Chicago. Finn also created a knockout drink that became world-famous.

Across State Street at Van Buren are two buildings that used to be the flagship department stores of Sears and Goldblatts (originally Rothschild's). Both chains were started by Chicago families. Now Sears (south of the El) is a city office building while Goldblatts is part of De Paul University's expanding Loop campus. (See Walk 7.) V.I. Warshawski's favorite newspaper snitch Murray Ryerson of the *Herald-Star* slobbered over De Paul's basketball-playing Blue Demons. But V.I., in spite of playing on a state championship team in high school and going to the University of Chicago on an athletic scholarship, didn't really care if the Blue Demons ever scored another basket, although she knew that in Chicago that was heresy, like saying you hated the St. Patrick's Day Parade, when Chicago dyes the river kelly green.

Speaking of green, look up at the huge metallic owls of wisdom crowning the new library, which was named for the late Mayor Harold Washington. (The downtown library for many years was located in what is now called the Cultural Center, at Randolph and Michigan. See Walk 1.)

In Sara Paretsky's *Guardian Angel,* V.I. had to use the temporary storage area on the west edge of the Loop where the library's books were housed until the Washington Library was built. V.I. approved of the fact that after two decades of dickering, Chicago was actually building a new public library, but she thought the building itself had the unfortunate look of a Victorian mausoleum.

Decide if you agree with V.I.'s assessment and either go inside the elegant marble and brass lobby and take the regular tour, or explore the library on your own from the lobby to the Winter Garden and Washington Collection on nine. To do so, you take the escalators to the third floor, then either elevators or escalators to the top. There are restrooms on each floor near the elevators.

The library is lavishly decorated with contemporary Chicago artists' work. On three in the Thomas Hughes Room, named for the Mayor of London who sent Chicago books after the Great Chicago Fire of 1871, you can find juvenile mysteries by Chicago writers Mary (Shura) Craig and Marion Markham. On seven is a Chicago Authors Room with *no* mention of Chicago's many mystery writers. But seven is also the court of last resort when trying to locate old or out-of-print Chicago mysteries. The Inter-Library Loan Department, for example, found me the Edgar Wallace mystery *On the Spot* at the University of Alabama. First try the stacks, then the computer, then ask at the desk. The books donated in honor of Mary Craig, who had been president of Mystery Writers of America, Midwest and was national MWA president at the time of her death, are listed in the computer system and identified by special bookplates.

On nine, in addition to the Winter Garden and the Washington Collection is Special Collections, where there are copies of works by Allan Pinkerton, Chicago's first police detective, who was also Abraham Lincoln's bodyguard and a Union spy during the Civil War. In 1883 Pinkerton wrote a story about a bank robbery, called *The Burglar's Fate and the Detectives,* and according to Kenan Heise and Ed Baumann in *Chicago Originals,* Pinkerton's motto "We never sleep" with the logo of a wide-open eye, led to the name "private eye" (aka P.I., "private investigator"). A well-known Pinkerton agent was mystery writer Dashiell Hammett, whose Nick Charles in *The Thin Man* is also an ex-P.I.

East Loop

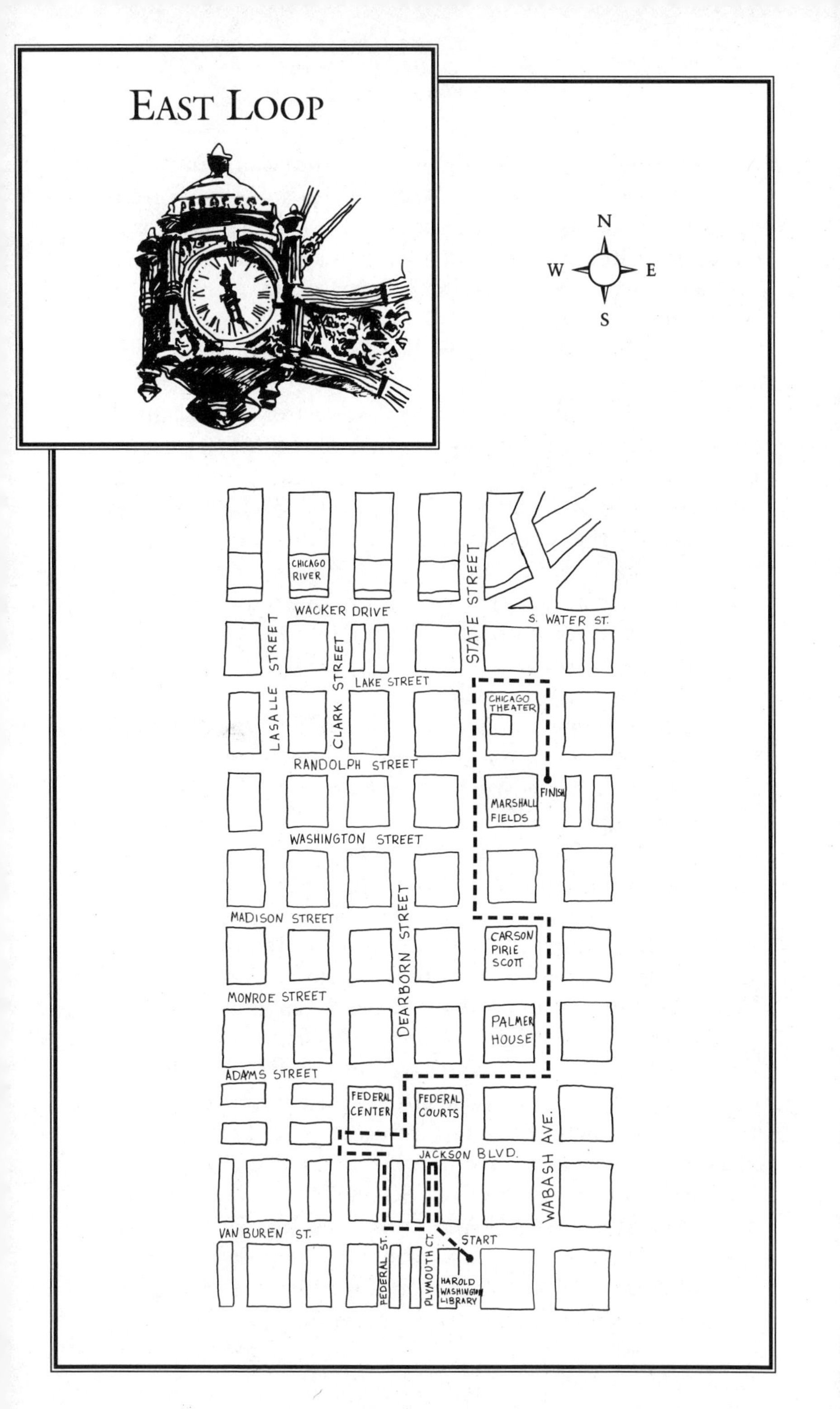
N
W
E
S
CHICAGO RIVER
WACKER DRIVE
STATE STREET
S. WATER ST.
LASALLE STREET
CLARK STREET
LAKE STREET
CHICAGO THEATER
RANDOLPH STREET
FINISH
MARSHALL FIELDS
WASHINGTON STREET
DEARBORN STREET
MADISON STREET
CARSON PIRIE SCOTT
MONROE STREET
PALMER HOUSE
ADAMS STREET
FEDERAL CENTER
FEDERAL COURTS
WABASH AVE.
JACKSON BLVD.
VAN BUREN ST.
START
FEDERAL ST.
PLYMOUTH CT.
HAROLD WASHINGTON LIBRARY

But more important for many mystery fans, in Arthur Conan Doyle's *The Valley of Death,* Sherlock Holmes investigated the mysterious murder of a Pinkerton agent sent from Chicago to infiltrate a mining gang. As a result P.I. Birdy Edwards was pursued across the Atlantic to end up in the moat of an English country manor.

Harold Washington's first race for mayor in 1983 began with an all-out Democratic primary fight between Mayor Jane Byrne, Washington, and fledgling State's Attorney Richard M. Daley in which Daley and Byrne canceled each other out. Michael Cormany's *Red Winter* took place during that primary fight when a lot of the old guard Democratic Machine were pro-Byrne because they knew Richie Daley couldn't win. One tough precinct captain tried to force free spirit P.I. Dan Kruger to register to vote. Ironically, Kruger was working for "connected" business contractor Nicholas Cheyney whose "Chinaman"—i.e., patron—was the sleazy 55th Ward alderman. (There actually are only fifty wards in Chicago.)

After exploring the library, come out of the Plymouth Court entrance on the northwest side of the lobby. Across the street (really alley) is a small bar-restaurant in the landmark Old Colony Building at 407 S. Plymouth. Called Karl's Pub, this bare narrow bar that goes through to Dearborn is another place V.I. might hang out, but not as fancy as her favorite bar, the Golden Glow.

Cross Van Buren at Plymouth Court to the tiny park created by tearing down junky shops. Walk north along Plymouth Court past the park and parking garage to Binyon's.

Binyon's is an old Chicago institution famous for its turtle soup and its legal clientele who have patronized it since Prohibition. It is not open on weekends, so plan accordingly if you want to lunch there. The monthly meetings of Mystery Writers of America Midwest have been held there on the second Wednesday of the month from September to May since they were moved there by MWA Midwest President Sara Paretsky.

Binyon's is also a broker hangout during the day, so it is appropriate that in Bill Granger's *The El Murders,* two young runners at the Board of Trade always went to Binyon's for a Friday night drink before they headed for State Street and the Near North side. One Friday when it was very cold and the wind slapped around the canyons of buildings, the two went to the bar on the second floor of the old restaurant with its wood-paneled walls and clublike atmosphere. They talked about going to the Biograph Theater (shades of bank robber John Dillinger), but decided to eat at Gordon's at 500 N. Clark Street, just north of the river, then take the El home. Members of a Humboldt Park gang attacked them when they got off the El. If you read Granger's mystery, you will never ride the El again!

In Max Allan Collins's *Dying in the Postwar World* P.I. Nate Heller had lunch there with Ken Levine, the attorney who got him together with Bob Keenan over the kidnap-murder of Keenan's 6-year-old daughter JoAnn. This story is a fictionalized replay of the Suzanne Degnan murder case. For a more factual account read Delores Kennedy's story of the convicted killer, *William Heirens: His Day in Court*.

Nate Heller observed that the restaurant was a businessman's bastion with wooden booths and spartan decor. For years Heller had been an occasional customer, but postwar business was good and his suits were Brooks Brothers not Maxwell Street, so he could afford to hobnob on a more regular basis with the brokers, lawyers, and other well-to-do thieves who ate there.

If you don't want to try the turtle soup, walk past Binyon's to John Marshall Law School and the Tigerman-McCurry 1991 mix of Gothic and Mies van der Rohe Chicago Bar Association Building. At Jackson Boulevard there is a Dunkin' Donuts if you want a snack.

In Michael A. Kahn's *Grave Designs* Chicago Police Detective Kevin Turelli, who worked his way through John Marshall, had been a first-year law associate at Abbott & Windsor with Rachel Gold. They became good friends and after he went back to the Chicago police department as a detective, Rachel sought his help when her investigation into the odd will of Abbott & Windsor senior partner Graham turned lethal.

Turn left to cross Plymouth Court and walk back down the west side of Plymouth Court. You pass the plain limestone facade of the Standard Club, the most prestigious Jewish club in Chicago. In Richard Himmel's *The Twenty-Third Web,* hotshot lawyer Irving Feldman was trying to end a blackmail conspiracy against his clients which was aimed at keeping them from giving money to Israel. Feldman dined there with his wife and clients like banker Livingston Stonehill, whose ex-son-in-law was an Arab sympathizer.

In Shelby Yastrow's *Undue Influence* Leon Schlessinger, the lawyer for Beth Zion Synagogue, takes younger lawyer Phil Ogden there to talk about the Ben Stillman will. In the will Stillman, who was not Jewish, had left Beth Zion $8 million. The two men met in the majestic lobby, then ate in the grill, not the main dining room. They liked each other, but were disappointed that they had no clue why Stillman left the money that way. They both knew, too, that Stillman's creditors or even rival claimants might get the money.

Just south of the Standard Club is the salmon-colored terracotta Fisher Building. An 1896 landmark, it is an early example of a Gothic-style skyscraper. Walk past it to Van Buren again and turn right to walk to Dearborn. In the corner of the Fisher Building is Morry's Old-Fashioned Deli, but prize fighter Barney Ross's speakeasy is no longer hidden behind the deli for the convenience of Prohibition drinkers.

In Max Allan Collins's *True Detective* and *True Crime,* ex-cop Nate Heller had his office (and a bed) on the fourth floor of the Fisher Building. Barney Ross, with whom he grew up on Chicago's West Side, hired Heller to be a live-in nightwatchman. Heller had a series of strange visitors there. One who may have been bank robber John Dillinger, sent Heller to "mob-connected" lawyer Louis Piquott. (See Walk 3.)

Cross Dearborn at Van Buren. To your left across Congress you can see Printers Row and the old Dearborn Street Station at Polk Street. (See Walk 8.)

The Monadnock Building on the northwest corner of Van Buren and Dearborn is the tallest wall-bearing "skyscraper" in Chicago (sixteen stories), with walls that are six feet thick at the base. It has been lovingly rehabbed and houses government agencies and not-for-profit organizations.

Go in the Van Buren door and walk through the block-long corridor. In John D. MacDonald's *One Fearful Yellow Eye* Travis McGee, in Chicago to help out an old girl friend recently widowed, heard about a P.I. firm called Allied Services run by a Francisco Smith. Allied Services had offices in the Monadnock Block on West Jackson, and McGee and Francisco Smith met for lunch in the restaurant because Frankie thought his office was bugged. He told McGee he was keeping track of Geis's mistress Gretchen Gorba and her kids because one of them was Geis's own daughter. McGee was in Chicago to help Geis' widow solve his death.

Half way down the corridor you come to Cavanaugh's Bar and Restaurant on the left side of the building with a street entrance on Federal Street. Its modern furnishings look old-fashioned and it has a polished wood bar. This is about the location of V.I. Warshawski's favorite bar, the Golden Glow. In Paretsky's *Blood Shot,* V.I. meets reporter Murray Ryerson there. Ryerson's mythical Chicago newspaper had its offices across from the *Chicago Sun-Times,* accessible to the Billy Goat, a lower-level restaurant patronized by reporters, meaning his paper was actually the *Chicago Tribune.*

In *Deadlock* the Golden Glow was tucked away in the DuSable Building, an 1890s skyscraper, and had the horseshoe-shaped mahogany bar that came from the old Cyrus McCormick mansion. It had seven tiny booths (Cavanaugh's has no booths) and was run by Sal, a big black and beautiful bartender/owner who lets V. I. run a tab for her Johnny Walker Black Label drinks. In addition to Cavanaugh's there is a Jacobs Bros. Bagel Bakery at the Jackson entrance.

Leave the Monadnock at Jackson and turning left, cross Federal Street to the Union League Club at 51 W. Jackson. Unless you are the guests of a member, you will not be able to go inside to admire the dining rooms or the magnificent library and art collection.

In Michael A. Kahn's *Grave Designs* WASP Kent Charles, an Abbott & Windsor partner, played handball there very day. A poor boy who had made his own way, Charles lived alone in a Gold Coast highrise. He also was an eligible widower who owned his own sailboat, so he could not understand why Rachel Gold did not like him.

In Paretsky's *Bitter Medicine,* V.I. went to night court at Police Headquarters and found her ex-husband Richard Yarborough in court to represent Dieter Monkfish. Monkfish was the head of pro-life IckPiff, which had vandalized Lotty Herschel's clinic. V.I. was surprised that Dick was representing someone like Monkfish and Yarborough replied, "I certainly wouldn't invite him to the Union League Club with me."

In Yastrow's *Undue Influence* Phil Ogden met Max Kane there. Kane was the lawyer for the brokerage firm where Yastrow's dead client Ben Stillman worked. As they ate Kane was busy writing on a yellow pad in spite of the Union League Club rule: no open display of business papers.

Cross Clark Street at Jackson and walk back past the Kluczynski Federal office building, which has a row of handsome bronze plaques along the Dearborn Street corridor.

Either walk through the building or go into Federal Plaza to look more closely at the huge red Calder statue called *Flamingo.* Bill Granger remarked that it looked more like a red lobster.

Cross Dearborn Street at Jackson and go into the lobby of the Dirksen Federal Courts Building. It is a massive bare gloomy hallway of gray and black marble. If you want a snack, head for the elevators to your right and go to two. The general public is welcome and you will see lots of court personnel like marshals and bailiffs and jurors and lawyers and cops. Two is also the location of the jury assembly room, where the federal and grand jurors wait to be called.

If you want to watch a trial, go past the elevators to the right to the Security Desk where you must go through a metal detector like an airport's. (There was a shoot-out in an elevator with a prisoner brought from the Metropolitan Correctional Center that left a guard dead.) Then go to floors 17–25 where the federal judges have their chambers and courtrooms. (If you have a particular judge in mind, see the directory in the main lobby.)

Just in case, keep an eye on the other people in the elevator. In Andrew Greeley's *The Patience of a Saint* trial lawyer Eileen Ryan Kane—sister of Father Blackie Ryan of Holy Name Cathedral and wife of newspaper columnist Red Kane—was attacked in one of the elevators. She was defending Hurricane Houston, an unbusinesslike black athlete whom the State's Attorney wanted to "railroad" to win himself both media fame and election to higher office.

The FBI has its offices on the ninth floor. In Paretsky's *Killing Orders,* V.I. went there to hassle her old law-school classmate Derek Hatfield about the phony stock certificates found in her Aunt Rosa's church safe. V.I. twitted Hatfield about his good view of the federal lockup, better known as the Metropolitan Correctional Center, on Clark and Van Buren. (See Walk 3.)

In Bill Granger's *Drover,* ex-sportswriter Jimmy Drover, who had been fired for his mob connections, worked for a Las Vegas bookie. When his girlfriend's husband was killed for gambling debts, Drover vowed revenge. He came to Chicago and ran a highly successful scam at an old Mafioso's plush home in the western suburbs. Having taken the murderer for all he had, Drover went to the Drake Hotel where the FBI picked him up. They knew all about the game—proving somebody there was "wired." They took him to the "United States Interior Survey Division" and worked him over, then asked him to turn informer himself.

In Paretsky's *Blood Shot,* V.I. also visited the Department of Labor there to see another University of Chicago law school classmate, Jonathan Michaels. V.I. wanted to find out if any workers had tried to sabotage the Xerxes plant in South Chicago where her mother's friend Louisa worked and got cancer.

In Kahn's *Grave Designs,* lawyer Rachel Gold went to Judge Harry Wilson's courtroom on the twenty-second floor for morning motion call. While waiting, Rachel read the elaborate codicil to Graham Marshall's will which called for Abbott & Windsor to give his pet Canaan's grave perpetual care.

Come out of the Dirksen Building on Dearborn and turn right to walk north to Adams. Cross Adams and turn right to walk east to State Street. At State and Adams turn left and walk to a small alley. Across the alley, at 120 S. State, is a long narrow restaurant called the Ferris Wheel.

The Ferris Wheel is open seven days a week. It advertises gyros and pita bread and has old-fashioned sodas and sundaes. Wood paneled, it has booths and a long bar that stretches to the rear exit on the alley, and there is a State Street subway entrance at its front door.

In Sam Reaves's *Fear Will Do It,* cabbie Cooper MacLeish went to a restaurant called the "Carousel" on State Street just north of Adams with a lunch counter down one side, booths, and a front door near a subway entrance. He wanted to dicker with some strongmen who had his girlfriend Diana Froelich Vela locked up in a car trunk. When strongman Wes Czop came in with Diana in tow, there was a shoot-out. Have a cup of coffee in booth three, but keep an eye on the other customers.

Come out on State Street and go back to Adams. State Street, "that Great Street," was once the center of Chicago merchandising, with the world's busiest corner at State and Madison, but lately it's been overtaken by North Michigan Avenue. A mall since 1979, the city fathers are thinking of reopening it to traffic. State Street originally was a trail all the way from Vincennes to Chicago, laid out by Chicago pioneer Gurdon Hubbard. State Road became State Street in 1834 when the official milestones were put in, but its real development occurred when Potter Palmer built the Field & Leiter department store there in 1868 and opened his first hotel in 1871.

Cross State Street at Adams and walk east to Wabash Avenue, dark and dirty with the El racing past overhead. In Paretsky's *Deadlock* V.I. Warshawski had several places along Wabash from Van Buren to Monroe Street where she went to eat in a hurry. But Paretsky's names, like the Spot or Johnnie's Steak Joynt, won't match up with the ones you see.

As you walk along Adams look across the street. There is a public parking lot on the site of the original Miller's Pub at 23 W. Adams. After a fire a few years ago, Miller's moved around the corner to 134 S. Wabash, next door to the Palmer House. I had a drink at the old Miller's one night with MWA chapter president Mary Craig and British visitor Ian Stuart, both great mystery writers.

Turn left at the corner of Wabash and walk north on the west side of Wabash to the new Miller's Pub. (It sometimes is hard to tell which Miller's Pub a mystery means, since this one also has stained glass windows, wood paneling, a long bar, and their autographed Celebrity Photo Gallery. Go inside and see for yourself. They are very hospitable.)

In Bill Granger's *The El Murders,* Chicago Police Sergeant Terry Flynn and his partner Karen Kovac ate lunch at Miller's. In Granger's *The Newspaper Murders,* Jack Donovan from the State's Attorney's Office and Police Lieutenant Matt Schmitt met at Miller's long bar to discuss their strategy for dealing with the gang murder of newspaper reporter Francis X. Sweeney.

In Sam Reaves's *Fear Will Do It,* cabbie Cooper MacLeish called *Maverick Magazine* owner Moss Wetzel, who agreed to meet at Miller's to cut a deal: trading the evidence incriminating Wetzel in return for Cooper's girlfriend.

In Michael Cormany's *Red Winter,* P.I. Dan Kruger was told by a source that he'd been in Miller's Pub and heard about a videotape that showed a cop was having kinky sex. The cop, a 25-year man, was about to retire with full perks. Later Kruger returned to Miller's to wait out the night until meeting with his rich client Nicholas Cheyney on the top of a Wells Street parking lot.

In Crabbe Evers's *Murder in Wrigley Field,* old newshorse Duffy House took his visiting niece Petey for drinks at Marina City, then back to Miller's Pub for a real steak. Since Petey was a sports bug, House figured she'd like the best sports photo gallery this side of Cooperstown, N.Y.

Look inside, then come out of Miller's Pub and cross the small alley to the Palmer House Hotel. This major mystery hotel occupies most of the block from Wabash to State, Adams to Monroe, and is the oldest continually operating hotel in the United States. Potter Palmer, a Chicago founding father, built the original Palmer House in 1871 as part of his development of State Street. His Field & Leiter building was the beginning of the State Street row of major department stores that once included the flagship stories of Field's, Carson's, Wieboldt's, Rothschild's, Lytton's, the Fair Store, Mandel's, Sears, and Goldblatts.

On October 7, Palmer's 225-room hotel burned to the

ground during the Great Chicago Fire, but Palmer had built a new hotel guaranteed fireproof by 1873. The present structure, now owned by the Hilton Hotel chain, was built 1925–27. The hotel has had many famous writers as guests, among them Mark Twain, Oscar Wilde, Rudyard Kipling, and Charles Dickens, as well as Presidents Grant, Ford, and Carter.

Palmer's wife Bertha, whose portrait by Zorn hangs in the Art Institute, was not only a famous Society matron but the energetic organizer of the Women's Building at the 1893 Columbian Exposition. An internationally known hostess, she also invested in French Impressionist paintings, helping to establish Chicago's collection at the Art Institute as one of the world's best. (See Walk 1.)

Walk past the main Wabash entrance to the Palmer House to the restaurant called Palmer's Steak and Seafood House. In Reaves's *Fear Will Do It,* con artist Tommy Thorne, in town to blackmail the owner of *Maverick Magazine,* used Cooper's girl Diana. Thorne went past the main entrance with its liveried doormen into a long and narrow restaurant/bar and found a place to sit, ordered a beer and pulled out a *Christian Science Monitor* to read (a high sign for Diana). Diana came in and ordered a drink, then Moss Wetzel himself came into the bar and Diana laid a thick manila folder on the table and left by the Arcade door.

Go in the Wabash Street entrance to the Palmer House. You are in the shop-filled Arcade which runs from Wabash to State Street. Once upon a time there was also a barbership with 250 silver dollars embedded in the floor. In *American Gothic* Chicagoan Robert Bloch, author of "Yours truly, Jack the Ripper," who went to Hollywood and wrote Alfred Hitchcock's *Psycho,* described the scene as it was in 1893. Newspaper editor Charlie Hogan had a regular Saturday appointment but tradition was shattered when his young female reporter Crystal turned up. By putting him at a disadvantage, she talked him into letting her do a story on the Castle, a hotel near the 1893 Columbian Exposition in Hyde Park. (See Walk 9.)

Inside the Arcade the stairs to your right take you to the

basement where you can find the Palmer House Coffee Shop and Trader Vic's. Or take the escalator to your left to the lobby where the elaborate ceiling with its naked women was recently restored. There are plenty of places to sit and wait for someone, phones, and restrooms. Straight ahead across the lobby are the steps leading up to the fabled Empire Room. It was once the most famous big-name entertainment spot in Chicago. In Ron Levitsky's *The Innocence That Kills,* lawyer Nate Rosen was unimpressed by the opulence which condensed centuries of European art into one room!

In Arthur Maling's *Dingdong,* after returning from a crazy trip to Switzerland to collect $400,000, actor Mike Wiley and his bodyguard stayed at the Palmer House because Dingdong was still at large. The next day Wiley's girl, actress Holly Simmons, was kidnaped during a fire Dingdong set at her Loop theater. (It could have been the Shubert on Monroe between State and Dearborn.)

In Michael Sherer's *Death Came Dressed in White,* freelance writer Emerson Ward met and fell for Catherine McCrae, a designer, at a fashion show at the Palmer House. They were lovers until she was murdered on a buying trip to California. Then Emerson got involved in finding out why.

On your right is Windsor's Lobby Bar and Cafe, once the scene of a live radio show. In William McGivern's *Very Cold for May,* Jake Harrison went to the Palmer House to meet his client's wife Denise Riordan. Harrison got her a drink at the private bar run by radio station WXL and Denise let slip the fact that Riordan's alibi for the death of his old mistress May Laval was no good.

Reporters Vincent Starrett and Robert Bloch used to meet at the Palmer House for drinks after work. Starrett, a world authority on Sherlock Holmes who wrote the classic *The Secret Life of Sherlock Holmes,* also wrote "The Eleventh Juror" about a criminal trial at 26th and California. The story has a nice chauvinist touch: in 1937 only men served on Chicagoland juries, but the Cook County League of Women Voters under President Ursula B. Stone opened juries to women shortly afterwards. Another Chicago Sherlockian, Dr. Eli Liebow, is a former "Sir Hugo" who wrote *Dr. Joe Bell, Model for Sherlock Holmes.*

When I checked out, the Palmer House lobby was full of saffron-robed monks from the Parliament of the World's Religions, to which Mother Teresa and the Dalai Lama came. In Clyde Clason's 1937 *The Man from Tibet* wealthy Adam Merriweather was murdered after buying a sacred Buddhist manuscript that had been stolen. Amateur sleuth Theocritus Lucius Westborough, a spry 70-year-old ancient historian with gold-rimmed bifocals went with police Lieutenant Mack to "Prescott House" to interview Tsongpun Bonbo, the lama who was robbed of the sacred book and came to Chicago with $20,000 to buy it back. Tsongpun Bonbo was a nice little fellow who reminds you of ET. The two men found the lobby full of an Antelope convention.

In Elliott Roosevelt's *The President's Man,* set during the Democratic convention of 1932 at which Franklin D. Roosevelt was nominated for the first time, Roosevelt's childhood chum "Blackjack" John Endicott stayed at the Palmer House. Endicott had come to tell Chicago gangsters that Prohibition was dead no matter who won, so it would be a waste of time to kill FDR.

Mobster Murray (the Camel) Humphries took Endicott out for a night on the town at Capone-controlled nightclubs. They visited the Cotton Club with black musicians and white hookers, and Endicott brought one called Tiffany back to his Palmer House suite. Next day while Endicott was meeting Frank Nitti, Capone's lieutenant, at his Loop office, two hoods came in and beat up Tiffany. They were then eliminated by Murray and Nitti, angry that outsiders had muscled in, and their bodies were dumped in front of the Palmer House. Endicott also had a visit from gangster Dutch Schultz–aka Mr. Arthur Flegenheimer of New York (see *Mystery Reader's Walking Guide: New York*).

In Roslynn Griffith's historical mystery *Pretty Birds of Passage,* architect Aurelia Kincaid went with her aunt to the reception at the Palmer House celebrating the opening of the Women's Building at the 1893 Columbian Exposition. At the reception Aurelia met Bertha Palmer, Buffalo Bill, Susan B. Anthony—and her new boss, Liam O'Rourke.

In D. J. H. Jones's academic mystery, *Murder at the MLA,* the Palmer House was mentioned as a replacement for the Fairfax Hotel if senior faculty continued to be murdered. In 1979 an MLA convention was held at the Palmer House with a special session on British mystery maven Dorothy L. Sayers.

In Leslie Charteris's novella "The King of the Beggars" the Saint came to Chicago on a clean-up mission. A knight errant, but debonair man of the world, the Saint was a prototype James Bond. Hoppy Uniatz was his strong-armed, weak-brained sidekick, who had some Chicago gangster connections. The pair spent three days in a State Street hotel suite watching the street with binoculars because a number of beggars had been found dead or beaten up across from the hotel. Lately the "pitch" had been taken—except on Wednesday and Saturday afternoons—by a beggar lady. When they saw a man with a gun take the beggar lady up the alley, the Saint and Hoppy dashed to the rescue. They smuggled both the lady and her attacker up in the service elevator. She turned out to be Monica Varing, a leading actress from a great theatrical family.

In Dorothy B. Hughes's short story "The Spotted Pup," young war vet Kip Scott was trying to find a missing spotted pup that belonged to his dead GI buddy Don. Kip visited the Palmer House to see a gangster who worked for his dead buddy's father (a racketeer). As Kip left he saw a mysterious blond who dived into the State Street subway at the sight of him, but he followed her and found out that she was the secret wife (widow) of his dead buddy.

In John Malcolm's *Mortal Ruin,* British investment banker cum art expert Tim Simpson came to Chicago to investigate some supposedly worthless gold mine shares belonging to Winston Churchill's American uncle. After having been mugged at O'Hare Airport Simpson was put up at the Palmer House by his counterpart, Chicago banker Andy Casey, and finally got two good nights sleep.

At the end of Barbara d'Amato's *Hardball,* free-lancer Cat

Marsala reached her apartment and heard the voices of her two boyfriends on her answering machine. Mike, the crazy one she liked best, said don't call him, he'd call her. John the stockbroker said "I was thinking maybe you'd need some babying. . . . How about a slow, luxurious weekend at the Palmer House? A play one evening, maybe a blues club. Quiet dinners. Breakfast in bed . . ." Listening, Cat thought: the lady or the tiger?

Go across the lobby and turn right to take the stairs to the Monroe Street exit. This is the entrance where the airport buses arrive and depart. In Arthur Maling's *The Snowman*, department-store executive Ches Novak took the limo there from O'Hare when he came back from Mexico. He had gotten his boss's son Scott and his girl out of Mexico, only to have them run away again. The Carson Pirie Scott department store, which is the model for Maling's Carter & Benson's, is right across the street.

To your left across State Street is the Shubert Theater at 23 W. Monroe. It is a probable site for the mythical Martin Beck Theater in Charteris' mystery where Monica Varing was starring in *The Doll's House*. The Shubert now is one of the few theaters left in the Loop, majestically decorated with terra-cotta, ornate and imposing with an authentic stage door alley.

Go right on Monroe to Wabash. This street got its name from the Indiana teamsters who used to park there with their goods. It is at Wabash and Monroe that Sara Paretsky put the old Pulteney Building where V.I. Warshawski had her office, next to the Monroe Street Tobacco Store.

Paretsky gave V.I. the quintessential private eye's threadbare city office, first occupied by Hammett's Sam Spade, so it doesn't matter much if it's located above the Footlocker or Florsheim's, the two stores at that corner favored by John Blades of the *Chicago Tribune*, or near Iwan Ries & Co. at 19 S. Wabash, a block north of you. In *Indemnity Only* Paretsky describes it as an old building with a lobby of chipped and dirty mosaic tiles that smelled of mold and urine. The manual elevator often did not work and V.I.'s fourth-floor office was right at El level.

In "The Maltese Cat," V.I. got a call from Brigette

LeBlanc, an ex-model who ran her own PR firm and coached the vice president of the U.S. (probably Dan Quayle). V.I. came back from doing research at the County Building to find a very irritated and irritating female in a Chanel suit who came on strong with "You find my sister. She ran away to my ex-husband" (who turns out to be a great ex-Bear). But the client really wanted her Maltese cat back. In *Bitter Medicine* V.I. found Sergio Rodriquez of the Latin Lions there. When Sergio went for her with a knife, it was especially annoying because as public defender V.I. had got him off on a charge of carrying a knife. In *Tunnel Vision,* V.I. found a homeless family living in the Pulteney's basement and had to rescue them from the great Chicago Flood.

Cross Wabash at Monroe Street to the flagship Kroch's and Brentano's bookstore at 29 S. Wabash. In Marc Davis's *Dirty Money,* P.I. Frank Wolf was investigating the murder of his childhood chum, broker Abel Nockermann. Wolf needed some books on the commodities business, so he went to Wabash where the El trains screeched and rattled. This probably meant Kroch's because Wolf was coming from the Board of Trade on south La Salle. (It could have been B. Dalton's near Randolph, too.)

In William Targ's *The Case of Mr. Cassidy* Hugh Morris, an overweight bon vivant crime writer, was trying to find a cheap reproduction of Edgar Allan Poe's *Tamerlane.* Unable to find it in the Loop bookstores, Morris went to the original Kroch's on North Michigan across the Chicago River. (See Walk 4.)

Explore Kroch's and Brentano's, then turn right to walk up Wabash to Madison Street. As you walk along, check out the older buildings on either side of the El for a good "Pulteney" model. Among the possibilities on your side are Walgreens' building and Iwan Ries, the famous tobacco shop. Across Wabash on the west side is Jewelers's Row, which includes the Wabash Jewelers Mall, the Mallers Building with its famous Mallers Coffee Shop (reuben sandwiches supreme) on the third floor, the Chicago Jewelers Building, and the Silversmith's Building at 10 S. Wabash, all suitable for V.I.

Cross Wabash at Madison Street and walk one block west to

State Street. You are at the "World's Busiest Corner": State and Madison, where the city street numbering begins. Originally, this was the point where the Chicago River entered Lake Michigan. Later, the McVickers Theater was built nearby. It had live theater performed by famous nineteenth century actors like Joseph Jefferson, Edmund Keane, and in 1862, John Wilkes Booth, who played there in Shakespeare's *Richard III*.

For many years this intersection was Chicago's Times Square, the celebration center of the city, alive day and night with gleaming plate glass windows, neon signs, and theater marquees. At Christmas newspapers ran photos showing it "wall to wall" with shoppers. When State Street became a mall, city festivals and demonstrations moved to Daley Plaza, making Dearborn the new parade street.

In Craig Rice's *The Wrong Murder* two people were shot dead at this corner during the Christmas rush. It was the perfect time for the perfect crime because, as criminal lawyer John J. Malone said, no one was paying any attention to anyone. The first murder victim was a minor crook/kidnaper named Gumbrill, who turned out to have surprising ties to Gold Coast celebrity Mona McClane; the second was a Gold Coast matron called Fleurette Ogletree. Both murders also concerned Malone and bridegroom Jake Justus because Mona McClane had bet Jake that she could commit a murder and get away with it. The stakes were her nightclub called the Casino, which Jake Justus wanted to own.

At the southwest corner of State and Madison you come to Louis Sullivan's world-famous ornamental iron facade of the Carson Pirie Scott department store at 1 S. State Street. Built in 1899 as the Schlesinger and Mayer department store it was one of the first in the country with a fireproof steel-frame structure designed with strong horizontals. The cast-iron ornamentation, painted green over red, helped the ground level display windows attract customers.

Samuel Carson and John T. Pirie came to Chicago from Belfast, Ireland, in 1854. Joined by John E. Scott in 1894, the two men opened their first store in 1864, were burned out in 1871, and took over this famous building in 1899. In Arthur

Maling's *The Snowman,* a department store called Carter & Benson's was built on State Street frontage bought by owner Tony Benson's great grandfather two weeks after the Chicago Fire in 1871. Benson had a falling out with his son and heir Scott, which Ches Novak, his protege, tried to troubleshoot when Benson had a serious heart attack.

In the Gordons' *Case File: FBI,* one case involved Kate Martel who was a buyer for the Pierce-Cabot department store. Kate was a young Korean war widow who was warned that her small daughter would be kidnaped if she didn't pay up her $10,000 GI insurance. She bravely went to the FBI, then was visited in her Loop office by FBI agent Jack Ripley who wanted her to let her daughter be used for a stakeout.

Explore Carson's and then turn right to cross Madison and walk north on State Street. You will pass a number of miscellaneous shops and office buildings, but it is a war zone these days on the west side of State Street where older buildings are few and far between.

In Kirby Williams's *The C.V.C. Murders,* on a November afternoon in 1926 William Hill Banning, a Loop lawyer, looked out his State Street office and saw a man shot dead on the street. Profoundly shocked, Banning founded the C.V.C., the Citizens' Vigilance Committee, made up of a group of influential and rich businessmen and professionals who decided they must rid the city of crime because crime had become professionalized. Kirby's fictional C.V.C. hired Dr. Thackeray Place, a Sherlockian type with a Watson, P. W. Tracy, who was like Philo Vance's S. S. Van Dine.

In Dennis E. Hoffman's *Scarface Al and the Crime Crusaders,* he describes the group of real Chicago businessmen known as the "Secret Six" who were organized to stop Capone and his organization. Among those still known today were Julius Rosenwald, chairman of Sears, Roebuck (and grandfather of Bobby Franks, who was murdered by Leopold and Loeb); Frank Loesch, president of the Chicago Crime Commission; Robert Isham Randolph, president of the Chicago Association of Commerce; and utilities millionaire Samuel Insull. *Chicago Tribune* owner Robert McCormick became an associate after his crime reporter Jake Lingle was murdered in the Randolph I.C. station. (See Walk 1.) FBI agent Alexander Jamie, the brother-in-law of Eliot Ness, who organized the Untouchables, was the Secret Six's chief investigator.

You can see the landmark Reliance Building across State Street at Washington at 36 North State. It might have held Banning's law offices. Now scheduled to be rehabbed instead of torn down, the Reliance Building was considered very advanced when it was built in 1895 by Daniel Burnham, using a steel framework so it could be sheathed almost entirely in glass. Before it was built, that site was occupied by Crosby's Opera House, whose opening night was delayed by news of Lincoln's assassination in 1865.

Look up at the famous trademark Marshall Field's Clock. There is a duplicate at the corner of Randolph and State. Then cross Washington to walk along State Street, making sure to look in Field's famous show windows. In Phyllis Whitney's very first mystery, originally called *Red Is for Murder,* now reissued as *The Red Carnelian,* Linell Wynn, a copywriter at Cunningham's department store went into the store's show window to add some finishing touches to a sports display. She found the store Lothario, Michael Montgomery, whom she had dated, lying dead beside a steel-headed golf club. Not only was Linell a prime suspect, but shortly afterwards another buyer turned up murdered as well. Phyllis Whitney's first job was working at Marshall Field's and the ambiance is very authentic. Phyllis Whitney herself appeared in William Targ's *The Case of Mr. Cassidy* when Hugh Morris visited Max Siegel's bookshop in the Pittsfield Building.

Across from Marshall Field's on State Street, together with the Skate on State—Block 37 Ice Rink, is the Hot Tix booth, where you can get half-price day of the performance tickets.

Stop at the corner of Randolph and State to look left toward Ronny's Steak Palace, located in a dingy white gingerbread building between State and Dearborn that used to be Old Heidelberg. In Vera Caspary's *Evvie* two bachelor girls, Evvie and Louise, were taken there for dinner by their beaus.

Cross Randolph Street. To the west you once could see a

row of theater marquees, among them the RKO Grand, the RKO Palace, the Garrick, the LaSalle, and the Oriental. The famous Iroquois Theater fire occurred there on December 20, 1903 when Eddie Foy was appearing in *Mr. Bluebeard*. Over 600 people died because the theater doors opened inward instead of pushing out—as they must do today.

Walk north on State to the famous Chicago Theater at 175 N. State. It was built in 1921 as the flagship of the Balaban and Katz theater chain in Chicago. For the next forty years virtually every well-known performer appeared there, commanding astronomical salaries. In 1982 there were plans to tear it down but a special move to save the palace was successful and it was refurbished—in some cases with decorations from other movie houses. Reopening night Frank Sinatra performed, backed by the Count Basie Band. Admire the triumphal-arch facade of the theater, then go inside and look around the renovated and elegant lobby.

In Jonathan Latimer's *The Lady in the Morgue*, P. I. William Crane and his two sidekicks went there to see the chorus girls in hopes of identifying the body in the morgue. After interviewing a number of the girls, Crane and his chums walked west to Henrici's, past all the brilliantly illuminated theater marquees on Randolph.

Across State Street in the middle of the block is the old State-Lake Theater building, now housing ABC's Channel 7. You can see where its arched doorway/marquee was filled in. In Harry Keeler's *Behind That Mask* the offices of Chicago detective Terrence O'Rourke were in the State-Lake building above the theater. O'Rourke used his phone switchboard to juggle calls while minding murder cases. He was a friend of magazine writer David Rand, who was trying to solve the murder of his boss, editor Jack Kenwood.

In Bill Granger's *The Infant of Prague* Devereux, the November Man, was trying to ride herd on a Czech defector and got mixed up with a young actress, Anna Jelinak, known as a Czech Judy Garland. Anna was on tour to promote Prague for filming movies. (It must have worked because the Brother Cadfael mysteries of Ellis Peters are being filmed there.) Anna came to the studio to appear on a black TV hostess's show. Since Oprah

Winfrey is on Channel 7, she came to that station, but Oprah actually records in a building west of the river. On a studio monitor Anna saw a weeping statue of the Infant of Prague and became hysterical, appealing for asylum and declaring that Christ was her only friend.

In Charles Merrill Smith's *Reverend Randollph and the Wages of Sin* the Reverend C. P. (Con) Randollph walked a few blocks from his Church of the Good Shepherd, passing Marshall Field's State Street windows. He was scheduled to appear on the TV talk show of Samantha Stack, who had asked him because his church represented old powerful WASP money. By the date Con Randollph was due to appear, however, a choir member whose husband was on the church's board of trustees had been found murdered in the choir room, making him a celebrity.

Walk to the Lake Street corner where you will see the 1872 Page Brothers building with a pre-Fire cast-iron front. Long John Wentworth, one of Chicago's more colorful politicians and scoundrels who, with Hinky Dink Kenna "ran" the Levee south of the Loop, unwisely picked a fight on this corner with an immigrant Scot named Allan Pinkertown who came to Chicago about 1842. Bigger but drunk as a lord, Wentworth was licked by Pinkerton, who later went to work for Abraham Lincoln as a bodyguard and then as a spy during the Civil War.

This is also the Loop area where nightclubs once were found. Fritzel's, a well-known nightclub in the '40s and '50s used to be across the street at Lake and State. It appeared in mysteries like Dorothy B. Hughes's story, "The Spotted Pup." Some of them were like the Wilde Spot run by Tony Wilde in Edward D. Hoch's "The Theft of the Overdue Library Book." The owner, Tony Wilde, was engaging in a little drug dealing on the side (a special menu) and another crook who wanted a piece of the action had him kidnaped while walking his dog in Lincoln Park. (See Walk 7.)

Turn right to walk east to Wabash. This is the corner where the El once jumped off its tracks making the turn west, spilling people and cars into the street below. Turn right again to walk south to Randolph Street and cross Randolph Street back to Marshall Field's.

Don Roth's famous Blackhawk Restaurant used to be across Wabash south of Randolph next to B. Dalton's. In *The Snowman* Maling's department store executive Ches Novak went there for lunch from Carter & Benson. He had two soothing martinis, but back at work heard that his small son Buzz had been kidnaped by drug dealers.

Standing outside Field's, marvel that in Craig Rice's *The Wrong Murder,* zany heiress Helene Justus parked her big car on Randolph Street and left it there while demonstrating to John J. Malone and her new husband Jake Justus how to lose a police tail in Field's basement. (It is now called Down Under and links up with the Loop Pedway system.) Helene would have more trouble diving into the Pedway, but so would the Chicago police.

Marshall Field's book department is now Down Under. Before the move, the department occupied a large part of the third floor overlooking State Street. In Targ's *The Case of Mr. Cassidy* Hugh Morris went there looking for Poe's *Tamerlane* and saw Carl Sandburg who was busily autographing his books. Morris bought a copy of Dorothy B. Hughes's thriller *The Fallen Sparrow* (see *MRWG: NY*).

On one of his American lecture tours, G. K. Chesterton of Father Brown fame met Sinclair Lewis in Marshall Field's book department and they concocted a silly play about Mary Queen of Scotch. (Chesterton did not approve of Prohibition because he considered it hypocritical. He agreed with Al Capone who said that "when I sell liquor, it's called bootlegging. When my patrons serve it on Lake Shore Drive, it's called hospitality.")

In Mignon Eberhart's *The Glass Slipper,* Rue Hatterick, who had recently married her boss, went to Field's to shop on the day that her maid Rachel was found murdered in their Gold Coast house. Rue went with her new stepdaughter Madge and Alicia Pelham, an old family friend. Inside they went their separate ways: Madge to the fifth floor for dancing slippers and Alicia to seven for a fitting, so any of them could have grabbed a cab back to the Gold Coast and done in the maid.

In Carolyn Haddad's *Caught in the Shadows,* Becky Belski, a computer hacker who uncovered her own past researching a juicy North Shore divorce case, discovered that her mother, convicted of murdering her stepfather, had met an old friend at Field's where they had sundaes together.

In D. C. Brod's *Murder in Store* Quint McCauley was head of security at Hauser's Department Store. Founded by the present family's grandfather, it was now run by Preston Hauser whose sister Grace knew she could do it better. First Hauser's sexy young wife Diana shoplifted at the family store, then Hauser asked McCauley to investigate some death threats he had received, only to be murdered in his own store. Brod put the Hauser store on North Michigan Avenue, but its description of dark floors, massive columns, and a five-story ceiling matches Marshall Field's State Street store better. Be sure to see Field's Tiffany dome and the new atrium.

In Nancy Pickard's *Bum Steer,* Jenny Cain was the director of the Port Frederick Civic Foundation which was unexpectedly given a Kansas cattle ranch. She came west to find out why. In Chicago to interview some of the heirs of the rancher who willed her foundation the ranch, Jenny drove from O'Hare to the vast and famous old store downtown where she bought some clothes for the Southern climate, a mystery novel, and a box of Marshall Field's famous candy (Frango mints). Then she ate a late lunch at the store. On her way out Cain saw some jigsaw puzzles in the toy department and got one for each niece and nephew. Then she asked the clerk how to get out fast so she wouldn't buy anything more!

In Dan Crawford's short story "Father's Day Special" in *Ellery Queen's Mystery Magazine,* a reporter spent the day in Field's in a hollow mirror column. He was trying to catch a necktie-killer buying more murder "supplies."

In Craig Rice's *Knocked for a Loop,* John J. Malone found the dead body of a client named Leonard Estapool in his Loop office. Then two mobsters who had kidnaped Estapool's 9-year-old stepdaughter Alberta dumped her back on Malone and he asked his secretary Maggie to suggest places to take Alberta for lunch or tea. Ever resourceful–if unpaid–Maggie gave him the following list: Marshall Field's, Walgreens, Henrici's, Jacques',

Le Petit Gourmet. Only Field's and Walgreens still exist, but luckily Field's has been The Place to take kids for generations.

End your walk by visiting the third floor's old-fashioned ice cream parlor, where you can try Field's special Frango flavor in ice cream, pie, or candy, or go to seven and try out the many Field's restaurants. The Walnut Room is still the classiest place, especially at Christmastime, when it is jammed with people having its chicken pot pie and admiring the Christmas tree.

3

WEST LOOP WALK

LaSalle Street and City Hall

BACKGROUND

The Loop West walk covers Chicago's business district, centered on the city's two most important industries: trade and government. Both offer the visitor a lot of action, whether you watch the trading floor at the Board of Trade or a City Council meeting. Discovered by the French as a portage that could control an empire and named "wild onion" by the explorer LaSalle, by the time Chicago became a city in 1833, there were already seventeen lawyers and land speculation had become big business. The first combined City Hall/County Building was built in 1858, while the Board of Trade, organized in 1848, moved to LaSalle Street in 1865.

Chicago's financial district, known as "LaSalle Street," just as the lower tip of Manhattan is called "Wall Street," is the focus of the brokers and dealers and their lawyers and bankers. Their businesses are either housed in landmark buildings like the Chicago School's Rookery and the Art Deco Board of Trade, or located in the many sleek new skyscrapers lining the Chicago River. When walking the west Loop look up to see the tops of the buildings, because you are in the midst of a world-class architectural museum. Surrounding you on every side are examples of the Chicago School like the Marquette Building or more recent glittering, glassy wonders like the world's tallest, the Sears Tower.

The center of Chicago politics had been at Clark Street long before the 1871 Chicago fire. The fire razed what is now the

Loop, but instead of destroying the city, it acted as a giant urban renewal project, allowing the area to be quickly rebuilt as a commercial area without residential enclaves or manufacturing.

Both trade and politics are vitally important settings for Chicago mysteries because Chicago authors retain a strongly American belief in the value of the ordinary guy and the venality of his elected rulers. To use FDR's telling phrase, Chicagoans are still deeply suspicious of "malefactors of great wealth," and make many murderers live in the northern and western suburbs or on the Gold Coast. Chicago writers from Nelson Algren and Saul Bellow to Bill Granger and Sara Paretsky also mistrust their politicians and policemen who often turn out to be "connected," that is, allied with gangsters, or "the Mob." Far from drawing a portrait of the Puritan city shining on a hill, they describe a city that is beautiful but "bent." They say that even in the '90s, the legacy of Al Capone and his friend, Mayor William Hale "Big Bill" Thompson is alive and well.

LENGTH OF WALK: About 2 miles

See the map on page 77 for the boundaries of this walk and page 341 for a list of the books and detectives mentioned.

Note: Because it follows the south bank of the Chicago River, Wacker Drive runs both east/west and north/south.

PLACES OF INTEREST

Chicago Board of Trade/Chicago Mercantile Exchange, 141 W. Jackson Boulevard. Fifth-floor Trading Floor Visitors Gallery open Mon.–Fri. Tours 8:30 A.M. to noon on the half hour. Free. Call 435-3500.

Chicago Temple (First United Methodist Church), 77 W. Washington Street. World's tallest church. Sky Chapel tours weekdays at 2:00 P.M. Call 236-4548.

County Building/Chicago City Hall, Randolph, Washington, Clark, and LaSalle Streets.

Civic Opera House, 20 N. Wacker Drive.

Richard J. Daley Civic Center, Randolph, Washington, Dearborn, and Clark Streets. Picasso Statue. Call 346-3278.

First National Bank Plaza, The Four Seasons (Marc Chagall mosaics). Dearborn, Madison, Clark, and Monroe Streets.

Metropolitan Correctional Center, 71 W. Van Buren Street.

Northwestern Station, Canal, Clinton, Madison, and Washington Streets.

The Rookery, 209 S. LaSalle Street. Burnham and Root 1885–88 with cast-iron framing, light court and elevator.

Sears Tower, 233 S. Wacker Drive. Jackson Street Skydeck open daily Mar.–Sept. 9:00 A.M.–11:00 P.M., Oct.–Feb. 10:00 A.M.–10:00 P.M. Fee. Call 875-9696.

State of Illinois Building, (James R. Thompson Center), 100 W. Randolph Street. Call 814–6660.

Union Station, Canal Street between Adams and Jackson Streets.

PLACES TO EAT

The West Loop is full of fast food restaurants like Wendy's, McDonald's, submarine shops, and Chinese places. Most of these have public restrooms. There are also small bars and private spots tucked away inside the buildings and in good weather al fresco cafes on the riverside. (Chicagoans can thank attorney Marshall Patner for bringing a lawsuit that made it legal for restaurants to serve outdoors.)

Berghoff Restaurant, 17 W. Adams Street.

Bismarck Hotel, 171 W. Randolph Street. The Chalet, Old Vienna Coffee Shop, the Walnut Room.

Ceres, Board of Trade Building, 141 W. Jackson Boulevard. Coffee shop with pleasant ambiance.

Lou Mitchell's, 565 W. Jackson Boulevard (west of the Chicago River).

Greektown (See Walk 10).

WEST LOOP WALK: LA SALLE STREET AND CITY HALL

Begin your walk at the unnamed Picasso statue in the Daley Center Plaza at Dearborn and Washington Streets. Designed in 1965 by Skidmore, Owings & Merrill, both the Daley Center and its Picasso are made of self-rusting Cor-Ten steel. Originally known as the Civic Center, the plaza was renamed after the death of Mayor Richard J. Daley, although it reverted to being the Civic Center during Jane Byrne's administration. Older City Halls stood on this site, which occupies the entire block from Dearborn to Clark Street, Randolph to Washington Street. Today it is Chicago's center, taking over from Daniel Burnham's lakefront plaza at Congress and Michigan Avenue as the site of the city Christmas tree, violent demonstrations, and ethnic celebrations. Since State Street was made a mall, city parades usually march from Wacker Drive down Dearborn to Congress past the plaza.

The Picasso weighs 163 tons and has been called many things: Picasso's wife, his Afghan hound, a baboon, or a dodo bird. It is now Chicago's major symbol. In Andrew Greeley's *Lord of the Dance,* a Board of Trade broker observed that "Himself was taken in on that one. He fell for Picasso's joke. But then I suppose if you have to fall for somebody's joke, it might as well be Picasso's."

In Martin Blank's thriller *Shadowchase*, an IRA terrorist turned informer who had been given a new identity murdered two Irish immigrants who recognized him. The murders were investigated by an odd couple of homicide detectives, Lieutenant John Lamp, small, neat, and cerebral; and Hutch, fat, heavy, and streetwise. They both were summoned to a high-level meeting at the State's Attorney's Office whose windows overlooked the "goofy Picasso sculpture in the plaza."

In Robert J. Campbell's *The Junkyard Dog,* 27th Ward precinct captain Jimmy Flannery said that the stuff in a junkyard was as interesting as the thing Picasso gave the city. "Nobody can tell what it is with its steely eyes—a bird, a dog, or a Chicago lawyer."

Look at the Picasso yourself, then at the Eternal Flame, a city memorial to President John F. Kennedy.

Walk to the corner of Washington and Clark and look across Washington to the 1913 Conway Building (old Chicago Title and Trust). Built by Daniel Burnham in his handsome Beaux Arts style, it is one of the few structures nearby that would have older (and cheaper) offices.

In Michael A. Kahn's *Grave Designs*, young lawyer Rachel Gold had her office about Clark and Washington in one of the oldest buildings in the Loop. Rachel looked down on the Daley Plaza with the rusty Picasso sculpture, which looked less like a work of art than a bizarre spoof on Soviet technology.

In Yastrow's *Undue Influence,* Phil Ogden also had a low-rent law office at Washington and Clark, across from the "Cook County Courthouse." Accountant Ben Stillman had come there to draw up a will and when he died, his cleaning woman brought Ogden a letter instructing Ogden to handle Stillman's will and estate. Stillman had left all his assets to Beth Zion Synagogue, an estate worth $8 million.

Cross Washington. One block south on Clark Street between Madison and Monroe Streets is the tapered 1969 skyscraper First National Bank Building with Chagall's Four Seasons mosaics in its plaza. Detour now to see them if you like and then return to Clark and Washington.

In Kahn's *Grave Designs* Rachel Gold and fellow lawyer Benny Goldman walked north from the offices of Abbott & Windsor in Sears Tower to the First National Bank. In the shadows of the setting sun Chagall's mosaics looked like giant slabs of moldy cream cheese, splotched with pastel greens and blues.

In Richard Himmel's *The Twenty-Third Web*, the Stonehill Bank Building was built in the late '60s at Adams and Clark. A family-run bank, it was a quality structure, classy, but not the tallest or largest Loop bank. Like other prominent Jewish leaders, its president Livingston Stonehill was being threatened with Arab retaliation for his financial support of Israel.

At Madison Street you can look right and see the pink marble modernist facade of St. Peter's Roman Catholic Church. In

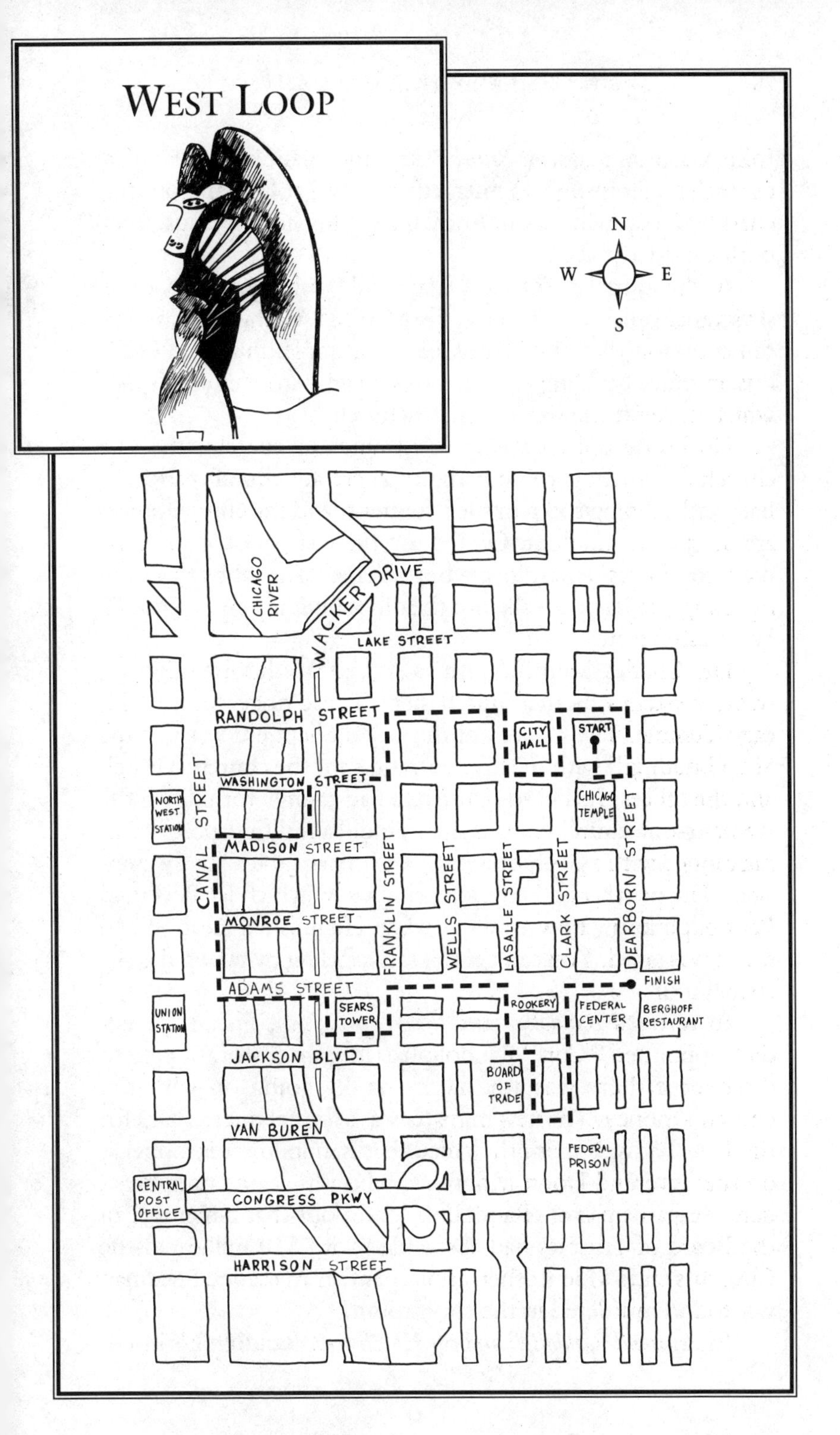
WEST LOOP
N
W
E
S
WACKER DRIVE
CHICAGO RIVER
LAKE STREET
RANDOLPH STREET
WASHINGTON STREET
MADISON STREET
MONROE STREET
ADAMS STREET
JACKSON BLVD.
VAN BUREN
CONGRESS PKWY
HARRISON STREET
CANAL STREET
FRANKLIN STREET
WELLS STREET
LASALLE STREET
CLARK STREET
DEARBORN STREET
NORTH WEST STATION
UNION STATION
CENTRAL POST OFFICE
CITY HALL
START
CHICAGO TEMPLE
FINISH
SEARS TOWER
ROOKERY
FEDERAL CENTER
BERGHOFF RESTAURANT
BOARD OF TRADE
FEDERAL PRISON

John Malcolm's *Mortal Ruin*, British merchant banker cum art expert Tim Simpson was mugged on arrival at O'Hare, but rescued by a cop who knew Andy Casey, his host, because they both went to St. Peter's.

At the southeast corner of Clark and Washington is a Gothic skyscraper officially called the First United Methodist Church, but commonly known as the Chicago Temple. Put up in 1923, it is an office building crowned by an eight-story church spire, which makes it the world's tallest church.

Go inside the Clark Street entrance to the church. The church sanctuary is to your right. There are church parlors, a hall, and a dining room in the basement, and the church offices are on the second floor. On the top there is not only an apartment for the resident minister but a chapel. The lobby turns at a right angle to let you walk into the office building entrance at 77 W. Washington.

Dr. Charles Merrill Smith, a retired Methodist minister, wrote mysteries about a church that is a dead ringer for the Chicago Temple. The Church of the Good Shepherd was in "the Shep Building" with separate entrances for the church, a hotel, and the offices. Its board of trustees had cannily torn down the Romanesque church on this site to build a multipurpose building capped with a Gothic pinnacle with a penthouse for the minister. The penthouse had a stunning view, which let Reverend Randollph know how God felt when He finished creation and saw it was good. You can get the same feeling by taking the sky chapel tour.

In *Reverend Randollph and the Wages of Sin*, Bishop "Freddie" appointed "Con" Randollph as interim pastor, hoping to discover if there was any hanky panky going on with the church's money. The new minister was a former quarterback for the L.A. Rams, but Smith denied that Randollph was modeled on the Reverend Donn Moomaw, who was at one time President Reagan's pastor. Randollph found out that a member of the Board of Trustees had absconded with $10 million of the Church's endowment; then choir member Marianne Reedman was found murdered in the choir room.

In *Reverend Randollph and the Holy Terror* Randollph's installation was an ecumenical extravaganza attended by her honor the peppy blonde lady mayor (Jane Byrne), but marred by the shooting of Roman Catholic Bishop Terence Kevin O'Manny. In *Reverend Randollph and the Avenging Angel*, Randollph performed the wedding of Hollywood movie star Lisa Julian, only to have her murdered in her bridal suite at the Drake Hotel. (See Walk 5.) In *Reverend Randollph and the Unholy Bible,* he had the funeral services for murdered old miser Johannes Humbrecht, who left him a Gutenberg Bible.

Admire the church, then walk through the lobby to Washington Street. The office of Craig Rice's criminal lawyer John J. Malone was at 79 W. Washington, which would be about here. Across the street, where the Daley Plaza is now, was Joe the Angel's City Hall Bar.

Malone kept a bottle in his desk drawer for emergencies, often slept on the couch, and had a rarely paid secretary called Maggie who covered for him. He was famous for getting guilty clients off, but he and his pals Jake and Helene Justus often saw to it that real justice was done.

In Rice's *Knocked for a Loop*, Malone made a date to see a tycoon named Leonard Estapool at midnight. Estapool had a folder of criminal names he was going to give the Grand Jury, but Malone found Estapool dead and the folder gone. He arranged to hide the body but when Malone left the office, two gangsters picked him up. They had kidnaped Estapool's stepdaughter Alberta but wanted to get rid of her. (Alberta was a female "Ransom of Red Chief" kid who adored being kidnaped.)

In Craig Rice's *The Fourth Postman,* Chicago Homicide Captain Von Flanagan (who added Von to his name so he wouldn't be a typical Irish cop) came to find Malone across the street at Joe the Angel's bar to take him along as defense attorney for sweet old Rodney Fairfaxx, the Gold Coast millionaire accused of murdering postmen.

Go out the Washington Street entrance and turn right into the tiny plaza where a Miro statue called *Miss Chicago* glares at the Picasso. Dedicated in 1980, the Miro is said to be a Spanish lady with a comb in her hair. Along the wall of the Chicago

Temple there are stained glass windows with scenes from Chicago Methodist history beginning at Fort Dearborn in 1825. You may hear the Temple chimes which Sara Paretsky's V.I. Warshawski heard in *Killing Orders* as she burgled offices at the old Midwest Stock Exchange.

Walk east (right) on Washington Street past the Miro to the Brunswick Building at 69 W. Washington, built in 1965 by Skidmore Ownings & Merrill with column-free floors. It is a modern office building across from the Picasso, so it is probably the place where Arthur Maling's Go-Between (who is never named) visited big businessman Oliver Lambert. Lambert told the go-between that his son Pete was blackmailing him for a secret report on some Alaskan oil fields Pete had stolen. Lambert hired the go-between to get the reports back.

Across Dearborn at 33 N. Dearborn, however, there is another tall, modern building that could house lawyers and big companies. It has the offices of the British Consulate General, where you find yourself in a reception room with bullet-proof windows to protect the staff.

Another old building whose windows currently look out at the Daley Plaza is the Reliance Building at the corner of State and Washington. Built by Burnham and Root in 1891, it is a landmark structure trimmed with terra-cotta and having "walls of glass"; that is, multistory bay windows. There are plans afoot to rehab it.

Turn left to cross Washington at Dearborn, returning to the Daley Center. Along Dearborn you pass the site of a number of other old buildings, torn down for future development. Chicago politicians and other mob-connected types used to gather there. The best known was the old—slightly tilting—Unity Building at 127 N. Dearborn, built in 1892 by former Governor John Peter Altgeld. Altgeld pardoned some of the defendants in the famous Haymarket Riot in which seven (some sources say eight) policemen were killed. Lawyer Clarence Darrow, an Altgeld protege who defended "perfect murderers" Nathan Leopold and Richard Loeb in 1924, had his offices there. The Unity Building also housed a restaurant called Mayor's Row, near but not the same as the notorious Counselors Row restaurant where the feds bugged Booth Number One to catch politicians with mob "connections." Currently it is known as "Skate on State"—Block 37 Ice Rink.

In Robert J. Campbell's *The Junkyard Dog,* Jimmy Flannery took lawyer Walter Streeter to lunch at the "famous old grill over on State Street which is used as a second office by half the lawyers and judges in the city." Flannery politely accuses the lawyer of having fixed up a young married hood named Danny Tartaglia with a hooker named Helen Brickhouse, who was later found murdered in Jimmy's precinct.

In Shelby Yastrow's *Undue Influence,* two sleazy lawyers who heard about Ben Stillman's will meet at the "Courthouse Square Cafe" across the street from the Daley Center to plan a class action suit against Stillman's estate and his employers Barnett Brothers for letting Stillman defraud their clients.

Before going inside, recall the last scene in Chicagoan John Belushi's movie the *Blues Brothers,* where mayhem reigned supreme in Daley Plaza. As Belushi and Dan Aykroyd drove up in the Batmobile to pay the back taxes on their foundling home, they were being pursued by SWAT Teams, Nazis, a Good Old Boys band, and Chicago's finest, armed with everything from uzis to tanks and helicopters. Made during the Byrne administration, that film marked the end of old Mayor Daley's rule that no one could portray Chicago as a violent, gangster-hoodlum heaven. Filming has become a Chicago habit, with *The Fugitive*'s Harrison Ford dashing through City Hall and other real Loop sites. Its director, Andrew Davis, like Belushi, is home-grown.

Go inside the Daley Center's south doorway. It houses over 120 courtrooms, hearing rooms, a law library, and offices. Since a defendant shot a judge in court, you must go through a metal detector if you want to go upstairs.

On the ground floor there are exhibits of art by school children and noontime concerts. To your right there is a desk with tourist and visitor information. The elevators are in the center, while on the west side, facing the County Building on Clark Street, are escalators that will take you to the two lower levels and the tunnel that connects the Daley Center with County/ City Hall.

The Daley Center houses the offices of the Cook County State's Attorney. In Andrew Greeley mysteries the D.A. is always a highly competent Rich (now Mayor) Daley. But in Bill Granger's *The Priestly Murders,* it was the Civic Center, never the Daley Center, and the State's Attorney was a stupid Irishman named Bud Halligan.

In Yastrow's *Undue Influence,* Phil Ogden went to the Daley Center to file Stillman's will for probate. Judge Lloyd ruled there must be a search for unknown heirs; there turned out to be some: an unscrupulous couple who ran the cancer clinic where Stillman died. The judge called Ogden into his chambers on the twelfth floor where Ogden could see the Shedd Aquarium, the Field Museum, and Lake Michigan out the windows.

The law library is open to the public but you must go through the metal detector. In Sam Reaves's *A Long Cold Fall* cabbie Cooper MacLeish, who was investigating the death of his old college flame, Vivian Horstmann, went to the Daley Center on the twenty-ninth floor to use the Cook County Law Library. It occupies the whole floor and has views of Chicago on three sides. There Cooper finally figured out what would happen legally to the money when there was a legacy coming to a deceased legatee like Vivian.

Explore the Daley Center and then go out the Randolph Street entrance. Henrici's restaurant used to be here on Randolph. In Mignon G. Eberhart's *The Glass Slipper,* Rue Hatterick and her escort Dr. Andy Crittenden, en route from the Gold Coast to the opening night of the opera, turned on Randolph Street. They passed Henrici's, which Eberhart called "the heart of Chicago; it had been there and it would be there, catching the flow and pulse of the life of a great city."

Henrici's was still there in Dorothy B. Hughes's story "The Spotted Pup" when World War II vet Kip Scott went there to meet his dead buddy's widow. They found the restaurant warm, sedate, and dignified, with marble-topped tables with heavy linen and wood-paneled walls with gold-framed paintings, and they had some of its famous coffee with whipped cream.

In Jonathan Latimer's *The Lady in the Morgue,* New York

socialite Kathryn Courtland followed a married band leader with mob connections to Chicago. Several girls's bodies turned up at the morgue, so P.I. William Crane was hired to see if one was Kathryn. Crane lunched at Henrici's with her brother Chauncey Courtland III. He had a double martini, very dry, seven Vienna rolls and a combination salad, and three bottles of imported Pilsener beer. Courtland had a club sandwich and three beers.

In "The Play's the Thing," Robert Bloch's theater critic went to Henrici's to lunch with actor Richard Barrett, whose version of *Hamlet* he disliked. Barrett had just gotten his big chance to take *Hamlet* to Broadway but was encumbered by a show girl with one gold tooth who wanted to play Ophelia.

Across Randolph at Dearborn is the Delaware, built in 1874 with high Victorian bays, a cast-iron facade and an interior sky-lighted court. It has a McDonald's where you can stop for some coffee. The Delaware is the only likely building left on Randolph where young Jon Chakorian could have had a small business, Chakorian Enterprises, in James Michael Ullman's *The Venus Trap*. Jon held a news conference there to announce that every year on his birthday since his father, shady financier Rudy Chakorian had disappeared, he had received two thousand dollars. His father had skipped with a million dollars worth of diamonds.

In Ullman's *Lady on Fire* P.I. Julian Forbes of Forbes and Associates also had an office with a window overlooking Randolph Street near City Hall. Forbes returned there after meeting an elderly new client, Walter St. Clair, on a park bench in Lincoln Park. St. Clair wanted Forbes to find his missing girl friend, Iris Dean.

Turn left to walk west to Clark Street. Across Randolph at 60 W. Randolph you can see the Garrick Garage. It was built on the site of the 1892 Schiller Building, designed by the famous partners Dankmar Adler and Louis Sullivan, which housed the Garrick Theater. When the building was torn down, the parking garage was decorated with terra-cotta panels from the Garrick.

Clark Street used to be known in mysteries as Chicago's

"Mean Street" but it has changed greatly since James Michael Ullman's Edgar winning *The Neon Haystack*. In her 1945 story "The Spotted Pup," Dorothy Hughes wrote that at the corner of Clark and Randolph you would see "the honkytonk that is Randolph . . . the glare of movie marquees . . . Chinese restaurants and hole-in-the-wall gyp joints called night-clubs . . . cafeterias and greasy hamburger stands, hat shops, pawn shops, candy shops, junk jewelry shops, book shops, phonograph record shops, everything scribbled up with neon, everything blaring with noise, glaring with light. . . ."

In Hughes's story, Kip Scott's seedy Grimsley's Confidential Agency was located at Clark and Randolph over a drugstore, where one Saturday night a girl in a mink coat appeared to hire Scott to find her dead brother's spotted pup.

Across Randolph on the northeast corner is the new Chicago Title and Trust Center. It was built in 1992 on the site of the old Greyhound Bus Station where hopefuls came to the big city looking for adventure.

In John D. MacDonald's *One Fearful Yellow Eye*, after Dr. Fortner Geis died mysteriously, P.I. Travis McGee met Dr. Geis's nurse there, and took her to gallery owner Heidi Geis's apartment. In Robert Campbell's *The Junkyard Dog,* Helen Brickhouse, the hooker who died in an abortion clinic bombing, had arrived at the bus station looking for the big time. In Michael Raleigh's *Death in Uptown,* P.I. Paul Whelan drove Donnie, who had been working in an Uptown mission, there to get a bus home. Whelan remembered having come back from war to the same station.

Directly across Randolph on Clark's northwest corner is Helmet Jahn's trendy blue glass State of Illinois Building. In Chicago mysteries it has a bad press, with few agreeing with former Governor James Thompson that it is "the first building of the twenty-first century." It is governmental red, white and blue with a gigantic atrium seventeen stories high and offices located around the edges at each floor. In front there is a Dubuffet fiberglass statue called *Monument with Standing Beast.* Andrew Greeley's Father Blackie said the Dubuffet in front of the ugly State of Illinois Building was designed for children of all ages to play on.

In Paretsky's *Bitter Medicine,* V.I. Warshawski thought the State of Illinois building was one of the worst monstrosities ever paid for by herself and her fellow taxpayers. She went there to talk to a friend of Dr. Lotty Herschel's about the Schaumburg hospital where Consuelo Alvarado died in childbirth.

In Barbara D'Amato's *Hard Luck,* free-lancer Cat Marsala thought the State of Illinois Building was a real weirdo, a huge stepped and rounded Mayan pyramid, made out of reflective glass and cut vertically in quarters. Despite all the ducts, wiring and plumbing showing pink and purple inside the atrium, the building has had monstrous heating and cooling problems.

Historically, the old Sherman House was on the site of this State of Illinois Building. In Latimer's *The Lady in the Morgue,* P.I. Bill Crane stayed at the hotel because it was air-conditioned. Crane and his two partners drank a lot of scotch and tried out the famous restaurants like the College Inn and the Well of the Sea. A gun-toting gangster invaded their hotel room because he wanted to get his girl's body from the morgue so he could bury her properly at Calvary Cemetery.

If it's raining or snowing, walk through the Daley Center from Dearborn to Clark and take the escalators down to the tunnel to County/City Hall. (There is a tunnel connecting the State of Illinois Building with County/City, too. When it was dug, the two parts didn't meet and there was a fine old Chicago row over who had to re-dig.)

In the lower level there are restrooms, a cafeteria, and more county and city offices. In Paretsky's *Indemnity Only,* V.I. went to Gun Registration in CL 90 to register her gun. In Robert J. Campbell's *Hipdeep in Alligators* Jimmy Flannery went to the Department of Health (level LL) to check out the alligator-bitten corpse he found in the sewers. (See Walk 9.)

If you stay outside, cross Clark and turn left to walk to the County Building. As you do so, keep a weather eye out to be sure no one is falling from one of the massive sash windows.

In D'Amato's *Hard Luck,* a lottery convention was being held at City Hall and Cat Marsala, doing an article on the state lottery, interviewed members of the politically-connected family who ran it. The next day, as she was taking her mother to a rehab session, one of the Lottery staff—PR man Jack Sligh—was pushed out a City Hall window and landed in front of them on the sidewalk. (This neatly canceled Cat's 11 o'clock appointment with him.)

The County Building/City Hall are the main mystery focus of the west Loop because Chicagoans tend to assume there is a criminal connection between the government and the mob ("Outfit"). The building was put up in 1911 by Holabird and Roche, with eleven very high stories and massive columns so it would *not* look like a skyscraper. Before 1917 the Office of the Coroner (now the Medical Examiner) was in the County Building, but bodies were sent to Cook County Hospital. (See Walk 10.)

Go into the County Building entrance. You are in an arched hallway which leads through the building to City Hall. To your left is the office of the Recorder of Deeds. In Paretsky's *Deadlock,* after V.I.'s cousin Boom Boom was murdered, she went into the "Title Office" on the first floor of County to find out who owned dancer Paige Carrington's condo. Paige had dated Boom Boom, but she was also the playmate of shipowner Niels Grafalk.

In D'Amato's *Hard Luck,* Cat walked down the first floor thinking the building was a fine example of the "Intimidate the Public" school of interior decoration. The arches looked like bleached rib bones, so you might as well have been swallowed by a rococo whale.

Walk through to City Hall. It was at this city crossroads that Mayor Richard J. Daley and Mayor Harold Washington lay in state while the aldermen and women played politics on the second floor in the City Council Chambers. Remember also that in Max Allan Collins's *Kill Your Darlings,* the Chicago Crime bus tour leader told his tourists "City Hall was the scene of many a Chicago crime."

Take the stairs on either side at the LaSalle Street entrance to see the aldermen's offices and the City Council Chambers on two. The public entrance to the Council Chambers is to your right, the offices to the left as you face LaSalle Street. In D'Amato's *Hard Women,* Cat Marsala watched Channel 3 telecast a City Council meeting as a group of aldermen known as the Sinless Seven debated the image problem Chicago had with streetwalkers.

In Mark Zubro's *Political Poison* murdered Fifth Ward Alderman Gideon Giles was a "lakefront liberal" and a professor of English at the University of Chicago. The Fifth Ward had such an alderman, Professor Charles Merriam, in the 1930s. (See Walk 9.)

In most Chicago mysteries, however, City Hall is clout city. In Michael A. Kahn's, *Grave Designs,* even Abbott & Windsor's honest senior partner Ishmael Richardson could use his pull with "City Hall" when Rachel Gold reported that a group of Chicago VIPs were being blackmailed by a member of his law firm.

The Board of Elections is on the third floor. In Ross Thomas's *The Porkchoppers,* corrupt union leader Donald Cubbin said Chicago was a town where they had made a fine craft out of stealing elections.

The office of the mayor is on the fifth floor, so the phrases "the Man on Five" or simply "the Fifth Floor" always means "Da Mare." In Robert J. Campbell's mysteries the twenty-seventh ward's lesbian Alderwoman Janet Cantaris was elected mayor with help from Jimmy Flannery, but that is not likely to happen in the near future. Mark Zubro also had a bright lesbian alderwoman in *Political Poison.*

In Stuart Kaminsky's *You Bet Your Life,* P.I. Toby Peters, hired by Louis Mayer of Metro Goldwyn Mayer to extricate Chico Marx from trouble with the mob, went to the Mayor's office. Peters told the mayor's secretary that MGM was thinking of doing a Chicago film, to be called *A Song in the Fire,* but the secretary still called the cops. Peters ducked down the staircase to the first floor and into the nearest office, where he found State Senator Richard J. Daley. Daley told Peters that this gangster city would be cleaned up by the righteous Bridgeport Democrats.

In D. J. H. Jones' *Murder at the MLA,* "connected" Police Lieutenant Mulcahy told detective Boaz Dixon that "the Man on Five gets the blue nasties if a convention gets screwed up in

Chicago." (Three tenured professors had been murdered at the Modern Languages Association's annual convention.)

In Robert Campbell's mysteries precinct captain, later ward committeeman, Jimmy Flannery often visited Wally Dunleavy, head of Streets and Sanitation *and* top patronage boss, who redrew the city ward map to suit himself. Since the Shakman decree outlawed patronage, the courts would not be amused, but "political connectedness" has not disappeared. It's just been privatized, as Sara Paretsky in *Burn Marks* and Michael Cormany in *Red Winter* make very clear.

In Campbell's *Hipdeep in Alligators,* Flannery carried the "master sewer map" in his pocket, but in fact there is a wall full of atlases not one map. The Deputy Commissioner (not Superintendent) also reports that he can't send naughty employees to walk the sewers because the sewers are too small. Nor does the city empty sewage in Lake Michigan because, as every school kid knows, Chicago reversed the flow of the Chicago River to avoid that sanitation problem.

In D'Amato's *Hard Luck,* Cat Marsala was snooping about the seventh-floor Lottery offices at night when she figured out who had murdered Lottery PR man Jack Sligh. She called her friend Deputy Police Commander Harold McCoo at 11th and State but just as McCoo told her to get out of City Hall a shot hit her phone. Cat escaped by climbing into an air duct. (You can't see the ducts on the first three floors.)

If you have been exploring the upper floors of City Hall, take the stairs back to the LaSalle Street entrance, noting that there are public phones under the stairways at the ground level. In Arthur Maling's *The Snowman,* the kidnapers of department store executive Ches Novak's son Buzz told Novak to go to City Hall, find a telephone, and wait for instructions. Novak was then told to go to the Greyhound Bus Terminal where a blue Dodge would pick him up.

Leave City Hall by the LaSalle Street exit. In Collins's *True Crime*, he commented that LaSalle Street was the Wall Street of the West, a concrete valley where money and power lived. Collins added that LaSalle Street had devoted an entire city block to City Hall, another place where money and power resided.

LaSalle Street is the centerpiece of the city's financial district, as well as the generic name for Chicago's banking, brokering, and trading industries. It is richly appropriate that it should be named after French explorer Robert Cavalier, Sieur de LaSalle, who saw Chicago's potential in 1682 when he said "This will be the gate of the empire." Of course, LaSalle is also the person who christened it *Checagou* ("wild onion"), according to Kenan Heise and Mark Frazel in *Hands on Chicago*.

Turn left to walk one block south on LaSalle Street to Washington Street. Across Washington is the '20s Art Deco American National Bank Building, faced with golden bricks. In Collins's *True Crime,* Heller went to see Capone lawyer Louis Philip Piquett in a sleek gold-brick skyscraper that looked down on City Hall. Piquett was representing bank robber John Dillinger, and Heller asked if Piquett ever represented anybody who wasn't a gangster or a thief. Piquett told him they were the only ones with money.

Turn right to cross LaSalle at Washington. On the west side of LaSalle was the site of the old Stock Exchange, an Adler and Sullivan landmark torn down in 1972. (Photographer Richard Nickels was killed by debris taking shots of it during demolition.) The Stock Exchange arch is now at Columbus Drive outside the Art Institute, where the original Trading Room has been reconstructed, too. (See Walk 1.)

Then turn right to walk back to Randolph. In the middle of the block at 120 N. LaSalle there is a modern building with a mosaic of two flying Icarus/Daedalus figures. It stands about where the LaSalle Hotel used to be.

In Stuart Kaminsky's *You Bet Your Life,* when P.I. Toby Peters arrived in Chicago Police Sergeant Chuck Kleinhans, who picked him up, ordered him to stay at the LaSalle Hotel. Shortly afterwards Peters discovered a corpse in his closet.

In Thomas B. Dewey's *A Sad Song Singing,* a young girl called Crescentia (Cressie for short) hired P.I. "Mac" to find a folk singer called Richie Darden who left her with only an empty suitcase. Mac put Cressie in a "medium-sized commercial hotel" downtown for safekeeping. That kind of hotel doesn't exist in the Loop these days, but it would have been near the LaSalle.

Craig Rice's criminal lawyer John J. Malone also lived in a mid-Loop hotel, considerably less elegant than the Palmer House, Midland, or Bismarck, the main choices today.

The modern 120 N. LaSalle with its mosaics is about the right location for the Ashmore Building, described as a "modern monstrosity" in Jay Robert Nash's *A Crime Story.* The body of Governor-elect Maitland Ashmore's chauffeur Oreste was found inside the Ashmore limo in the building's parking garage. Oreste had been shot and the limo filled with cement. It was suggested that the car and the chauffeur be buried together, but the Medical Examiner said he had to do an autopsy.

Continue back to Randolph where Paretsky put the Grafalk Steamship Company offices in *Deadlock.* V.I. and her English friend Roger Ferrant, the expert on Great Lakes shipping from Lloyds of London, were investigating Grafalk's finances.

Turn left to walk west on Randolph to the Bismarck Hotel at 171 W. Randolph. It is still the de facto stronghold of the Democratic Party, where the party elders slate candidates, but recent fancy celebrations like the second Mayor Daley's victory gathering have been held at the Hyatt Regency. (See Walk 1.) Stop for a cup of coffee or a hot fudge sundae in the Old Vienna coffeeshop or go upstairs to the lobby where you can sit down or use the restrooms. At the Bismarck you see lots of foreign tourists as well as an occasional politician. On the lobby level the (Swiss) Chalet restaurant and the famous Walnut Room are open to the public.

In Bill Granger's *The Newspaper Murders,* his stupid States Attorney Bud Halligan was very upset when he was ignored by the mayor in the Bismarck's Walnut Room, where all the Democratic politicians ate lunch.

Come out of the Bismarck and go left to Wells Street where the El rattles by overhead. Wells is named for Captain William Wells, who arrived at Chicago just in time to lead the Fort Dearborn garrison on retreat. Wells painted his face black because he was sure the garrison would be attacked by the Potawatomi. He was right. (See also Walks 4 and 8.)

Cross Wells and continue west to Franklin Street. At Franklin look right for a grand view of the "postmodern" green glass skyscraper at 333 Wacker Drive. In Andrew Greeley's *The Patience of a Saint,* newspaper columnist Red Kane said it was the color of his wife Eileen's eyes. Walking back from Old St. Patrick's across the river, Kane was nearly killed by a big Cadillac limousine driven by an old gangster. The near hit reinvolved Kane (and his brother-in-law Father Blackie Ryan) in the mysterious disappearance of his newspaper mentor Paul O'Meara. It also changed Red Kane's life.

Cross Franklin. Four blocks west of you is Haymarket Square. In 1886 there was a workers' demonstration there and some unknown person threw a bomb, causing a riot that resulted in the hanging of four anarchists. When Governor Altgeld pardoned the others he was labeled John "Pardon" Altgeld, and lost a chance to become senator.

Turn left on Franklin and walk south to Washington Street. At 300 W. Washington is the old Midwest Stock Exchange building. (The Exchange, now housed in a new building behind the Board of Trade, has been renamed the Chicago Stock Exchange.) In *Killing Orders,* V.I. broke into the old Midwest Stock Exchange Building to investigate a Roman Catholic secret society called Corpus Christi. V.I. was caught but, dressed liked a cleaning woman, shouted insults in Italian at the cops until they let her go.

Turn right at Washington to walk west to Wacker Drive's north/south extension, which was built over the old Market Street at the river's edge. Cross Wacker Drive to the west side. Then cross Washington to the Civic Opera Building, built in the shape of a throne by utilities czar Samuel Insull to showcase his mistress Mary Garden. Insull, who died penniless, was also a member of the Secret Six, the group of prominent citizens organized to get rid of Al Capone.

Walk under the arcade past the Civic Opera Building's entrance to Madison Street and turn the corner to the entrance to the opera house itself. In Paretsky's *Killing Orders,* V.I. remembered that her Italian mother, Gabriella, took her to the Lyric Opera every fall. In Mignon G. Eberhart's *The Glass Slipper,* Rue Hatterick, a nurse who had just married her boss, went to the opera on a rainy opening night, escorted by her husband's young assistant, Dr. Andrew Crittenden. Their limousine crossed Washington to draw up to the entrance where women, their gowns shimmering below their furs, were crossing the wide walk quickly, the men assisting their ladies and clutching their top hats. Once in the Hatterick box, Andy told Rue that the Chicago Police thought her husband's first wife had been murdered.

After looking at the elegant lobby, walk west on Madison across the Chicago River. The Madison Street Bridge, like the other Loop bridges, was built in the days of the last Republican mayor of Chicago, boisterous, gangster-loving Big Bill (William Hale) Thompson. Although the Chicago River is not very wide, it has more movable bridges than any other city in the world. On St. Patrick's Day it is dyed kelly green, but it doesn't deserve the crack by John D. MacDonald in *One Fearful Yellow Eye,* that "Chicago is divided in the middle by a sewer with nine bridges called the Chicago River."

Just across the Chicago River on your right at 400 W. Madison is the old *Chicago Daily News* Building. Designed by Holabird and Root in 1929, it echoes the '20s style of the Civic Opera House. The *Daily News*—now defunct—was founded in 1875.

Before World War II, what was known as "newspaper row" had a Wacker Drive/Madison Street axis, until the surviving *Chicago Sun-Times* moved to the north side of the Chicago River across from Tribune Tower. Other Chicago newspaper buildings nearby included the *Chicago Daily Times* at 211 Wacker (in a building built for the *Chicago Evening Post*) and the Hearst Building at 326 W. Madison, home of the *Chicago Herald and Examiner* and the *Chicago American.* In *The Devil's Card,* Mary Mayer's young Irish reporter Tom Martin worked at the *Chicago Tribune* during the 1880s, when its offices and presses were at Dearborn and Madison.

Chicago mysteries often use the names of long-gone papers. In Andrew Greeley's *The Patience of a Saint,* Father Blackie's brother-in-law, columnist Red Kane, works for the *Herald Gazette* in a building at Wacker and Dearborn on the south side of the Chicago River, while Paretsky's Murray Ryerson works for the *Herald-Star* near the *Sun-Times* (probably the *Chicago Tribune*).

In Harry Stephen Keeler's *The Face of the Man from Saturn,* reporter Jimmie Kentland worked for the *Sun* "Chicago's Only Socialist Newspaper." Kentland was left in charge as city night editor by Editor-in-Chief August L. Fornhoff, but got a mysterious note and left his post to find murder done in an old Curio Shop in Crilly Court. (See Walk 7.) Although Kentland scooped the *Tribune,* the *Herald-Examiner,* and the *Times-Star,* he was fired for leaving his post.

One block west at Canal and Madison is the glitzy Northwestern Station. Its new multistory atrium, built by Helmut Jahn over the old tracks of the Chicago and North Western Railroad has a neon decor very like Jahn's United Airlines terminal at O'Hare Airport, but the lobby's exposed steel skeleton is supposed to remind you of London's nineteenth-century train sheds, so beautifully evoked in Margery Allingham's *Tiger in the Smoke.*

Many mysterious characters come and go from this station. Among them are Fredric Brown's young Ed Hunter in *The Fabulous Clipjoint.* When Hunter's father was found dead in an alley he went to get his Uncle Am who worked for a Wisconsin carnival (like the Ringling Bros. Barnum and Bailey Circus?).

In Fredric Brown's *The Screaming Mimi,* reporter William Sweeney went to Northwestern Station after bullying the fare from a gangster who ran a string of Chicago nightclubs. Sweeney took the milk train north to track down the story behind the exotic Yolanda, who did a burlesque act with her dog Devil.

In Clyde B. Clason's *The Man from Tibet,* Vincent Merriweather met his explorer Uncle Jed there. Bored by working for his father, young Merriweather saw the track gates as meant for "smug commuters, blasé salesmen, frenzied businessmen, and vacationers." He wanted adventure, which he got when his father was murdered in his Tibetan collection.

In Harry Stephen Keeler's *Thieves' Nights,* the man with gray eyes arrived there, checked his luggage, and walked downtown, where he got mugged and lost his memory. In Craig Rice's *Trial by Fury,* John J. Malone caught the milk train to Wisconsin to bail out Helene and Jake Justus, and in Frank Gruber's *The Scarlet Feather,* pitchmen Johnny and Sam went to suburban Baker Hill to watch an illegal cock fight. They got a ride back to the city with the police. In Eleanor Taylor Bland's *Dead Time,* black Detective Marti MacAlister discovered that the murdered Lauretta Dorsey had taken the train to Chicago to sell some jewels on the day she was killed.

Look inside, then you can either take the side trip described on page 105 or go left on Canal Street and walk south to Adams. Along the way you pass many skyscrapers on sites where there used to be seedy, cheap office buildings. In O. G. Benson's *Cain's Wife,* P.I. Max Raven (aka Maxim Ravensky) had his office in an old building with a manual elevator, two tiny rooms painted off-white and a window overlooking the Chicago River and the West Side. A gorgeous client Naomi Cain (née Norma Dupkovitch—a Kim Novak look-alike) came there and hired Raven to find out who was blackmailing her. (Naomi had married Jedediah Cain of Cain Pharmaceuticals, then two-timed him with her stepson.)

In Bill S. Ballinger's *Portrait in Smoke,* Danny April bought Clarence Moon's small-time collection agency, housed in a two-room office in an old loft building near the Civic Opera Building. With the business April also inherited the mystery of Krassy Almauniski, who had become socialite Candice Powers. (See Walk 6.)

At the corner of Adams looking west you can see a water tower marked "Greek Islands." If you walked about four blocks to Halsted you would be in Greektown, where many people from the west Loop go for lunch. You can also see the green spire of old St. Patrick's on DesPlaines. Chicago's oldest existing church building, built in 1852, it has become a "society" church, attended by the mayor and upscale characters in Andrew Greeley's mysteries like *Wages of Sin.*

Cross Adams and go left across Canal Street to go inside Union Station to see its huge, domed 1913 waiting room, recently renovated. Scenes from the 1987 movie of Eliot Ness's *The Untouchables* were filmed here. The station is one of the few great railroad stations left in the country.

In John Ashenhurst's *The World's Fair Murders,* reporter

Allison Bennett of the evening *Journal* was sent by his city editor to Union Station to cover the arrival of world-famous Professor Arturo del Grafko of Almania. Bennett never liked the station because it was so large there were too many chances a celebrity might escape you. This particular celebrity was not murdered until he got to the fairgrounds.

In Eleanor Taylor Bland's *Dead Time* Detective Marti MacAlister told her partner that her mother had done day work in Lake Forest and her father had cleaned trains in Union Station. In Stuart Kaminsky's *When the Dark Man Comes,* psychologist Jean Kaiser's ex-husband Max and her daughter Angie saw her off here for New York and a job with the CBS network because Jean wouldn't fly. Author Barbara D'Amato won't fly either if she can help it.

Come out of Union Station on Canal Street and turn left to return to Adams, unless you want to detour one block south to Jackson and one block west to Clinton to get something to eat at Lou Mitchell's. It is a favorite spot for breakfast (or lunch) with good coffee, fresh cream, double-yolked eggs, omelets with hash browns, and much else, served at cafeteria-like tables.

In D. J. H. Jones's *Murder at the MLA,* the coroner's toxicology division's night shift came to Lou Mitchell's to take a break from figuring out what had poisoned English Professor Susan Engleton. Later detective Boaz Dixon and professor Nancy Cook went there, too. In Bill Granger's *The Priestly Murders,* Criminal Division's Jack Donovan ate a "business" breakfast there with Police Lieutenant Mathew Schmidt. They were planning a stake-out at St. Alma's Roman Catholic Church. (See Walk 9.)

Two blocks south across the river you can see the Central Post Office, which straddles the Congress Eisenhower Expressway. In Paretsky's *Killing Orders,* V.I. drove under it on her way to Aunt Rosa's home in suburban Melrose Park, thinking the expressway looked like a prison exercise yard, lined with rundown houses and faceless projects and barbed wire fences.

M. S. (Mary Shura) Craig's *The Third Blond* was set in the post office's Dead Letter Office. Nina Hayward took a personal interest in tracing and returning lost and found items, but one snowy day she was killed on her way to a small cafe run by her boyfriend Charlie B.

Cross Wacker Drive at Adams, passing the main Rand McNally store. Walk east to the 110-story Sears Tower at 233 S. Wacker, labeled the world's tallest white elephant by *Chicago Magazine*. Either go inside on Adams to walk through the lobby or walk south to Jackson to use the elegant glass tourist entrance to reach the Skydeck Observatory on the 103rd floor. In the lobby on the Wacker Drive side is Alexander Calder's huge mobile *Universe,* which he set in motion in 1974.

Half empty or not, Sears Tower is still a notable landmark. In Barbara D'Amato's *Hardball,* reporter Cat Marsala used its beacon as a landmark when swimming to shore after being dumped in Lake Michigan wearing cement boots.

In Yastrow's *Undue Influence,* lawyer Philip Ogden went there to meet with members of the firm of Schlessinger, Harris & Wade, who represented synagogue Beth Zion. As executor of Stillman's will, Ogden met with the suave head honcho Leon Schlessinger and his attractive associate Maggie Flynn, whom the firm hoped Ogden would take as bait.

In Brian Michael's *Illegal Procedure,* Station WBCC-TV3 was located on the twentieth floor of the Sears Tower. A bomb planted in a Cougar football had been caught by the Cougar quarterback who was blown to bits, an event seen on WBCC-TV in living color. Police Lieutenant Frank Lesniak and Sergeant George Corvello came here to interview the people who did the TV coverage, but got a runaround.

Most exciting of all, in Eugene Izzi's *The Booster,* old pro Bolo and his young protege Vincent Martin made a deal to burglarize the Sears Tower offices of a Mafia (Outfit) leader to get some incriminating tapes. The old boss was locked away but his capo, Angelo "Tombstone" Paterro, had entered the federal witness protection program (i.e., squealed). Booster Martin and his old mentor had always prided themselves on their independence from the mob, but this one job would make them both terminally rich.

The job called for them to climb down Sears Tower from

the ninety-first floor in subzero weather one February morning to break into a lower floor, get the tapes, and go back up. In real life, "Spider Dan" Goodwin scaled the tower on May 25, 1981, with thousands of spectators watching.

Izzi's burglars broke into the suite of a recently dead lawyer, cut out a circle of glass to open the window, and climbed out into blinding wind and snow. One floor down, they robbed the safe—and went back the way they came. They made it down safely, but their mobster lookout man turned out to be a stoolie and shot at them, scaring pedestrians.

Come out of the Sears Tower on Franklin and look about for a likely-looking old loft building. In Martin Blank's *Shadowchase,* homicide detectives Hutch and Lamp went there to find Randy Hennessey, who was related to two recent IRA murder victims in Chicago. His drama coach, Lidiya Petrov, had a studio in a building with a dark vestibule of broken ceramic tile and flaky walls, where Randy was hiding out from the media. The cops took the freight elevator to the third floor, where they found a whitewashed room the size of a basketball court, with armchairs and a sofa at one end, and met young Randy, a new stand-up comic admired by Gene Siskel.

Cross Franklin and walk east on Adams to Wells Street, passing the Midland Hotel. A renovated '20s hotel, it has several restaurants catering to the stock exchange crowd, including the Ticker Tape Bar and Bistro and the Exchange Restaurant. You can walk through the lobby and up the stairs to the restaurant area where there are also restrooms, or stop at another McDonald's on the corner of Adams and Wells.

Mystery writer Ian Stuart and his wife Audrey stayed at the Midland when they came to Chicago. Ian had been very kind to Barbara Hendershott and me when we ventured into a meeting of the British Crime Writers Association in Shoe Lane, London. But shortly after their USA trip, Ian published *Stab in the Back,* in which an extremely pushy Chicago lady turned up in a tiny English village determined to locate her ancestors at all costs!

Walk past the Midland to the corner of LaSalle Street. In detective stories, as in real life, LaSalle Street is inhabited by bankers, stockbrokers, lawyers, and other malefactors of great wealth, many of whom do turn out to be crooks and/or murderers in Chicago mysteries. Bankers are rarely good guys, but greedy and crooked. They live on the North Shore in wealthy suburbs like Kenilworth, Lake Forest or Winnetka and most are WASPs, but in recent mysteries Roman Catholics and Jews have joined the action. Real banks are not often mentioned by name but fictional banks are put on real bank sites.

For example, one block north at Monroe and LaSalle there are banks on three corners. In *Indemnity Only,* Paretsky's mythical bank, the Fort Dearborn Trust, had buildings on all four corners of Monroe and LaSalle.

In Michael A. Kahn's *Grave Designs* the third oldest and second largest law firm in Chicago—Abbott & Windsor—had its spacious offices on the 41st floor of the "Lake Michigan Bank Building" at Monroe and LaSalle. Rachel Gold had worked there on a case called "in re Bottles and Cans," the largest civil law suit in American legal history, which went on forever like the Chancery case in Charles Dickens's *Bleak House.* Gold got so bored she quit to set up her own practice.

In Yastrow's *Undue Influence,* the "First Illinois State Bank & Trust" at Dearborn and Monroe was one of the Loop's oldest and most conservative banks. Phil Ogden and the Attorney General's representative met there to open Ben Stillman's strong box.

Cross LaSalle Street. On the northeast corner is the LaSalle National Bank. In John Malcolm's *Mortal Ruin,* Tim Simpson, the British investment banker cum art expert, was sent to track down the story behind some gold-mine shares belonging to Winston Churchill's Aunt Clara Jerome with the help of brokers Owens, McLeod, and Casey. Their offices were in the LaSalle Bank building. Simpson noted that the bank was in an older sort of skyscraper and when you leaned out the back window, you looked out over the (Loop) Post Office with its modern red iron sculpture resembling a sagging anchor (Calder's *Flamingo*). Intrigued by Chicago history, Simpson also noted that he could see Michigan Avenue where it met the Chicago River and squint at the site of Fort Dearborn, where Captain John Whistler, an Anglo-Ulsterman (Scotch-Irish), put up the palisades one hundred and eighty-odd years ago. (Nice to have a Brit more interested in Fort Dearborn than in Al Capone.)

Turn right to cross Adams. The famous Rookery Building is on the southeast corner. After the Chicago Fire in 1871 a temporary City Hall with lots of pigeons (and politicians) was built here, hence its nickname, the Rookery. This massive dark red building trimmed with terra-cotta and turrets was built by Burnham and Root in 1886. Its masonry structure was combined with internal cast-iron columns and beams. First renovated by Frank Lloyd Wright, it has recently been refurbished again. Go inside to see its skylight but you won't get past the main lobby without a guard asking your business.

An alley east of the Rookery separates it from the Bankers Building at Adams and Clark Street. In Max Allan Collins's *True Crime,* on the Friday after the Biograph Theater shooting of bank robber John Dillinger, a James Probasco fell nineteen stories from the Bankers Building to the alley below as he was being interrogated by the FBI. (See Walk 2.)

In Max Allan Collins's *Dying in the Postwar World,* vet Nate Heller, back from Guadalcanal and married with a baby on the way, moved his A-I Detective Agency into the prestigious old Rookery Building. Heller got a call from OPA (Office of Price Administration) executive Bob Keenan, whose daughter JoAnn had been kidnaped from her bedroom. JoAnn's body was later found in pieces in city sewers.

This is a fictional version of the real life murder of Suzanne Degnan, for which William Heirens, then a University of Chicago student, is serving a life sentence. In *William Heirens: His Day in Court,* Delores Kennedy insists on Heirens's innocence. Craig Rice, brought back to Chicago to cover the story, interviewed Heirens and also decided he was not guilty.

In Frank Gruber's *The Scarlet Feather,* Johnny Fletcher and his partner Sam Cragg pulled society girl Lois Tancred from the lake, then drove her Cadillac to the Crocker Building at LaSalle and Adams where her wealthy father had his offices. Tancred's secretary's office was only a few feet smaller than a city square, and his office was the most luxurious they had ever seen. Tancred gave the odd pair his card, which allowed Johnny to re-outfit himself at an expensive State Street store, then sell his old clothes to redeem their pawned muscle-building books and do their sales pitch. (See Walk 8.)

Turn right and walk past the Rookery down LaSalle to tiny Quincy Street. Across LaSalle is the Federal Reserve Building with all flags flying. Cross Quincy and continue south on LaSalle past the 1924 Continental Bank Building. It has a mezzanine lobby with Ionic columns and a painted frieze topped by a coffered ceiling. Below the lobby at ground level is a handsome arcade filled with shops.

Cross Jackson to the Board of Trade Building at the foot of LaSalle Street. (LaSalle actually continues south with a jog to the left.) You are in front of the Queen of LaSalle Street, a triumphant and majestic forty-five-story Art Deco building. The roof is a pyramid supporting the thirty-foot aluminum statue of Ceres, Greek goddess of grain, who used to look down on all she surveyed. (The trendy Helmet Jahn rear end was added in the '80s.)

The Chicago Board of Trade was founded in 1848 to stabilize grain prices. It moved to LaSalle Street in 1865, but this massive building was only built in 1930. Today the whole area seems to be filled with young men and women wearing lightweight, colorful, jackets, name tags and athletic shoes—the traders and runners.

On the Jackson side the Board of Trade has a tall, elegant lobby decorated in agricultural motifs in bronze with black and buff marble. To your left is the Ceres Cafe, a pleasant coffee shop. The elevators and building directory are straight ahead. The Chicago Board Options Exchange and the Midwest Stock Exchange (now the Chicago Stock Exchange) are all connected both physically and electronically from Van Buren to the Congress Expressway.

If you have time, go to the Visitors Gallery on the fifth floor where you can look down on the trading floor and watch the wild rainbow-jacketed traders waving their hands in occult signals. There are regular morning tours during the week, but a good way to learn what is going on is to read William Brashler's *Traders*, the story of a bright young girl learning the trade. So far no one has caught a murderer on Chicago's Trading Floor as happened in Emma Lathen's New York mystery *Death Shall Overcome*.

In Marc Davis's *Dirty Money*, P.I. Frank Wolf was a childhood friend of broker Abel Nockerman who took Wolf on a tour of the Board of Trade, telling him you can win or drop a million here, just like that. As Wolf stared down into the swarming mass of humanity he thought that the inmates of Bedlam might seem sane by comparison. But Nockie told him that this was Vegas, only bigger and faster. When Nockerman was found dead, shot gangland style, his wife hired Wolf to investigate.

In Andrew Greeley's *Ascent into Hell*, Hugh Donlon came to work here after he quit the priesthood. He considered the Chicago Board of Trade one of the last of the pure marketplaces in the world. But in Scott Turow's *Burden of Proof* the deaths hinged on the shady deals made by lawyer Sandy Stern's broker brother-in-law Dixon Hartnell. Hartnell ran a vast commodities-futures trading empire called Maison Dixon with sumptuous offices in the Board of Trade Building.

In Bill Granger's *The El Murders*, two young gays named Brandon Cale and Lee Herran, who worked as runners for different brokerage houses, had a Friday afternoon custom of meeting in the Jackson Boulevard entrance and going to Binyon's for a drink. One terribly cold and windy Friday night, they walked to Binyon's, then took the El home. Getting off the El they were attacked by gang members and Herran was killed.

Walk through the building to Van Buren and go out the new Jahn entrance. Look across Van Buren to the new building that houses the Chicago Board Options Exchange and the Chicago Stock Exchange. Then turn left and cross LaSalle Street.

Walk one block east to Clark on Van Buren. Across the street at Clark you can see the odd, triangular Metropolitan Correctional Center at 71 W. Van Buren. A federal prison, it was built in 1974 by Harry Weese and looks exactly like a computer card. The windows were supposed to be too narrow for a prisoner to escape, but several have, so bars were added.

In Paretsky's *Killing Orders*, when V.I. was investigating

why phony stock certificates were found in the safe of St. Albert Magnus Dominican Priory in Melrose Park, she went to visit a University of Chicago classmate named Derek Hatfield who worked for the FBI. Looking out his office window, V.I. sarcastically commented that Hatfield's view of the Metropolitan lockup must be a great inspiration to him.

Look down Clark. Just south of the corner there are two old bars. The second is Z's Sports Bar and Grill at 410 S. Clark. It is next to a single-room-occupancy (SRO) hotel and has apartments above it. In Eugene Izzi's *The Booster*, old booster (thief) Bolo owned Bolo's Bar at Clark and Van Buren. Bolo's bar was filled with retired thieves, and Bolo lived upstairs in an apartment furnished with "old country" heavy Victorian furniture.

Turn left to walk north up Clark to Jackson. On the southeast corner is the Metcalf Building, another federal office building designed by Mies van der Rohe, the "main man" in Chicago's modern architectural era. Cross Clark to peer in the first floor window to see Chicago's most recent addition: the mass of silvery steel and mesh welded together by Frank Stelle called the *Town-Ho Story*. That was the phrase used in Melville's *Moby Dick* for sighting a whale. The art object looks more like trash than fish, suitable for Campbell's Jimmy Flannery in *The Junkyard Dog*.

Cross Jackson and go north on Clark past the Federal Center's Loop Post Office and Calder's scarlet *Flamingo*. In Michael Cormany's *Red Winter*, P.I. Dan Kruger went there to mail crooked cop Thomas Lord a videotape of Alderman Nilardo cavorting with some black hookers. Kruger then called Lord from a pay phone to tell him it was coming. Kruger reminded Lord that Nilardo's northwest ward wouldn't like its alderman to patronize *black* hookers.

Stop at the corner of Clark and Adams to look across Clark at the Bankers Building, where the FBI offices were located before they moved into the Dirksen Building. Across the street, the U.S. Courthouse was also located where the Federal Center is. WBEZ, Chicago's public radio station, and businesses like ELEK-TEK are now in the Bankers Building.

In the Gordons' *Case File: FBI*, federal agent Jack Ripley reported to the FBI offices in the Bankers Building. He was given the three cases his friend and coagent Zack Stewart had been working when he was murdered. Gordon Gordon had worked with the FBI in Washington, DC, and Chicago and his wife Mildred wrote suspense novels, so they teamed up in 1950. Many of their mysteries like *The Cat* were made into movies.

In *Behind That Mask* Harry Keeler put the Interstate Life Building on the site of the Bankers Building. Jack Kenwood, a racketeer who published the *Ultrapolitan* had his offices there. Kenwood had run a $500 ad for Chinese wax artist Yin Yi. On Halloween, Yin Yi—dressed as an American Indian—came to demand his money back and Kenwood was later found dead in his office. Across the hall from Kenwood's office was Dr. Hippolytus Zing, who published the *Numerological Gazette* and taught courses on numerology. Zing's prosperous younger brother Sebastian had suggested Hip predict a murder and confess, but when Sebastian heard on the radio that his brother had confessed to the axe murder of Jack Kenwood he was still amazed.

Turn right and walk east on Adams towards Dearborn. Across Adams is the Marquette Building. Built in 1895, it is an archetypical Chicago School structure with a superb doorway decorated with bronze bas reliefs of Father Marquette's life by Edward Kemeys, who also did the Art Institute lions. In the lobby there is a double row of bronze heads and a mosaic mural depicting the French settlement of Chicagoland.

Cross Adams to take a look inside. The Marquette is the kind of building where prestigious old law firms have offices, although recently a client shot his lawyer and his brother here. In Charles Merrill Smith's *Reverend Randollph and the Unholy Bible,* the offices of Knox, Knox, and Elder, who were handling the estate of the murdered miser Johannes Humbrecht, were in an office building near the Church of the Good Shepherd. Bishop "Freddie" and the Reverend "Con" Randollph walked from there to a substantial old building with an ornate lobby. The law firm occupied the two top floors, decorated with pine walls and a long walnut table, hooked rugs and pictures of clipper ships, giving an aura of New England's understated success and integrity. Everyone named in Humbrecht's will was there: Reverend Con, Prior Simon of the Order of St. Thomas Apostle, and Art Institute curator Dr. Joyce Compton. The big ticket item in the will was a genuine Gutenberg Bible.

The Marquette Building would also make a good site for the law offices of Cohen, Kahn, Cohn, and Kahane in Haddad's *Caught in the Shadows,* a mystery about two generations of North Shore WASPs. No class was shown by either the upper classes or the smart Jewish lawyers who took advantage of the mess (incest and murder) to make money hand over fist. This firm's office had Persian carpets, paintings by Modigliani, Klee, and the ever-present David Hockney, durable and comfortable leather furniture, and Kleenex in needlepoint boxes all about the place for weepy clients.

Cross Dearborn to the south side of Adams and walk east to the Berghoff Restaurant at 17 W. Adams to end this walk. The Berghoff is housed in the kind of 1880s building you used to see all over the Loop. Its oak-paneled restaurant with old gilt-framed paintings has a carefully maintained beer-hall atmosphere, with aproned waiters in black who still make their own change. The place can be very noisy if full but the German cooking—and the beer—is very good. It has been run by members of the same family since it was founded as a beer garden at the 1893 Columbian Exposition in Hyde Park. (See also Walk 9.)

Max Allan Collins's Nate Heller liked to come to the Berghoff when he was tired or cross. It was about a block away from his first office in the Fisher Building on Van Buren. (See Walk 2.) In Collins's *Dying in the Postwar World,* a more prosperous Heller treated suspended Chicago cop Bill Brury to lunch there while they planned how to get the inside details on the JoAnn Keenan kidnap-murder. Heller and Brury ate veal, German fried potatoes, and red cabbage.

In Paretsky's *Killing Orders,* V.I. treated herself to a stein of their private label dark draft and a plate of sauerbraten as she worked her way through the Loop's stockbrokers, looking for a clue to the dealing in Ajax Insurance Company shares.

In Martin Blank's thriller *Shadowchase,* while chasing a small

Hispanic murder suspect through Pilsen, Detective Hutch thought lovingly about "the things in this world you can count on, like Wiener schnitzel at the Berghoff."

In Michael Raleigh's *Death in Uptown,* P.I. Paul Whelan, whose specialty was looking for lost kids, took his client Jean Agee there to dinner. Whelan was trying to locate Jean's brother Donnie. They ordered two historic favorites on the Berghoff menu: sauerbraten and Wiener schnitzel.

In Michael Cormany's *Red Winter,* P.I. Dan Kruger, the ex-cop with the "quirky" social conscience, ate there with his "connected" client, contractor Nicholas Cheyney, who was being blackmailed. They went first to the bar downstairs, then back up to the noisy dining room and sat at a table in the corner under two paintings of the 1871 Chicago fire. Kruger ordered a steak sandwich and beer, but Cheyney had Hungarian goulash. Looking about, Kruger saw many people dressed for success like Cheyney. Kruger was in jeans and jacket.

Go into the Berghoff to enjoy its food and end your walk.

POSSIBLE SIDE TRIP

Skid Row/Presidential Towers. Walk four blocks west on Madison Street from Northwestern Station, crossing the Dan Ryan Expressway to Halsted Street. This used to be Skid Row (Chicago's Bowery), where there were plenty of bums and bars and flophouses. In older mysteries, suspects hung out on West Madison, and P.I.s and cops came here to find them.

In Bill Granger's *The Public Murders,* Sergeant Terry Flynn went to a Skid Row flophouse called the Red Lion Hotel looking for a couple of feuding southern migrants whom the Chicago police thought had murdered Swedish tourist Maj Kirsten.

In Phyllis Whitney's first mystery, *The Red Carnelian,* Linell Wynn, a copywriter for Cunningham Department Store (aka Marshall Field's) teamed up to solve a murder with Bill Thorne. Thorne had inherited the Universal Arts Company on West Madison from his father. The company supplied show windows all over the country. Wynn took the streetcar west on Madison to meet Bill at the plant. She then went exploring while Bill worked until she realized someone else was hiding there, yelled, and they both gave chase. But the suspect got away.

In the mid '80s the four monumental brown Presidential Towers were put up at Madison and Clinton with city and federal subsidies. They were supposed to include some low-income housing, but have not to date. Even so, Presidential Towers is the biggest HUD defaulter in the country.

In Paretsky's *Burn Marks,* after the SRO hotel where her Aunt Elena lived burned down, V.I. told Democratic fundraiser Marissa Duncan to find Aunt Elena another place to stay or she would go to County Board President "Boots" Meagher's fundraiser to ask Congressman Dan Rostenkowski about finding room for Elena in Presidential Towers. (Rosty had made the Presidential Towers' deal.)

At 600 W. Madison you can see the Claes Oldenburg *Batcolumn,* a sculpture which stands in front of the Harold Washington Social Security Administration. In D'Amato's *Hardball,* Cat Marsala, going to LaSalle Street from 11th and State by a very indirect route, stopped to rest near Oldenburg's whimsical *Batcolumn,* unaware that she was being followed by a brown Chevy. Cat then walked back to LaSalle Street to visit her broker boyfriend John in the Board of Trade Building.

4

NEAR NORTH SIDE WALK

Michigan Avenue

BACKGROUND

Daniel Burnham's 1909 Chicago Plan proposed creating a grand Parisian boulevard north of the Chicago River. But it was not until 1920 that Pine Street was widened and renamed Michigan Avenue, the imposing double-decker bridge connecting it to the Loop was built, and new buildings like the Drake Hotel, the Wrigley Buildings and Tribune Tower sprang up to make Chicago's Boul' Mich a rival to the glamorous Parisian one.

A second great growing spurt occurred in the 1970s when the John Hancock and Water Tower Place appeared, dwarfing the old Water Tower, symbol of Chicago's sturdy survival. The flappers' and reporters' Boul' Mich became the tourists' Magnificent Mile, lit at holiday time with millions of tiny lights, thronged with serious shoppers, with skyscraper after skyscraper rising up to remind you of New York's Fifth Avenue. The same rich aura extends for blocks east or west, so that walking Rush Street today, most of its bohemian "Greenwich Village" flavor is long gone, while Streeterville, once sand dunes and squatters, rivals the Gold Coast.

North Michigan Avenue from the Chicago River to Oak Street is *the* shopping street in Chicago today, appropriately nicknamed the "Magnificent Mile" by developer Arthur

Rubloff. This walk includes those stores and boutiques and galleries and eateries mentioned by name in a mystery, but there are many, many others. If you want to cover them all, the best thing to do is stop in the Chicago Welcome Center at Michigan and Pearson Avenue where you will find lists and maps galore.

To the west of Michigan Avenue "River North" is the relatively new name of the territory south of Chicago Avenue and west of Wells Street. Originally factories and warehouses, it has gradually become a haven for artists and artisans because its deserted lofts make good living and working space. This walk only touches the eastern edge of Chicago's "SuHu"—Superior and Huron—but there are regular tours to the many galleries. The district's anchor is still the gigantic Merchandise Mart, a wholesale store built by the Marshall Fields and bought in 1945 by the Joseph P. Kennedy family who still own it. The Mart remains the world's largest commercial building.

Since there is plenty to see, you may want to divide the walk in half to allow more time for shopping and dining. Start at the Michigan Avenue Bridge, easy of access by bus, taxi, foot or Metra. Check out the Chicago River and Wacker's Lower Level, then "do" Michigan Avenue north to Oak Street. After refreshments, you can head west on Oak to see the rest of the Near North side and end by sampling some of the tourist spots like Capone's gangsterland show or River North's art galleries.

LENGTH OF WALK: About 3 miles

See the map on page 113 for the boundaries of this walk and page 345 for a list of the books and detectives mentioned.

PLACES OF INTEREST

Capone's Chicago, 605 N. Clark Street. Open 7 days a week 10:00 A.M. to 10:00 P.M. Shows every half hour, refreshments, Four Deuces Gift Shop. Fee. Call 654-1919.

Chicago Sun-Times Building, 401 N. Wabash Avenue. Call 321-3000.

Courthouse Place (Old Criminal Courts Building), 54 W. Hubbard.

Fort Dearborn site, Wacker Drive and Michigan Avenue.

John Hancock Center, 875 N. Michigan. Skydeck Observatory on ninety-fourth floor. Fee. Open daily 9:00 A.M.–11:00 P.M. Call 751-3681.

Holy Name Cathedral (Roman Catholic), 735 N. State Street. Open daily 6:00 A.M.–6:00 P.M. Call the Rectory at 787-8040.

Michigan Avenue Bridge, Wacker Drive and Michigan Avenue. Built in 1920 under Republican Mayor William Hale (Big Bill) Thompson.

The Newberry Library, 60 W. Walton Street. Open Tue.–Thur. 10:00 A.M.–6:00 P.M., Fri.–Sat. 9:00 A.M.–5 P.M. Public tours Thur. 3:00 P.M., Sat. 10:30 A.M. Call 943-9090.

St. James Episcopal Cathedral, 65 E. Huron Street. Church Offices open Mon.–Fri. 9:00 A.M.–5:00 P.M. Call 787-7360.

Stuart Brent Books, 670 N. Michigan Avenue. Run by the "Orpheus of Chicago booksellers" according to Nobel Prize winner Saul Bellow. Call 337-6357.

Tribune Tower, 435 N. Michigan Avenue. Call 222-3200. Plant tours are given at Freedom Center, 777 W. Chicago Avenue.

Washington Square Park, Chicago's oldest park, donated to the city in 1842. Also known as Bughouse Square because of bums and soap box orators.

Waterstone's Booksellers, 840 N. Michigan at Chestnut. New superstore. Call 587-0808.

Water Tower, 806 N. Michigan Avenue. Victorian gingerbread survivor of Chicago's 1871 fire.

Water Tower Place, 835-845 N. Michigan Avenue. Most stores open Mon.–Fri. 10:00 A.M.–7:00 P.M., Sat. 10:00 A.M.–6:00 P.M., Sun. 12:00 P.M.–6:00 P.M. On the third level is ***Rizzoli International Bookstore and Gallery***. Open Mon.–Sat. 10:00 A.M.–10:00 P.M., Sun. 11:00 A.M.–6:00 P.M. Call 642-3500.

Water Tower Pumping Station, Pearson Street and Michigan Avenue. See *Here's Chicago!* multimedia introduction to city, get maps, brochures, and flyers about Chicago events, shopping, etc., or board a tour. Call 467-7114.

Wrigley Buildings, 400–410 N. Michigan Avenue.

TOURS

Chicago Architecture Foundation, Tours by bus, foot, or boat. Call 922-3432.

Chicago Horse and Carriage Company, Water Tower Pumping Station. Horse-drawn buggy rides with top-hatted drivers. Call 944-6773.

River North Association, 229 W. Illinois Street, Suite 4W. Call 645-1047.

Untouchable Tours, Water Tower Pumping Station and Capone's Chicago. Two-hour circuit of gangster sites. Call 881-1195.

Wendella Sightseeing Boats, Michigan Avenue bridge. One- and two-hour river and lake cruises. Call 337-1446.

PLACES TO EAT

You will pass by many fast food places, including, of course, McDonald's, Burger King, Wendy's, and trendier spots. Most of the ones listed below either are mentioned in mysteries or are on the site of a place that was.

Billy Goat Tavern, 430 N. Michigan Avenue (lower level). Old reporter hangout where Chicagoan John Belushi got his "Cheeseborger, Cheeseborger" bit for *Saturday Night Live.*

Chez Paul, 600 N. Rush Street. French.

House of Hunan, 535 N. Michigan Avenue. Chinese.

Lawry's The Prime Rib (formerly the Kungsholm), 100 East Ontario. Fine roast beef in the remodeled McCormick mansion.

Lenox Hotel, 616 N. Rush Street: Andrews coffee shop, Houston's.

Pizzeria Uno, 29 E. Ohio Street; Pizzeria Due, 619 N. Wabash Avenue. The original Chicago deep-dish pizza; celebrity haven.

Riccardo's, 437 N. Rush Street. Palette-shaped bar; outdoor cafe tables in summer. Italian.

Rock 'n' Roll McDonald's, 600 N. Clark Street (at Ohio). Open 24 hours.

Signature Room at the 95th, John Hancock Center, 875 N. Michigan Avenue. Spectacular views of the city.

Water Tower Place, 835–845 N. Michigan Avenue: several restaurants.

NEAR NORTH SIDE WALK: MICHIGAN AVENUE

Begin your walk at Wacker Drive on the south side of the Michigan Avenue Bridge. This is the site of Fort Dearborn, whose shape is shown in the pavement with brass markers on either side of Michigan Avenue. There is a small model of the fort at the Chicago Historical Society, as well as a piece of the lifesized replica built for the World's Fair of 1933. (See Walk 7.)

In John Malcolm's *Mortal Ruin*, visiting British banker cum art expert Tim Simpson looked out the window at the LaSalle Bank, trying to see Michigan Avenue where it met the Chicago River because he wanted to squint at the site of Fort Dearborn. Surprisingly, Simpson knew the fort was built by Captain John Whistler, an Anglo-Ulsterman (Scotch-Irish), one hundred and eighty-odd years ago. The Methodist Church of the Good Shepherd was founded in Fort Dearborn in Charles Merrill Smith's mysteries about the Reverend "Con" Randollph. (So were the real Chicago Temple and First Presbyterian Church.) (See Walk 3.)

In 1812 the entire garrison, including women and children, had to evacuate the fort, led by Indian scout Captain William Wells. Knowing he was as good as dead, Wells blackened his face and marched them out to the "Dead March." They were attacked by five hundred unfriendly Potawatomie Indians at about 16th Street, losing twenty-four soldiers, twelve civilian males, two women and a dozen children. Others were captured and later ransomed. (See Walk 8.) The classic account—or accepted version—is still *Wau-Bun*, written by Juliette Kinzie, the daughter-in-law of John Kinzie, Chicago's first white settler.

Cross Wacker Drive to the southwest corner where you will see a sign for the Mercury Cruise Skyline Tours and possibly a red double decker London bus of the Chicago Motor Coach Company's tours. Locate the steps that go down to the dock (or lower) level, where you will find the ticket office for the Chicago Architecture Foundation boat tours.

In good weather you can sit there and watch the river traffic go by. There are a number of riverside cafes, but there is no continuous walk along the Chicago River west of the Michigan Avenue Bridge. Chicago cop Hugh Holton, author of *Presumed Dead,* does *not* recommend wandering about the nooks and crannies of Lower Wacker Drive, especially in the colder months when the homeless set up housekeeping down there. Read Barbara D'Amato's chilling tale about derelicts called "The Lower Wacker Hilton" or for a futuristic twist, Dan Crawford's "The Dark, Shining Street" where P.I. Gordon McGregor was chased there by a ghost cab.

If you don't have time for a Chicago Architecture cruise, cross the Michigan Avenue Bridge. Chicago has the most movable bridges of any city in the world, but bridges are no longer raised and lowered for a single sailboat. Paretsky's V.I. Warshawski, sitting at a riverside cafe, thought it was nice when Chicago did that.

Daniel Burnham's 1909 Chicago Plan called for this bridge to connect to what was then Pine Street, but it was not until 1920 that it was built under William Hale "Big Bill" Thompson. According to Kenan Heise and Ed Baumann in *Chicago Originals,* Thompson's talent for the spectacular made most Chicagoans regard him with dismay and ridicule. Elected to three nonconsecutive terms, Big Bill also associated with Al Capone, whose gangsters helped him win reelection in 1927. He lost to Democrat Anton Cermak in 1931, but according to Max Allan Collins in *True Crime,* Cermak then reorganized the Democratic machine so well—using the Capone model—that there has not been a Republican mayor since.

The Michigan Avenue Bridge is a popular mystery site. In John Ashenhurst's *The World's Fair Murders* Almanian Professor Arturo del Grafko had checked his suitcase carrying a lethal invention through to Chicago. When the professor was shot at the World's Fair the suitcase came into the hands of the Chicago police. After five cops died examining it, the Police Chief ordered the suitcase taken to the Michigan Avenue Bridge where a police launch waited. The launch went out several miles past the (water intake) crib and the cops tossed out the suitcase, weighted with three hundred pounds of iron. (Today environmentalists would have fits.)

NEAR NORTH

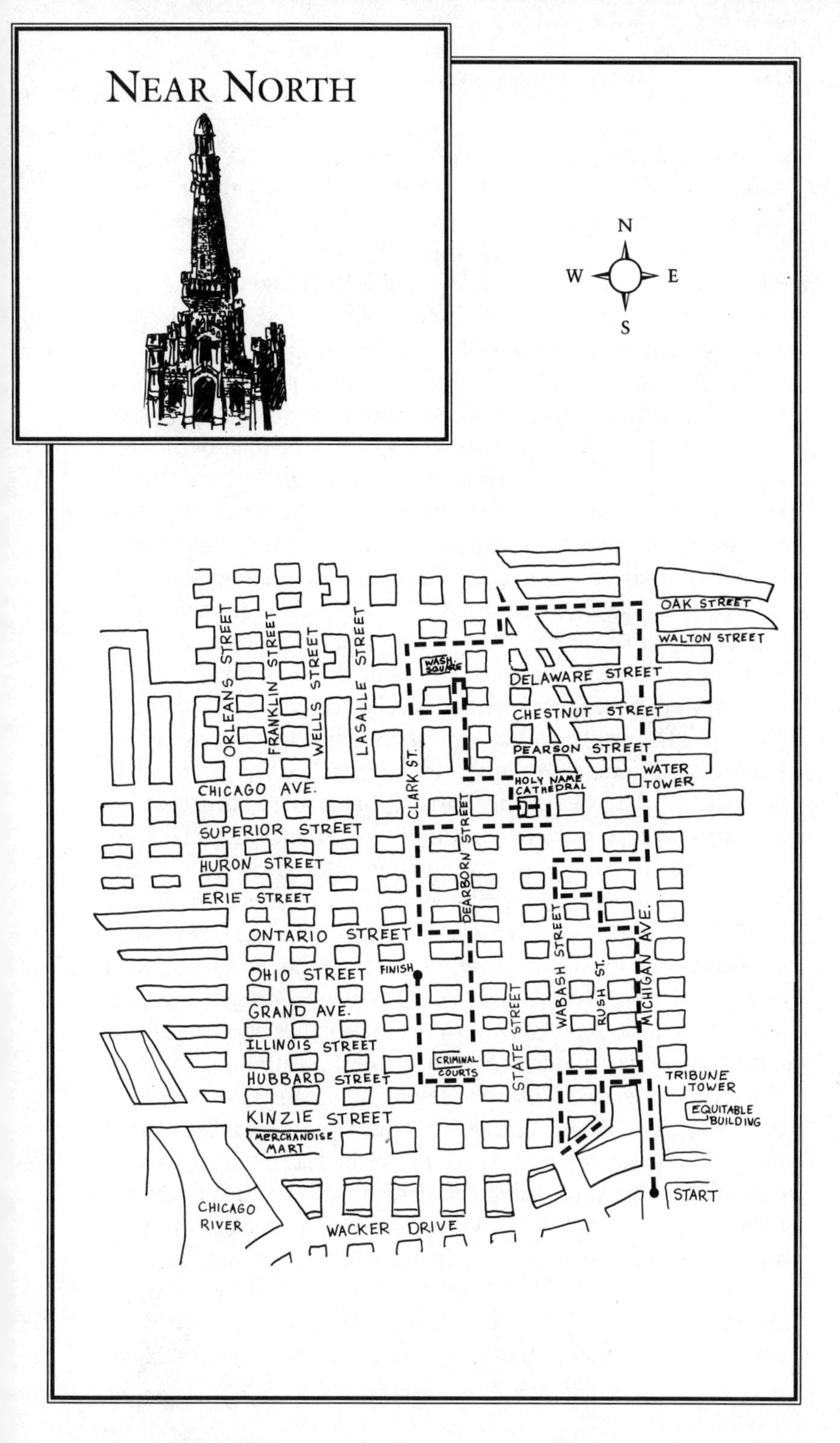
N
W
E
S
OAK STREET
WALTON STREET
DELAWARE STREET
CHESTNUT STREET
PEARSON STREET
WATER TOWER
HOLY NAME CATHEDRAL
WASH. SQUARE
ORLEANS STREET
FRANKLIN STREET
WELLS STREET
LASALLE STREET
CLARK ST.
DEARBORN STREET
STATE STREET
WABASH STREET
RUSH ST.
MICHIGAN AVE.
CHICAGO AVE.
SUPERIOR STREET
HURON STREET
ERIE STREET
ONTARIO STREET
OHIO STREET
FINISH
GRAND AVE.
ILLINOIS STREET
HUBBARD STREET
CRIMINAL COURTS
TRIBUNE TOWER
EQUITABLE BUILDING
KINZIE STREET
MERCHANDISE MART
START
CHICAGO RIVER
WACKER DRIVE

In Jonathan Latimer's *Heading for a Hearse,* P.I. William Crane was trying to prove the innocence of stockbroker Robert Westland, on Death Row for the murder of his wife. Crane hired a cab to drive back and forth across the lower level of the Michigan Avenue Bridge while he tossed a monkey wrench into the Chicago River for a diver to find. After a few false tries, the diver actually came up with the murder weapon.

In Arthur Maling's *The Snowman*, kidnapers drove department store executive Ches Novak and his son Buzz to Wacker Drive on the lower level so the car couldn't be seen by the FBI helicopter. They turned towards the Michigan Avenue Bridge, then headed instead into the new Wacker Drive east extension and the construction area and warehouses near Lake Michigan.

Cross the Michigan Avenue Bridge on the upper level, but don't try to beat the warning bell that tells you when the bridge is going up. In Rice's *The Corpse Steps Out,* Jake Justus and Helene Brand had just removed the body of Nelle Brown's lover from a warehouse fire when a bystander accused them of setting the fire. Helene ran to her big car followed by Jake, and they headed for Michigan Avenue. As they reached the approach to the bridge, they heard the warning bell. Jake yelled that she couldn't make it, but Helene reminded him that they had a passenger and crossed the bridge, just missing the last barrier. She shot into the lower level, waited until the bridge went down and took it north on the lower level. Shades of *The Blues Brothers*!

Take the stairs down to the Wendella Cruise dock if you want to take their trip. In Bill Granger's *The Public Murders,* Mr. and Mrs. Omar Dalrymple of Duluth, Minnesota, decided to skip the meetings of the American Pharmaceutical Association to take a Wendella cruise. Mrs. Dalrymple was the first person to see the body floating in the Chicago River. Since Police Area Six is on the north side of the river and Area One on the south side, the police dispatcher insisted on being told which side the corpse was on. Eventually, the body was pulled out by the fire department boat and taken to the morgue with an army bayonet in the back.

In the movie *V.I. Warshawski,* starring Kathleen Turner, Paretsky's intrepid P.I. got involved in a wild boat chase along the river. The chase led past the Wendella dock with the Wrigley

Building looming up behind and ended with a major explosion in the river instead of Lake Superior's locks, as it did in Paretsky's *Deadlock*.

You are at the southern end of Chicago's Magnificent Mile, which stretches north to Oak Street and the Drake Hotel. Known in the '20s as the Boul' Mich (nicknamed after the street in Paris) North Michigan Avenue has become the Mecca of the Middle West, where twenty million people come yearly to shop and dine.

Walk north to the gleaming Wrigley Buildings, joined by an overhead walkway and connected by a tiny plaza at ground level. Long a symbol of modern Chicago, the Wrigley Buildings were completed in 1924, faced with white terra-cotta tiles. William Wrigley of the chewing gum clan wanted to bring Chicago the "new" vertical look of Manhattan, while putting up a building that fitted the traditional dignity of the earlier Burnham era's buildings. The southern building is taller and has a famous clock tower. At night spotlights across the river highlight the facade.

Chicago's nighttime glamour was often suggested by the Wrigley Building in older mysteries. In Mignon G. Eberhart's *The Glass Slipper,* Rue Hatterick was driven in the family limousine to the opening of the opera along Michigan Boulevard where the Wrigley Building rose white and wraithlike under its floodlights. The bridge was up so they waited for it as a freight boat tooted hoarsely from the river below.

There is no longer any public area in the buildings except the Boulevard Bank. The Wrigley Bar and Restaurant at the end of the northern building's gleaming brass and marble lobby is now the private 410 Club. To visit it you must be a member or come to one of the monthly programs sponsored by the oldest Chicagoland writers' group, the Society of Midland Authors. William Brashler and Reinder Van Til, coauthors who are "Crabbe Evers," gave a talk there on how to collaborate in crime. Appropriately, since Wrigley once owned the Chicago Cubs and the *Tribune* does now, they talked about *Murder in Wrigley Field,* with retired Chicago sports writer Duffy House as an amateur sleuth.

The Wrigley Bar was a hangout for ad men, reporters, and

radio-TV staff, and its martinis were famous. In Arthur Maling's *Bent Man,* ex-football player Walter Jackson, who was kicked out of professional sports for throwing a game, drank there a lot. So did Maling's New York broker Brock Potter when he came to town to investigate *The Koberg Link* murders.

In Craig Rice's *The Corpse Steps Out* red-headed Jake Justus had his PR office in the Wrigley Building, so Justus often met Helene Brand and his pal lawyer John J. Malone in the bar. Both CBS and WIND radio stations were there, and Jake Justus's client, singing star Nelle Brown, had her own coast to coast show on CBS. In *The Corpse Steps Out,* Nelle found a blackmail note from a former lover tucked in her script.

In Rice's *My Kingdom for a Hearse,* Jake Justus wanted to do packaged TV shows. Justus wanted to hire gorgeous Delora Deanne who did cosmetics commercials but became less enthusiastic when parts of her body started arriving in gift boxes.

Admire the gleaming decor, then walk past the south Wrigley Building and turn left into the plaza between the buildings. Walk by the fountain to the riverside walk. On your right is a McDonald's, handy for a quick coffee or pit stop. Then walk on west past the Sun-Times Building at 401 N. Wabash Avenue. You can go inside and walk along a corridor with windows where you can see the presses at work or walk by the river.

Chicago mysteries do not always use the names of real newspapers. The classic Chicago newspaper story is Charles MacArthur and Ben Hecht's *The Front Page.* Hecht worked for the *Chicago Daily News* while MacArthur worked first for the *Tribune,* then the *Examiner.* In James Michael Ullman's story "Dead Ringer," crime reporter Barney Lear worked for the *Chicago Express,* where he competed with Chester Moon of the *Chicago Journal* to solve a hit-and-run murder. In Barbara Gregorich's *Dirty Proof,* the *Chicago Truth-Examiner,* where gymnastic redhead Suzanne Quering read proof, was located near the *Chicago Sun-Times,* but its loading docks were near the *Chicago Tribune*'s. The same "mix" occurs in Bill Granger's *The Newspaper Murders,* where a Chicago paper with a new Canadian publisher, has both *Tribune* and *Sun-Times* aspects.

Come to the Wabash Avenue Bridge and look across. Andrew Greeley's fictional *Herald Gazette,* where Pulitzer-winning columnist Red Kane worked in *The Patience of a Saint,* was across the river here. Columnist Red Kane was married to Eileen Ryan Kane, one of Father Blackie's bright sisters. Andrew Greeley's syndicated column used to be published in the *Sun-Times.*

Across Wabash is the aluminum-slab IBM headquarters, the last Loop office building designed by "form-follows-function" Mies van der Rohe. A block west at the State Street Bridge you can see the "corncobs" of Marina City which occupy the space from State to Dearborn. Begun in 1959 as Chicago's first "city within a city," Marina City combines residential, commercial, and recreational facilities. It was designed by Bertrand Goldberg, like River City, to house the single yuppie who wanted to live "downtown."

In Michael A. Dymmoch's *The Man Who Understood Cats,* police detective John Thinnes and psychiatrist Dr. James Caleb went to Marina City because an apparent suicide who was Caleb's patient had been doing the books of Margolis Enterprises. They visited Vincent Margolis's plush Marina City office, then later tagged along when the FBI caught Margolis sneaking a smuggled piece of art out of his apartment there with the help of a pizza delivery man.

Past Dearborn Street is the Clark Street Bridge. In Michael Cormany's *Red Winter,* P.I. Dan Kruger told his client the sad story of the Eastland disaster in 1915 when the cruise ship capsized with terrible loss of life. To Kruger it was typical of what befalls "the little guy." In *Chicago Originals,* Heise and Baumann relate that "Papa Bear" George Halas was scheduled to go on the cruise but arrived too late but Halas was not exactly a little guy.

In Les Roberts's *Seeing the Elephant* California actor/P.I. Saxon, in town for the funeral of his mentor, ex-cop Gavin Cassidy, figured out Cassidy was murdered. He and the murderer then fought on the Clark Street Bridge and one of them went into the river.

After enjoying the river front, turn right at Wabash to walk around the *Sun-Times*'s loading docks to Kinzie Street. It was named for John Kinzie, who bought black Jean Baptiste Point du Sable's cabin–trading post. (See Walk 5.)

Cross Kinzie and continue on Wabash to Hubbard (named for another Chicago pioneer, Gurdon Saltonstall Hubbard, or Swift Walker). Up ahead is the Medinah Temple, the 1912 Islamic-style home of the Shriners.

In Jay Robert Nash's *A Crime Story,* crime columnist Jack Journey drove into the lower level of Michigan Avenue near *The Record*'s loading dock at Clark and the Chicago River. A car with a shotgun came up on Journey who ran, yanking open a steel door to find himself inside an old tunnel system filled with the facades of ancient buildings, cobblestone streets, and iron gas lamps, mute survivors of the Great Fire of 1871. Journey was shot at by a monstrous seven-footer as he ran up the tunnel. You are standing above part of the old freight tunnel system at Hubbard that flooded Chicago in April 1992.

Turn right at the Lake Shore Athletic Club and take the stairs down to the lower level. Walk one block east to Rush Street. There is no longer a Thai restaurant at the corner of Rush and Hubbard but there are others in the vicinity. In Sam Reaves's *A Long Cold Fall,* cabbie Cooper MacLeish went there to consult his newspaper source, a college friend called Melvin Moreland. Cooper was trying to solve the murder of their classmate, Vivian Horstman.

Cross Rush to a Chicago institution: Riccardo's, at 437 N. Rush Street. Famous as a hangout for hard-boiled reporters and slick advertising types, it has a palette-shaped bar with a mural by original owner Ric Riccardo. It is not a big place, but in good weather it has outdoor tables and chairs.

In Craig Rice's *The Corpse Steps Out,* singer Nelle Brown was married to elderly, ex-tycoon Henry Gibson Gifford. Nelle was being blackmailed by an ex-lover who turned up dead and her agent, Jake Justus, was trying to keep it quiet. They met at Riccardo's with Helene Brand and John J. Malone along to help. The waiter kept giving them menus, but they went on drinking until the waiter gave up and went home to bed.

In William Targ's *The Case of Mr. Cassidy,* fat young sleuth Hugh Morris went to Riccardo's. He was greeted by Ric himself and ordered spaghetti and anchovies with meat sauce and a crate of breadsticks. He saw two publishers, B. D. Zevin (the mystery is dedicated to him) and Bennett Cerf, drinking martinis and radio actors from CBS and WGN. At another table were Chicago's literary critics: Dave Appel, A. C. Spectorsky, Frederic Babcock, and Fanny Butcher of the *Tribune* (who lived in the same Astor Street building as Mignon G. Eberhart; see Walk 6.)

In Bill Granger's *The Newspaper Murders,* obnoxious columnist Peter Markk collected groupies. He also took them home and beat them because one tried to sue the paper. Markk finally admitted to detective Karen Kovacs that he had heard murdered reporter Francis X. Sweeney being threatened by a West Side mobster called Mr. Theodore, who always wore purple, at Riccardo's and at the Billy Goat next door.

Come out of Riccardo's to walk east along Hubbard to the Billy Goat Tavern at 430 N. Michigan. Inside it is just the way mysteries describe it, with a square grill in the center, a Wall of Fame to your left, and a bar to your right. Stop to have some coffee or a beer to feel the atmosphere. During the Cubs' 1945 World Series Greek owner Billy Sianis got a series ticket to Wrigley Field for his lucky goat Sonovia but P. K. Wrigley refused to let the goat inside. As a result, Sianis cursed the Cubs, saying they would never win another pennant. (They haven't yet). The Billy Goat was also made world-famous by Chicago's John Belushi shouting "Cheezborger, cheezborger, no Coke, Pepsi," on TV's *Saturday Night Live.*

In Nash's *A Crime Story* the Billy Goat was called The Fallen Angel and run by Greek Homer Pippoupolus, a good-hearted Zorba in a long dirty bartender's apron. Columnists in expensive suits mixed with pressmen wearing little hats made of the day's newspaper. Crime columnist Journey found his legman, Champ Rimmel, nodding over a book by Solzhenitzen and hired him to track down a photographer who knew the governor-elect's murdered son.

In Michael A. Kahn's *Grave Designs* (originally called *The Canaan Legacy*) Rachel Gold, hired to find out what the strange "Canaan" codicil in the will of Graham Marshall III meant, called a council of war at the Billy Goat with Abbott & Windsor associate Benny Goldberg, call girl Cindi Reynolds, and pet cemetery owner Maggie Sullivan. Rachel pushed past crowded tables to a small one in the corner directly beneath a photo of the late Mayor Daley.

In Michael A. Dymmoch's *The Man Who Understood Cats,* Detective John Thinnes met Harry, his source at the *Tribune,* at the Billy Goat. It was not a favorite spot for the cops, whose feelings about reporters could be summed up by saying that reporters were like mystery writers, never letting the facts get in the way of a good story! Thinnes wanted to know how the *Tribune* had gotten the story of psychiatrist James Caleb OD'ing. Harry reported it was that frequent contributor, "Mr. A. Nonymous."

Come outside and take the stairs up to the west side of North Michigan Avenue. You come up about where the old Kroch's Bookstore used to be (where the Vance Gallery is today). A Chicago tradition, "Papa" Kroch sold German-language books on Monroe Street, then took over Brentano's. His son Carl Kroch took over in the mid '50s, but the chain has recently been sold to a Florida-based corporation.

In Targ's *The Case of Mr. Cassidy,* Hugh Morris, hunting for an old Italian book with a watermarked page torn out, gave up on the Loop to go to Kroch's. Morris saw Carl Kroch, but had no luck with the old book and left to lunch at Riccardo's.

Cross Michigan Avenue to Tribune Tower. (Cross carefully because cabbies U-turn here and as a young advertising gofer I was nearly hit by Colonel McCormick's limousine). The *Tribune*'s Colonel Robert M. McCormick was a member of the McCormick reaper clan. He was also a grandson of Joseph Medill, who bought the paper in 1855, and helped found the Republican Party and elect Abraham Lincoln president. After McCormick served in World War I he took over the Tribune Company. At his death it included the *Tribune,* the *New York Daily News* (founded and run by his cousin Joseph Medill Patterson), WGN Radio-TV, paper mills, and a fleet of ships.

In 1922 an international competition was held for the design of Tribune Tower. The winning design gave the skyscraper a Gothic cathedral top, a perfect reminder of the Colonel's extreme belief in the sanctity of the First Amendment. But his faith was badly shaken when one of his reporters, Jake Lingle, was shot in the Randolph Street I.C. station in 1930. McCormick offered a reward until it came out that Lingle was mob-connected. The whole story, including the Colonel's, is well told in Howard Browne's *Pork City.* The *Tribune* syndicated many comic strips like *Dick Tracy,* long drawn by Chester Gould in his Tribune Tower studio, later scripted by mystery writer Max Allan Collins. In *True Crime,* Collins wrote his version of the Jake Lingle story.

Many *Tribune* reporters were known as writers, among them Harriet Monroe of *Poetry Magazine,* John T. McCutcheon, Charles MacArthur, and Ring Lardner, who wrote "You Know Me, Al" and a series called *Own Your Own Home,* starring Fred Gross, a Chicago detective. The doyen of book reviewers was Fanny Butcher. Robert Goldsborough, who is continuing the Nero Wolfe mysteries, and John Fink, whose *The Leaf Boats* has a Chicago locale, also worked there, as do Bill Granger and columnist Mike Royko, who wrote *Boss* about the first Mayor Richard Daley.

The *Tribune* is Chicago's paper of record so it is often mentioned–by name–in mysteries. In Arthur Maling's *Go-Between, Tribune* reporter Al White gave the go-between useful information about the Lambert family fortunes. In Charles Merrill Smith's *Reverend Randollph and the Unholy Bible* the *Sunday Tribune* wrote that the Reverend "Con" Randollph had been kidnaped while on a pastoral visit to Wesley Hospital. His kidnaper turned out to be a gangster who wanted a Gutenberg Bible.

In Edgar Wallace's British version of Al Capone's story *On the Spot,* Tony Perelli (aka Al Capone) met his arch rival North-sider Mike Feeney outside Tribune Tower after Feeney's brother-in-law Shaun was killed. Shaun (aka O'Banion) had been an altar boy at Holy Name Cathedral. But Tribune Tower was alive with cops, so they went to Perelli's apartment where he agreed to put two of his men "on the spot," that is, have them killed by Feeney's gunmen.

In *Tunnel Vision,* Paretsky's V.I. and her old snitch, reporter Murray Ryerson, went spying together at a senator's farm near Morris. Ryerson's paper, the *Herald Star* was also "across the street" from the *Sun-Times.*

In Jay Robert Nash's *A Crime Story,* the *Chicago Record* was located about where Tribune Tower is and was run by Lucian de Barent—a fair-haired boy wonder hired to rejuvenate the paper. When Journey offered de Barent the scoop about the governor-elect's cover-up of his family murder, de Barent turned it down, saying "This isn't *The Front Page.*"

Walk to the southwest corner of Tribune Tower, to the right of the main entrance. WGN Radio is back at the Tower and you can see an operating studio. Years ago WGN Radio was housed in the newer building to the north. In Jon L. Breen's story "Malice at the Mike," the radio show was probably transmitted there from the ball park where sportscaster Buzz Rizzleston was working.

Walk into Tribune Tower's lofty, inscribed lobby to the corridor at the back and turn left to walk into the lobby of old WGN. Although the editorial offices are still here, the Tribune tours now are given at Freedom Center because the presses are there.

Walk out through Nathan Hale Court. Directly across Michigan Avenue you see a Rand McNally store, handy for buying *Mystery Reader's Guides* to England, London, New York, and Chicago. Their larger store is on S. Wacker Drive across from the Sears Tower. (See Walk 3.)

Turn right to walk "up" Michigan Avenue to Illinois Street. (You actually are going downhill because you are coming to the end of the lower level.) Cross Illinois Street to the Hotel Continental at 505 N. Michigan Avenue. It is another '20s building and was originally designed to be the Medinah Athletic Club for Shriners. Olympic swimmer Johnny Weismuller, who later played Chicagoan Edgar Rice Burrough's Tarzan in the movies, practiced there.

Just beyond the hotel at 535 N. Michigan is the House of Hunan. In Marc Davis's mystery *Dirty Money* about commodities traders, Tina Nockerman's father Abel was shot gangland style. Tina ran a North Michigan Avenue art gallery, and after interviewing her, P.I. Frank Wolf took her to the House of Hunan for lunch. The restaurant was packed but the waiter found them a small table where they ordered Bombay martinis on the rocks and Kung Bao shrimp for two and told each other the story of their lives.

Walk to Grand Avenue and cross Michigan Avenue.

Cross Grand Avenue to walk past the Chicago Marriott Hotel on the site of the old Time-Life Building at 540 N. Michigan. It is a modern blob, popular with conventioneers. Keep walking to Ohio Street, and cross Ohio to go one more block north to Ontario.

On the second floor at 620 N. Michigan is the Richard Gray Gallery, a showcase for modern paintings, drawings and sculpture by Picasso, Moore, Matisse et al. It makes a good substitute for Tina Nockerman's second-floor Quest gallery located at 618 N. Michigan in Davis's *Dirty Money.*

Across Michigan Avenue was the apartment of Christopher Morley's *Kitty Foyle.* Morley was another famous Sherlockian whom Targ's Hugh Morris met at Argus Books. (See Walk 1.) Look further east past Michigan Avenue. You can see a few older houses of the kind that used to line those side streets to the Outer Drive. Such houses have long been upscale businesses like the Delora Deanne cosmetics company with the pink and green reception room in Craig Rice's *My Kingdom for a Hearse.*

Cross Ontario and turn left to walk west to Lawry's The Prime Rib at 100 E. Ontario. Now known for its beef, this restaurant used to be the Kungsholm, famous for its Swedish smorgasbord, and its puppet opera productions. It was much appreciated by the overweight Hugh Morris in Targ's *The Case of Mr. Cassidy.* The modern front was built around the Edwardian palazzo of Hamilton McCormick, one of the numerous McCormick reaper clan that gave this neighborhood its nickname "McCormickville."

In Mark Zubro's *A Simple Suburban Murder,* high-school English teacher Tom Mason and his celebrity lover, Cubs baseball pitcher Scott Carpenter, liked to go to Lawry's to eat because they were left alone by the other customers. In *Why Isn't Becky Twitchell Dead?* they took young Jeff Trask whom they were "minding" there, too.

In Paul Engleman's *To Catch a Fallen Angel* P.I. Mark Renzler, in town to find a lost angel for *Paradise Magazine*'s Hefner-like Arnold Long, said it *claimed* to serve the best prime rib in town. He didn't argue because Arnold Long was paying.

If you don't want to eat at Lawry's, cross Rush to the southwest corner to the Lenox Hotel, where you will find Andrews, a coffee shop with a modern steel and plastic look, or the upscale restaurant/bar called Houston's at 616 N. Rush.

Houston's has English pub decor with a polished bar, dark wood paneling and etched glass. In Hugh Holton's mystery *Presumed Dead,* a swinging singles dentist called Sam Sykes spotted a gorgeous Amazon in black at Houston's circular bar and tried to pick her up. But he discovered that museum curator Evelyn Vaughan was too busy spying on another group there. They included crime writers Jamel Garth and Barbara Zorin and Chicago Police Commander Larry Cole, who were exchanging information about the bizarre happenings at the National Science and Space Museum. (See Walk 9.)

You can see both Su Casa and Pizzeria Due one block west of you. Due's sister restaurant, Pizzeria Uno, a block south at 29 E. Ohio, is the original home of Chicago-style deep dish pizza. In Gregorich's *Dirty Proof* murder suspect Suzanne Quering bought takeout pizza at Uno, which she warmed up to feed to her newly-hired P.I., Frank Dragovic, who was a gourmet cook.

If you're not hungry, turn right past the side of Lawry's building. At the back you can see the red brick windows of the old McCormick mansion rising above the modern facade. Walk along Rush to Erie, then cross Erie to the restaurant Chez Paul at 600 N. Rush. Another Chicago institution, it originally was a McCormick mansion built in 1875 for Robert Hall McCormick, brother of the inventor of the reaper. The two mansions were even connected by a tunnel.

In Edith Skom's *The Mark Twain Murders* English Professor Beth Austin was taken to the very exclusive Near North Club LaCache in a restored mansion, run by a Roumanian emigre called Victor Bilescu. Austin's host was FBI agent Gil Bailey who specialized in stolen art objects and was investigating the disappearance of rare books from Midwestern (Northwestern) University's Library. Chez Paul is not the Club LaCache, but it is in about the right location and its elegant Edwardian decor showed to advantage in *The Blues Brothers* when Belushi and Aykroyd upset the regular clientele.

Turn left on Erie to walk past the McCormick coach house and the auditorium of the American College of Surgeons to the corner of Wabash. Now the R. H. Love Gallery, the mansion at 40 E. Erie was built in 1883 by Samuel Mayo Nickerson, a (pre-Capone) distiller and president of the First National Bank. Its heavy sandstone exterior with a columned entrance hides a gorgeously opulent hallway with alabaster, onyx, marble and wood inlays. The entire house was designed to show off Nickerson's art collection, making it perfect for the Love Gallery's nineteenth-century American art. No murders have been set here yet but a peek inside the gallery will give you a good idea of the departed splendor of Chicago's stately homes, where Mignon Eberhart often set murders.

Walk around the Nickerson mansion to your right to St. James Episcopal Cathedral. An old church of soft yellow sandstone with wooden trim put up in 1857, the fire-damaged church was rebuilt in 1875. Inside, the chancel and nave have colorful stencils done by a student of William Morris that have been beautifully restored. On June 13, 1993, a Choral Evensong was held there in honor of the 100th birthday of British mystery maven Dorothy L. Sayers. Sayers never set foot in Chicago but her papers are in the Wade Center at Wheaton College, just west of the city.

St. James itself will not be open, so turn right on Huron and walk past the basement entrance to St. Andrew's Chapel to the Episcopal Church Center at 65 E. Huron if you want to go inside.

Or continue to Rush Street. The Rush Street neighborhood, known as Chicago's Greenwich Village or "Towertown" in the '20s and '30s when it was home to writers like Sherwood Anderson, Ben Hecht, Carl Sandburg, Edgar Lee Masters, Edna Ferber, et al., is still a mixed-use street.

This is where psychiatrist John Carmody took Sir Guy Hollis, who had come to Chicago seeking London's Jack the Ripper in Robert Bloch's story "Yours Truly, Jack the Ripper." Sir

Guy insisted that Jack the Ripper was a vampire, still alive, who killed on certain days and would be found among Chicago's "intelligentsia–the lunatic fringe from the near north side." When an arty party did not produce a murder, Carmody took Sir Giles to a dingy black bar at 29th and Halsted.

You still see some older buildings where Gregorich's P.I. Frank Dragovic could have afforded an office. In *Dirty Proof,* Suzanne Quering appeared at Dragovic's shabby office to hire him to defend her from a murder rap. She figured that a defense lawyer would just hire a detective and then she'd have to pay for both. In Barbara D'Amato's *The Hands of Healing Murder,* Doctor Gerritt De Graaf lived on Rush Street above an Italian grocery where he had a bar with stools made from merry-go-round horses. A consulting specialist in forensic pathology, De Graaf also had a knack for solving unsolvable murders.

Cross Rush Street and go east to Michigan Avenue again. To your right between Erie and Huron Streets are two more Chicago institutions: Stuart Brent Books and the Terra Museum of American Art. Across Michigan in the old Saks Fifth Avenue building is the improbable kiddie/adult heaven called Niketown.

The old Saks was probably the best choice for Hauser's, the family-owned department store in D. C. Brod's *Murder in Store.* Hauser's looked a lot like Marshall Field's State Street store, although Brod insists her model was Liberty's of London. (See *MRWG: London.*) Quint McCauley was the chief security officer at Hauser's. He had to deal first with his boss's young wife who liked to shoplift–at Hauser's, then with the poisoning death of the boss, Philip Hauser, which happened "in store."

Cross Michigan at Huron to the Allerton Hotel whose lobby entrance is at 140 E. Huron. It was put up in 1923 as a residential "club" for single men and women. Go in the main door and up a flight of stairs to the small Art Deco lobby where you can sit down. There are restrooms to your left, and to your right is the lobby entrance to the coffee shop called the Avenue Cafe, located where L'Escargot used to be.

Years ago the *Breakfast Club,* a radio show that was Chicago's answer to New York's Algonquin Round Table, was broadcast here. Its host was Don McNeill, with TV ("Kukla, Fran and Ollie") star Fran Allison as Aunt Fanny. Another lost Allerton institution was the Tip Top Tap on its top floor, which had a glorious view of Chicago. The unlit sign is still visible from below.

At the end of Fredric Brown's *The Fabulous Clipjoint* young Ed Hunter's uncle Am took him to the Tip Top Bar to show him the city, telling him to remember that Chicago is "the most fabulous clipjoint" of them all. H. R. F. Keating in *Crime & Mystery: The 100 Best Books,* called *The Fabulous Clipjoint* ". . . a splendid mingling of the realistic and the romantic with Chicago seen in all its unvarnished brutality and squalor by an urban Holden Caulfield."

Come out of the Allerton Hotel on Michigan Avenue. Across the street is the new Saks Fifth Avenue in towering Chicago Place, a multi-use building at 700 N. Michigan with an eight-level atrium filled with escalators and elevators and—more shopping. It has a food court on eight, while across Superior is another McDonald's, always a safe refuge for a pit stop and coffee.

Turn right and walk north on the east side of Michigan to Superior, passing Brooks Brothers and other elegant shops. Just before Superior Street you come to the brown facade of Neiman Marcus, which Father Blackie's nieces called the Needless Markup Building in Greeley's *Happy Are the Clean of Heart.* (Father John Blackwood Ryan and his family are very conservative architecturally, not unlike Britain's Prince Charles.)

Cross Superior Street and walk one more block to Chicago Avenue. In Richard Engling's futuristic *Body Mortgage,* escaping P.I. Blake and his client were driven by his secretary past Michigan Avenue shoppers to Chicago Avenue, then west on Chicago to his office building. It was just east of Cabrini-Green in a building owned by ex-hippie Quiller, who had won his fortune in the national lottery.

To your left across Chicago Avenue in a tiny green space is the celebrated Water Tower. Built in 1866 and miraculously left standing after the Great Chicago Fire, its Victorian Gothic towers became the symbol of the rebuilt city, although British satirist Oscar Wilde labeled it a "castellated monstrosity with salt and pepper boxes stuck all over it."

The Great Chicago Fire began on Sunday, October 8, and lasted until Tuesday, October 10, 1871. It destroyed the city's near south side, the Loop, and the north side to Fullerton Avenue, from DeKoven Street to Lake Michigan. The fire began in the O'Leary's barn where the Fire Academy of Chicago stands today, but official opinion says the O'Leary's cow was not to blame. People escaped by heading for Lake Michigan or using the recently emptied graves in the city cemetery (Lincoln Park). The red glow could be seen as far away as Lake Geneva in Wisconsin and across the lake. Chicago mystery writer Mary (M.S.) Craig's *Dust to Diamonds* gives a very accurate description of the Fire, and the best place to see surviving artifacts is the Chicago Historical Society. (See Walk 7.)

In Craig Rice's *The Corpse Steps Out,* Jake Justus was standing at noon on the southwest corner of Michigan and Chicago Avenue where there used to be an ice cream parlor called Charmet's. (Rickett's, popular with ad and showbiz types, was just west of Charmet's). Jake had paused to stare at the old Water Tower when a familiar voice said "It looks just the way it does on the postcards." Turning, Jake found a drunken Helene Brand, wearing a low-cut chiffon evening gown, beside him. She then fell asleep, so he took her back to his apartment by way of the freight elevator.

Cross Chicago Avenue and walk past the Pumping Station to Pearson. The Pumping Station now is a combination Visitor Information Center and museum. If you have time, see the film presentation called *Here's Chicago.* You can also take a carriage ride or catch the Untouchables Tour here. Across Michigan on Pearson you can get red double-decker sightseeing buses.

Cross Pearson to Water Tower Place. This vertical shopping mall forever changed Chicago shopping by taking the leadership away from the Loop stores. It has both Marshall Field's and Lord & Taylor as anchor stores, an atrium front and a vertical mall behind. On the mezzanine level there is a trendy cafeteria called Foodlife where you get to sit at tables with great views of the neighborhood. On the third level is Rizzoli's

Bookstore which has a good mystery section, including the *Mystery Reader's Walking Guides* to London, England, New York, and Chicago.

In Sam Reaves's *Fear Will Do It,* cabbie MacLeish drove a lady with more packages than she could carry from the Conrad Hilton Hotel to Water Tower Place (twenty-five city blocks). Then she gave a long suspicious stare at his meter and no tip.

In Carolyn Haddad's *Caught in the Shadows,* Becky Belski, went Christmas shopping here with her newly rediscovered stepbrother Billy Townsend III before they went to a River North gallery party.

In Michael A. Kahn's *Grave Designs,* when the group led by Rachel Gold decided to make a fake video of Abbott & Windsor senior partner Ishmael Richardson as bait for the murderer, they sent a policewoman to Field's at Water Tower Place to buy call girl Cindi Reynolds a sexy outfit.

In Eugene Izzi's *The Take,* partners Doral and Fabe Falletti amused themselves at Water Tower Place before making their "hit." Fabe and Doral spotted a couple of New Wave types; the guy had a spike haircut, a gold ring in his nose and a shabby old army coat and his girl had a multicolored waterfall hairdo, sprayed in place. The twosome were unnerving the other shoppers but Doral stopped and said in a loud voice, "Well, look at these two motherfuckers here." People smiled openly, feeling safer because now the two would attack Doral. In Izzi's *Bad Guys,* undercover cop Jimbo Marino, who had become a valued member of the mob, reported to Detective Commander Franko Lettierri at Water Tower Place by going to level seven, then taking the private elevators to the penthouse.

After casing the joint, come out of Water Tower Place and cross Chestnut Street to the John Hancock Center ("Big John") at 875 N. Michigan. Although it is only the third tallest building in the city (Sears and the Amoco Building beat it) the Hancock's massive shape with its dark, tapered profile and the huge X's up its sides seems to suit Chicago. It is also a mixed-use building with shops, parking, offices, condos, a rooftop restaurant and an observation deck.

But to Frank Wolf in Marc Davis's *Dirty Money,* the Hancock was an "aborted obelisk of 100 stories" where Tina, the daughter of murdered broker Abel Nockerman, had an apartment. P.I. Frank Wolf, hired by her mother to find the killer, went with Tina to her apartment, which was filled with blown-up photos of her and her daddy.

In Sara Paretsky's *Deadlock,* V.I. Warshawski stayed in the Ajax Insurance Company's apartment overnight with British insurance whiz Roger Ferrant, who was investigating the bombing of the grain ship in a Lake Michigan lock. V.I. was not terribly impressed with the company decor but liked the view of the steel mills where she grew up.

In Charles Merrill Smith's *Reverend Randollph and the Wages of Sin,* talk show host Samantha (Sam) Stack took the Reverend "Con" Randollph, an ex-quarterback for the L.A. Rams, to the restaurant on top of the Hancock Building and told him that she hadn't yet decided whether to seduce him.

After seeing the city from Big John's 94th-floor Skydeck Observatory, go back down to Michigan Avenue. Across Michigan you can see the gigantic teddy bear in FAO Schwarz's window. Around the corner on Chestnut is Waterstone's Booksellers, which also features big mystery and travel sections.

Cross Michigan Avenue at Chestnut, then cross Chestnut to the beautiful Gothic revival style buildings of the Fourth Presbyterian Church, designed by Howard Van Doren Shaw. The church together with the cloister and garth, was built in 1914. The manse on the corner of Chestnut was built later, in 1925. "Fourth Pres" is famous for its music and its annual Festival of the Arts. The offices are at 126 E. Chestnut behind the manse.

Walk along Michigan Avenue past the garth to the church door to go inside to see the sanctuary. In Mignon G. Eberhart's *The Glass Slipper,* the "Third Presbyterian Church" on North Michigan Avenue was the site of the wedding of "Cinderella" nurse Rue and Chief of Staff Dr. Brule Hatterick.

Come out and turn left to walk past the church on Delaware. Behind it there are some steps leading to other church buildings. Walk up the steps and peek in the bay windows where there was a church parlor, known as the Westminster

House lounge, until recent renovations turned it into a chapel. Louise Howe of Fourth Pres says that it was the closest to the one described in Paretsky's short story, "The Case of the Pietro Andromache."

The "Michigan Avenue Presbyterian Church" at Delaware and Chestnut was the site of Dr. Lewis Caudwell's funeral. Caudwell, the much hated Chief of Staff at Beth Israel, turned out to have a statue that had been stolen from Dr. Lotty Herschel's family, so when he was found dead, the Chicago police arrested Lotty. To save her, V.I. staged a classic confrontation here over the funeral baked meats.

Cross Delaware at Michigan. You are at Bloomingdale's, another mixed-use highrise development with an Art Deco atrium and four lanterns on top. This building replaced the old 900 N. Michigan Building with its elegant duplex apartments.

In Andrew Greeley's mystery *Happy Are the Meek* Father Blackie bemoaned the destruction of 900 N. Michigan to build this superbuilding. In Greeley's *Angels of September,* gallery owner Anne Reilly had a duplex apartment there.

Walk north past Bloomingdale's to Walton. Across the street is the 1929 Art Deco Palmolive Building, later known for a while as the Playboy Building, with the (Lindbergh) beacon on top. In Max Allan Collins's *Stolen Away,* which deals with the Lindbergh kidnaping, P.I. Nate Heller was sent east to help solve the case. Collins's conclusions about the murder are intriguing, while a recent study by Noel Behn, *Lindbergh: The Crime* suggests another: that the Lindbergh baby was murdered by his Aunt Elisabeth.

Until the 1950s its penthouse housed Arnold Gingrich's *Esquire Magazine,* for which both lawyer Clarence Darrow and reporter Meyer Levin wrote. (Both later were involved with murderers Loeb and Leopold.) In Sam Reaves's *Fear Will Do It, Maverick* Magazine (aka *Playboy*) was owned by Southwest sider Moss Wetzel, who had an elegant office with a broad teak desk and plush leather executive chairs. He sat there looking at porno photos and ordering up girls until a blackmailing scheme threatened his lifestyle.

Go one block north to Oak and turn left past the pink granite facade of One Magnificent Mile, another mixed-use '80s highrise, to walk west on Oak. You pass some more old brownstone mansions but they are all elegant businesses now.

Greeley's Anne Reilly had her Reilly Gallery here. Anne was suffering from guilt, believing that she had started the Mother of Mercy parochial school fire in which nearly a hundred kids died—including her two sisters. (In spite of Greeley's protests, this *is* a replay of Chicago's ghastly 1958 Our Lady of the Angels fire.) Later when Anne showed the works of the gifted but insane priest-artist Des Kenney at her gallery, there was a terrible fire and a cosmic storm. Blue electrical current raced down Oak Street, across Michigan Avenue, and up into the sky. The marquee of the Esquire Theater collapsed, the glass windows of a bridal shop dissolved, the beacon on the Playboy Building tore loose and one of the TV antennas on top of the John Hancock Tower cracked and hung like a broken toothpick. The "Angels of September"—Father Blackie Ryan, his sister the shrink Mary Kate Ryan, Patrol Officer Deirdre Lopez, and former Deputy Police Commissioner Mike Casey—rode to the rescue and saved Anne's sanity. There must be something to this story, for Michael Raleigh also described a similar storm near here in *A Body in Belmont Harbor*.

Go along Oak to Rush Street. You are about halfway through the walk and coming up on Hamburger Hamlet, moved from Walton to 1024 N. Rush Street. It would make a good place to stop and/or decide if you want to save the rest of the walk for another day.

In Gregorich's *Dirty Proof* South Chicago Croatian P.I. Frank Dragovic had trouble making up his mind if his client Suzanne Quering had murdered a newspaper executive or not. His mother would tell him he needed some good Croatian cooking, but with none handy, Dragovic went to Hamburger Hamlet and ate a chiliburger and fries.

If you continue the walk, cross Rush and go west to State Street. State Street still has older buildings and small businesses and trendy restaurants, mixed with cleaners and an adult entertainment show or two, keeping alive the "mean street" ambiance.

Cross State Street and go left one block south to Walton. Go one block west to Dearborn. At the southeast corner of Dearborn and Walton is the Scottish Rite Cathedral. Built in 1867, the limestone Gothic cathedral was rebuilt in 1873 after the Chicago Fire. South of the cathedral there are some late nineteenth-century townhouses that are now office buildings.

Somewhere near here Monica Quill (aka Ralph McInerny) put the convent of the Order of Martha and Mary, founded by the blessed Abigail Keineswegs. The Order had fallen upon reduced circumstances, its college and property was sold off in the '60s and there were only three nuns left, Mother Superior Sister Mary Theresa Dempsey (known as Emtee) and two younger nuns who did not wear habits. Out in the world, they brought cases to Emtee, a former college professor, who, like Nero Wolfe, preferred to gather the suspects in her parlor. The Order still lived in a Frank Lloyd Wright house, but there are none near the Newberry Library. The nearest one is the James Charnley House at 1365 N. Astor. (See Walk 6.)

Cross Dearborn at Walton and walk to the Newberry Library on the north side of Washington Square Park. The massive Richardson Romanesque building has a front entrance with a triple arch based on the twelfth-century church of Saint Giles-du-Gard. Inside the mosaic-tiled lobby, the rebuilt chandelier has light bulbs that point down, indicating that it was one of the first buildings in the city to be electrified.

Built by Henry Ives Cobb in 1893 with an addition by Harry Weese in 1981, the Newberry Library houses the "uncommon collection of uncommon collections" established under a bequest of Walter Loomis Newberry, who died in 1868. It is one of the great research collections of the Middle West, with 1.4 million volumes, 5 million manuscript pages, and 75,000 maps. The collections are noncirculating, but anyone seventeen or older may become a reader. It is especially famous for its genealogical materials, as well as for lectures, concerts, art exhibits, and Lyceum courses on subjects like "Mysterious Chicago."

In Jay Robert Nash's *A Crime Story*, when the son of Governor-elect Ashmore was found murdered crime columnist

Jack Journey sent his researcher to Newberry Library to check out the Ashmore family fortunes.

In *The Case of Mr. Cassidy*, Hugh Morris walked to the Newberry Library and took the elevator to the main reading room. He was trying to track down the source of the fake "Fiend" note found next to Cassidy's body. Since Cassidy, a noted book collector, also had a rare copy of Poe's first work, *Tamerlane,* when Morris saw rare book dealer Frank Doherty come in, he asked if Doherty had ever seen a facsimile reprint of *Tamerlane.* Doherty offered to sell him one for five bucks and Morris accepted because Cassidy's copy of *Tamerlane* had smelled like coffee, making him suspect it had been deliberately aged.

After looking about and checking out the bookstore in the lobby, go outside to cross Walton to Washington Square Park, the city's oldest park, better known to natives as "Bughouse Square" from the days when it was a soapbox speakers' heaven like London's Hyde Park. (See *MRWG: London*.) The park opened in 1842 as the centerpiece of a new housing development and by the 1890s was an elegant place to promenade. It suffered hard times when the eastern buildings were sold to the Scottish Rite Order and the other houses about the square were converted into rooming houses. Finally, during the Great Depression, it became a bum's hangout. The area around it is gentrifying again, but the Park District stipulates that it must be maintained as a public forum, so the Newberry Library sponsors annual debates there each summer.

Targ's *The Case of Mr. Cassidy* opened with a young blond walking across Washington Square who was caught by the Fiend and had her throat cut. But Morris still thought fondly of Bughouse Square as the Hyde Park of Chicago, where summer crowds sat on curbs, listening to soapboxers and drinking warm bottles of pop.

Fredric Brown's *The Screaming Mimi* opened with Irish Bill Sweeney, the *Blade*'s star reporter, getting over a monumental hangover. Sitting on a park bench next to "God" (Godfrey), an old alcoholic in Bughouse Square, Sweeney told God he wished he had another drink and left to cadge one. On State Street

Sweeney found a crowd staring at an apartment lobby where a gorgeous girl lay unconscious with a huge dog with yellow eyes guarding her. Next day when Sweeney reported for work he was put on the story.

In Harry Stephen Keeler's *Thieves' Nights,* the Man with Gray Eyes, a down-and-outer who lost his memory, met with a club of bums at Bughouse Square. They gave him the idea of burglarizing a Gold Coast mansion to find something to sell.

Walk to Clark Street on the western side of the park. Originally an Indian trail that became Green Bay Road, North Clark Street used to be notorious for cheap hotels, boarding houses, porno shops, dance halls and bars, as well as secondhand bookstores and antique shops. It was the site of James Ullman's *The Neon Haystack* in which a man disappeared (for good). But Chicago's favorite "mean street" is upscaling fast and no one would look there for a missing person now.

Walk halfway down Washington Square on Clark Street. Across Clark there used to be a Locust Street (it still exists a block west) but it has been swallowed up by the new development.

In Mary Mayer's historical mystery *The Devil's Card,* which takes place in the late 1880s, young apprentice reporter Tom Martin, who worked for the *Chicago Tribune,* lived just west of Clark on Locust, one of the poor streets behind the square with frame boarding houses and working-men's cottages. Tom daily walked to Washington Square to buy any newspaper but the *Tribune,* which he got free at work. He studied the papers before heading south to work. His Irish nationalist friends, who were implicated in the murder of "lace-curtain" Irish Dr. Patrick Cronin, lived nearby.

Clark Street was somewhat seedy in Kirby Williams's *The C.V.C. Murders.* The Citizens Vigilance Committee were a group of rich businessmen and professionals who decided they must rid the city of crime (like the real life "Secret Six" that included Samuel Insull and Julius Rosenwald). They hired Dr. Thackeray Place, a Sherlockian criminologist with a German Ph.D. who had taught sociology at the University of Chicago. His Watson was a former assistant D.A. named P. W. Tracy, who was an "S. S. Van Dine type."

Dr. Thackeray Place's apartment on North Clark Street was in a fairly modern building left stranded in a backwash of cheap family hotels, run-down rooming houses, garages and stores. His large suite had a laboratory and a library where Tracy came home to find Dr. Place in a leather armchair with a massive German meerschaum reading S. S. Van Dine's *The Canary Murder Case*.

In Stuart Kaminsky's *When the Dark Man Calls* detective Abe Lieberman warned Jean Kaiser, a radio talk-show host, not to follow the released convict who murdered her parents. But Jean tracked Parmenter by car all the way down Clark Street from Rogers Park to Bughouse Square, parked near Newberry Library, walked down Clark to a porno theater, and went inside for a confrontation.

Walk south to the corner of Chestnut Street. Across Clark at 100 W. Chestnut is a red highrise. Beyond the highrise on LaSalle Street is the campus of the Moody Bible Institute and across Chestnut at 830 N. Clark are the Chestnut Station Theaters.

In Eugene Izzi's *The Take,* safesman Fabe Falletti went past the Chestnut Station Theater to check the "hit," which was the elegant condo of drug-dealing Dr. Javier Chacona, thirty stories high across the alley. Fabe and his black partner Doral broke in and found the dead sister of a mob drug dealer called Francisco Ortiz.

In Sara Paretsky's "The Case of the Pietro Andromache" Deborah and Steve, the children of murdered Dr. Caudwell, told the police the night of the crime they went to the staff party at their father's condo, then to the Chestnut Station Theater, had pizza, went dancing and came in about 2:00 A.M. to find dear old Dad dead.

Turn left at Chestnut to walk east one block back to Dearborn. Turn left again to walk north past some elegant townhouses that were built as part of the Newberry estate; 839 N. Dearborn once housed Grant's Seminary for Young Ladies. You pass by the vacated headquarters of the Salvation Army, due to be torn down for another highrise and townhouse development.

Continue until you reach the park's southern boundary at Delaware and cross Dearborn to Delaware Place. To your left is a brownstone Victorian mansion with a coach house and on your right is the highrise Dearborn Place at 875 N. Dearborn. Beyond Dearborn Place there is an alley, but it does not go to State Street. Sinai Temple plans to tear down the older buildings east of Dearborn Place to build a new temple.

In Bill Granger's *The Newspaper Murders,* drunken reporter Francis X. Sweeney, having worked the bars of Old Town, ended up taking a leak in an alley between Delaware and Chestnut near Bughouse Square. The murderer clobbered him with a baseball bat and left him dead, with the red gang symbol of the South Side Brotherhood of Mecca sprayed on the wall above his head.

In Harry Stephen Keeler's *The Washington Square Enigma* Ford Harling, fired by a California bank, had come to Chicago to clear his name. He found Chicago huge, unfriendly, and cheerless. Sitting on a wooden bench in Washington Square on a freezing November day Harling noticed that Delaware Place at the south end of the park had a row of dilapidated old four-story brick houses and went to steal something to sell.

He broke into the house at 63 W. Delaware, where he found the body of a well-dressed man with an ornamental hat pin jammed through his right eye. When Harling saw two policemen coming, he dashed into the alley as a girl driving a purple coupe came past. He caught hold of the back of the car and rode north on Dearborn to her Gold Coast mansion.

Explore the alley, then return to Dearborn and walk south past Chestnut. In Targ's *The Case of Mr. Cassidy,* Hugh Morris's apartment was at Dearborn and Pearson above a French restaurant (Pearson now ends half a block east of Dearborn). Morris was writing up *The Cassidy Murder Case,* which he thought would be a swell title for a murder mystery by S. S. Van Dine.

Continue south on Dearborn to Chicago Avenue past more townhouses. In James Michael Ullman's 1968 *Lady on Fire,* P.I. Julian Forbes's son Eric lived in a three-story brownstone on Dearborn. The rent was cheap, and it was an easy walk to the night life of Rush Street. Eric had been to see Forbes's secretary (and mistress) the night she was found murdered and left marijuana there which the cops found, making him a suspect.

The Lawson YMCA at 30 W. Chicago Avenue is a brick and limestone skyscraper with Art Deco trimmings built in 1930. In Izzi's *The Take* Fabe Falletti walked north past the Lawson YMCA in an area where apartments went for $100,000 to start, with jewelry stores next to secondhand shops and boutiques with trendy names and $4.00-a-night flophouses.

In Michael Raleigh's *Death in Uptown,* P.I. Paul Whelan's client's kid brother Gerry stayed at the Y when he came to Chicago. When he disappeared, his big sister Jean came to Chicago to find him. She hired Whelan, who specialized in finding lost kids. The Lawson Y's desk clerk remembered Gerry Agee and the guy in the room next to Gerry thought he was kind of crazy because he talked to himself.

Go left on Chicago Avenue past the Lawson Y to State Street. If you are ready for some refreshments, across State Street are a Submarine Station and a Burger King. On Chicago Avenue a little east of State is the Chicago's McDonald's, with a polished bar-like counter and a most amusing mural of Chicago's recent mayors: Jane Byrne, Harold Washington, Richard J. Daley, and Michael Bilandic. All four are wearing cowboy getups and riding fiery steeds, rushing forward like the hired hands in the Frederic Remington bronze called "Coming to Town." None of the mayors is shooting, but Washington is the only one on a white horse. Go in to see the mural and use the restrooms if you like.

Then have a cup of coffee or a snack, and sit in a window looking out at the parking lot occupying the entire block across State from Holy Name Cathedral. There is no civic marker, but in the 1920s there was a flower shop there, owned by Dion O'Banion, the head of the North Side bootleggers and Capone's chief rival. O'Banion, once an altar boy at Holy Name Cathedral who reputedly hated the taste of beer, was shot dead in his flower shop after sending his former boss and partner, Johnny Torrio, to jail. Both Torrio and his lieutenant, Al Capone, sent fabulous wreaths to O'Banion's funeral.

In British Edgar Wallace's *On the Spot,* South sider Tony

Perelli was taking over Chicago. He had a mobster retinue, expensive clothes and lifestyle, and a love for Italian opera. Perelli got his start in "Cosmolino's Orchestra." His main rivals were North siders Mike Feeney and his brother-in-law Shaun O'Donnell, who was once an altar boy at Holy Name Cathedral. When O'Donnell was shot, it began a gang war.

Cross Chicago Avenue to the Cathedral School and walk down the block to the cathedral. According to Chicago legend, the land for the cathedral was given to the archdiocese by two of Chicago's founding fathers, William B. Ogden and Walter L. Newberry. They were developing the area and needed a bridge over Clark Street. The gift of land assured the Catholic vote for the bridge.

In another round of gangland strife, Earl Wajciechowski, who changed his name to Weiss and was known as "Little Hymie" was shot dead on the steps of Holy Name Cathedral by orders of Al Capone. Weiss's boss had been O'Banion, so Weiss tried to avenge him with a series of attacks on Capone, who finally got him instead. For years you could see the nicks in the cathedral cornerstone caused by the bullets.

Built in 1874 of limestone in late Victorian Gothic, Holy Name Cathedral replaced an earlier Roman Catholic church lost in the Chicago Fire. It is 233 feet long with a spire 210 feet high. It seats 1,350 people. Walk up the steps and push the lever that opens the massive metal front doors and go inside. It will be open, although in Bill Granger's *The Priestly Murders,* the Cardinal himself was held up on the street in front of the Cathedral by a young black who told him "I don't care if you're a turkey buzzard, gimme your . . . wallet or you ain't going to whistle no more."

As a cathedral—the seat of the cardinal archbishop of Chicago—it has the Cathedra, or Bishop's chair, on the back wall of the sanctuary and hanging from the ceiling above the altar are the hats (galeros) of the previous cardinals: Meyer, Stritch, Mundelein, and Cody.

In Ralph McInerny's *Bishop As Pawn,* anticlerical Andy Pilsen kidnaped Auxiliary Bishop Arthur Rooney when he came to Father Dowling's suburban parish for confirmation. Dowling and Rooney had worked together here on the Archdiocesan marriage tribunal. The ransom note demanded that the archdiocese distribute $100,000 worth of food to the poor. The Cardinal talked with Father Dowling and Fox River police Captain Phil Keegan about the distribution and suggested that a renegade priest, Ambrose Chirichi, might be behind the plot.

In Andrew Greeley's mysteries Cardinal Sean Cronin, a Chicago product, was too courageous, honest, and outspoken to be archbishop (Cardinal) of Chicago. He lived in the rectory instead of the North Avenue mausoleum, so he could order Father Blackie to "See to it, Blackie" whenever murder occurred. In *Happy Are the Clean of Heart,* the Cardinal rushed over in person to Northwestern Hospital to anoint Lisa Malone, then came back to tell Blackie himself because Lisa was an old flame from Beverly.

In Mary Mayer's historical mystery *The Devil's Card, Tribune* reporter Tom Martin attended the lavish funeral of murdered Dr. Patrick Cronin. After lying in state with various Irish groups standing ceremonial guard, Dr. Cronin's ornate casket was brought through the streets in a hearse with four black horses and honorary pallbearers past packed crowds to Holy Name.

Walk around and admire the ornate interior. In Thomas McCall's *A Wide and Capable Revenge,* Nora Callum, a one-legged Chicago detective (who in real life would be retired on disability) went to Holy Name Cathedral to the scene of a crime on a Saturday afternoon. The victim, a young Hispanic woman, had been shot in a confessional booth to the left of the high altar. Callum discovered the victim Eva Ramirez was not dead, so they rushed her to the hospital while the police searched the cathedral.

Walk down a side aisle past the confessionals to the side door on the left and go out into the paved area between the Cathedral School and the cathedral; then turn right to walk through the courtyard to Wabash Avenue. On Wabash to your left is the convent of the Sisters of Charity and on your right is the Cathedral Rectory at 730 N. Wabash where a sign on the gold door reads "Walk in."

In Andrew Greeley's mysteries, all his suspects, sooner or later, come knocking on Father Blackie's door. Father Blackie, who has become the Most Reverend Bishop John Blackwood Ryan in *Happy Are the Peacemakers,* considers the North Side his "parish," but actually deals with murder and mystery worldwide. Greeley's other characters often compare Father Blackie to G. K. Chesterton's shabby but shrewd little Father Brown, but Father Blackie has more in common with Rex Stout's portly and sedentary Nero Wolfe. Like Wolfe, Blackie specializes in holding sessions with victims and suspects here in his room at the Cathedral Rectory. Unlike Wolfe's elegantly maintained brownstone, which Robert Goldsborough suggests might be found on Arlington Place in Chicago if Wolfe moved from New York, Blackie's room is messy and decorated with familial and intellectual clutter. On the walls there are three photographs of his heroes: Pope John XXII, President John F. Kennedy, and football star Johnny Unitas, and supplicants of all kinds are plied with Jameson's liquor served in Waterford goblets.

By contrast, in Mark Zubro's *The Only Good Priest,* amateur P.I.s Tom Mason and Scott Carpenter paid a formal call on Bishop John Smith at the Cathedral Rectory and were offered tea. They were investigating the suspicious death of Father Sebastian, a priest who ministered to the gay community.

In Greeley's *Happy Are the Peacemakers,* Blackie's niece and sister were being initiated into Father Blackie's North Wabash Avenue Irregulars, a reminder of Sherlock Holmes's legendary group of London street urchins called the Baker Street Irregulars (See *MRWG: London*). Chicagoan William F. Love also borrowed the idea for his New York City mysteries where Bishop Regan and his sidekick Davie Goldman have their Delancey Street Irregulars.

Walk south to the corner of Wabash and Superior. Turn right and walk west three blocks on Superior to Clark Street.

Much of the area is parking lots today, but in Craig Rice's '40s mystery *The Lucky Stiff* there was a North Clark Street joint called The Happy Days near here. It had a bar along one side of the big room, booths on the other, a juke box, and a sign over the bar that read "Whisky, 30 cents a drink, Double 50 cents."

Mobster Big Joe Childers was shot there and his girlfriend Anna Marie St. Claire was convicted of his murder but reprieved at the last minute. Jake Justus was there when Childers was shot because he was paying Childers protection money for his nightclub, the Casino. (See Walk 5.)

North Clark was still sleazy in the '50s and '60s. In Jonathan Latimer's *The Lady in the Morgue,* P.I. Bill Crane went to the Clark-Erie Ballroom where Miss Udoni worked. (A female body was missing from the morgue and he needed to make sure it was not hers.) Crane found Angela Udoni alive but there was a raid, so he sneaked her off to his Loop hotel.

Cross Superior to walk south on Clark. This is now the center of what the *Chicago Tribune*'s architecture critic called "The Blurbs, where Victorian brownstones run smack into the plastic chic of the Golden Arches." It is full of nouveau tourist entertainment joints with gaudy signs and club-restaurants named for celebrities of our day, like Michael Jordan's or Harry Caray's.

As you walk south on Clark you also see blue street banners advertising River North, an area located just west of "the Blurbs," beginning about Wells. Filled with older warehouses and loft buildings that now house galleries, art supply stores, and other art-connected activities such as restoration, this neighborhood is also called SuHu—for Superior and Huron—in imitation of New York's SoHo. (See *MRWG: NY.*) The Gold Coast Art Fair is now held in River North, and there are regular gallery tours. (See Possible Side Trips.)

Walk south on Clark to Erie. You can see the gigantic mirrored billboard front of Planet Hollywood, the newest celebrity hangout with fake palm trees and Hollywood-style searchlights. Keep going to Ontario. Further west, at 223 W. Ontario, there used to be (Mike) Ditka's City Lights, now closed. In Eugene Izzi's *The Booster,* Detective Bigum, the black partner of white Chicago Detective Sean, took Sean to Ditka's to celebrate his promotion.

At Ontario you will also see Chicago's Hard Rock Cafe. Turn left to walk east to Dearborn, where you will pass the granite castle that once housed the Chicago Historical Society; most recently it is a nightclub called Excalibur. Cross Ontario and go south on Dearborn three more blocks to Illinois.

At Illinois you will see a 1968 fire house, built on the site of the old Cook County Jail. In 1921 a murderer called Terrible Tommy O'Connor, who had shot a cop, escaped from the jail and was never caught. The authorities kept the gallows just for him and when the old jail was torn down and the Criminal Courts moved to 26th and California in 1927, they stored them there until 1977. That year Chief Judge Richard J. Fitzgerald looked at the gallows, then ordered it destroyed. But according to Heise and Baumann in *Chicago Originals,* Larry Donley, owner of the Seven Acres Museum in Union, Illinois, drove into town and took the six-person gallows home.

Walk one more block south on Dearborn to Hubbard. Now you will see *brown* banners proclaiming that this is the Court House District. Turn right to walk along Hubbard towards Clark. In the middle of the block on the north side of Hubbard is Courthouse Place, which is really the old Cook County Criminal Courts Building. It is built of Romanesque Victorian limestone with arched windows resembling the Loop's Rookery. You can't miss it: it is flying the flags of Chicago and the USA. Inside is a magnificent double stairway of marble with brass handrails and iron posts.

The Courthouse was built on the site of an earlier court building where the Haymarket Anarchists were tried and the insanity trial of Mary Todd Lincoln was held. This building was the scene of such famous Chicago trials as that of murderers Richard Loeb and Nathan Leopold in 1924, ably defended by Clarence Darrow. John Ashenhurst, who wrote *The World's Fair Murders,* was the *Daily News* reporter on that story. Poet Carl Sandburg was also a reporter assigned to the fourth-floor press room where Charles MacArthur and Ben Hecht dreamed up their comedy *The Front Page.* In this amusing expose of the Chicago newspaper world, the reporters hid an escaped murderer in a desk in the press room to get an exclusive on his story. (If you can't find a copy of the book rent either the movie starring Adolph Menjou and Pat O'Brien or the take-off, *His Girl Friday,* starring Rosalind Russell and Cary

Grant. There are newer versions like *The Picture* and a musical *Windy City,* too.)

The classy old building languished until 1985 when it was bought by a River North developer and rehabbed. Be sure to go inside to admire the lobby and see the photographs of the famous reporters and criminals associated with it. Then turn right to walk back to Clark Street. Go north three blocks to Ohio. There is a block-square post office on the site now; across Ohio are Capone's Chicago and the Rock 'n' Roll McDonald's. But in Targ's 1939 *The Case of Mr. Cassidy* Ohio and Clark was the site of Thaddeus Todd's bookshop. In the final scene all the suspects came to the Todd Bookshop, where Hugh Morris identified the murderer.

In Michael Dymmoch's *The Man Who Understood Cats,* psychiatrist James Caleb and Chicago detective John Thinnes stopped at the Clark and Ontario McDonald's for a dinner of quarter pounders. While they sat in the unmarked police car eating, Caleb noticed a black man roughly dragging a small boy along and told Thinnes the boy was being abused. He offered to sign a citizens complaint, the cops roared off, and it ended in a chase into Cabrini-Green where Caleb was proved right.

McCall's detective Nora Callum stopped at that McDonald's for lunch in *A Wide and Capable Revenge.* She was on her way from the morgue where she had watched the autopsy on a butchered (literally) Russian émigré called Lugotov. Go see the Roaring 20's show at Capone's Chicago or stop and have something to eat at McDonald's or the Hard Rock Cafe to end your walk.

POSSIBLE SIDE TRIPS

River North. This is the area from Chicago Avenue west of Wells to the Chicago River. You can walk there at the end of this walk or go another day. There are regular tours of the River North galleries and the yearly Gold Coast Art Fair is held here.

In Barbara D'Amato's *Hard Women,* Cat Marsala lived near the El where it turns at Chicago and Franklin in the heart of

River North. Marsala was doing a story on prostitutes, working with an undercover detective called Ross Wardon. Cat made a date with a hooker for an interview at the Chicago Avenue/ Franklin Street El stop, but a modern-day Jack the Ripper stalked Cat, who escaped by lying down on the track as the El went past.

In Sam Reaves's *A Long Cold Fall,* cabbie MacLeish came to River North to check out his dead girlfriend Vivian Horstmann's art gallery on a third floor between Wells and Franklin. Cooper felt most modern art is like the Emperor's New Clothes.

The Merchandise Mart, between Wells and Franklin on the Chicago River, is part of River North too, although it predates the name. It occupies the entire block from Wells to Franklin and is the world's largest commerical building, built by Marshall Field and owned by the Joseph P. Kennedy family since 1945. To visit the Mart, walk west on Hubbard or Kinzie to Wells, or hop the El and ride it around the Loop to Merchandise Mart station. You can see it separately or in combination with a River North gallery tour.

In Harry Keeler's *Behind That Mask,* the office of Mr. Nisaku Sato, the head of the Chicago Branch of the Japanese Secret Service, was in the Mart. Chief Chosoburo Kusumoto ordered Sato to get the Coin of Confucius back by putting operatives on the streets of Chicago on Halloween night wearing costumes. One of them killed Jack Kenwood.

West of the Mart on Kingsbury is the trendy East Bank Club. In Marc Davis's *Dirty Money,* P.I. Frank Wolf went there, climbing up the atrium stairway and out on the roof to talk to Abel Nockerman's steady girlfriend Rita Baronette. She told Wolf the murdered Nockerman had a cocaine habit and dealt it, too. In Shelby Yastrow's *Undue Influence,* lawyers Sarah Jenkins and Maggie Flynn, representing the two opposing clients for the estate of Benjamin Stillman, met at the East Bank Club to discuss who would give up the chance to get the $8 million for their clients.

5

STREETERVILLE WALK

BACKGROUND

Streeterville was named for the enterprising Captain George Wellington Streeter, whom Chicago historians Kenan Heise and Ed Baumann called Chicago's "Don Quixote." In reality, Streeter, an ex–ship's captain whose scow ran aground in 1886 about where Michigan Avenue's Hancock Building sits today, was a clever promoter who used the press to establish his own kingdom by the sea.

Originally, this area east of old Pine Street (Michigan Avenue) was part swamp and part sand dunes. But when he was unable to get his excursion ship the Reutan off the sandbar, Cap'n Streeter built a gangplank to shore and lived there. He encouraged other builders to dump landfill about his new home, building up the territory, then staked out 186 lakefront acres and sold lots to his saloon buddies for one dollar each. Streeter ended by creating a shantytown which he called the District of Lake Michigan and defended with a rifle. There were many ups and downs in Chicago's fight with Streeter, but it was not until the 1940s that the city finally got legal possession of the territory, which has become some of Chicago's most valuable real estate.

The southern part of Streeterville along the Chicago River and the Ogden Slip was built up in the 1890s with warehouses and docks, while the Gold Coast residential neighborhood began to move south across Oak Street before World War I. After the war, the opening of the Michigan Avenue Bridge speeded up the gentrification process, then Northwestern University built its Chicago campus along the lakefront, expanding as the hospital complex grew.

Today there are only a few reminders of Cap'n Streeter, or the nightclubs like the Chez Paree that used to be here, or the newspapermen and dock workers who frequented the older diners and bars. Most of Streeterville is high-class highrises. But the rehabbing of Navy Pier for a major city amusement center—perhaps with gambling boats docking there—will keep alive the memory of old Cap'n Streeter's circus.

LENGTH OF WALK: About 2 miles

It will be more when Navy Pier reopens completely and you can walk all the way out. This neighborhood is a curious mixture of highrise luxury living, hospitals and universities, tourist attractions, and media headquarters.

See the map on page 151 for the boundaries of this walk and page 348 for a list of the books and detectives mentioned.

PLACES OF INTEREST

CBS Building (old Arena-Riding Club), 630 N. McClurg Court. 1924 building adapted to house television studios. No tours.

Drake Hotel, 140 E. Walton Place (at Michigan Avenue). Built in 1920 in Italian Renaissance style, now the grande-dame of Chicago hotels. Afternoon tea in its Palm Court lobby is popular with VIPs and mystery fans. Call 787-2200.

James Jardine Filtration Plant, 1000 E. Ohio Street. Metropolitan area water purification plant.

Museum of Contemporary Art, 237 E. Ontario Street. Open Tues.–Sat. 10:00 A.M.–5:00 P.M., Sun. noon–5:00 P.M. Fee. Admission free on Tuesdays. Call 280-5161. (New building going up on Chicago Avenue.)

Navy Pier, 600 E. Grand Avenue. The Chicago Plan of 1909 called for five piers, but only one was built in 1916. World's largest pier, it remained an important passenger/freight terminal until the 1930s. During World War II, it was a naval training center, then from 1946–65 the Chicago branch of University of Illinois. It is being refurbished for an amusement center. It is 5/8 of a mile long. Open 6:00 A.M.–8:00 P.M. daily. Call 791-7437.

NBC Tower, Cityfront Center, 454 N. Columbus Drive. Gorgeous 1989 Art Deco (postmodern) skyscraper. No tours; call 321-5365 for free show tickets.

North Pier, 435 E. Illinois Street. Former exhibition center for wholesale products, now a three-story mall.

Northwestern Memorial Hospital, Huron to Superior, Lake Shore Drive to St. Clair Street. The old Wesley, Northwestern, and Passavant Hospitals are now pavilions of Northwestern Memorial Hospital.

Northwestern University Chicago Campus, Chicago Avenue to Huron Street, lakefront to St. Clair. Original 1924 Gothic campus plan, modified in recent years. Includes the Schools of Law, Business, Medicine, and Dentistry.

Milton J. Olive Park, dedicated to Chicago-born African-American winner of the Medal of Honor. Ohio and Lake Michigan.

Ritz-Carlton Hotel, 160 E. Pearson Street (part of Water Tower Place). Only hotel in the city to get AAA Diamond Award year after year. Call 266-1000.

University of Chicago Graduate School of Business, East North Water Street.

PLACES TO EAT

Because Streeterville backs up to some very elegant North Michigan Avenue hotels, there are marvelous choices for lunch, dinner or afternoon tea. Otherwise, your choices are mostly fast food vendors, arcade-style restaurants, and a few older places that cater to the news media. Most people are not thrilled by hospital cafeterias, although mystery characters get to spend anxious hours in them.

Chris's Cafe, 201 E. Grand Avenue (lower level). Old-fashioned diner with counter and booths, outdoor tables.

Drake Hotel, 140 E. Walton Street: Coq d'Or Lounge, Cape Cod Room (seafood), Oak Terrace Room, Palm Court lobby (afternoon tea, cocktails).

Moosehead Bar & Grill, 240 E. Ontario Street. Landmark Chicago jazz club, live entertainment.

North Pier, 435 E. Illinois Street. Several restaurants.

Ritz-Carlton Hotel, 160 E. Pearson Street: The Dining Room (French), The Green House (atrium setting for lunch, afternoon tea, or cocktails).

West Egg Cafe, 620 N. Fairbanks Court. Order breakfast all day, or sandwiches, salads, pasta.

STREETERVILLE WALK

Begin your walk on the east side of Michigan Avenue at the Equitable Building at 401 N. Michigan, which stands behind Pioneer Court on the north bank of the Chicago River. Pioneer Court is built on the site of the cabin of Jean Baptiste Point du Sable, whose mother was a Haitian black and his father a French Canadian. DuSable's business was trading with the Indians. He settled at Chicago about 1770 and married a Potawatomie chief's daughter. In 1800 du Sable sold his extensive property to a representative of John Kinzie. Kinzie was called the "Father of Chicago," but according to Heise and Baumann, Kinzie got the credit because his daughter-in-law Juliette Kinzie wrote one of the first "histories" of Chicago, called *Wau-Bun*.

To the south along the Chicago River you will see stairs leading down to the lower level of Michigan and the river bank. Below you on the lower level of Michigan Avenue are the old *Tribune* loading docks. There are some riverside cafes and boats along the river and since the University of Chicago Graduate School of Business's downtown campus just east of the Equitable Building has been completed, you can also walk along the river on North Water Street from Michigan Avenue to Columbus Drive.

The university built on the site of the old Mandel-Lear Building at 425 N. Michigan, where the central public library's books were stored for nearly twenty years while the city argued about where to put a new library. In Michael A. Kahn's *Grave Designs* (originally *The Canaan Legacy*), Rachel Gold was hired to find out what was behind the weird bequest for the care of Canaan's grave in the will of dead Graham Marshall. An associate, Benny Goldberg, went to the Mandel-Lear library to dig up facts about the New England town of Canaan, where Graham Marshall's ancestors ran a lottery.

In Martin Blank's *Shadowchase,* police lieutenant John Lamp brought a piece of newspaper found at murder victim Tom Hennessey's shop to the library. All Lamp had was a headline "Orioles Sweep Series," which meant it had to be October 1966. He searched the big dailies like the *Tribune, Sun-Times,* and *Daily News,* and found nothing. Next Lamp went to Bridgeport, the Back-of-the-Yards Irish neighborhood, to visit the offices of the *Bridgeport Review* at 3100 S. Morgan, and found a story about the murderer, an IRA informer now living in the Chicago area.

Cross Pioneer Court and walk right between the Equitable Building and Tribune Tower. (This is a good time to admire the bits of famous stone embedded in its walls. They were collected by *Tribune* publisher Colonel Robert M. McCormick, one of the McCormick reaper family and the grandson of the *Tribune*'s Joseph Medill.) Pioneer Court leads into Cityfront Plaza where you can walk to the new NBC Tower.

The sparkling Art Deco NBC Tower at 454 N. Columbus Drive was built in 1989. It is sometimes called "postmodern" but really has echoes of Tribune Tower's '20s Gothic and New York's Rockefeller Center. (See *Mystery Reader's Walking Guide: New York.*)

Go left on Cityfront Plaza Drive to Illinois Street. Cross Illinois Street and go left about half a block to find the stairway to the lower level. Take the stairs down. You come out near a parking lot, all that's left of the older and much larger random parking area under the S Curve of the old Lake Shore Drive.

Streeterville

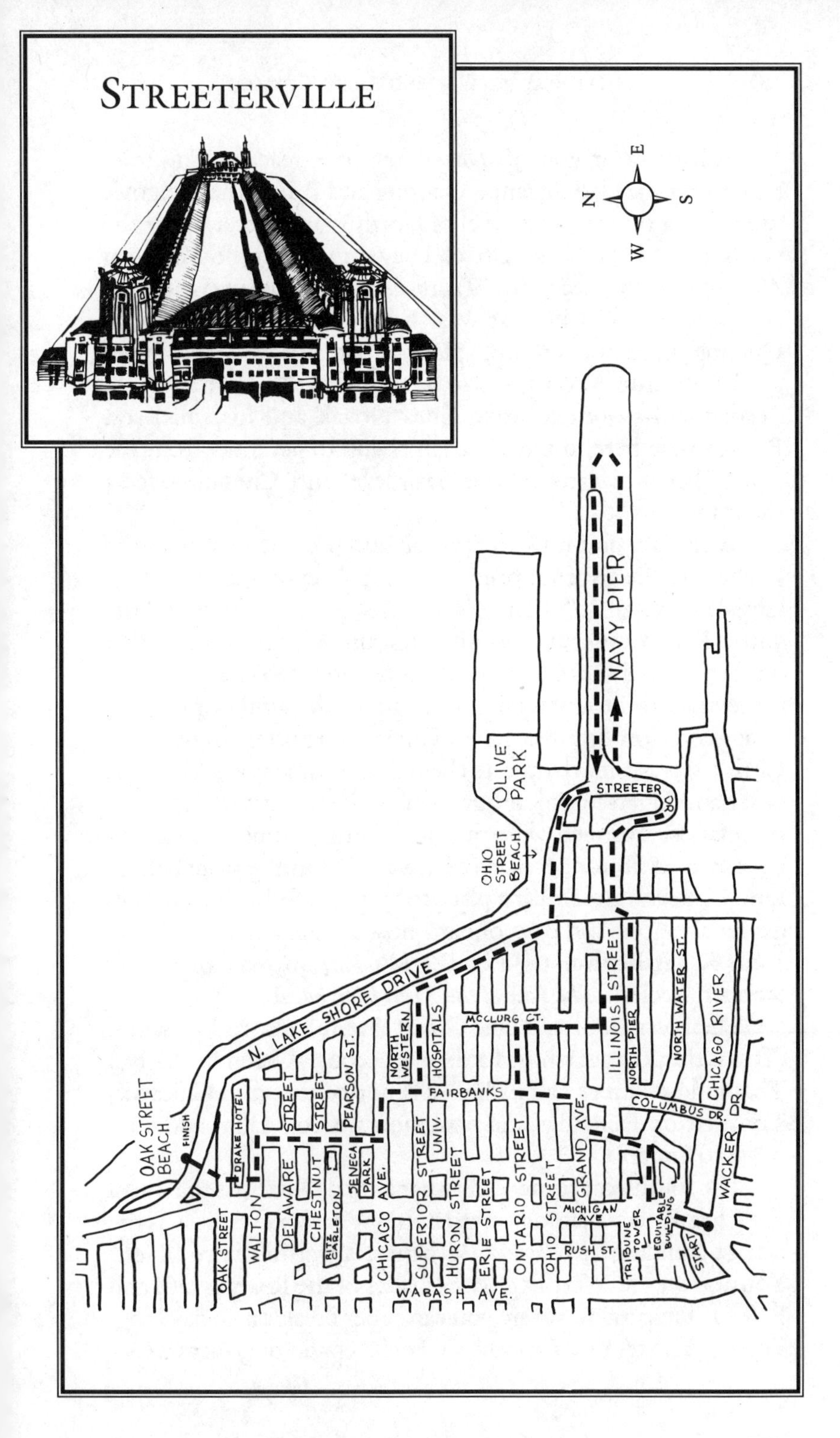

In Barbara Gregorich's *Dirty Proof*, proofreader and murder suspect red-headed Suzanne Quering and P.I. Frank Dragovic walked east on the lower level of North Water Street under the old route of Lake Shore Drive. They came from the Michigan Avenue docking area for the *Truth-Examiner* (*Tribune*) and were checking to see if her car was still there. Dragovic warned Quering that it was a terrible place to park.

In Arthur Maling's *The Snowman*, the kidnapers of department-store executive Ches Novak and his small son Buzz, drove here in a blue sedan trying to get away from the cops. They drove around the lower level until Ches managed a showdown fight.

Turn right and walk to St. Clair and take St. Clair north to Grand Avenue. At the corner of Grand Avenue and St. Clair is Chris's Cafe, at 201 East Grand. It is an old-fashioned diner with a long counter and booths, still run by Chris himself, that has now added the tourist touch of outdoor tables and chairs.

It used to be a newsman's hangout–the kind of place Bill Granger or Jon Breen or James Ullman's reporters went. Now Chris's serves a more upscale clientele the same good food: the best hamburgers in Chicago and rice pudding, served in tall sundae glasses, seasoned with nutmeg. Chris told us that he had never served liquor because there was a bar in the store behind him. Chris's is an excellent place to stop and feel a bit of nostalgia for the good old days of hard-nosed reporting as shown in John M. Ashenhurst's *The World's Fair Murder* or Henry Stephen Keeler's *The Face of the Man from Saturn.*

Then come out and take Grand Avenue east to Fairbanks. (This is the point at which Fairbanks becomes Columbus Drive. That kind of street name change is not common in Chicago.) Turn left on Fairbanks and walk north. Cross Ohio and continue to Ontario.

The southwest corner of Fairbanks and Ontario is the site of the Chez Paree, a famous nightclub. (What you see now is the Schatz Building at 610 N. Fairbanks, advertising live blues.) You also see the West Egg Cafe (shades of the Roaring '20s and F. Scott Fitzgerald), where you can order breakfast all day long. You can also try out Timothy O'Toole's patio or go across Ontario to the Moosehead Bar and Grill, known for live jazz. No doubt intentionally, this block has a real Greenwich Village feel to it. (See *MRWG: NY*.)

The Chez Paree, which used to feature stellar talent like Tony Bennett, appears in many mysteries. In Targ's *The Case of Mr. Cassidy* Ruth Bell, the girlfriend of murdered Mr. Cassidy, worked in the chorus line. Amateur sleuth Hugh Morris took Helen Todd, the daughter of his favorite bookseller Thaddeus Todd, there to talk with Ruth. The maitre d' put them at a table near the dance floor and Morris pointed out celebrities to Helen. The chorus line was made up of blonds with wide grins in tights and brassieres, dancing burlesque style to a swing version of "Loch Lomond." They were followed by jigging Negroes in purple silk full dress suits and a suave magician.

In Jonathan Latimer's *The Lady in the Morgue,* P.I. William Crane went to the Chez Paree to get a list of the chorus girls. The Chez was then run by Mike Fritzel, who had another place at Lake and State in the Loop. (See Walk 2.) Crane was hunting a New York socialite named Kathryn Courtland who had followed a married mob-connected band leader to Chicago. There was a mix-up at the coroner's and the body of a young woman disappeared before Crane could identify it.

In Craig Rice mysteries Jake and Helene Justus and their pal lawyer John J. Malone often went to the Chez. In *My Kingdom for a Hearse,* Malone took cosmetics company receptionist Tamia Tabet there, as well as to Jake Justus's own nightclub, the Casino.

The Casino appears to be located on top of the Chez Paree. But according to Rice in *The Right Murder,* the nightclub was in a restored and remodeled mansion. It was painted white with a chaste neon sign, and there were artificial trees on either side of the entrance.

Inside, the ghost of the original owner would have been lost. The gambling rooms on the third floor still had old marble fireplaces, and the original staircase still went up from the ground floor, but that was all. The first floor with an orchestra and dance floor was softly lighted and paneled, with dove-gray benches along the walls.

The Casino had been owned originally by top mobster Max Hook, who lost it on a bet with Gold Coast heiress cum adventuress Mona McClane. Mona then made a bet with Jake Justus that he could not prove she had murdered someone, with the stakes the Casino. (Justus lost the bet in *The Wrong Murder,* but won it in *The Right Murder.*) By *The Lucky Stiff* Jake Justus was being forced to pay protection money to gangster big Joe Childers. When Childers was shot, his mistress Anna Marie St. Clair just missed going to the electric chair, only to do a "ghost show" at the Casino to scare the real killer.

In the middle of the block at 237 E. Ontario is the Museum of Contemporary Art. It occupies an old 1915 building, remodeled in 1967 for the museum by Dan Brennan, with a Cafe Bookstore on the lower level where you can get a cup of coffee. In a few years the museum's new building on Chicago Avenue will be completed and it will move there.

Turn right and cross Fairbanks to walk east on Ontario to McClurg Court. Ahead of you is Harry Weese's 1970 golden glass Time and Life Building. Past the Holiday Inn you come to the McClurg Court Center at 333 E. Ontario. It is a fancy multiple use building with movies, apartments, and shopping.

The CBS studios are located in the block north of Ontario, in the old Arena Ice Rink/Chicago Riding Club. CBS does not offer tours, but you can get tickets to watch a live show. In earlier mysteries like Craig Rice's *The Corpse Stepped Out* and Targ's *The Case of Mr. Cassidy,* WBBM (CBS radio) operated out of the Wrigley Building, but now it, too, is located here.

In Stuart Kaminsky's *When the Dark Man Calls* Jean Kaiser, a psychologist who did a call-in radio show for small Evanston station WSMK was offered a one-hour show by WBBM. She arrived on time for her appointment with VIP Mr. Alexian, after visiting the sister of the man convicted many years earlier of murdering her parents. In the CBS lobby Jean saw Johnny Morris, a former Chicago Bear now a local sports newscaster.

There is a Starbucks Coffee House on the southeast corner of McClurg and Ontario, and a McDonald's across from CBS, handy places for a snack or a pit stop.

Then turn right on McClurg and walk back to Ohio and

cross it. You are surrounded by new highrise luxury condos like Lakeshore Plaza and 400 East Ontario. Keep walking south on McClurg to Grand Avenue, looking right at the Michigan Avenue skyline. On your left you pass the old Art Deco Kraft Building. Kraft gave it to the Board of Education but Mayor Jane Byrne took it for the city. It now is used by the Police Department, but may be torn down for parking.

Cross Grand and walk to Illinois where you will reach North Pier Market, the old redbrick warehouse at 435 E. Illinois Street. The redevelopment of this part of the city, which was once industrial-commercial, is part of a master plan called Cityfront Center. Its boundaries are the Chicago River, North Lake Shore Drive, Grand, and Michigan Avenue.

Cross the railroad tracks that used to run on Illinois at street level from the docks to the lower level of Michigan Avenue. The North Pier Terminal has been redeveloped into something touristy like Seaport in New York, Pike's Market in Seattle, or Ghiradelli Square in San Francisco. Its old buildings along the north side of the Ogden Slip now hold several levels of shops and fast food places and a couple of small museums, over forty establishments in all. In good weather lake/river tour boats depart from the Ogden Slip on the south side of the building. There are also public restrooms on the lower level. Several of the North Pier restaurants feature live bands and dancing.

Go inside to check out the shops and snacks, then go down to the water level. Weather permitting, walk left along the Ogden Slip, looking across it to the still undeveloped no-man's-land between the slip and the Chicago River. The Baby Ruth/Butternut candy factory used to be there, but now it hosts circuses and other open-air entertainment.

The slip itself—into which a pair of young women drove by accident and drowned—was named for the family of Chicago's first mayor, William B. Ogden, who owned much of the land about here. Ogden reestablished Chicago's first railroad, the Galena and Chicago Union, in 1848. Its first engine, the Pioneer, is at the Chicago Historical Society. (See Walk 7.) Ogden lost both his Chicago mansion and his lumber business in Peshtigo, Wisconsin in tragic fires on the same day: October 8, 1871.

There used to be a Maritime Museum at North Pier, but it has been replaced by a Bicycle Museum. In Paretsky's *Deadlock,* the family of Niels Grafalk, who owned a grain shipping company, gave the city the Grafalk Maritime Museum, which was located next to the Shedd Aquarium. (See Walk 1.) You can buy tickets for Architectural and Historical River Cruises here. Other river tours are run from the west side of the Michigan Avenue Bridge. (See Walk 4.)

At the eastern end of North Pier, there are a number of new highrises that could have been the Rapelec Towers, the scene of the crime in Sara Paretsky's *Burn Marks.* One is the 1991 North Pier Apartment Tower at 474 N. Lake Shore Drive, another is the Parkshore, under construction in 1990, the year *Burn Marks* was published. (Another possibility is the Sheraton Chicago Hotel and Towers at 301 North Water Street.)

In *Burn Marks* V.I. Warshawski found herself investigating the political deals cut for the Rapelec complex, an office-condo combination. It was being built on the west side of Lake Shore Drive facing Navy Pier beside a strip of decaying warehouses between Illinois and the river.

Although terrified by heights, one night V.I. worked her way up the half-finished building to check out the death there of Cerise Ramsey, the daughter of her Aunt Elena's SRO chum. (Warshawski had been pulled in to view the body at the morgue because Cerise had V.I.'s driver license, which she and Aunt Elena had stolen.)

On the building site V.I. bumped into the security guard, whose boss booted her out fast. But later Warshawski returned to the complex to rescue her alcoholic, trick-turning aunt. She mixed it up with the politically connected contractors, one of whom got knocked over the side.

At the eastern end of North Pier there is a flight of steps up to the lower level of the Outer Drive (the name Chicagoans use for Lake Shore Drive). If you don't want to climb, go back inside North Pier to take the elevator.

At the top of the stairs turn left to go past North Pier. You are back on Illinois. Cross the Drive with the light and go by the high brick facade of Lake Point Tower at 505 N. Lake Shore

Drive. You cannot get inside unless you know someone living there. It was built in 1968 from a design originally intended by Mies van der Rohe for Berlin in the 1920s. Under different names it appears in many mysteries as the prime urban "nest" for malefactors of great wealth.

In Michael A. Kahn's *Grave Designs,* former beauty queen cum call girl Cindi Reynolds owned her own condo at "Shore Drive Tower." There she serviced VIP lawyers and other executives for about $900 a night ($1,100 with videotape included). Cindi and Rachel Gold got acquainted because the senior partner of Abbott & Windsor died in Cindi's apartment, leaving a strange will with perpetual care for his pet Canaan's grave. Later, a big explosion occurred there and the two people in Cindi's apartment were killed, but Cindi had loaned her condo to a fellow hooker who was also a University of Chicago grad student! (The new GSOB building would be very handy for her.)

In Marc Davis's *Dirty Money,* commodities trading broker Abel Nockerman was found shot gangland style in his glass-and-steel tower on Outer Drive near Navy Pier. It had its own pool, health club, shops, restaurants, doctors, dentists, even a psychiatrist. His ex-wife hired his childhood pal P.I. Fred Wolf to find out who did it. Wolf and Nockerman's daughter Tina went to investigate the scene of the crime. Nockerman's apartment was full of museum-quality paintings and lavish furniture, and had a library with floor-to-ceiling books and an electronic amusement center.

As you walk around Lake Point Tower to Streeter Drive, you have a great view of the Chicago Yacht Club, lighthouses, breakwaters, and the cribs, as well as boats in season. In the movie *V.I. Warshawski,* starring Kathleen Turner, the Grafalk family's shipping business was relocated from the Port of Chicago to Navy Pier. Going after the killer, V.I. had a terrific boat chase west from Lake Point Tower under the Michigan Avenue Bridge, past the Wendella Cruise dock and the Wrigley Building and down the Chicago River.

In Barbara Gregorich's *Dirty Proof,* Suzanne Quering parked by the old S Curve; later, heading north, she and Frank

Dragovic took Illinois to Streeter and turned left to take the Outer Drive to the North Avenue exit.

Follow Streeter Drive and walk straight ahead to look at Navy Pier. Originally named Municipal Pier, it was part of the Burnham Plan of 1909, which called for a spectacular lakefront with a matching pier on either side of the mouth of the Chicago River.

Navy Pier was built in 1914 with excursion boats that went from there to Lincoln and Jackson Parks, its own streetcar line, a dance hall, theater, restaurant and recreational facilities as well as docks for commercial shipping. The pier also helped Montgomery Ward's successful effort to keep the lakefront south of Randolph "open, clear and free" for the public. (That fight goes on and on—Navy Pier is being renovated as a land-based amusement center, and may have lakefront gambling boats docking here.)

In Sam Ross's *He Ran All the Way,* Navy Pier was called Municipal Pier. Two punks, Nick Robey and Al Molin, cased the area, planning to heist the payroll of a lake cruiser. They got off the streetcar and hid by the main entrance where they could see the ship's upper decks. They waited there for a paymaster and when he came they held him up. The paymaster gave them his briefcase, but a cop came by and shot Al, so Nick grabbed the briefcase and hopped on a passing truck, leaving his wounded partner behind.

In Craig Rice's *The Corpse Steps Out,* after collecting the body of blackmailer Paul Martin from a burning warehouse near Navy Pier, Jake and Helene Justus stopped to watch the fire. They were spotted by the waitress who had seen Helene start a fire in her ashtray at Rickett's, who shouted that Helene was a pyromaniac, forcing the Justuses to make a mad getaway. (See Walk 4.)

Navy Pier is being renovated, but you can jog, bike, or walk its 5/8 mile length. The Skyline Stage is already open. Or go left and take Streeter Drive to Ohio, passing the James J. Jardine Filtration Plant at 1000 E. Ohio. Then go west along Ohio to Milton J. Olive Park. This tiny park/beach was named in honor of African-American Medal of Honor winner Milton J. Olive, who fell on a live grenade to save his comrades' lives during the

Vietnam War. The view from Olive Park of the Chicago skyline is one of the best there is.

In Arthur Maling's *Dingdong,* ex-Hollywood actor Mike Wiley spent a cold, damp day at Olive Park making commercials for spring clothes. There was a ten-mile-an-hour wind sweeping in from the north and in a lightweight suit he was freezing at sixty dollars an hour.

Dr. James Caleb did some of his five-mile daily running past Olive Park in Michael A. Dymmoch's *The Man Who Understood Cats.* Unlike many mysterious dogs, Caleb's cats Freud and Skinner did not come along for the run.

Walk along the Ohio Street Beach past the north side of Lake Point Tower to the pedestrian walkway under Lake Shore Drive leading to Grand Avenue. Cross under the Drive, turn right, and walk to Ontario.

Cross Ontario by the Days Inn (originally a Holiday Inn) at the corner. In Arthur Maling's *Go-Between,* Pete Lambert stayed at this Holiday Inn while he tried to negotiate a deal with his father, successful business executive Oliver Lambert. Pete wanted to be paid to give back some Alaskan oil papers he had stolen from his dad's Loop office. The motel overlooked the Outer Drive, the frozen lake, the dark bulk of Navy Pier, and the filtration plant. The go-between (an ex-professional golfer who had known Pete in school) was going to meet him there. But Lambert had checked out so instead the nameless go-between walked four times around the filtration plant.

Keep going north on the Inner Drive to Erie. Cross Erie to the old Furniture Mart, which has been turned into condos, and go one more block to Huron where you come to the beginning of Northwestern University's Chicago Campus.

Built in the 1920s in Collegiate Gothic, most of the major campus buildings are along Chicago Avenue, but the law, business, medical and dental schools have spread to cover the territory between Huron and Chicago Avenue from the lakefront to St. Clair.

Go one more block north to Superior. Across Superior is the modern American Bar Association Building. Turn left on

Superior to walk past part of the medical complex which appears in mysteries far more often than the West Side Medical Center or the hospitals of the University of Chicago. Now part of Northwestern Memorial Hospital, the hospitals are called "pavilions."

A lot of mystery characters get attacked in their hospital beds or are sent there when attacked. In Dymmoch's *The Man Who Understood Cats,* Dr. James Caleb was taken there when he tried to OD on drugs in his Gold Coast apartment. In Mignon G. Eberhart's *Dead Men's Plans,* Reg Minary was attacked outside the family's Gold Coast home, then again at "Central Hospital" on Lake Shore Drive.

In Barbara D'Amato's *Hard Case,* Cat Marsala, doing a health care story, found Director Dr. Hannah Grant dead in University Hospital's Trauma Center.

Walk west to Fairbanks. Across Fairbanks on your left is Passavant Pavilion. In Robert J. Campbell's *The Junkyard Dog* Jimmy Flannery went to Passavant after an abortion clinic in his ward was bombed, killing a young girl and an old lady volunteer. (It is not clear why the victims were taken to Passavant, bypassing the entire West Side Medical Center.) Flannery also gave Mary Ellen Dunne–a half Jewish, half Irish nurse who volunteered at the abortion clinic–a lift to Passavant where she worked, and they began a romance.

Cross Superior at Fairbanks. On the north side of Superior the Northwestern University Medical Center stretches to Chicago Avenue. In Arthur Maling's *The Koberg Link,* Brock Potter of the New York brokerage firm of Price, Potter and Petacque came to Chicago to investigate the murder of the grandson of the Koberg heiress. Elissa Koberg was dying at Northwestern Hospital. She had lived a sort of Barbara Hutton life; her current husband, Comte Henri de Garonne, was minor nobility. Trying to get in to see her, Brock was shot in a corridor at the Drake Hotel and ended up at Northwestern himself.

In Andrew Greeley's *Angels of September,* Anne Reilly's Polish assistant Sandy was mugged at Reilly's art gallery and taken to Northwestern Hospital. When her estranged husband arrived from Poland no one could translate for him until Anne finally called Holy Name Cathedral, and Cardinal Sean Cronin came to the rescue.

In Greeley's *Happy Are the Clean of Heart,* singing star Lisa Malone, an old flame of Father Blackie, was hospitalized at Northwestern's Olson Pavilion after a murder attempt at the Westin Hotel. She was attacked again at the hospital although only her nearest and dearest could visit her. Naturally, Father Blackie's brother-in-law Joe Murphy was a psychiatrist on the staff of Northwestern Medical Center, giving the family access.

In Barbara D'Amato's *The Hands of Healing Murder,* rich and arrogant Chief of Staff Dr. Adam Cotton was murdered while playing bridge in his Gold Coast house with family and friends, among them amateur sleuth Dr. Gerritt De Graaf. Doctor Cotton's daughter Melanie had graduated from Northwestern Medical School, where De Graaf taught two days a week.

In Michael A. Kahn's *Grave Designs,* Graham Anderson Marshall III, senior partner at Abbott & Windsor law firm was DOA at Northwestern Hospital. Officially, Anderson had been working late at the office, but actually he was enjoying his usual Wednesday fling with call girl Cindi Reynolds at her condo, and died wearing an orange wet suit and black flippers.

In Thomas McCall's *A Wide and Capable Revenge,* disabled Detective Nora Callum was first on the scene when a young Hispanic woman was shot in the confessional at Holy Name Cathedral. Callum discovered the victim was not dead, shipped her to the hospital, then went to see her in Northwestern's Intensive Care Unit. While there, Callum stole the bullet that had struck the victim.

In Arthur Maling's *The Snowman,* Chicago merchant prince Tony Benson, who owned Carter & Benson, had a falling out with his son and heir. When Benson had a heart attack and ended up at Northwestern his ad manager, Ches Novak, tried to troubleshoot for Benson's son Scott who was wanted by the Feds for drug dealing.

Turn right to cross Fairbanks and go north one block to Chicago Avenue. Ahead of you is a big hole where the Armory used to be and where the Museum of Contemporary Art will be. In Mark Zubro's *Why Isn't Becky Twitchell Dead?* when schoolteacher Tom Mason and his lover pro baseball pitcher Scott Carpenter went to Northwestern Memorial Hospital to pay a visit to an old gay friend, they parked on Chicago Avenue by the Armory.

To your left is the Wesley Pavilion. In Shelby Yastrow's *Undue Influence,* Darlene Newman DuPres had left her downstate hometown and family to train as a nurse at a major Near North hospital. Darlene then married a doctor and talked him into running their own cancer clinic, where elderly accountant Ben Stillman died, leaving synagogue Beth Zion $8 million that the DuPres coveted.

In Charles Merrill Smith's *Reverend Randollph and the Unholy Bible,* the Reverend made a pastoral call at Wesley in the middle of the night where a parishioner's only son was dying. On his way out Con Randollph was kidnaped by two hoods, Junior and Pack, who worked for a "Mr. Jones." Mr. Jones was a top Italian gangster who wanted a Gutenberg Bible to buy his way into heaven. Jones thought Randollph had stolen one from Johannes Humbrecht, an old recluse parishioner of the Good Shepherd Church who had been murdered.

To your right along Chicago Avenue is the Northwestern University Law School. In J. A. Jance's *Dismissed with Prejudice* shyster Seattle lawyer Chris Davenport had gone there. His dad, Chris Senior, was the personal lawyer for Chicago mobster Aldo Pappinzino, so young Davenport had been hired by Pappinzino to acquire a nice high-tech Seattle company for his daughter and her new husband. But Seattle detective J. P. ("Beau") Beaumont decided the death of the original owner, Kurobashi, was not a suicide. On hearing that one of the out-of-town hit men had a "Chicago accent," he thought to himself that there were lots of lawabiding citizens in Chicago, but with all due respect to them, Eliot Ness didn't spend his career busting mobsters in Hoboken, New Jersey. As a result, Beaumont contacted Chicago police and found his man.

Shelby Yastrow who wrote *Undue Influence* went to Northwestern Law School, as did his fictional Judge Verne Lloyd and the senior lawyer for the brokerage house where Ben Stillman had worked. Professor Tony D'Amato, who worked with his wife (mystery writer Barbara D'Amato) on the real life murder case of Dr. John Branion, teaches here. Barbara D'Amato wrote up the Branion case in *The Doctor, the Murder, the Mystery* which won both the Agatha and Anthony mystery awards. (See also Walk 9.)

Cross Chicago Avenue and look east to see the famous pair of steel and glass Mies van der Rohe buildings at 860 and 880 Lake Shore Drive. Then turn left and walk west on Chicago Avenue past the Armory site to tiny Seneca Park just east of the Water Tower Pumping Station.

In Andrew Greeley's *Happy Are the Clean of Heart* after the murderous attack on superstar Lisa Malone, Father Blackie walked from Holy Name Cathedral Rectory to Seneca Park, taking her husband George Quinn's manuscript to read. It was October, "the finest month for our city—brisk, clean, deep-blue," and he enjoyed sitting in his favorite little park, surrounded by the giant canyon walls of the John Hancock Center, Water Tower Place, the partially finished Olympia Center (Neiman Marcus) and Loyola University.

At Seneca Park, a little green oasis behind iron railings, turn right on Mies van der Rohe Way to walk one block north to Pearson and cross Pearson to the Ritz-Carlton Hotel, which is part of the Water Tower Place complex. Father Blackie, who has strong views on architecture in what he thinks of as his parish commented that, "a Water Tower is a Water Tower is a Water Tower, to paraphrase Ms. Stein. Whereas Water Tower Place, the grotesque marble skyscraper across the street from our beloved gingerbread Water Tower, is an insult to the eye."

Go into the Ritz's ground floor lobby and take the elevator to the twelfth floor where you will find the elegant but cozy Green House with an atrium and fountain. It is the perfect place for lunch or an elegant afternoon tea. This is one of Chicago's classiest hotels, but there is no restaurant on the forty-fourth floor despite the fact that Father Blackie ate there in *Happy Are the Meek.* He must have been across the street at John Hancock's 95th restaurant or in the Ritz-Carlton's Dining Room.

In Eugene Izzi's *The Booster,* an important secret luncheon meeting of the eleven main members of the mob was held in a banquet room here. The meeting was an elaborate ploy to keep the coast clear for the "boosters"–i.e., thieves—Bolo and his protege Vincent Martin, who were climbing Sears Tower to steal some vital tapes of mob testimony.

In Michael Cormany's *Red Winter,* P.I. Don Kruger and his client, mob "connected" contractor Nicholas Cheyney, met at the Green House. They were there to discuss a blackmailing threat from Cheyney's former Communist comrades that might blackball him from membership in the most exclusive club in Chicago. Kruger, in his usual '60s garb, was sitting near a table of women wearing fur hats and expensive jewelry who had spent the day shopping at Water Tower Place and were relaxing over white wine and Perrier. The Green House was not Kruger's cup of tea, but he finally agreed to meet the blackmailer's messenger at Dearborn Station at eleven o'clock that night. (See Walk 8.)

In Andrew Greeley's *Happy Are the Clean of Heart,* when Father Blackie talked to Lisa Malone's entourage, most of them suspects, he met her singing partner Tad Thomas in the Grill at the Ritz-Carlton. Tad Thomas was neat gray perfection, even wearing makeup.

Take the elevator down from the twelfth floor and leave the Ritz to walk back to van der Rohe. Walk north, cross Chestnut and go one more block to Delaware. Look about for some old row houses, but there are almost none left. In Craig Rice's *My Kingdom for a Hearse,* the Delora Deanne cosmetic firm was located just east of Michigan in a little marble building with a pink and green reception room with satin furniture. The firm symbol, Delora Deanne, was actually five models—one each for her face, body, feet, hands, voice—making it hard to put "Delora Deanne" on TV, especially when parts of her body began to arrive in the mail.

On the southeast corner at 195 W. Delaware there is a strange little old mansion painted dead black. It has no sign but it is actually the Casino, a very private club, whose old building was preserved from demolition by its high-powered members. Painted black, not white, it cannot be Jake Justus's Casino, but by using its name, it seems quite possible that Craig Rice was pulling high society's leg.

Cross Delaware and go into the main entrance to the Westin Hotel. The lobby is done up in very contemporary glitz. In Richard Whittingham's *State Street,* detective Joe Morrison, investigating the nasty death of a drugstore owner on the West Side, met attractive Linda Tate, the ex-girlfriend of suspect broker Dennis Courtland, at the Westin. They had some Jack Daniels together while Morrison tried to find out why Courtland drove to the West Side to get Valium when he lived on the Gold Coast.

In Greeley's *Happy Are the Clean of Heart,* the scene of the crime was a Westin fourth-floor suite where Lisa Malone had a secret rendezvous with her estranged husband, George the Bean Counter. Her murderer found her first, torturing her for several hours until surprised by George.

Come out of the Westin's Delaware entrance and go left on van der Rohe one block north to Walton. Cross Walton to the Drake Hotel.

Go in the entrance to the hotel, which rightly is known as the grande dame of Chicago hotels, Chicago's answer to New York's Plaza and equally popular with mystery characters. (See *MRWG: NY.*) The quietly elegant and comfortable Palm Court Lobby is up one flight and you can have a sumptuous afternoon tea or a drink there in an atmosphere much like that of the Plaza. (The difference is that you no longer can sit down in the lobby of the Plaza.) At the Drake you can stay in a room with a view, not of Central Park, but of Lake Michigan and the Outer Drive, which are handsomer. The Oak Terrace restaurant is up another flight to your right from the lobby.

You can also go downstairs and walk through the street-level arcade to the Drake's main bar, called the Coq d'Or, which features live music. The Coq d'Or has a sign saying that it served the second drink made in Chicago after the end of Prohibition, so it clearly is not only classy but Craig Rice's kind of place. Her characters appear and reappear here in all her mysteries.

In *The Corpse Steps Out* Malone's pal, Police Captain Daniel Von Flanagan, complained to him about a big advertiser named Givvus, who flew into Chicago, registered at the Drake, went up to his room, washed and went downstairs, had lunch and walked out the door, only to turn up dead on a bench in Lincoln Park. In *The Wrong Murder,* newly married Helene and Jake Justus arranged to meet at the Drake bar, but Helene was arrested and spent the night in jail instead.

In Greeley's *Happy Are the Clean of Heart,* Lisa Malone's nasty surgeon brother Roderick, in town to borrow money from her, stayed at the Drake. He had no alibi for the murderous attack on Lisa at the Westin Hotel across the street. In John D. MacDonald's *One Fearful Yellow Eye,* P.I. Travis McGee, called to Chicago to help out a widowed old flame, checked into the Drake Hotel. As he left to walk on Michigan Avenue, McGee admitted that Chicago was not on the list of his favorite places; most of it was strictly hinterland-hick.

In Smith's *Reverend Randollph and the Avenging Angel,* Lisa Julian, a Hollywood movie star, was found murdered in her honeymoon suite at the Drake. She had just been married by Con Randollph at his Loop Church of the Good Shepherd. (Shades of Craig Rice's *Having a Wonderful Crime,* in which the bride lost her head in the bridal suite.)

In Maling's *The Koberg Link* broker Brock Potter stayed here and was shot at in a corridor. He ended up in Northwestern Hospital near the elderly Koberg heiress he came to see.

In Stuart M. Kaminsky's *You Bet Your Life,* P.I. Toby Peters was hired by Louis Mayer of Metro-Goldwyn-Mayer to contact the mob who claimed Chico Marx owed them a $120,000 Las Vegas gambling debt. The Marx Brothers, who often played in Chicago, also arrived in town to help and registered at the Drake as the Rothsteins of Ohio. They played gin rummy until Groucho got bored and went to the American Psychiatric Association meeting at the hotel. When Toby Peters saw some gangsters coming for him he joined Groucho at the convention. Mistaken for the main speaker from Australia, Peters gave an impromptu lecture, then Groucho got into the act. Back in their suite they finally had a message to be at the New Michigan Hotel at eleven that night to meet Frank Nitti, bringing Chico Marx with them. (See Walk 8.)

In Richard Whittingham's *State Street,* a murder suspect, broker Dennis Courtland, told Chicago detectives Sawyer and

Morrison that he might have stopped off at the Coq d'Or Bar at the Drake the night of the West Side rape and murder. But the bartender said Courtland never came in that night.

In Edgar Wallace's *On the Spot,* Jimmy McGrath, a college student being taught the gangster's trade by Tony Perelli (Capone) had tea at the most fashionable hotel in Chicago. Coming out of the hotel McGrath saw Perelli himself on Michigan Boulevard. On a little shopping trip, Perelli had four killers with him, two in front, two behind and, Jimmy suspected, four across the street. McGrath saw Perelli shot at from a closed car but Perelli's gunmen got the attackers.

In reporter John Ashenhurst's *The World's Fair Murders,* visiting Professor Arturo del Grafko of Almania was to be put up at the Drake but before he ever got there, he was shot dead at the World's Fair. Allison Bennett, the reporter covering the story, had a source who worked at the Drake Travel Bureau and went with a pretty Almanian girl, so Bennett arranged to go out as a foursome with reporter Helen Maynard. (Ashenhurst's wife ran a travel agency at the Drake Hotel when her reporter husband was writing his mystery.)

In Max Allan Collins's *True Crime,* P.I. Nate Heller was the bodyguard for the World's Fair's most celebrated star, fan dancer Sally Rand, who lived at the Drake. When Nate and his chum Barney Ross, the ex-prize fighter, were attacked Sally Rand put Heller in a cab and took him to the Drake, where she left him to recover while she did her bubble matinee. Heller enjoyed looking down at Lake Shore Drive and the people on Oak Street Beach as he listened to WGN broadcasting Wayne King, the Waltz King, from the Drake itself.

In Bill Granger's *Drover,* former Chicago sportswriter Jimmy Drover, fired for his mob connections, came to Chicago to avenge the murder of his girlfriend's husband. He carried it out in a crap game at a Mafioso's mansion in the western suburbs. Staying at the Drake, Drover was picked up by FBI agents in a black Buick; they took him to a highrise office in the South Loop and beat him up. (See Walk 3.)

In Paul Engleman's *Catch a Fallen Angel,* New York P.I. Mark Renzler, brought to Chicago to find a missing "angel"—

i.e., Bunny—for *Paradise* magazine owner Arnold Long, was put up at the Drake Hotel. Renzler was kidnaped, but got free, and worked his way through north side alleys toward his hotel just as the Chicago Police drove the hippies, demonstrators, SDSers, and fellow travelers of the 1969 Days of Rage out of Lincoln Park. As a result, Renzler got to watch the mob rampage through the Gold Coast, en route to the Drake where Judge Julius Hoffman lived. The Inner Drive looked like *Guernica,* Picasso's famous painting of the Spanish Civil War.

Go out the Drake's street-level entrance on Oak Street. Turn right and walk past the Mayfair Regent Hotel, now being rehabbed into condos, and walk along East Lake Shore Drive, admiring the handsome older buildings lived in by the city's ultra plus ultra. Like Astor Street, this is a street with some shady—if rich—inhabitants.

In Paretsky's *Blood Shot,* V.I. Warshawski came here to meet with Gustav Humboldt, a German immigrant who was chairman of Humboldt Chemical and lived on the twelfth floor of the Roanoke Building. The Roanoke was one of six or seven old dowagers on Oak Street (sic) bordering the strips between the lake and Michigan Avenue. According to V.I., if you had a million to invest in housing and were related to the British royal family, they might let you live here after a couple of years's intensive checking!

Humboldt's pad had a lobby with mosaics and wood-paneled walls, and a manned elevator. The library had books lining three walls and opulent red-leather furniture. Humboldt offered V.I. cognac but still wanted her to stop the investigation of his plant's toxic products.

In Craig Rice's *Knocked for a Loop,* Malone went there to the apartment of mobster Max Hook, a large fat individual who never went out, but sat wheeling-dealing behind his battered rolltop desk. (There is a strong resemblance to Rex Stout's sedentary sleuth, Nero Wolfe.) Malone had a healthy respect for mobster Hook's power, and when he borrowed money from Hook he always repaid it immediately. The only people who discomfited Max Hook were his interior designers, who kept changing his decor, and possibly wealthy Mona McClane, who had won the Casino from him in three nights of roulette.

In Rice's *The Fourth Postman* Malone, having acquired a mutt in the Gold Coast alley off Astor Street, took the dog to Max Hook's apartment to cash a ten thousand dollar check written by Rodney Fairfaxx. Hook would not cash the check—everyone thought Fairfaxx was looney, but he made Malone get the mutt he'd left downstairs in the cab. Hook gave the dog a saucer of beer and a small kitten to fight with.

In Rice's *Knocked for a Loop,* Malone asked Hook to provide him with a murder suspect to keep the cops from arresting his client Jane Estapool. Hook obligingly produced a very proper young gangster called Frank McInnis who was quite willing to confess to the murder of financier and do-gooder Leonard Estapool so long as he would only be locked up for twenty-four hours.

Walk through the small park across from the Drake and then cross Lake Shore Drive (use the pedestrian underpass at Michigan Avenue) to the Oak Street Beach. This is the most prestigious beach in the city, kept alive each season by mighty dumping of sand. It's very narrow, but you can walk (or jog) along the lakeshore to North Avenue Beach. (See also Walks 6 and 7.)

In Sam Ross's *He Ran All the Way* Nick Robey, the punk who shot the paymaster of the ship at Navy Pier and ran with the money, worked his way around the lake to the Oak Street Beach. There he bought some swim trunks from a kid and mingled with the crowd, finally picking up a northwest-side girl whom he took home in a cab. He then held her entire family hostage.

In Harry Stephen Keeler's *Behind That Mask,* reporter David Rand and his girl Aline Creston were walking on the Oak Street Beach on Halloween when Rand's boss Jack Kenwood was murdered in his Loop office. (See Walk 3.)

In Keeler's *Thieves' Nights* Ward Sharlow, pretending to be missing heir Calvin Atwood, attended the funeral of Calvin's father, wealthy John Atwood. He met an Atwood country cousin called Rosegail and after the funeral they walked along the Oak Street Beach and sat on a secluded concrete bench to listen to the breakers. Rosegail asked Sharlow why he was impersonating Calvin Atwood and he explained that John Atwood had hired him to do so.

In Mark Zubro's *Sorry Now,* detectives Paul Turner and Buck Fenwick were sent to the Oak Street Beach on a homicide call. Christina, the daughter of TV evangelist Bruce Mucklewrath, who was also a senator from California, had been shot near the playground. Three muggers had come up on them while father and daugher were walking on the beach, and shot her. Then they asked the Reverend Mr. Mucklewrath whether he was sorry now and escaped through the pedestrian underpass.

In Michael Raleigh's *Death in Uptown,* P.I. Paul Whelan drove east from the Lawson Y to the Magnificent Mile watching the pedestrians. He turned on Lake Shore Drive and cruised past Oak Street Beach where hundreds more young women were sunning themselves—or playing volleyball with young men—in an utterly different way of life from his Uptown habitat.

In Greeley's *Happy Are the Clean of Heart,* Father Blackie went to the Oak Street Beach because he needed to see the gracefully dancing whitecaps, lightly teasing the empty beach.

End your walk at the Oak Street Beach. If it is a pleasant day, buy an ice cream cone as a reward and sit and enjoy Lake Michigan yourself. You have walked about two miles.

6

GOLD COAST WALK

BACKGROUND

The Gold Coast, a narrow strip along Lake Michigan from Oak Street to North Avenue, and west to Dearborn, has been *the* place to live ever since entrepreneur Potter Palmer left the South Side's Prairie Avenue in 1882 to fill in a frog pond and swamp later called North Lake Shore Drive. Palmer built his forty-two-room brownstone castle on Lake Shore Drive between Schiller and Banks to match his wife's position as top social arbiter. By the 1890s the Palmers were being followed north by Chicago's other merchant princes, many of whose descendants live here in apartments today. In a March 1989 article entitled "Lake Shore Drive Confidential," *Chicago Magazine* detailed who lives where, showing that the area is still socially "it."

In spite of the bodies dug up when each new mansion was built (leftovers from the old city graveyard) by the 1920s the Gold Coast was the natural habitat of the truly rich. New building stopped during the Depression and many mansions were cut up, but by the 1950s new highrises began to appear, and the old mansions and townhouses were regentrified as condos. Home to McCormicks, Rockefellers, Pritzkers, and Crowns who prefer not to do the suburban commute, the Gold Coast is still the wealthiest community in the entire Chicagoland area as well as the second wealthiest community in the country. Its benign well-heeled ambiance has spread west across Old Town and is even threatening the grim environs of public housing's notorious Cabrini-Green.

With its elegant, landmark houses the Gold Coast is a delightful place to explore, but mystery writers tend to make things difficult by being purposefully vague about exact addresses—not wanting, no doubt, to offend the mighty. As a result, this walk contains a number of educated guesses and as many of the most architecturally renowned houses as possible. Just walking its peaceful, narrow tree-lined streets gives you a strong feeling of "Old Chicago" in the days when its movers and shakers were proud of being "native" Americans, often Yankees, who had moved here from the East Coast to better themselves. Nowadays, in mysteries, a number of ethnic, gangster-like characters live here, too.

You can reach the starting point at Michigan Avenue and Oak Street easily by bus or cab (or on foot) to begin the walk. You can also drive and park your car a block west on Rush where there are a number of parking garages. At the end of the walk take a bus south on State Street to the Loop or walk west to get the El (subway) at Clark and Division Street.

LENGTH OF WALK: About 1 mile

See the map on page 177 for the boundaries of this walk and page 350 for a list of the books and detectives mentioned.

PLACES OF INTEREST

Note: The stately homes mentioned are nearly all private residences and can be viewed only from the outside. Most of them do not sport plaques but you can find their street numbers.

Ambassador East Hotel, 1301 N. State Street. One of Chicago's top hotels with romantic and elegant old-world charm. The major celebrity spot is its Pump Room, and it once housed mystery movie mogul Alfred Hitchcock and the entire cast of *North by*

Northwest in the days before Chicago became a hot film spot. Call 787-7200.

Ambassador West Hotel, 1300 N. State Street. Older sister of the Ambassador East with the ambiance of a small European hotel. Oak-paneled lobby with seventeenth-century decor. Connected by underground passage to the Ambassador East.

Astor Street Historical District. Landmark homes designed by world-famous Chicago architects.

The Fortnightly (Club) of Chicago (Bruce Lathrop House), 120 E. Bellevue Place. New York's famous McKim, Mead and White built this as a private residence in 1892. Since 1922 the home of the Fortnightly Club, the most exclusive women's club in Chicago.

Carl C. Heisen House and Mason Brayman Starring House, 1250 and 1254 N. Lake Shore Drive. Two single-family mansions that came to symbolize the "good old days." In 1990 the insides were gutted to form four residences.

George S. Isham House (Playboy Mansion), 1340 N. State Parkway. Built for law partner of Abraham Lincoln's son Robert Todd Lincoln, in the 1960s it became the unlikely pad of *Playboy*'s Hugh Hefner.

Potter Palmer's Castle (site of) 1350–1360 N. Lake Share Drive. The gigantic Henry Ives Cobb striped stone castle built in 1882. Now occupied by two redbrick highrises.

Residence of the Roman Catholic Archbishop (Cardinal) of Chicago, 1555 N. State Parkway (at North Avenue). 1880 redbrick Queen Anne mansion with nineteen chimneys.

Rush/Division Streets. Chicago's old nightclub entertainment center, celebrated in song and story.

St. Chrysostom's Episcopal Church, 1424 N. Dearborn. 1913–25. Early English (Prairie) Gothic. Locked unless you go to the Church Offices.

PLACES TO EAT

This is not a restaurant area except for the hotels and the western border along Rush and Division Streets. So eat first, do the walk, then stop at a hotel or bistro afterwards. Along State Street are the usual fast food places.

Beau Nash, Ambassador West Hotel, 1300 N. State Street. International cuisine.

Butch McGuire's, 20 W. Division Street. The granddaddy of all singles bars since 1961.

Dublin's Pub, 1050 N. State Street. Polished bar, big-screen TV, and leather-jacketed clientele.

Gibson's Bar and Steakhouse, 1028 N. Rush Street. Trendy "surf and turf" spot, conventioneers' hangout. Live piano music, outdoor tables.

Hamburger Hamlet, 1024 N. Rush Street. Fancy hamburger place; one of the booths was originally Winston Churchill's elevator.

The Original Pancake House, 22 E. Bellevue Place. Little white house just off Rush Street.

Pump Room, Ambassador East Hotel, 1301 N. State Street. Low-numbered booths (especially Booth One) reserved for the rich and famous. Irv Kupcinet wrote in the *Sun-Times* that a gathering of stars was an almost daily occurrence in the 1930s and '40s before air travel put an end to the stopovers. Check out the celebrity photos in the foyer and take a look at the famous decor: dark blue walls, white leather booths, and red-coated waiters.

Goose Island Brewing Company, 1800 N. Clybourn Avenue (see Possible Side Trips). Best beer in town at this mini-brewery west of the Gold Coast, Old Town, and Cabrini-Green.

GOLD COAST WALK

Begin your walk at the corner of Oak Street and Michigan Avenue across from the Drake Hotel by the pink granite skyscraper called One Magnificent Mile. Cross Oak Street and walk along the Inner Drive one block north to Bellevue Place.

Cross Bellevue and turn left to go west past the dark brick Georgian Revival mansion at 120 E. Bellevue Place. The New York firm of McKim, Mead & White built this double house in 1892, starting a Gold Coast trend away from Richardson Romanesque. Partner Stanford White was notorious for his Manhattan love nest with its red velvet swing; he was shot by a jealous husband in Madison Square Garden. (See *Mystery Readers' Walking Guide: New York.*)

Since 1922 this building has been the home of the oldest women's club in Chicago, the Fortnightly. Called the most truly highbrow women's organization in the city, its members were—and are—the wives and sisters and mothers and daughters of the city's major movers and shakers since the Great Chicago Fire. (Its counterpart for men, the Chicago Literary Club, was founded two years later.) Dedicated to improving their minds, the club members have invited such speakers as Mary Craig and Barbara D'Amato to discuss the mystery story.

Muriel Beadle, whose husband George was President of the University of Chicago, wrote a history of this Chicago institution, *The Fortnightly of Chicago: The City and Its Women, 1873–1973.* It had an introduction by member Fanny Butcher, the city's most famous book reviewer. Butcher, who lived north of the Fortnightly on Astor Street, appeared as herself in William Targ's *The Case of Mr. Cassidy.*

Walk west on Bellevue to Rush Street, admiring the lovely block of mansions, mixed with highrises. Since Chicago mystery writers use the term "Gold Coast" generically, often you can choose a house to suit yourself. Any one of these would do nicely for a suspenseful Mignon G. Eberhart novel like her 1933 *The Dark Garden.* Eberhart herself lived nearby in the same Astor Street building as Fanny Butcher.

At Rush Street you find a totally different ambiance. As Barbara D'Amato reported in *Hard Women,* Rush Street is still the tourist area, where out-of-town conventioneers looking for "Chicago After Dark" are brought by cabbies. (See Chicago Jack's *A Cabbie's Guide to Chicago at Night.*)

D'Amato's Cat Marsala, working on a TV piece on hookers, roamed the area looking for interviews. She was escorted by Ross Wardon, an undercover cop, courtesy of her police chum Captain Harold McCoo. Wardon sardonically pointed out to Cat that the territory was bounded by Holy Name Cathedral, Cabrini-Green, and the new highrise condos on Michigan Avenue—all within walking distance of one another.

The "Rush Street" ambiance goes north to Division Street

and then spreads west. In addition to bars and nightclubs, you will find fast food places suitable for a pit stop and/or coffee. The Original Pancake House has its own little white house at 22 E. Bellevue, across the street from Le Meridien Hotel. A small place, it might once have been the cozy little "cottage" of sleuth Susan Dare in Mignon G. Eberhart's *The Cases of Susan Dare*.

Turn right on Rush and walk one block north to Cedar, where Rush Street ends. Michael Cormany's *Lost Daughter* opened in a bar on Rush Street near Cedar. P.I. Dan Kruger, a skinny ex-cop and rock musician who played guitar in several bands, was there tailing "The Kid." The Kid, a rookie righthander from Arkansas, was a nine-day Cubs pitching wonder who had bombed out. (A younger version of Crabbe Evers's star pitcher "Dream" Weaver, who was shot in the Cubs' ballpark tunnel in *Murder in Wrigley Field*.)

Kruger's client, who had lost money betting on The Kid, wanted to know what happened. Kruger quickly figured out that The Kid was into too much wine, women and song. Kruger then walked out of the bar and was accosted by a "drunken gorilla" called Dawson. Dawson, a beefy suburban contractor, offered Kruger two hundred a day to find his run-away teenage daughter Asia.

There are several choices for Kruger's bar. One is Gibson's Steakhouse at 1028 N. Rush Street, next door to Hamburger Hamlet at 1024 N. Rush Street. There is also a place called Melvin B's across State Street near Cedar. Melvin B's has been a singles bar for over twenty years, popular with the advertising crowd. Perhaps the most likely is the very Irish Dublin's Pub at Maple and State with a big polished bar, TV, and plenty of leather-jacketed customers.

Look them all over, then go right on Cedar to walk back to the Inner Drive. Along Cedar there are luxury apartments, some old, some new, then more townhouses of limestone, brownstone, and brick. The buildings get newer and taller as you get nearer the Drive. In terms of who's who, it's a good guess that the older the building, the older the money, except that many of the mansions have been converted into expensive

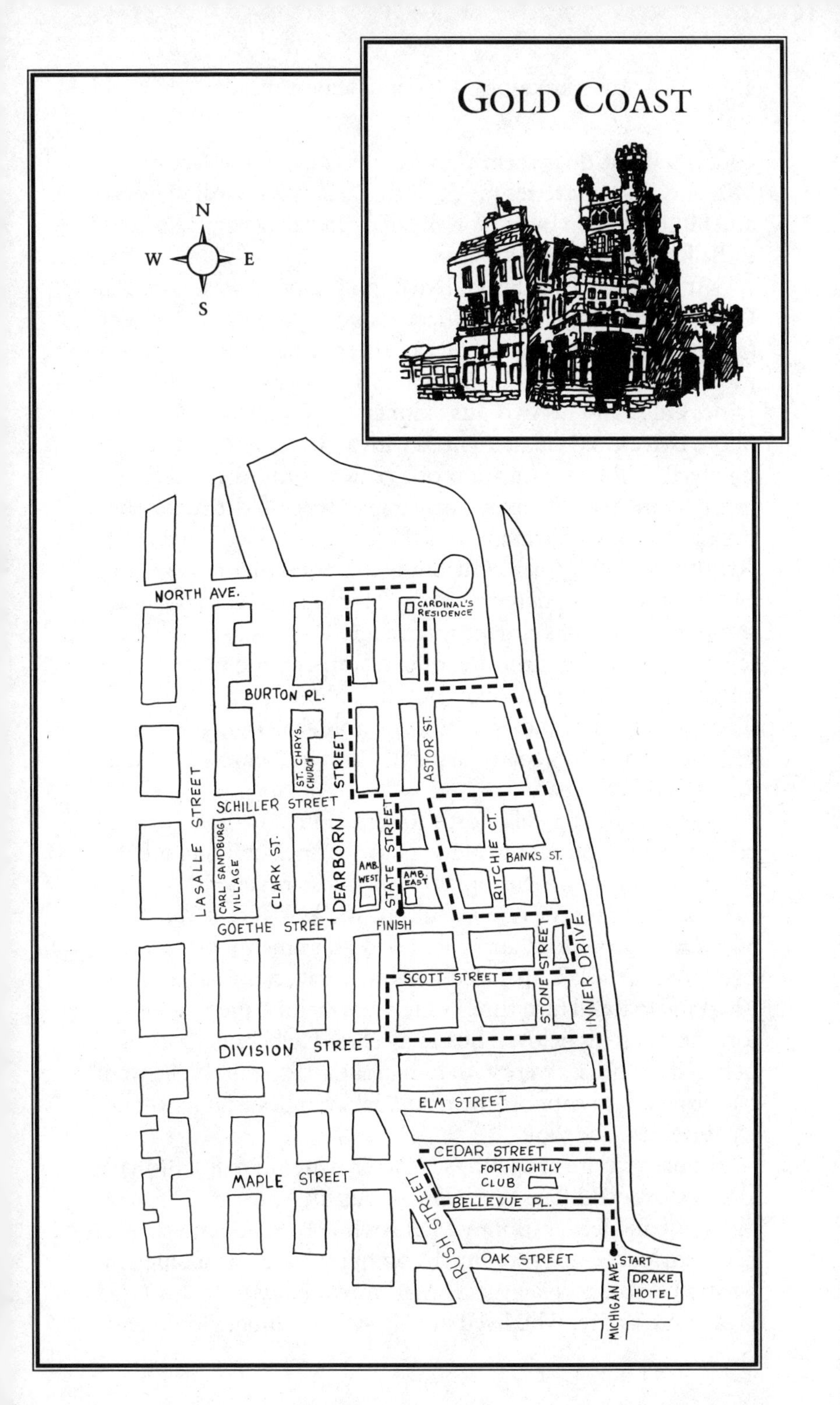
GOLD COAST
N
W
E
S
NORTH AVE.
CARDINAL'S RESIDENCE
BURTON PL.
ST. CHRYS. CHURCH
ASTOR ST.
LASALLE STREET
DEARBORN STREET
SCHILLER STREET
CARL SANDBURG VILLAGE
CLARK ST.
AMB. WEST
STATE STREET
AMB. EAST
RITCHIE CT.
BANKS ST.
GOETHE STREET
FINISH
STONE STREET
INNER DRIVE
SCOTT STREET
DIVISION STREET
ELM STREET
CEDAR STREET
FORTNIGHTLY CLUB
MAPLE STREET
RUSH STREET
BELLEVUE PL.
OAK STREET
START
MICHIGAN AVE.
DRAKE HOTEL

condos. What does seem unbelievable now is the fact that in '40s and '50s mysteries much of this area was boarding houses and SROs, lived in by kids on the make like the characters in Bill S. Ballinger's *Portrait in Smoke*.

At 1100 N. Lake Shore Drive, on the northwest corner of Cedar and the Inner Drive, there is a new building with underground parking (not common along here). In Michael A. Dymmoch's *The Man Who Understood Cats,* wealthy psychiatrist Dr. James Caleb and his two cats Skinner and Freud lived in a Lake Shore Drive Gold Coast highrise with a garage. After he became involved in the investigation of a patient's murder, Caleb was jumped in his own parking garage, force-fed drugs, then dumped in his apartment and the police notified. Rushed to Northwestern Hospital, Caleb was also arrested for possession. But his new friend detective John Thinnes, convinced it was a setup, rechecked his elegant apartment. Thinnes found that Caleb had solid wood furniture, oriental carpets, and many books, ranging from Americans like Faulkner, Hemingway, Steinbeck, Cheever, Updike, and Bellow to a whole shelf of mystery writers, including Chicagoans Granger, Paretsky, Turow, Engling, Zubro, and D'Amato.

Cross Cedar to walk north towards Elm. At the southwest corner of Elm you pass an older, gracious brick building suitable for the lavish apartment of radio singing star Nelle Brown and her husband Henry Gibson Gifford. In Craig Rice's *The Corpse Steps Out,* the Gifford apartment had an immense living room overlooking the lake, paneled walls, a massive fireplace, and polished and graceful furniture. Nelle's elderly husband first lost his fortune, then his beloved horses in a fire. He became dotty and believed the horses were with him in the apartment. Nelle went back to work to support them and behaved beautifully to him, whatever else she did.

In nasty contrast to Rice's Nelle Brown, in Fredric Brown's 1950s story "I'll Cut Your Throat Again, Kathleen," former big time band leader Johnny Marlin who played sax and clarinet had been locked up for trying to commit suicide—by slashing his wrists. Unable to play again, Marlin was released to his Gold Coast wife Kathy, who lived in a classy Lake Shore Drive apartment. She had thrown out his beloved instruments and was looking forward to having Johnny "all to herself."

In Marc Davis's *Dirty Money,* P.I. Frank Wolf drove south along Lake Shore Drive, watching the glass towers on the right and the heaving waters of blue and green on the left. He felt inspired by the harmonies between the man-made and the natural, which were especially beautiful along these few miles of urban shoreline. Wolf was heading for a Lake Shore Drive condo between Elm and Division where the ex-wife of murdered commodities broker Abel Nockerman lived. She wanted Wolf to find out who had killed Nockerman execution-style in his lakefront condo, so she asked him to dine. Her living room overlooked the lake and the dining room showed the gentle curves of Lake Shore Drive as it veered past the Drake and the ornate facades of splendid old buildings that faced Oak Street Beach.

Cross Elm. In Sara Paretsky's *Indemnity Only,* V.I. Warshawski's newly acquired Ajax Insurance Company boyfriend Ralph Devereux had been living in a furnished apartment on Elm since his divorce. Thanks to Devereux's stupidity, the murderer staged a shoot-out there, and V.I. had to rescue Ralph, which ended their relationship.

Continue walking north to Division Street. At the corner at 110 E. Division Street there is a handsome older building with a penthouse visible from across the street. In William Targ's *The Case of Mr. Cassidy,* murdered James Cassidy lived in a Lake Shore Drive penthouse apartment. Amateur sleuth Hugh Morris went there with elderly bookseller Thaddeus Todd. Cassidy's living room had vaulted ceilings and paintings by Rembrandt, Van Dyck, Constable, and Reynolds. A noted collector, Cassidy was found dead in his library with its floor-to-ceiling books.

Among other items Cassidy owned a first edition of Edgar Allan Poe's play *Tamerlane,* sold to him by Todd. (A valuable work by Poe was the cause of murder in John Dickson Carr's *The Mad Hatter Mystery.* See *Mystery Readers Walking Guide: London.*) After viewing the scene of the crime, Morris asked to see the *Tamerlane,* commenting that Vincent Starrett would give his eyeteeth to see it.

Vincent Starrett was a *Chicago Daily News* reporter and a

friend of Harriet Monroe, the Gold Coast founder of *Poetry Magazine.* An internationally acclaimed authority on Sherlock Holmes and author of *The Secret Life of Sherlock Holmes,* Starrett also wrote mysteries, notably his classic Chicago story "The Eleventh Juror."

In Barbara D'Amato's *Hardball,* Cat Marsala attended a meeting on legalizing drugs where the principal speaker, Louise Sugarman, was blown up. At the conference Cat had noticed Charles Jaffe, a mobster's debonair son, whom she arranged to interview. Driving to his apartment, Cat mused that if Chicago was a city of neighborhoods, the Gold Coast was its longest, narrowest neighborhood, one building wide, a strip of beautiful light sand bordered on one side by water and on the other side by wealth.

Cat had pegged Jaffe as a Hancock Center type, but Jaffe lived on the two top floors of a traditional Lake Shore Drive building overlooking the lake, with a walnut-paneled elevator and a doorman. His corner office had highly polished floors, a dark Oriental rug, floor-to-ceiling glass-fronted oak bookcases, leather sofa and chairs. There was nothing to excess, but the room whispered money.

Cross Division and turn left to walk west. Along Division you see many more old-fashioned townhouses, suitable for Gold Coast mystery characters, who tend to be murderers or murder victims, as befits their grand way of life.

Keep walking along Division to tiny Stone Street which runs north and south for two blocks. On the south side of Division there is another tiny house that would be perfect for Mignon G. Eberhart's *The Cases of Susan Dare.* Dare's little house had a small library with a fireplace, a dog to whom she explained when she left on a case, and a maid Huldah. Dare was listed by Ellery Queen as one of the Great Women Detectives in 1941 when such characters were very thin on the ground. She was a single young woman who wrote mysteries and solved cases for the police, with the help (and admiration) of newspaper reporter Jim Byrne.

At Stone Street you really are in Eberhart territory. In Eberhart's *Dead Men's Plans,* the Minary family who owned a

Great Lakes shipping business lived in a brick mansion on "Game Street," a short street near the lake. Stone Street is the best location because at the east end of Division there is a pedestrian walkway to the lakefront. But no dogs are allowed to cross there, while in Eberhart's mystery, the Minary's poor relation Sewal was always out walking the dogs to the beach while murderers ran amok up and down Game Street. Sadly, Stone Street's houses are all gone, leaving it an alley of highrises.

Walk past Stone Street to Astor Street. In Paretsky's *Indemnity Only,* a pair of hoods picked up V.I. Warshawski at her apartment and took her to visit a mobster named Earl Smeissen, who lived off Astor on Division in a stately old home of dull red brick with elegant wrought-iron railings. It was now a three-flat where Smeissen lived on the second floor with Louis Quinze furniture. He told V.I. to lay off the Thayer murder case, hit her in the face, then let his doorman work her over. They didn't kill her even though V.I. figured that with his City Hall and police connections, Smeissen could get away with murder. V.I. hobbled to Lake Shore Drive and persuaded a cabbie to drive her home.

To move from the sublimely rich to the desperately poor, walk west on Division to State Street. This is the symbolic "great divide," east and west, north and south described by WFMT's oral historian Studs Terkel in *Division Street: America.* In 1949, Terkel's friend, writer Nelson Algren had described the saloons of West Division through the eyes of Frankie Machine, the drug dealer, in *The Man with the Golden Arm.* Today the area is a scene of yuppie serendipity with spots like Butch McGuire's. When Terkel wrote in the late '60s, the Gold Coast was north and east of Division, while south and west along Division was the honkytonk extension of Rush Street, mixed with the working-class houses of Old Town. But the glittering boundaries are moving so fast that gentrification may soon attack Cabrini-Green.

In Fredric Brown's *The Screaming Mimi,* Raoul's Gift Shop was located one block west at Dearborn and Division. Raoul Reynarde sold art objects and upscale imports like foo dogs, thunder birds, and brass candlesticks. Lola Brent, one of the murder victims, had worked there and stolen a copy of the Screaming Mimi, a ten-inch statuette of a naked, terrified girl.

Turn right at State Street and go one block north to Scott Street, then turn right and walk east on Scott Street back to Lake Shore Drive. Turn left on Scott to walk north along the Drive past still more elegant highrises.

The second building north of Scott Street is 1242 N. Lake Shore Drive. Its '20s style is very suitable for the penthouse of society do-gooder Mrs. Laura Wingate in Leslie Charteris's *Call for the Saint*. Invited to a party there, Simon Templar (aka the Saint) found broad acres of terrace covered with tables, beach umbrellas and trays of cocktails. He grabbed two—one for himself and one for celebrity actress Monica Varing, with whom he was investigating the murder of some Loop beggars. As always, Simon Templar was a debonair, suave man of the world playing knight errant—a sort of prewar James Bond, crossed with Lord Peter Wimsey.

In Sara Paretsky's story "The Case of the Pietro Andromache" Beth Israel's Chief of Staff Dr. Lewis Caudwell had a condo in a '20s building at East Scott Street. It housed his art collection which included a Pietro d'Alessandro alabaster of Andromache. Looted by his father after World War II, it had belonged to the family of Dr. Lotty Herschel and at a staff party she recognized the statue and made a scene. When Caudwell was found dead, Lotty was picked up and put in County Jail.

Keep walking north on Lake Shore Drive. At 1250 and 1254 N. Lake Shore Drive there are a pair of Richardson Romanesque mansions protected by a wrought iron railing. In 1990 they were connected inside to make four residences but so far have survived demolition. The redstone Carl Constantine Heisen house at 1250 was built about 1891; the gray limestone Mason Brayman Starring house in 1889. It is in the wrong location but it looks like the parental home of John Banks, Cat Marsala's staid stockbroker beau. In *Hardball* D'Amato described it as built of Toyota-sized blocks of granite with slits for windows.

The third house in this surviving row at 1258 Lake Shore Drive is a three-story Venetian Gothic house with balcony, designed by Holabird and Root in 1895. It is one of several Gold

Coast palaces that could be the one in Arthur Maling's *Lover and Thief,* owned by rich widow Anita Danton. (Reading Maling's mystery makes you think of Helen Brach, a candy heiress, who disappeared in 1977. Brach's body has never been found but a man has been accused of her murder.)

When Anita Danton's young lover disappeared with some jewels, she called in P.I. Calvin Bix to recover the jewelry, not to prosecute the thief. Bix came to her Venetian palazzo with its Gothic interior and three excited Yorkshire terriers; later Peter Ives's body was found in his car in the Danton garage.

When you reach Goethe Street, turn left to walk to Stone Street. On the northwest corner of Goethe and Stone Street, at 1300 Goethe, there is a towering highrise suitable for the apartment of model/dancer Nadia Meade in Jay Robert Nash's *A Crime Story.* Crime columnist Jack Journey and his researcher Charlie Lindquist went to Nadia's classy rabbit warren after photographer Hamilcar Ball was murdered. They suspected Nadia had another copy of a photograph taken the night of the first murder. When Nadia didn't answer, they broke in and found her naked body strung up on the balcony like a plant.

Beyond Stone Street there is a tiny street called Ritchie Court with a small playground called Goudy Square Park. It is very much like a London square with nannies and kiddies all about. (See *MRWG: London.*) Take a look, then keep walking west on Goethe to Astor Street.

At Astor Street you have reached *the* Gold Coast Street, named for John Jacob Astor. Astor never lived there, but Astor's American Fur Company had its headquarters in Chicago. (See also *MRWG: NY.*) This is the Astor Street Historical District, filled with landmark houses by Chicago's famous architects.

On one corner at 1300 N. Astor is the Astor Tower Hotel, one of the first Gold Coast skyscrapers, built in 1963. Across the intersection is 1301 Astor, a sedate '20s Art Deco highrise. The second generation of Potter Palmers lived in its three-story penthouse, establishing a new vogue for apartment living.

Cross Astor Street and walk west to the alley between Astor and State Parkway. Numbers 19–21 are a group of brownstones, one of which would be perfect for the old Hatterick family mansion in Eberhart's *The Glass Slipper*. The Hatterick house was a narrow five-storied brownstone built at about the time of the 1871 Chicago Fire, with a wide, carved mahogany door, plate-glass windows with beveled edges, and a basement entrance down a flight of steps. Rue Hatterick, a nurse who married her boss, came there to live with Brule's teenage daughter Madge and his brother-in-law, Stephen.

One of these brownstones also could have been the Chakorian house in James Michael Ullman's *The Venus Trap*. International wheeler/dealer Rudy Chakorian brought his son Jon and his mistress Bess to Chicago to live in a Gold Coast brownstone while he promoted the Venus Corporation. Then one Christmas Eve when Jon was ten, Rudy disappeared. Jon later found his way back here from his aunt's house in Rogers Park. He got into the house through the back alley, but he met a man his father had known who was armed with a knife and was scared off.

Walk back to Astor Street, then go left (north) along the west side of the street. You pass several landmark houses like 1308–10–12 Astor, three connected sandstone and redbrick houses where the famous architect John Wellborn Root, of Holabird and Root, lived. After he died his widow lived there with her sister, Harriet Monroe. Monroe, who looked like a New England schoolmarm, came home from circling the globe in January 1911 and found Chicago surging with life, except it was not celebrating poetry. So Monroe founded *Poetry Magazine*, in which she published Modernist Middle Western poets like Ezra Pound, Carl Sandburg, and T. S. Eliot. Monroe also wrote an art column for the *Chicago Tribune* when the city editor was Walter Howey, featured in MacArthur and Hecht's *The Front Page*, and her colleagues included Ring Lardner, Marquis James, and Finley Peter Dunne. Among Monroe's writer friends were Edna Ferber, Susan Glaspell, and Sherwood Anderson, all part of the "Chicago Renaissance" which won H. L. Mencken's praise in 1917. The group broke up during the Roaring Twenties when many writers went to New York, and bootlegging and mysteries about gangsters became Chicago's favorite literary activity.

At 1316–1322 Astor there is a group of blocky limestone Romanesque Revival mansions, built by Potter Palmer. They, too, could be the house made of "Toyota-sized chunks" that D'Amato's Cat Marsala described in *Hardball.* On the west side of Astor at 1318 there is a redone graystone townhouse with a small alley south of it, where once there were coach houses, but now are garages and other buildings. This is about the right place for the mansion with coach house in Bill Ballinger's *Portrait in Smoke* that Danny April broke into to use as a base to woo Krassy Almauniski, a West Side girl on the make. (There are amazingly few coach houses left in the Gold Coast, so you have to use what you can find.)

Ironically enough, top mobsters lived on Astor in Eugene Izzi's mysteries. In *The Take* independent operator and burglar Fabe Falletti was being escorted there by two toughs called Elmo and Lloyd to see the Outfit's Roland DiNardo when he disarmed them. Fabe then escorted them to their boss's very comfortable pad where he also met Angelo "Tombstone" Paterro, DiNardo's boss. The Outfit wanted Fabe to do a job for them, but he declined and still left in one piece.

Keep walking north along Astor Street to Banks Street. On the southwest corner at 25 E. Banks there is a beige-colored mansion with a connected coach-house apartment at 25 E. Banks Rear. This mansion is between Astor and State behind some older highrises on Lake Shore Drive, where Krassy and her rich old husband could have lived, so it, too, might have been the elegant bachelor pad April used for a love nest while its real owner was on a Florida vacation in Ballinger's *Portrait in Smoke.*

Across Astor you can see 1335 Astor Street, for many years the home of Irna Phillips, the Queen of the Soaps, who invented the genre by writing such memorable serials as *As the World Turns* and *The Guiding Light.* At 1345 Astor there is another Romanesque mansion made of varieties of sherbet-colored sandstones.

One or the other of these mansions would be excellent for May Laval's plush Victorian home on Astor Street in William P. McGivern's *Very Cold for May.* May had a two-story brownstone with wide bay windows and a long elegant parlor done in rococo modern Victorian. When she had parties, it was always crowded with politicians, judges, gamblers, newspapermen, and a handful of derelicts picked up from west-side soup lines. May knew everybody and everybody knew May, a beautiful show girl who married an elderly meat packer. But when she decided to write her memoirs and showed guests her thick, leather-bound diary, which she kept in her bedroom, she was soon murdered.

Numbers 1349–53 Astor are called the Court of the Golden Hands; you can see some of the golden hand doorknobs. Astor Court at 1355 is a Howard Van Doren Shaw Greek Revival mansion with animal-skull keystones. It was the home of the Goodman family, who gave the city the Goodman Theater in memory of their son Kenneth who died in World War I. (See Walk 1.)

Cross Banks Street and continue north to Schiller. At 1443 Astor, at the corner of Astor and Schiller, is the May House. It is another Richardson Romanesque "castle," built in 1891 on a colossal scale.

Turn right on Schiller and cross Astor. At 1364 you pass the James Charnley House, built in 1891 by Chicago architects Adler and Sullivan. Young Frank Lloyd Wright was working for the firm and this mansion has his unmistakable touch, including a skylight the length of the building.

In Monica Quill's (aka Ralph McInerny) *Let Us Prey,* Sister Mary Theresa Dempsey (known as Emtee) was the Mother Superior of the Order of Martha and Mary, founded by the Blessed Abigail Keineswegs. The Order, much reduced in circumstances, was housed near Newberry Library on Walton in a (fictitious) Frank Lloyd Wright house. There were only three nuns left in the order after their College and other property was sold off in the '60s and the money given to the poor. Since there are no Wright houses on Walton, the Charnley house makes an acceptable substitute.

Walking east towards the lake along Schiller you pass another group of elegant townhouses on the north side of the street. One, at 36 E. Schiller Street, was the home of Mayor Carter Henry Harrison, Jr. He was elected mayor five times, in part because his very popular father Carter Henry Harrison, Sr., had also served five terms as mayor. (The senior Harrison was murdered by a disappointed office seeker just as the 1893 World's Columbian Exposition ended in a shower of fireworks.) In *American Gothic,* Robert Bloch described the genial mayor and his "wide-open" city. After Harrison, the next owner of the house was William Wrigley, Jr., the chewing gum manufacturer who built the Wrigley Buildings, and once owned the Chicago Cubs.

At Schiller and Lake Shore Drive there are two large modern redbrick apartment buildings at 1350–1560 Lake Shore Drive. They are on the site of Potter Palmer's castle, which occupied the entire block from Schiller to Burton Place. In these highrises, built from 1949–51, each apartment was designed to have a tiny view of Lake Michigan.

The Victorian castle built by Potter Palmer in 1882 marked the beginning of the Gold Coast. Palmer, who had developed State Street, aided and abetted his wife in her role as unquestioned queen of Chicago society. Their striped and turreted castle was filled with art; in fact, many of Chicago's famous Impressionist paintings at the Art Institute came from the Palmer collection.

Bertha Honore Palmer grew up in Chicago and attended its select Dearborn Seminary. In addition to reigning as the hostess with the mostest till the day she died, she was also a leading light in civic duty and great supporter of women's causes. As chairman of the Board of Lady Managers of the World's Columbian Exposition Palmer chaired meetings and greeted visiting VIP women—including the silly and snobbish Infanta Eulalia of Spain. You can get a good picture of Bertha Palmer in action by reading Roslynn Griffith's historical mystery about the 1893 Fair called *Pretty Birds of Passage.*

In Craig Rice's *The Wrong Murder,* the ancestral mansion of celebrity heiress Mona McClane was on or near the site of the Potter Palmer castle. John J. Malone considered it a combination of a high-class undertaking parlor and 1880 government building. In *The Right Murder,* interrupting their honeymoon, Helene Justus stayed there as Mona's guest while she and Jake tried to figure out if Mona had killed her house guest Gerald

Tuesday, so Jake could win the Casino. (In *The Wrong Murder,* Mona had bet Jake she could murder someone and not get caught. See Walk 2.)

Mona McClane had one of the world's great fortunes and her marriages, divorces, and adventures were Sunday-supplement history. She had flown the Atlantic solo for a dinner party, climbed Mount Everest, and won the Casino from mobster Max Hook in three nights at roulette. She had a respectable suburban daughter and grandchild and was a damn good shot.

Mona did not physically resemble Bertha Potter (with dark hair and pale skin she looked more like Craig Rice) but Mona had Bertha's penchant for doing the unexpected—and getting away with it. Rice's biographies to date tend to suggest she, too, grew up in the Gold Coast, which is far from the truth. (See Walk 9.)

In Rice's *The Fourth Postman,* the police car taking sweet old Rodney Fairfaxx to Police Headquarters at 11th and State to be locked up for murder went past the McClane castle. Thanks to Captain Von Flanagan, Fairfaxx was being escorted by lawyer Malone and his stray dog as a defense team.

In Harry Stephen Keeler's *The Washington Park Enigma,* the down-and-out hero hitched a ride on the back of a purple car from a Washington Square alley to Dearborn. The car then turned east on Schiller and stopped at one of the massive and elegant mansions that lined the Drive, which turned out to be the home of heiress Trudel Vanderhuyden. The Vanderhuyden mansion must have been about where the Potter Palmer castle once stood.

In Keeler's *Thieves' Nights,* the "Man Who Mislaid His Memory," who was completely broke and homeless, burglarized a mansion on "Millionaires' Row." It had spirals, turrets, angles, and gargoyles and on each side of the driveway was a huge bronze table with the name "Algernon van de Puyster." When he broke in, the man banged his head and regained his memory, discovering that he was Algernon van de Puyster. His very proper servants ignored the fact that the master had broken into his own house.

There is no house at the address given in Frank Gruber's *The*

Scarlet Feather (*The Gamecock Murders*) for the Tancreds's mansion. An odd couple of attractive con artists—the brains and the brawn—were walking in Lincoln Park on a November morning when they saw Lois Tancred park her Cadillac, take off her mink coat and head for Lake Michigan. Johnny dived in after her, rescued her, wrapped her in her mink, and put her in her car. She lived at 1498 Lake Shore Drive in one of the last of the old-time castles, but Lois's starchy mother who opened the door, took the girl and slammed it in their faces, so they drove the Cadillac downtown to see Mr. Tancred.

Walk north past the Potter Palmer site to Burton Place. You pass by several more old limestone mansions, including the International College of Surgeons and the Polish Consulate, where there used to be major demonstrations before the Berlin Wall fell.

Turn left (west) on Burton to return to Astor Street. In John D. MacDonald's *One Fearful Yellow Eye,* Travis McGee went to interview Heidi Geis at 180 E. Burton (fictitious) where she had a studio apartment. Heidi painted very large abstracts which she marketed at an East Scott Street gallery called Tempo East. McGee was up from Florida to help out Heidi's widowed step-mother, a former girlfriend, who lived in a Lake Forest mansion.

At 40 E. Burton Place there is a huge colonial mansion with a coach house behind it. It is the kind of place where Chicago writer Vera Caspary's '20s bachelor girls lived in *Evvie.* Louise was a copywriter like Caspary herself at one time, while Evvie herself belonged to the flapper era, sleeping with anyone and everyone from stockbrokers to electricians until she was found murdered in the coach-house apartment. Caspary's most famous mystery about career girls was *Laura,* but it took place in New York. (See *MRWG: NY*.)

Continue walking towards 20 E. Burton (also known—confusingly—as 1500 Astor because it is on the northwest corner where the two streets meet). This is the Patterson–McCormick Mansion. A Georgian Revival/Italian palazzo designed by the New York firm of McKim, Mead and the notorious Stanford White, it also could be the Venetian residence of Maling's rich widow Anita Danton in *Lover and Thief.* Built of orange Roman brick with terra-cotta trim, the house was commissioned in 1914 by Joseph Medill, former mayor and part owner of the *Chicago Tribune,* as a gift for his daughter Cissy Patterson. The Pattersons had lavish parties there, with VIP guest lists. In 1927 Cyrus McCormick II, a member of another old Chicago family, bought the mansion and doubled its size. It has now been divided into condos.

Walk by the mansion one block north on Astor to North Avenue. To your left you come to an alley behind the Cardinal's residence on North Avenue that is still paved with wooden blocks. The alley, which also has a coach house, is the easiest alley in the neighborhood to explore, so go left and walk down it to look around.

What you are looking for is a harmless postman (or woman) to murder as he/she walks through the alley to deliver mail. (In the Olden Days of Long Ago there were many postmen walking the streets in the morning. Today, no postman would be caught dead in an alley, and it is sheer luck if they appear regularly on the streets of Chicago.) But in Craig Rice's *The Fourth Postman* a group of upper-crust old families lived in a row of houses just east of North State Parkway. On the east corner of the block was a brick wall that enclosed a garden belonging to a big house on Astor Place, and between the wall and the last of the three houses, there was a narrow alley like this one.

The alley was the scene of the crime where three postmen were murdered. Captain Von Flanagan was determined there would not be a *fourth* postman murdered, but Von Flanagan also brought John J. Malone along to serve as Rodney Fairfaxx's defense lawyer. They suspected Fairfaxx, who lived in one of the houses, because the sweet old gentleman believed his sweetheart, who had drowned on the Titanic, was still alive and writing him letters.

Before escorting his client to the clink, Malone snooped about in the fatal alley which was just as littered with rubbish, waste paper, empty bottles, tin cans, and battle-scarred cats as the far less aristocratic alleys a mile to the south. He ended up being adopted by a little stray mutt who liked beer.

Go back to Astor and walk past the green grounds of the Roman Catholic Archbishop's (Cardinal's) Residence. At North Avenue walk all the way around its many-chimneyed, redbrick Victorian splendor. It is the oldest surviving structure in the Astor Historical District. Across North Avenue is Lincoln Park. (See Walk 7.)

Since there are no other mansions left, the Archbishop's Residence will also have to represent the John Atwood mansion at 1516 Lake Shore Drive in Harry Keeler's *Thieves' Nights*. It was a massive corner house of gray stone, with rounded bay windows and a great lawn fronting both the main street and the side street. Ward Sharlow from London saw an ad for someone to impersonate Atwood's dead son for $10,000 and agreed. Then John Atwood had a heart attack and died. At his funeral an East Indian called Jagat Singh, Special Envoy from His Majesty, the Maharaja of Bahawalpur, called to demand the return of the Atwood emerald currently on loan to the Art Institute.

In Bill Granger's *The Priestly Murders* Sergeant Terry Flynn had to report to the Cardinal about the investigation into the murder of a young priest at early mass at St. Alma's Church on the South Side. He was not impressed by his Eminence, who was fat and self-important. In Granger's *The Infant of Prague,* when a statue of the Infant of Prague at St. Margaret of Scotland's Church began to weep tears and the media got the story, the Cardinal was not pleased. He was very big on social responsibility, racial justice, and the rights of the unborn, but he was not overjoyed about a miracle that was corny and flashy. (In real life, a statue of the Virgin has been seen to weep at St. Nicholas Orthodox Church in Chicago. In Eugene Izzi's *The Booster,* his punk gangster Teddy went there to pray that he wouldn't be wiped out for messing up a job by shooting a policeman.)

In the Father Blackie mysteries by Andrew Greeley, Chicago's Cardinal Archbishop Sean Cronin is a heroic person blessed with the common touch, whom Greeley says does not resemble any real cardinal living or dead. Cronin does not live in state at the mansion, but at Holy Name Rectory where he personally takes his turn at phone call duty, deals wisely and well with august personages of all kinds and shapes, and likes to tell Father Blackie to "See to it" when murder is involved.

Ralph McInerny's Cardinal in *Bishop as Pawn* was also both smart and affable when he discussed the kidnapping of Bishop Rooney with Father Dowling of St. Hilary's. Told that the ransom note demanded money to buy food for the poor, the Cardinal calmly said that he would give the equivalent in food, not cash, adding that such giving was not a new departure for the Archdiocese. He then suggested that Father Dowling and Police Captain Phil Keegan look for the maverick priest Ambrose Chirichi, who now operated out of a van in Old Town.

Walk west on North Avenue one block to State Parkway. Cross State, also the site of many elegant old mansions, to walk one more block west to Dearborn. In Charles Merrill Smith's *Reverend Randollph and the Unholy Bible,* the decaying mansion where old miser Johannes Humbrecht lived was somewhere near here. Since Humbrecht was a parishioner of the Loop Church of the Good Shepherd, Con Randollph, an ex-quarterback for the L.A. Rams, called on him, only to find him murdered. Unknown to everyone, Humbrecht was a direct descendant of Gutenberg and owned a Gutenberg Bible. A gangster known as "Mr. Jones" wanted one to give the Pope to buy his way into Heaven, so Mr. Jones kidnaped Randollph, thinking he had taken Humbrecht's missing Bible.

Turn left and walk south on Dearborn. Carl Sandburg Village is a block west of here between Clark and LaSalle, North Avenue and Division Street. Created by a massive 1960s urban renewal project, it contains highrises, lowrise apartments, and townhouses, surrounded by protective fencing which reminds some sardonic mystery writers of its mirror image, public housing's Cabrini-Green, due west at Sedgwick. (See Possible Side Trips.)

Go south one block on Dearborn to Burton. Cross Burton and walk to the middle of the block. On the west side of the street at 1424 N. Dearborn Parkway is a handsome '20s limestone Gothic church called St. Chrysostom's. It has a tower topped with a cross and there is a kind of quadrangle between the church itself and the parish house and offices. Except for the church office none of the doors are open on a weekday.

Built in 1894, the church itself is plain Early English style with wooden rafters and plastered walls, not at all glitzy. But St. Chrysostom's is a major Society church where very important people attend, wed, and are buried.

In Mignon G. Eberhart's *Hasty Wedding* south side heiress Dorcas Whipple married Jevan Locke at "St. Chrystofer's." But Dorcas took part in the elaborate wedding, presided over by a bishop, under protest because her boyfriend Ronald Drew had just been found murdered. During the brief ceremony the bride barely knew what was happening, then the bridal couple's limo drove back to the south side for a reception in the Whipple house in Hyde Park, followed by hordes of reporters. (See Walk 9.)

Walk past the church to Schiller and turn left on Schiller to return to State Parkway. There are any number of elegant mansions converted into apartments along here. Choose one you like for Marvel Leigh, the clever, conniving mistress of the governor-elect in Jay Robert Nash's *A Crime Story*. Leigh lived in one of those elegant turn-of-the-century mansions split into spacious apartments—with a canopy from entrance to street and a uniformed doorman.

In Joan Bard-Collins's short story "The Fowler Solution" Marge Blake had bought a vintage nineteenth-century townhouse on Schiller, where the neighborhood was quiet, not trendy, and the building affordable (not today). Blake bought the place with help from her ex-husband, real estate millionaire Harry Fowler, who owned a flashy Astor Street duplex. She ran her investigating business, CompSurch, from the English basement, lived on the first floor, and planned to rent the upper stories. Early one Monday morning Blake had a visitor called Rhonda Jean, who was Harry's latest wife, and built as well as her red Jag. Rhonda Jean came to hire Blake because she thought Harry was trying to kill her.

Turn right to go south on State Parkway to Banks Street. At 1340 State Parkway is the George S. Isham Mansion, built in French style in 1899 for the law partner of Abraham Lincoln's son Robert Todd Lincoln. Today it is better known as having been the home of Hugh Hefner who ran (and owned) the Playboy Club.

In Paul Engleman's *Catch a Fallen Angel* NYC P.I. Mark Renzler was hired to investigate the disappearance of an Angel (aka Bunny) called Sherri West. She had disappeared from Paradise, the club-mansion of Arnold Long where all the beautiful broads walked about nude.

In Sam Reaves's *Fear Will Do It,* there was a similar establishment run by Max Wetzel that published a magazine called *Maverick*. Wetzel was being blackmailed by cabbie Cooper MacLeish's girlfriend because he had killed a young hooker in Trinidad.

At the corner of Banks Street and State Parkway, look towards the lake. It is still lined with Victorian mansions, now expensive rental and condo units, but in the 1950s, Bill S. Ballinger in *Portrait in Smoke* described it as "a twilight fringe" of small rooms, studios, and tiny apartments, where the painters, musicians, and writers lived, together with the actors, radio people, young reporters, and newly-arrived secretaries and file clerks. Past Clark Street (now Carl Sandburg Village), the city again became dirty, filthy and vicious with grubby stores and bums.

Ballinger's gorgeous upwardly mobile Krassy Almauniski from Back of the Yards rented a room on Banks Street in an old brownstone with a high tower. Krassy paid six dollars a week for no cooking in her room and a bath down the hall, but in about six months, she had moved to a full-fledged apartment with a living room and a bath on east Delaware.

Walk one more block south on State Parkway to Goethe Street and cross State to the Ambassador East Hotel. Go into the main entrance and up to the elegant lobby, with its green and white Italian marble and crystal chandeliers. This is still sheer class and you will find the celebrities's haven, the Pump Room, with its famous Booth Number One.

In 1958 mystery moviemaker celebrity Alfred Hitchcock shot scenes from *North by Northwest* here, and the entire cast, including Cary Grant, stayed here, too. Many VIPs other than stage and screen stars have also been guests. Dr. Catherine Kenney and I once waited here all afternoon for Professor Carolyn H. Heilbrun (aka mystery writer Amanda Cross), who was flying in from New York, only to find out her plane had developed engine trouble and turned back. Like Marion Babson, Heilbrun hates to fly, which made it much worse.

In the basement you can make use of the restrooms and take the tunnel under State Street to go to the Ambassador West Hotel. There you come up in a comfortable wood-paneled English lounge that leads to the Guildhall, the Beau Nash, and the Sarah Siddons Dining Rooms.

In Stuart Kaminsky's *You Bet Your Life,* Hollywood P.I. Toby Peters, hired by Louis Mayer of Metro-Goldwyn-Mayer to stop the mob from disposing of Chico Marx for a bad gambling debt, came here to ask for help from his acquaintance Ian Fleming of the British Secret Service, future author of the James Bond thrillers. William F. Love in "Butler, Dabbler, Spy: Jeeves to Wimsey to Bond" suggested that Fleming "borrowed" James Bond from Wodehouse's Jeeves and Sayers's Lord Peter.

Fleming greeted Peters wearing a dark velvet smoking jacket. As they talked, they realized someone was lurking outside the room, opened the door, and gave chase up to the roof where Fleming slipped. He managed to hang on by his fingertips until Peters rescued him, debonair to the nearly bitter end.

In Michael W. Sherer's *An Option on Death,* writer Emerson Ward lived in a brownstone with a bay window across the street from the Ambassador East Hotel (across Goethe). Ward had just enjoyed a reunion with an old flame named Jessica Pearson when a stray bullet fired from the Ambassador East came through the bay window and killed her.

In Craig Rice's *The Wrong Murder,* newlyweds Helene and Jake Justus were sitting on the fire escape at the Ambassador East with her dad, George Brand, and a pitcher of martinis. George Brand had something important to say to them but he had forgotten what it was. Helene then drove him and his valet to Midway Airport, but got picked up for speeding and tossed in jail. Jake spent their wedding night first watching for Helene, then drinking with their next door neighbor, a gray haired Southern lady called Lulamay Yandry who mixed a cocktail with an incredible wallop.

The hotel has always been tops with theater people. Stage great Gertrude Lawrence stayed there and ate in Booth Number One ninety consecutive nights when she was playing in *Susan and God*. When she died, Booth One was draped in black for a week. In Leslie Charteris's *Call for the Saint,* actress Monica Varing, of a theatrical family like the Barrymores, was staying at the Ambassador East during a production. Simon Templar, aka the Saint, met Varing at the Pump Room for lunch the day after they met in the Loop alley. He ordered cocktails and sat back and enjoyed the usually expensive pleasure of gazing at her wonderful mutable face and the warm vitality that three generations of Varing had had. But the Saint worried that Varing, used to the limelight, would not be willing to play a lesser role in their search for a murderer.

In Arthur Maling's *Dingdong* ex-actor Mike Wiley, making commercials in Chicago for a living, took up again with his old love, Holly Simmons, now a major actress in town with a play. She was staying at the Ambassador East, where he came with her after the show. One night crossing Rush to walk north to the Ambassador East, Holly spotted Dingdong, a scary tough with long blond curls, tailing them. Outraged, Wiley went after him, past brownstones and into an alley where Dingdong disappeared, only to jump Wiley and knock him unconscious.

This walk ends at the Ambassador Hotels. You can stop for something to eat in the Pump Room or walk south on State Parkway to the crossroads of Rush/State and Cedar where you will find a variety of less expensive places, including Hamburger Hamlet, a Subway, the Original Pancake House, and Dublin's Pub at the corner of Maple and State. It has a big polished bar, TV, and leather-jacketed customers.

POSSIBLE SIDE TRIPS

Carl Sandburg Village: Clark to LaSalle Street, Division to North Avenue. Built as a result of massive Clark-LaSalle redevelopment between 1960 and 1975, creating a yuppie urban neighborhood of highrises, townhouses, and lowrise apartments. Mystery characters like Michael Raleigh's P.I. Paul Whelan compare this security-minded complex to a high-priced Cabrini-Green development.

Old Town: North Avenue and Wells Street. Since Old Town is an enclave all its own without any real connection to the Gold Coast, it is covered at the end of Walk 7. But you could go west on Geothe or Division Street to Wells Street and visit it when you finish this walk.

Cabrini-Green Public Housing Complex: Chicago Avenue to North Avenue, Sedgwick to the Chicago River. This is the public housing development most often mentioned in mysteries, but it is not safe to visit unless you are driving there with a native Chicagoan or have a police escort.

This area was once a port of entry area for Irish, Swedish, and Italian immigrants. The public housing development was built in the 1940s after the old tenements and workers' homes were demolished. Ironically, it was named for America's first saint and a governor of Illinois. St. Frances Xavier (Mother) Cabrini was a frail nun not unlike Mother Teresa, who founded Chicago Columbus Hospital and Mother Cabrini Hospital; Governor Dwight Green had been State's Attorney when the final fight to "get" Al Capone was launched.

In Fredric Brown's *The Fabulous Clipjoint,* this was the very seedy neighborhood where young Ed Hunter's family lived and where his drunken father was murdered in an alleyway.

In Michael Dymmoch's *The Man Who Understood Cats,* psychiatrist James Caleb rode one night with detective John Thinnes. They went together into Cabrini-Green to find the home of a youngster called Joey. They parked close to the building so snipers couldn't easily get at the car and walked up eight flights of stairs to find the boy's mother murdered.

In Bill Granger's *The Newspaper Murders,* drunken old pro reporter Francis X. Sweeney, working on a story about street gangs, headed on North Avenue away from O'Rourke's Public House, took Wells to Division, wandered west towards Cabrini-Green, turned at the edge of Old Town, went south on Larrabee, and finally went into an alley near Bughouse (Washington) Square where he was murdered with a bat.

According to Dennis L. Breo and William J. Martin's *The Crime of the Century*, while the entire Chicago Police force was conducting a massive manhunt, multiple nurse-murderer Richard Speck left the southeast side where he had committed his murders. He took a cab and asked to be dropped off at a parking lot at 1160 N. Sedgwick, right in front of a Cabrini-Green residential tower, where a witness later remembered seeing a white man get out of a cab and walk away. From there Speck walked east to Dearborn and Division and got a room in a flophouse called the Raleigh Hotel at 648 N. Dearborn. He stayed there several days, but the police finally came for him just after he had left for Skid Row on West Madison. Speck ended up in County Hospital's emergency room with self-inflicted knife wounds. (See Walk 10.)

Goose Island: North Branch of the Chicago River from about North Avenue to Chicago Avenue. Drive there or take a cab. Originally it was pasture, then it became a shipping and manufacturing area.

In Richard Engling's *Body Mortgage,* P.I. Gregory Blake's client Scott was hiding out from body mortgage creditors to whom he owed his organs. Blake took Scott by tunnel across the Chicago River and under Goose Island to Cabrini-Green (the tunnel probably was filled in after the Great Chicago Flood of 1992).

7

LINCOLN PARK/ DE PAUL WALK

BACKGROUND

The Lincoln Park neighborhood stretches along Lake Michigan from North Avenue to Diversey Parkway. Today it is considered one of the most desirable and expensive parts of the city, filled with historic districts of elegant old houses, restaurants, shops, and tree-lined streets, with Lincoln Park as its playground.

It started out as an immigrant neighborhood around North Avenue in the area now known as the Old Town Triangle. A largely German community, for years it was represented by Alderman Mathias "Paddy" Bauler, who ran the 43rd Ward from his saloon at North and Sedgwick. His most famous remark was that "Chicago ain't ready for reform."

To the north there are enclaves of handsome mansions and townhouses, DePaul University's campus encompassing the old McCormick Theological Seminary, and the trendy theater-restaurant-books-and-bars neighborhood at Halsted, Lincoln, and Fullerton Avenues.

The first major development occurred after the 1871 Chicago Fire when burned-out Chicagoans moved north. McCormick Seminary's arrival in the 1850s upgraded the atmosphere, and during the 1920s and '30s Lincoln Park remained a classy address. By the 1950s the city had declared it a blighted area and began a major urban renewal project. Like the major urban renewal projects carried out on the West Side and in Hyde Park, there was considerable liberal opposition, but under the leadership of the city's Urban Renewal Department, the community and developers came to an agreement and tore down or restored the old buildings and encouraged construction of the new, regentrifying the entire neighborhood.

By the 1970s DePaul University had bought the lovely campus of McCormick Seminary and begun an expansion program which continues today. Old Town with its many small frame houses boomed, too, becoming a popular tourist trap along Wells Street, but there are surprisingly few references to it in mysteries.

The greatest community asset is Lincoln Park, running north along the lakefront; it is the largest and busiest city park. Once a cemetery it was renamed for the assassinated president in 1865, but the graves were not all vacated before the Chicago Fire in 1871. Over 1,200 acres, much of which came from landfill, its landscaping, decoration, and institutions like the Chicago Historical Society, the Chicago Academy of Sciences, the Lincoln Park Zoo and the Conservatory were all added to the park over the next hundred years.

Getting to Lincoln Park is simple: take a Loop bus straight up Clark Street or drive yourself and park your car (by day) in the parking lots at the south end of Lincoln Park. There are also cabs about most of the time. The El runs farther west, near DePaul University where you can use the Fullerton stop.

LENGTH OF WALK: About 4 miles

You can do this walk in two parts, one day at a time, or make a day of it, stopping to eat at one of the places mentioned during the walk. The walk breaks down naturally into:

Lincoln Park: 2½ miles

De Paul: 1½ miles

See the map on page 205 for the boundaries of this walk and page 353 for a list of the books and detectives mentioned.

PLACES OF INTEREST

Biograph Theatre, 2433 N. Lincoln Avenue. Still shows movies. See the John Dillinger plaque on the alley side of the marquee. (One of very few gangster sites in Chicago publicly designated.) Call 348-4123.

Chicago Academy of Sciences, 2001 N. Clark Street at Armitage. Open daily 10:00 A.M.–5:00 P.M. Fee. Admission free on Mondays. Call 871-2668.

Chicago Historical Society, 1629 N. Clark, Open Mon.–Sat. 9:30 A.M.–4:30 P.M., Sun. noon–5:00 P.M. Fee. Admission free on Mondays. Call 642-4600.

Crilly Court, between Eugenie and St. Paul, Wells and North Park Avenues. Queen Anne enclave built by Daniel Crilly 1885–1893.

DePaul University, founded 1898 as St. Vincent College. Fullerton, Webster, Halsted, and Kenmore Avenues.

Lincoln Park Conservatory, 2400 N. Stockton Drive. Known as the Crystal Palace, it overlooks a formal French garden to the south and an English-style perennial garden on the west. Lovely shows at Christmas and Eastertime. Open daily 9:00 A.M.–5:00 P.M. Free. Call 294-4770.

Lincoln Park Zoo, 2200 N. Cannon Drive. Restrooms in Elephant House and Giraffe House. See especially The Great Ape House. Free. Call 294-4660. Open daily 9:00 A.M.–5:00 P.M.

McCormick Row House District, 1882–1889, faculty housing designed by Colton & Sons. Private street surrounding grassy square inside DePaul University Campus. Houses face Fullerton and Belden, Chalmers Place.

Piper's Alley, 1618 N. Wells (at North Avenue). Began as Piper family bakery in 1880s, became a cobblestoned mall in 1960s.

St. Valentine's Day Massacre garage site. 2122 N. Clark Street.

Second City, 1616 N. Wells Street. World-famous improvisational theater begun in Hyde Park during 1959. (See Walk 9.) Famous alumni include Mike Nichols, Elaine May, John Belushi, Alan Arkin, Dan Aykroyd, and Gilda Radner. Call 337-3992.

Victory Gardens/Body Politic, 2257–2261 N. Lincoln Avenue. Two off-Loop theaters share the building. Call 871-3000.

Zoo Rookery (Lily Pond). Fullerton Parkway between Stockton Drive and Cannon Drive. Natural habitat for birds.

TOURS

Richard T. Crowe's Tour of Haunted and Legendary Places. Covers major Chicago legends like Resurrection Mary, Indian burial grounds and other likely places for spooks. Tours depart Sat.–Sun. noon, Fri.–Sat. 7:00 P.M. from DePaul University's Lincoln Park Campus. Fee. Call 1-708-499-0300.

PLACES TO EAT

Places too numerous to list, including vendors in Lincoln Park, fast food places. The group below includes some mentioned in mysteries as well as others at good stopping points on your walk.

Note: A number of these places do *not* open until mid or late afternoon so plan accordingly.

Big Shoulders Cafe, Chicago Historical Society, Clark Street at North Avenue. Orange terra-cotta gateway from the Stockyards National Bank, designed by Holabird and Root. Original Chicago motifs: cow, horse, cowboy, and commission merchant.

Cafe Brauer, 2021 N. Stockton Drive in Lincoln Park. Designed by Prairie School Architect Dwight H. Perkins in 1908 and rehabbed in 1989, it has a cafeteria, ice cream parlor, restrooms, and public telephones.

Cafe Equinox, 2300 N. Lincoln (at Belden). Coffeehouse with old-fashioned drugstore ambiance. Great place for streetwatching.

John Barleycorn Memorial Pub, 658 W. Belden (at Lincoln). This old saloon fronted as a Chinese laundry during Prohibition.

Red Lion Pub, 2446 N. Lincoln Avenue (across from Biograph Theatre). Genuine British beer, Cornish pasties, steak-and-kidney pies. (See *MRWG: England; MRWG: London.*)

That Steak Joynt, 1610 N. Wells Street. Stick-to-the-ribs food; package deals with The Second City next door.

Wise Fools Pub, 2270 N. Lincoln (at Belden). Small, dark bar with live blues seven nights a week.

LINCOLN PARK/DE PAUL WALK

Begin your walk at North Avenue and Clark Street, outside the Chicago Historical Society. A visit here makes an excellent beginning or end to your walk, letting you see how Chicago grew. Founded in 1856, the Society has been documenting Chicago's social and cultural development ever since. In 1920 the Society bought caramel-candy maker Charles Gunther's eccentric personal collection, which included not only the table where Grant and Lee ended the Civil War, but Libby prison (part of whose walls still stand on the site of the Coliseum at 15th and Wabash). (See Walk 8.) Like all "family" museums it also has oddments, among them John Dillinger's death mask and Admiral Dewey's loving cup, made of 70,000 dimes.

The Chicago Fire began at the O'Leary barn on DeKoven Street, but the Chicago Historical Society is *not* convinced that the O'Leary's cow started the fire by kicking over a lantern. (See Walk 10.) Susan Hoelschen, a CHS volunteer who plays the part of Mrs. O'Leary, says that the legend was nothing but media hype to sell newspapers. But Kenan Heise and Mark Frazel in *Hands on Chicago* say the cow *may* have been responsible after all.

The CHS is probably the best place to locate a Lincoln authority, so this is the place Lieutenant Joe Leaphorn called in Tony Hillerman's *Sacred Clowns* when he needed information about the Lincoln canes from an expert called Bundy.

The Society's gift shop has an excellent selection of books on Chicago history and architecture, as well as Chicago classics like Nelson Algren's *Chicago: City on the Make,* James T.

Farrell's *Studs Lonigan* series, and Richard Wright's *Native Son*. Although Al Capone is not featured in its exhibits, there are, inevitably, some gangsterland mementos.

Across North Avenue is the new building of the Latin School of Chicago, founded in 1888. In Michael Cormany's *Lost Daughter* P.I. Dan Kruger, a skinny '60s type who was trying to locate a missing teenager, was shanghaied by two hulks called Angelo and Bern. When they stopped at the Clark Street light, Kruger hit one in the mouth and somersaulted out of the car in front of the Chicago Historical Society. He saw a distinguished-looking man in a pinstripe suit standing in front of the Latin School and crossed the street to ask him for a Valium!

After visiting the Chicago Historical Society, come out on Clark. Across Clark is the brick Dwight L. Moody Memorial Church, named for a famous Chicago evangelist. The church is designed like the Hagia Sophia in Istanbul.

Turn right to walk to the corner of Clark, LaSalle, and Lincoln Park. On your right you pass the Couch Tomb, the only one left when the city cemetery was vacated to create Lincoln Park. The chief mystery is who beside Ira Couch, who owned the Tremont Hotel, is inside? You can also catch a glimpse of the bronze standing Lincoln by Augustus Saint-Gaudens, an artist who had actually seen Illinois's favorite son. There is a pedestrian underpass beneath LaSalle Drive just beyond the Lincoln statue. It will take you across the heavy traffic without waiting for a light and is popular with park walkers.

In Eugene Izzi's *Bad Guys* undercover cop Jimbo, pretending to work for the mob, took his Doberman Sparky on a three-mile run east to the lakefront, using the underpass to Lincoln Park Zoo. In Michael Sherer's *An Option on Death*, freelancer Emerson Ward walked home through the park to his apartment across from the Ambassador East Hotel. (See Walk 6.) At North Avenue Ward ducked into the pedestrian subway where he caught a man following him. They had a fight and the cops arrested Ward.

In James Michael Ullman's *Lady on Fire*, P.I. Julian Forbes went through the Lincoln Park underpass near the Historical

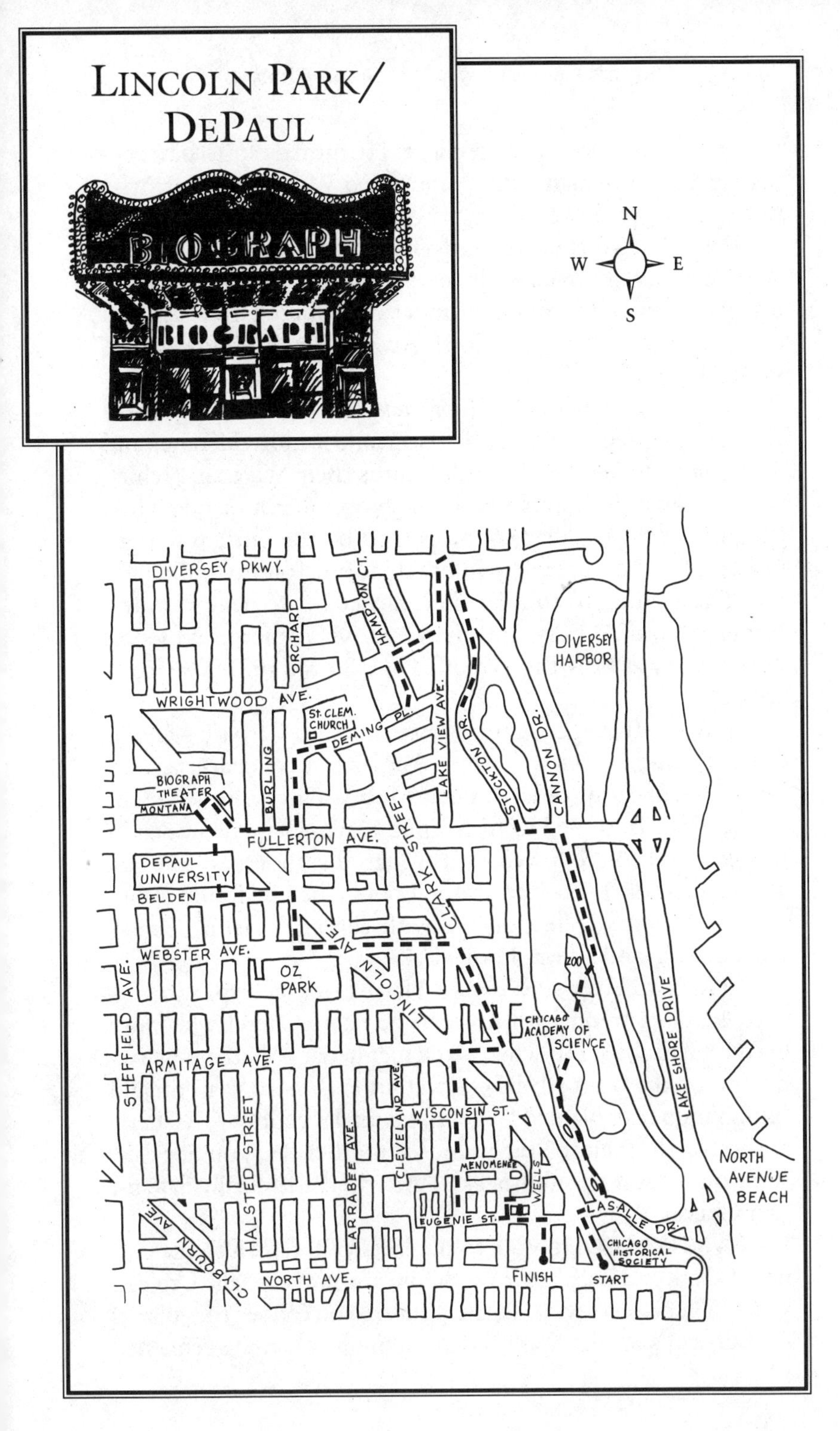
LINCOLN PARK/
DEPAUL
BIOGRAPH
BIOGRAPH
N
W
E
S
DIVERSEY PKWY.
HAMPTON CT.
ORCHARD
DIVERSEY
HARBOR
WRIGHTWOOD AVE.
ST. CLEM.
CHURCH
DEMING PL.
LAKE VIEW AVE.
STOCKTON DR.
CANNON DR.
BURLING
BIOGRAPH
THEATER
MONTANA
FULLERTON AVE.
STREET
DEPAUL
UNIVERSITY
BELDEN
CLARK
AVE.
WEBSTER AVE.
OZ
PARK
LINCOLN
ZOO
SHEFFIELD AVE.
CHICAGO
ACADEMY OF
SCIENCE
ARMITAGE AVE.
LAKE SHORE DRIVE
CLEVELAND AVE.
WISCONSIN ST.
HALSTED STREET
LARRABEE AVE.
MENOMENEE
WELLS
NORTH
AVENUE
BEACH
LASALLE DR.
EUGENIE ST.
CLYBOURN AVE.
CHICAGO
HISTORICAL
SOCIETY
NORTH AVE.
FINISH
START

Society to meet a prospective client. He turned out to be a dapper elderly gentleman with a cane called Walter St. Clair, who hired Forbes to find a missing girl called Iris Dean.

Four blocks east of you across Lake Shore Drive is the North Avenue Beach. If you have time, detour east to Lake Michigan, using the pedestrian viaduct under the Outer Drive. As you come out you will see the North Avenue Beach House, which looks like an ocean liner.

In Frank Gruber's *The Gamecock Murders* (aka *The Scarlet Feather*) con man and muscle man team Johnny Fletcher and Sam Cragg were taking a stroll (minus their overcoats, which were in pawn) in Lincoln Park one November morning when they noticed a Cadillac coupe parked by the curb and a girl heading for the water. She jumped in, but Johnny pulled her out. She hit him, he smacked her, carried her to her car, found her name and address, and delivered her to her Gold Coast home. She was Lois Tancred of 1498 Lake Shore Drive, a society deb.

In Bill S. Ballinger's gritty version of Vera Caspary's *Laura*, called *Portrait in Smoke,* Danny April ran a collection agency he'd bought from old Clarence Moon. One summer night Danny walked to the North Avenue beach where he noticed a gorgeous girl and followed her through the underpass to Clark where she took a streetcar for the Loop. Then he found a clipping in Moon's collection file with the girl's name—Krassy Almauniski—and he was hooked.

In Richard Hyer's *Riceburner,* Harry Dane, an explosives expert, had a reunion with his teenage flame Cheryl who once lived on Larrabee. But when Dane met her at a Vietnamese restaurant on the far north side, a riceburner (bomb) went off and the Chicago cops blamed Dane. In his final meeting with Cheryl at the North Avenue Beach House, another "Saigon Special" went off, causing headlines like "Are the Parks Really Safe for Our Children?"

If you detoured to walk to the lakefront, return to the corner of Clark and LaSalle Drive. Before you cross LaSalle Drive to Lincoln Park, look west. In the distance you can see the spire of St. Michael's Roman Catholic Church. Only its walls remained standing after the 1871 Chicago Fire, which burned all the way north to Fullerton and sent residents fleeing into Lincoln Park.

At this corner to the left you also can see highrises where Arthur Maling's P.I. Calvin Bix in *Lover and Thief* could stand to survey the neighborhood. He saw the eastern edge that bordered the park, the marinas, and Lake Michigan, lined with highrise buildings almost as classy now as they were a generation ago, when they were built. West of them, buildings that used to house Rotarians with their PTA wives and children now house a mixed bag of singles and two-income couples from many walks of life, including those who get nervous whenever they see a squad car.

Cross LaSalle Drive to Lincoln Park. Turn right to find Stockton and then walk north to the statue of Robert Sieur de LaSalle, one of the French explorers who came through the Chicago portage in the seventeenth century en route to the Mississippi. Stay on Stockton Drive which meanders north through Lincoln Park to Diversey. Across the park on the west side of Clark Street you will see a highrise called Eugenie Terrace, next to the shopping complex that has Bigsby and Kruthers, Ann Taylor, and other shops. (Just north of Eugenie, LaSalle Street crosses Clark and enters the park as LaSalle Drive.)

Other highrise condos are visible at regular intervals because this is *the* place to live. In Michael J. Katz's *Murder Off the Glass,* his nice Jewish boy Andy Sussman, who did radio broadcasts on WCGO for the Chicago Flames from the Stadium, was suspended for swearing on the air when the lights went out. (It turned out someone had shot the color man—an old sports has-been—during the blackout.) Sussman had a Lincoln Park condo, but he still used his Northbrook Bar Mitzvah crowd as an old boys' network. He hired Murray Glick, whose P.I. agency was in the Northbrook Court shopping mall, to solve the case, but he was furious when Glick easily picked the lock of his expensively "secure" building.

Lincoln Park fills one thousand acres of lakefront land and is the most popular park in the city for mystery writers and their characters. It opened officially in 1868 when the City Cemetery vacated it, but in 1871 it still had half-opened graves, many of which were used for shelter from the Chicago Fire. Its lagoons were a part of the Burnham Plan of 1909.

Surprisingly enough, mystery characters often head for Lincoln Park in lousy weather. P.I. Paul Pine in Howard Browne's *Halo in Brass* drove north through Lincoln Park at night; its trees and bushes were cold and lonely under the moon and Lake Michigan's surf pounded like heavy artillery. He was tailed by young Susan Griswald, whose stepmother was a prime suspect in a murder he was investigating.

Walk along Stockton Drive looking for big trees or park benches to dump a body. Craig Rice's sleuths use it frequently. In Craig Rice's *The Corpse Steps Out* Jake Justus and Helene Brand brought a murdered client from the Wrigley Building's CBS studios to Lincoln Park at dusk and left him on a park bench. In *The Lucky Stiff* Jake and Helene Justus and their pal John J. Malone met at night in Lincoln Park where they saw the ghost of Anna Marie St. Clair, executed for the murder of gangster Big Joe Childers. In *My Kingdom for a Hearse* Jake and Malone dumped the body of model Delora Deanne there.

In Stuart Kaminsky's *You Bet Your Life,* minor mobster Gino Servi, who looked a lot like Chico Marx (Toby Peters' client), was stuffed into the trunk of a friendly cabdriver who was showing P.I. Peters the sights. They deposited Servi's body on a bench in Lincoln Park for the police.

Next you come to the Farm-in-the-Zoo, which you may explore, then return to Stockton. Cross Lester Fisher Drive (named for the former head of Lincoln Park Zoo). You are behind the Chicago Academy of Sciences and coming up on the South Pond and Cafe Brauer at 2021 N. Stockton Drive.

Just before you get to the Cafe, you pass the Comfort Station, an 1888 cottage with restroom facilities. It makes a good spot for the mysterious disappearance of Tony Wilde, who ran the trendy nightclub called the Wilde Place in Edward D. Hoch's "The Theft of the Overdue Library Book." Wilde always took his German Shepherd Bruno for protection, but this morning Bruno slipped up.

Built by Prairie School architect Dwight H. Perkins in 1908, Cafe Brauer has a closed central pavilion two stories high and two open loggias, made of red brick with a green tile roof. It was rehabbed in 1989 and once again serves snacks or lunch in its cafeteria and ice cream parlor. It also has public phones and restrooms.

In Bill Granger's *The Newspaper Murders*, on a snowy January day Detective Karen Kovac and Sergeant Terry Flynn walked to Lincoln Park. They threw marshmallows at the polar bears in their outside cages, then ate hot dogs they bought from a stand near Cafe Brauer.

In Michael Raleigh's *A Body in Belmont Harbor,* P.I. Paul Whelan came there and ate lunch outside, enjoying the effect of one of Chicago's little-known resources on his bruised psyche: no exhaust fumes and pigeon guano. Then Whelan, who lived and worked in Uptown, walked all the way north past Belmont Harbor's Chicago Yacht Club.

Immediately west of Lincoln Park, the north/south street is no longer Clark Street but ritzy Lincoln Park West, a street with gorgeous modern highrises. In Paul Engleman's *Catch a Fallen Angel,* the mansion of *Playboy*-like *Paradise Magazine* was located there. Called the Garden of Eden, or just Eden, it was ruled by the Arnold Longs, father and son. An opulent pad, it had a huge foyer featuring a reception desk shaped like a fig leaf.

In Mark Zubro's *Sorry Now* the murderer had found the police snitch, Wilmer Pinsakowski, a homeless bum, sleeping in Lincoln Park. The bum had seen the murder and threatened to tell, so he ended up dead in the Chicago River.

Past Cafe Brauer on Stockton you come to the south end of the Lincoln Park Zoo (the main entrance is on Cannon Drive). The major zoo buildings were built in Georgian Revival '20s style, with habitats that allow the animals indoor and outdoor quarters and greater visibility for us. The Zoo occupies over 35 acres and is open every day in the year.

Walking north you pass the Waterfowl Lagoon and to your right is the Small Animal House, or Primate House, now called the Helen Brach Primate House because it was rehabbed by her foundation. Helen Brach is one of Chicago's real life celebrity mysteries. The widow of the head of Brach Candy who loved animals and automobiles disappeared in 1977. Her body has never been found, but her death was just linked to a rare horse racket which caused her murder.

Next you come to the Great Ape House, which is brand new with no heating problems whatsoever. But in Robert J. Campbell's *The 600 Pound Gorilla,* the Zoo's heating system was not working so the mayor made Jimmy Flannery, who worked for Sewers, take Babe to the Paradise Baths in his west-side precinct near the Chicago Stadium. Babe was the city's darling, outpolling the mayor in popularity. When Babe was accused of killing a man, Flannery saved her bacon. The scenario is like the one in Aaron and Charlotte Elkins's Agatha Award-winning short mystery "Nice Gorilla." Chicago's beloved gorilla was really Bushman, now stuffed and on display at the Field Museum (See Walk 1.)

Outside the Small Animal House go left to the Reptile House. In Eugene Izzi's *The Take,* safesman (thief) Fabe Falletti and his childhood buddy, Chicago narcotics cop Jimmy Capone, set a trap there for some drug dealing mobsters on Christmas Eve.

In Robert J. Campbell's *Hipdeep in Alligators,* Jimmy Flannery, now dealing with alligators found in the city sewer system, consulted Reptile House expert Dr. Angela Luger. He even took her to look at the body in the morgue, which she agreed had been chewed by an alligator.

To your right there is a memorial statue for Chicago newspaperman and poet Eugene Field. It has a bronze fairy leaning over two sleeping children, with Field's famous poem, "Wynken, Blynken and Nod" inscribed below. Many of Field's newspaper colleagues were also mystery writers, including Harry Stephen Keeler, Charles MacArthur, Bill Ballinger, Vincent Starrett, Fredric Brown, Howard Browne, James Michael Ullman, and William P. McGivern.

Many sleuths found the Zoo a restful habitat. In Arthur Maling's *Bent Man,* Walter Jackson, an ex-professional ball player who was barred from the sport, was worried about his missing teenage son, so he walked to the Zoo to see how baby elephant Rosalie was doing.

In Thomas McCall's *A Wide and Capable Revenge,* detective

Nora Callum, a one-legged widow, took her daughter Meg to Lincoln Park Zoo for some quality time. She had parked in a no parking zone, but when Meg asked if this was police business, moved their car. The Zoo was as jammed as the beaches and parks and the heat made the ape and lion houses smell.

In *A Body in Belmont Harbor,* Michael Raleigh's Whelan, waiting for his client Mrs. Fairs who lived in a fancy highrise on Lincoln Park West, went to the Zoo. It was a very hot day and the lion was a lifeless pile of hair and fur, one paw hanging down over a rock staring into space.

In Barbara Gregorich's *Dirty Proof* P.I. Frank Dragovic did a daily five-mile run through Lincoln Park to Diversey Parkway. But after his client Suzanne Quering was arrested, Dragovic got drunk and went to Lincoln Park to feed the brown bears Brick (Jack Brickhouse) and Kup (Irv Kupcinet).

In Michael A. Dymmoch's *The Man Who Understood Cats,* psychiatrist James Caleb attended a Friends of the Zoo benefit gala with drinks and hors d'oeuvres, a small orchestra, and "everybody who was anybody" being interviewed on TV. Caleb even saw Detective John Thinnes, who was investigating the murder of Caleb's client, studying the snow leopards.

Turn right to walk to the Zoo's main entrance on Cannon Drive. It overlooks the lagoon to the east which stretches north to Diversey Harbor. In James Michael Ullman's *Lady on Fire,* P.I. Julian Forbes and his associate Curley hoped to get Morris Maxwell, a scion of old Chicago money, and wily old Walter St. Clair to meet on the shore of the Lincoln Park lagoon. Curley thought he could pick up their conversation there with a shotgun microphone.

Go left (north) along Cannon Drive past the Zoo Rookery to Fullerton Parkway. In Engleman's *Catch a Fallen Angel* P.I. Mark Renzler and his client, *Paradise* publisher Arnold Long, got a ransom note for kidnaped "Angel" Sherri West. It told them Sherri was alive, but to get her back would cost $250,000. The drop was to be made by the bird sanctuary on Fullerton.

When you reach Fullerton Parkway, turn left to walk back to Stockton Drive. There you will find the Lincoln Park Conservatory, which was inspired by London's great Crystal Palace built for the Exhibition of 1856. (See *Mystery Readers Walking Guide: London.*) It is surrounded by a French formal garden and an English perennial garden, both there since the 1880s.

To your left across from the park is Lakeview Avenue, where you can see some elegant older buildings mixed with mansions. One handsome old place with a penthouse would do for the '20s skyscraper apartment building "on Diversey" where financier Thomas Chance's mistress, Madge Quigley, lived in Kirby Williams's *The C.V.C. Murders.* The redbrick building at 420 W. Wrightwood (the corner of Lakeview) would work, too. Chance was a member of the Citizens Vigilance Committee dedicated to eradicating Chicago's gangsters, but Quigley's absent husband had mob connections, which gave him a conflict of interest.

Cross Fullerton to Stockton and keep going north on Stockton past the North Pond. This is the part of the park where everyone does his or her jogging or biking. By day it's full of moms or nannies, small kids, dogs, and roller skaters—fulfilling its claim to be Chicago's Central Park. (See *MRWG: NY.*)

In Jay Robert Nash's *A Crime Story,* crime columnist Jack Journey picked up his girlfriend Eden and they drove to Lincoln Park for serenity (there had been four murders related to the family of Governor-Elect Maitland Ashmore). As they walked along the bridle path, Journey told Eden the famous story about Samuel J. "Nails" Morton (née Markovitz), one of Dion O'Banion's gang. (See Walk 4.) Morton died in Lincoln Park in 1922 when his horse kicked him. In revenge O'Banion's boys rented the same horse, brought it here, and shot it.

In Sara Paretsky's *Blood Shot,* V.I. Warshawski took Peppy jogging but left the dog near the lagoon to run toward the lake where she met some South-Side hoods in slickers. They snatched her and drove her south to dump her in a famous wetland known as Dead Stick Pond, full of murder memories from the famous Loeb and Leopold case. Nathan Leopold was a bird watcher who often went there. (See Walk 9.)

In Marc Davis's *Dirty Money* P.I. Frank Wolf had arranged to meet Erwin Osvald, Jr., at Lincoln Park at high noon, where he had to watch him eat bean sprout sandwiches. Abel Nockerman was the senior Osvald's broker so Wolf hoped Jr. knew something about the Nockerman killing.

In Raleigh's *Death in Uptown*, Paul Whelan went to the park to sit under an enormous old cottonwood and meditate about his growing relationship with his client Jean Agee, whose brother he was trying to find.

About halfway between Fullerton and Diversey to the west you see Columbus Hospital at 2520 N. Lakeview, but it is not far enough north to be Beth Israel Hospital in Paretsky's mysteries where Max Loewenthal is director and Dr. Lotty Herschel is on staff. (Paretsky probably meant either St. Joseph's Hospital at 2900 Lake Shore Drive or Weiss Memorial Hospital at 4646 N. Marine Drive.)

Lincoln Park is long and narrow, following the lakeshore all the way to Hollywood. There is a marker telling you that the edge of the sidewalk is the original shoreline of Lake Michigan. (Like the Dutch, Chicagoans have always been good at claiming back land from the sea.) The North Pond is to your right and east of it the lagoon runs north into Diversey Harbor. Just before you reach Diversey Parkway, there is a pedestrian underpass from Lakeview, presumably the one V.I. Warshawski used for her daily lakefront runs with Peppy.

At the corner of Lakeview and Diversey Parkway is the Elks National Memorial Building, with a circular dome. Built in 1926 in honor of the Elks who died in World War I, it is the city's most elegant memorial. Its colonnaded rotunda has a frieze carved with allegories of war and peace, appropriate symbols for mystery and murder. Many of Chicago's contemporary fictional P.I.s are 'Nam vets, cynical and tough, but pushovers for strays.

You pass the Alexander Hamilton Monument to reach Diversey Parkway. (There are too many monuments and statues in Lincoln Park to name them all.) In Paretsky's *Bitter Medicine,* V.I. commented that Diversey was the northernmost boundary of the Lincoln Park yuppies with their condo conversions and wine bars and designer running clothes. However, V.I. used the "thank you" money she got from mob capo Don Pasquale in *Killing Orders* to buy a co-op on Racine near Lincoln. Those streets meet at Diversey about a mile west of here, so V.I. is on the edge of yuppiedom herself. V.I.'s original apartment, which was destroyed by fire, was farther north past Belmont on Halsted.

In Barbara Gregorich's *Dirty Proof,* murder suspect Suzanne Quering, accused of shoving her former lover, *Tribune* executive Ralph Basingame, into the presses, lived in a highrise on Diversey Parkway. Quering only had one large room and a tiny kitchen, but when P.I. Dragovic visited her she told him the building was going condo.

Turn left on Diversey Parkway to walk to the corner of Lakeview Avenue. Cross Lakeview and turn left to walk one block to Wrightwood. Then turn right to walk west on Wrightwood and cross Pine Grove (one block long). The Second Church of Christ Scientist is across the street. Walk one more block to Hampden Court, where on the southwest corner you will find the huge 1896 limestone palace of Frances J. Dewes, a German brewer, at 503 W. Wrightwood. It makes the Gilded Age seem real with its exuberant Old World splendor. It has a high mansard roof and a fancy wrought-iron balcony supported by two caryatids—one male, one female—combined with classical columns. There are other elegant mansions on the block, worthy of the claustrophobic wealth described in Mignon Eberhart's mysteries like *The Cases of Susan Dare.*

Turn left to walk south on Hampden Court past some ugly modern houses and handsome old ones. One refurbished Victorian, recently for sale for half a million dollars, would be perfect for Eberhard's Hattericks in *The Glass Slipper.* (See Walk 6.)

Turn right to walk west along Deming Place to Clark Street. Clark is a typical Chicago commercial strip in pre-mall days. There are all sorts of fast food places where you can get some coffee and use the restrooms, as well as odd shops and dirty old office buildings, mixed with trendier places.

In Nash's *A Crime Story,* columnist Jack Journey had his office on north Clark Street in an old white building. The small entrance had a cracked marble floor, an elevator that only held three people, and loitering drunks. Journey's second-floor office was drab but had more crime background materials than most major police departments. After Journey started nosing about the murder of the governor-elect's son, he heard someone in the hallway, then two loads from a double barreled shotgun shredded his door frame and threw Journey against the desk.

In Marc Davis's *Dirty Money,* P.I. Frank Wolf had an office south on Clark near Fullerton on the second floor of a no-nonsense building without ornament or distinction. Wolf had a small steel desk and chrome couch, and no secretary, but he had a Smith & Wesson hidden under the desk and a homemade button to hit with his knee that made a light blink at the deli on the corner.

After stopping for a snack or looking around, cross Clark Street to walk west on Deming Place past Geneva Terrace to Orchard. On the north side of Deming there are more grand old houses, some divided into apartments, while on the south side there are '20s style highrises.

On the south side of Deming, there are several Art Deco buildings with penthouses. In Jonathan Latimer's *The Lady in the Morgue,* P.I. Bill Crane went to Deming Place to a penthouse party. Crane picked up a girl in the case and drove her around Lincoln Park until she admitted who she was. (There were several missing girls, some dead.)

Keep walking west past Ronald McDonald House to Orchard Place. Across Geneva Terrace you pass the Wieboldt mansion on the south side of the street at 639 W. Deming and the Jacob Gross House at 632 Deming on the north side.

At the northeast corner of Orchard Place is limestone St. Clement's Roman Catholic Church at 642 W. Deming Place. Its redbrick parochial school is across Orchard. Twin-towered St. Clement's is not open on a weekday unless you go around the corner to ring the office bell. Built in 1918, it is considered one of the handsomest churches in Chicago with a Byzantine dome and an interior embellished with marble and mosaics, and its bells dominate the neighborhood.

In Andrew Greeley's *The Patience of a Saint,* St. Clement's was the parish church of columnist Red Kane, and his children went to its parochial school. Perhaps if you mentioned having read about Red Kane's vision—which he called a "swat from the cosmic designated hitter" here on Christmas Eve, it might help get you a look inside.

Although it's neither shabby nor redbrick, St. Clement's is about the right place for twin-towered St. Stephen's Roman Catholic Church on a residential street near North Clark Street in Sam Reaves's *Fear Will Do It*. Cabbie MacLeish and "Stumps," a World War II vet, were drinking buddies. Stumps lived in the church basement, so he let MacLeish and his girl Diana crash there.

Turn left on Orchard to walk south to Fullerton. You are in the Arlington and Roslyn Park District, two tiny tree-shaded blocks of lovely Victorian townhouses. In "A Wolfe on Our Doorstep" Robert Goldsborough suggested that this is where Nero Wolfe would live if he moved to Chicago, which is very unlikely.

At Orchard and Fullerton you will see the world-famous Children's Memorial Hospital on the far corner. (The hospital actually occupies many buildings in the area.) This hospital specializes in solving mysteries about desperately ill or abused children.

Turn right (or west) on Fullerton and walk to Burling, cross Burling, and go one more block to the complicated three-way corner of Lincoln, Fullerton, and Halsted. Across Halsted is the Lincoln Park campus of DePaul University. Once a commuter college, it now has a handsome residential campus, having bought the old McCormick Theological Seminary buildings, and added others of its own, so you will find this a center of student-yuppiedom.

Lincoln Avenue goes on the diagonal northwest, intersecting here with both Halsted and Fullerton. Cross Halsted, turn right to walk north on Lincoln past a tiny park. Cross a small alley to the Biograph Theatre at 2433 N. Lincoln Avenue. It has a marker stating that it is a landmark, but the sign does not say why!

The reason is one all murder/mystery buffs know: on July 22, 1934, bank robber John Dillinger, hiding out nearby, went to a movie called *Manhattan Melodrama* with his landlady, the notorious Anna Sage (the lady in red). She fingered Dillinger for the FBI and Chicago police to keep from being deported, and Dillinger was gunned down in the alley you just crossed. Some passersby were hit, while others dipped handkerchiefs in Dillinger's blood for souvenirs. Dillinger's death mask is currently on display at the Chicago Historical Society.

There are also as many references to Dillinger in Chicago mysteries as there are to Jake Lingle and Al Capone. In Michael Raleigh's *A Body in Belmont Harbor,* Uptown P.I. Paul Whelan was tailing Rick Vosic up Lincoln Avenue until Vosic parked half a block from the Biograph Theatre. As Whelan waited, he could see into the alley where John Dillinger had been shot up by police and FBI agents some fifty years ago.

In Gregorich's *Dirty Proof,* P.I. Frank Dragovic accused client Suzanne Quering of wanting him to play Dillinger (i.e., get shot for her). In Edith Skom's *The Mark Twain Murders,* FBI art authority Gil Bailey, investigating the disappearance of books from Midwestern University's library and the murder of a grad student in the stacks, found himself daydreaming about working with Houlihan, who went all the way back to Dillinger days. In *True Crime* Max Allan Collins maintained the legend that it was not John Dillinger who was shot. But in Collins's mystery *Kill Your Darlings* mystery writer Mallory took the Chicago Crime Tour, where, tooling along Lincoln Avenue, the driver pointed out the site of John Dillinger's death, the Biograph Theatre.

Just north of here on Lincoln Avenue you would find used book heaven, better known as Booksellers Row at 2445 N. Lincoln, as well as Wax Trax and the Children's Bookstore. Across the street used to be the Guild Bookstore, mentioned in Michael Cormany's *Red Winter,* where you could get political, art, and literary books as well as folk records. Farther up the street at 2470 Lincoln is Earl's Pub, descended from the old Earl of Old Town where folk song artists like the late Steve Goodman and Bonnie Koloc performed.

Cross Lincoln at Montana Street to walk back down Lincoln to Halsted. You go past the 3 Penny Cinema at 2424 N. Lincoln and the Red Lion Pub, which serves authentic shepherd's pie, scones, fish and chips, and beer. It's a good place to stop if you're hungry, and on occasion they sponsor "Twilight Tales," readings by local mystery writers like Barbara D'Amato and Hugh Holton. (There are many other places, including Clarke's Pancake House and Restaurant which shares the building with the Biograph Theatre.)

Go by Uncle Dan's Army and Navy Store to the corner of Lincoln and Halsted where there is a Thai restaurant, the nearest thing to a Korean restaurant around there. In Nash's *A Crime Story* porn photographer Hamilcar Ball lived on Lincoln over a Korean restaurant. Realizing that Ball had a vital negative of the murder of the governor-elect's son, Jack Journey wangled his way into the cheap, dirty place which was filled with expensive photo equipment, evidence that Ball had been into blackmail. Journey came back later to find Ball dead in his own wet vat.

At Fullerton/Lincoln/Halsted you have gone 1 mile from Diversey Parkway and 2½ from North Avenue. This is a good place to stop and eat or to end this walk for the day. You can easily get a bus back to North Avenue or the Loop on Halsted or take the El a block west.

DePaul

From the Fullerton/Lincoln/Halsted intersection, walk west on Fullerton along the north side of the DePaul University Lincoln Park Campus. (For the Loop Campus see Walk 2.) Founded as St. Vincent's College in 1898 and renamed DePaul in 1907, this campus had only two big buildings until it bought the McCormick Seminary campus east of the El in 1973. More development in the '80s made it more of a residential campus, and in 1992 the university closed a block of Seminary Avenue to create a quadrangle.

As you walk along Fullerton you can see the Fullerton El Stop ahead of you. In Bill Granger's *The El Murders,* the Humboldt Park gang riding the El got off here and waited for two young gays who worked at the Board of Trade. After jumping the pair, the gang murdered one. Later one of the gang tracked down the survivor, Brandon Cade, who lived just off Sheffield north of DePaul University.

In Paretsky's *Bitter Medicine,* Dr. Lotty Herschel's storefront clinic was on Damen near Seeley, west of DePaul University. There were demonstrations led by Dieter Monkfish of IckPiff (the Illinois Committee to Protect the Fetus) and V.I. Warshawski's neighbor Mr. Contreras brought some old union buddies to protect the clinic. But Contreras got jailed, so V.I. had to spring him. Lotty Herschel lived on Sheffield in a five-room walk up on the fringes of Uptown, by choice, not need.

Turn left at the Fullerton entrance to DePaul University and enter the campus through the old wrought-iron McCormick gate. You pass buildings of various periods. To your left are the charming McCormick Row Houses, built in 1882 to help provide more income for the seminary and housing for its faculty. Now a historic district, the redbrick row is in its own square, like a private London park or the Chelsea campus of General Theological Seminary in New York. (See *MRWG: London; MRWG:NY.*) The Presbyterian Seminary opened in Indiana, but in 1859 Cyrus McCormick gave them $100,000 to move to Chicago and locate here. It was renamed McCormick Seminary after his death. Some of the gray Gothic buildings date from the late 1920s, but the original academic buildings on Halsted were demolished during the 1960s. In 1973 McCormick Seminary moved to Hyde Park, selling its remaining buildings to DePaul and the houses to private owners.

In Michael J. Katz's *Murder Off the Glass,* radio sports commentator Andy Sussman drove to DePaul University where the Chicago Flames (aka the Bulls in pre 3-peat days) practiced when the hockey team was using the (old) Chicago Stadium. The Flames practiced in a tiny gym near Alumni Hall on the western edge of the campus under the El. Sussman found the whole team there, including black star Sly Thomas who was arguing with a redhead and a funny little guy who was "Señor Flame," the team mascot.

Walk through the campus to the exit at Fremont and turn left to go east on Belden. Cross Dayton and continue walking along Belden past Burling to Halsted. Halsted once ran all the way to "Little Egypt" in downstate Illinois. It originally was called Dyer Street in honor of a famous Abolitionist who helped thousands of blacks along the Underground Railway; later it was an immigrant trail, settled by many different groups at different parts of the city. Its present name came from Philadelphia's Halsted brothers, who helped William B. Ogden, Chicago's first mayor, finance his real estate ventures.

Cross Halsted on Belden and walk east to the corner of Orchard and Lincoln. This is a great corner for a little R & R. You are standing next to a coffee house called the Cafe Equinox, at 2300 N. Lincoln, on the site of one of Chicago's oldest drugstores. Cafe Equinox still has the drugstore's original oak cabinets and woodwork and tile floors. The restrooms are behind the counter and downstairs, a la London.

It is perfectly safe to stop here, because the murderous pharmacist E. Gordon Gregg in Robert Bloch's *American Gothic,* who made away with hundreds of young women, ran his lethal pharmacy on the south side near the 1893 Columbian Exposition. (See Walk 9.) Cafe Equinox is a great place to sit and people-watch and enjoy some of the cafe's delicious coffees or have lunch. You can sit inside or out depending on the weather.

If you prefer, kitty-corner across Lincoln is the John Barleycorn Memorial Pub. An 1890 saloon, during Prohibition it fronted as a Chinese laundry, with deliverymen who rolled in the booze in laundry carts! It serves good hamburgers and has about a dozen varieties of beer on tap, but there's no big screen TV.

Across Belden on Lincoln is the Wise Fools Pub with its dark, old-fashioned space that jumps with live blues every night. In Michael A. Dymmoch's *The Man Who Understood Cats,* detectives Crowne and Thinnes took Dr. James Caleb with them on a ride-along in an unmarked car one night. Their first stop was the Wise Fools Pub where they were looking for a blues player who might or might not have seen the fatal beating of a drug-buy witness. Thinnes went in and questioned the bartender, who shook his head a lot and told him not to bother the musicians.

Beyond the Wise Fools Pub you can see the modern, multi-colored building that houses the Victory Gardens/Body Politic theaters. Founded to revitalize Chicago arts with the work of Chicago playwrights like David Mamet, both are part of the renaissance of Chicago's off-Loop theater. But murders onstage occur rarely in Chicago mysteries, unlike New York and London scenes of the crime. (See *MRWG: NY*; *MRWG: London*.)

Turn right to take Orchard south to Webster and Oz Park. Walk a little way into the park on the left, which goes east to Geneva Terrace. This was where L. Frank Baum lived when he wrote his first books (later plays) about Dorothy and the Wizard of Oz. Baum was one of Chicago's famed trio who created classic American fantasies. The other two were Walt Disney of Mickey Mouse fame and Edgar Rice Burroughs who invented the ape-man Tarzan. (Both Baum and Burroughs later lived in Oak Park, where writer Ernest Hemingway grew up. See Walk 10 side trips.)

At the south end of the park is Lincoln Park High School, one of Chicago's magnet schools. The first weekend in August the Lincoln Park Chamber of Commerce used to sponsor an old English pageant known as the Oz Park Medieval Faire, with over two hundred costumed volunteers and Shakespeare productions. The Faire was not as authentic as Mary Monica Pulver's Society for Creative Anachronism in *Murder at the War* and now is called the Oz Park Festival.

Come out of Oz Park at the very confusing corner of Lincoln, Larrabee, Geneva Place, and Webster. Cross Larrabee and then Lincoln and continue walking east on Webster to Grant Hospital, which is at the corner of Webster and Geneva Place. Cross Geneva Place to continue walking east on Webster to Cleveland.

Once again you are in a historic district with some old and some very modern houses. In Harry Stephen Keeler's *Thieves' Nights,* his Excellency the Honorable Timothy O'Hartigan, governor of Illinois, lived on Cleveland. O'Hartigan, known as "Beef" or "Big Hammer of Tim," was a crook who planned to bribe a psychiatrist to declare murderer Frank Porley insane, so he would not be executed. But disguised jewel thief Bayard DeLancey came to call and kept the governor from making the deadline for the pardon.

In Dymmoch's *The Man Who Understood Cats* murder victim Allan Finley, who was a client of Dr. James Caleb, lived in a condo at 2123 Cleveland in Apartment 3B. Cleveland was a quiet, tree-lined residential street filled with exclusive, rehabbed yuppie homes. Finley's body was discovered in the dining room near his desk with a .38-caliber revolver near his empty hand.

Walk east to tiny Hudson where you should detour for a moment to look at Policeman Richard Bellinger Cottage, at 2121 N. Hudson. Designed in 1869 by W. W. Boyington, who built the Water Tower, this little wooden house is a Chicago Fire survivor and a legendary landmark. It was supposedly saved by pouring buckets of cider on the roof.

Cross Hudson and walk to Sedgwick. Here is a block of the kind of Victorian houses with stoops where Greeley's columnist Red Kane lived in *The Patience of a Saint.* Kane's wife, lawyer Eileen Ryan, sister of sleuth Father Blackie, bought it before Lincoln Park real estate boomed. Their oldest son John redesigned it by removing most of the walls and adding bright colors, cushions, and posters. (See the photo in *Andrew Greeley's Chicago.*)

Keep going to the corner of Clark Street. To the left across Clark is Frances W. Parker School, another of Chicago's well-known private schools with many famous Chicago alums, among them mystery writer Arthur Maling. Its new building was put up in the 1960s.

Turn right and walk south on the west side of Clark Street. Just past the building at 2136–2140 Clark is a tiny grassy yard enclosed by a low link fence, with a parking lot behind it. The address is 2122 N. Clark. This is the real site of the famous St. Valentine's Day Massacre. There is no historical marker, but the site is well known and is visited by the Untouchable Tour.

The actual crime was the gangland mass shooting carried out on Valentine's Day, 1929, supposedly by members of Al Capone's gang dressed as cops. They shot six members of Bugs

Moran's north-side gang and a neighborhood optometrist, leaving only a dog alive, but they missed Bugs himself, who had not yet arrived at the scene of the crime. This event focused the attention of public officials on the city's gangster problem and led directly to an organized effort to "get" Capone.

The building was finally torn down under city auspices while my brother George B. Stone was in charge of the Lincoln Park Urban Renewal Project. According to Stone the Department of Urban Renewal purchased the garage/warehouse. When it was determined that it was the real scene of the crime, he was told to tear it down. A contract was signed with a wrecking company which was then approached by a Canadian museum owner, to whom the wrecking company sold the actual wall. But during demolition, other people kept coming by wanting to buy bricks, especially bricks with bullet holes, so the wrecking company workers started knocking holes in the bricks and selling them. Many of the bricks were also stolen. As a result, the garage is scattered to the four winds.

In Collins's 1984 mystery *Kill Your Darlings,* mystery writer Mallory saw the site of the St. Valentine's Day massacre on his crime bus tour. His tour guide told them that those two white pillars are all that remain of S-M-C Cartage Company, but Stone says the garage itself was gone by the mid-'70s.

A typical comment about St. Valentine's Day occurs in Crabbe Evers's *Murder in Wrigley Field.* When the best friend of murdered star pitcher Dean "Dream" Weaver was asked who hated him he answered "Remember that line from the St. Valentine's Massacre? When Bugsy Moran heard about the bodies lined up against the wall . . . he said 'Only Capone kills like that.' "

Just beyond the site of the St. Valentine's Day massacre is a nice old cast-iron building with an antique shop and across Clark is a Starbucks Coffee shop where you can sit and contemplate the scene of the crime if you want to.

Then take Clark two blocks south to Armitage. Across Clark is the Chicago Academy of Sciences at 2001 N. Clark. Chicago's oldest museum, it was founded in 1857 to promote knowledge of Chicago's natural history and in 1893 Matthew

Laflin, a pioneer businessman, donated its Renaissance Revival building. If you have time, cross Clark Street to see the museum and hunt up the boulder south of the building that marks the grave of tall-tale teller and old settler David Kennison, who claimed to have been at *both* the Boston Tea Party and the Fort Dearborn Massacre. But experts on where the bodies are buried, Kenan Heise and Ed Baumann in *Chicago Originals,* cast doubt on this pioneer's credentials. Kennison died in 1851 at the supposed age of 115.

Or turn right at Armitage to walk west. You pass the Park West, a huge building at Armitage and Orleans Street with a modern facade put over an older movie house. It has been both a concert hall and a dance hall, featuring famous acts. Armitage is lined with typical older Chicago commercial buildings with storefronts below and three or four stories with bay windows and apartments above them. There are also many fast food places if you want to take a quick break.

At Sedgwick (where you meet Lincoln again) cross Armitage, then Lincoln, then turn left to walk south on Sedgwick to Wisconsin. You pass old houses that are small and mixed with new developments. You are at the north end of the Old Town Triangle, bounded by Wisconsin, Clark, Larrabee, and North Avenue. According to tradition, if you can hear the bells of St. Michael's Roman Catholic Church at 1633 N. Cleveland you are in Old Town. Although the area was first settled by German workers, the legend is clearly related to the old London saying that if you were born within hearing of Bow bells, you were a Cockney. (See *MRWG: London.*) The annual Old Town Art Fair, always held the second weekend in June, has been held along Wisconsin and Menomonee for nearly fifty years. (For the oldest Art Fair see Walk 9.)

Walk south one more block to Menomonee Street. Turn right to cross Sedgwick Fern Court and go to the Midwest Buddhist Temple at 435 W. Menomenee, pagoda-shaped with a traditionally Japanese gable and hip roof.

Old Town had developed a large Asian community during and after World War II and it was also the first north-side area to be revitalized after the war, changing the character of the area from working class to professional. Among others who live here are architect Walter Netsch who designed the University of Illinois at Chicago campus and his wife Dawn Clark Netsch. (See Walk 10.)

Go south on Fern Court to Eugenie Street; to your right is St. Michael's Church. Built in 1869, a treasure-house of German art and crafts, the church burned to the bare walls in the 1871 Chicago Fire, but was rebuilt and a steeple added. Outwardly Romanesque, its interior is Bavarian Baroque, with stained glass windows and a spectacular high altar where St. Michael, supported by Sts Gabriel and Raphael, stands victorious over Lucifer, the devil. The parish high school on Hudson was recently rehabbed into elegant condo duplexes.

After inspecting the church turn left to recross Sedgwick. Walk east on Eugenie to Orleans. On the other side of Eugenie there is a small white house with black shutters with an Illinois Bell Telephone sign marking the home of Joseph J. O'Connell, a telephone pioneer. Continue walking on Eugenie past one tiny frame house after another to North Park. The houses all have high basements and gabled roofs with Italianate trim, real workman's cottages that have gone up in the world.

Cross North Park and keep going about half a block to Crilly Court. In the late 1880s Daniel F. Crilly bought the block and cut a street through it. On the west side he built two-story Queen Anne rowhouses and on the east side a four-story apartment building, whose entrances have the names of his four children, Isabelle, Oliver, Erminie, and Edgar carved above the doors. He later added another building on Wells Street with a storefront and apartments above. It was the renovations made here by his son Edgar in the 1940s that started the neighborhood's revival.

At Crilly Court there are gateposts at either end of the row of limestone houses with their iron bannisters and gabled roofs. Turn left to walk along Crilly Court towards tiny St. Paul Avenue at the north end, looking for Number 1710. It has a black door and a knocker and it is certainly not a curio shop!

But in Harry Stephen Keeler's *The Face of the Man from Saturn,* there was a curio shop at 1710 Crilly Court. When reporter

Jimmie Kentland who worked for the *Sun,* Chicago's Only Socialist Newspaper, was left in charge as city night editor he got a note telling him to send a man to 1710 Crilly Court, so he went himself. There was no answer so Kentland and the cop on the beat broke in. They found the proprietor, coffee-colored Abdul Mazurka, lying dead in his shop with a long wooden spear in his chest. Above him on the wall was a weird painting. The face was missing, but there was one green-taloned hand with seven fingers and a title in its corner read "The Man from Saturn." Kentland scooped the *Tribune,* the *Herald-Examiner,* and the *Times-Star* with the murder story, but his editor fired him because he had left the office.

Walk east on Eugenie Street to Wells Street and turn right to walk south on Wells to North Avenue. You pass by Piper's Alley, a commercial mall, created here in the mid '70s by rehabbing a bakery and putting in a new retail complex. This is now the home of Second City, which is decorated with a terra-cotta frieze saved from Adler and Sullivan's Schiller Theater. Second City began as the Compass Players in a storefront in Hyde Park. (See Walk 9.) Next to Second City is the restaurant called That Steak Joynt, and there is an Arby's on the corner. Across the street is the big red Treasure Island complex which, like Piper's Alley, has a parking garage.

In James Michael Ullman's 1966 *The Venus Trap,* young Jon Chakorian lived near here in "Levee Court," an old commercial garage remodeled to contain an arcade of four shops on one side and a cabaret called The Den on the other. Afternoons, the Den served sandwiches but evenings it featured Dixieland combos. Jon, the straight but smart son of a very shady financier who had disappeared on Christmas Eve, owned 10 percent of Levee Court. In addition, as manager Jon was paid to maintain the place, collect rents, and help keep order in The Den. Jon lived above The Den, where one rainy night a blond appeared who offered to take him to meet the guy who had kidnaped his father.

In mysteries, Old Town itself is not so much the scene of the crime as a state of mind. In Jay Robert Nash's *A Crime Story,* Journey's girlfriend Eden lived in Old Town off Clark, "the place hopeful young professionals lived in sandblasted brownstones with open fireplaces that worked poorly and ancient clanking radiators that didn't work at all."

Old Town became famous in the '60s as the Chicago version of Haight-Asbury's home for flower children, mixed with folk music and improv comedy. By the '70s it was the home of quaint shops, restaurants and nighttime excitement—the heir of old Rush Street—but by the '90s much of the "action" has moved north.

In Ralph McInerny's *Bishop As Pawn* a renegade Roman Catholic priest called Ambrose Chirichi was running his own church, having tried to get his rectors to give up their parishes' worldly goods to the poor. Chirichi's parishioners now were the people who roamed Old Town, the pimps, girls, and hustlers. He operated out of a van he had won in a poker game. When Bishop Rooney was kidnaped in Fox Valley, the Cardinal suggested to Father Dowling and Police Captain Keegan that Chirichi might have done it.

In Eugene Izzi's *The Take,* safesman Fabe Falletti walked north on Clark Street to his final rendezvous with his partner Doral through Old Town, the 1960s folk music scene. He turned left to walk up Wells because he had loved it as a kid, sneaking into the Earl of Old Town to listen to Steven Goodman and Bonnie Koloc, going to Ripley's Believe It or Not Museum or the wax museum. Fabe saw old newsguy Morrie leaning against his stand, with his ancient cracked face, the philosopher of Old Town in suspenders and filthy green work pants, combat boots and long army coat.

In Harry Keeler's *Behind That Mask,* the enterprising young Chinese Yin Yi made wax figures of murderers for museums all across the country long before Chicagoans were into Madame Tussaud-style Wax Museums.

You can end your walk at Wells and North Avenue and go visit some of the well-known tourist sights of Old Town. Or you can walk two blocks east on North Avenue to Clark Street. There you can go to the Chicago Historical Society to see the collections and eat in its elegant restaurant. Or you can go to the Original Mitchell's kitty-corner across Clark where you can have a hamburger or a sandwich or an ice cream soda. Mitchell's is a comfortable old-fashioned Chicago institution, with friendly help and booths with a view of Lincoln Park.

In Paul Engleman's *Catch a Fallen Angel,* P.I. Renzler had escaped from the oddballs who had kidnaped an Angel from Paradise and made it safely to North Avenue and Clark Street, where he called his buddy Nate from the Original Mitchell's on the corner. While waiting to be picked up Renzler got to watch the Chicago Police driving the hippies, demonstrators, and fellow travelers out of Lincoln Park to begin the Days of Rage, which ended with a rampage down the Gold Coast and raising hell in the Loop. The street action as the SDSers spilled out of Lincoln Park to head south past yuppiedom's Carl Sandburg Village to the Gold Coast made it tough for Renzler's pals to pick him up.

POSSIBLE SIDE TRIPS

These mystery sites north of Lincoln Park may be visited by El, bus, or car.

Area Six Police Headquarters, Belmont and Western. The Chicago Police Department's Area Six Headquarters is located in a modern building on the site of the late, lamented Riverview Amusement Park; in fact, Ed Baumann reports it is on the site of Aladdin's Castle itself. Mysteries about the cops send their officers there almost as often as to the Central Police Headquarters at 11th and State.

In Michael A. Dymmoch's *The Man Who Understood Cats,* the detectives involved in the murder of CPA Allan Finley worked out of Area Six and much of the action took place there. The Department had even hired a resident shrink, Dr. Jeffrey Karsch, to advise the police on work-related emotional problems.

Wrigleyville (Lake View): centered at Clark and Addison. To reach Wrigleyville, the name the media coined for the Lake View area around Cubs Park, take Clark Street north to Addison. Wrigley Field, at Clark, Addison, and Waveland, is the oldest surviving National League ballpark. Built in 1914, it has only recently been allowed to host night games. In Crabbe Evers's *Murder in Wrigley Field* there is a lyrical description of the perfect stage for this country's pastime amid the ivy and the red brick of the venerable arena on Clark and Addison, where Hank Wilson autographed a ball for the son of Al Capone. Just before a game superstar Dean "Dream" Weaver, a big blond ox of a southpaw pitcher, was found shot to death in the tunnel from the dugout and Baseball Commissioner Granville Canyon Chambliss, former head of the Chicago Board of Trade, asked retired sports writer Duffy House to solve the murder.

In Marc Davis's *Dirty Money,* after P.I. Wolf was called in for questioning about murdered Abel Nockerman by Lieutenant Duffy of Homicide, Wolf told Duffy he was on his way to see the Cubs play Pittsburgh and offered to take him along to sit in the center-field bleachers, high up, under the scoreboard.

In Mark Zubro's mysteries from *A Simple Suburban Murder* to *The Principal Cause of Death,* high-school teacher Tom Mason's lover is star Cubs pitcher Scott Carpenter. Paretsky's V.I. Warshawski is a typical yuppie Cubby fan, forever fussing about their continual losing streak. In *Bitter Medicine* the Cubs were playing a doubleheader against the Mets, so Mr. Contreras, driving V.I. home from Beth Israel Hospital after her face was slashed, obligingly turned on WGN so she could hear Trillo ground out and Davis pop up in the infield.

In Kahn's *Grave Designs,* Rachel Gold went to the Addison El stop near Wrigley Field disguised as a blind person with her dog Ozzie to find out what the Canaan personals ad was about.

In many mysteries the characters live near Wrigley Field. In D. C. Brod's *Murder in Store* P.I. Quint McCauley, head of security at Hauser's department store on north Michigan Avenue, unexpectedly moved in with a young woman called Elaine Kluszewski who lived in a highrise just south of Addison at Lake Shore Drive with a view of Wrigley Field.

In Carolyn Haddad's *Caught in the Shadows,* computer hacker Becky Belski's klutzy love, divorce lawyer Michael Rosen, lived off Addison a few blocks from Halsted, but he was still tied to momma's Highland Park apron strings.

In Cormany's *Lost Daughter,* P.I. Dan Kruger was a north side White Sox fan, an ex-cop and rock musician, a loner who lived on Fremont off Addison near the LeMoyne Elementary School just east of Wrigley Field. But in *Rich or Dead,* Kruger, his Hispanic client Elvia Reyes, and his rabbit Bugs had to move out because they had unpleasant visitors like the Romeo Kings.

Graceland Cemetery, 4001 N. Clark Street (between Irving Park Road and Montrose Avenue). To reach Graceland Cemetery's main entrance, continue north on Clark Street to Irving Park Road. There is parking inside the cemetery and regular tours of the famous tombs. Graceland Cemetery is the 121-acre burial ground of Chicago's rich and famous. Its entrance gates and fence were built by Holabird & Root in 1896. Among the famous tombs are those of Mies van der Rohe, Marshall Field, Henry Harrison Getty, Daniel Burnham, Louis H. Sullivan, George Pullman, the Potter Palmers, Martin Ryerson, and Allan Pinkerton, the first Private Eye.

In Cormany's *Lost Daughter,* runaway Asia Dawson and her weird fellow high school student Mitchell Floridge–who collected guns and liked to shoot them–holed up in an apartment on Beacon Street just north of Graceland Cemetery. P.I. Dan Kruger went to find them there in a ten-story Jazz Age rat trap.

In D. J. H. Jones's *Murder at the MLA,* the academic murderer went to Graceland Cemetery to pick yew berries from the shrubs about the vaults and make poison.

In Evers's *Murder in Wrigley Field* Duffy House mentioned that Graceland Cemetery was within walking distance of Wrigley Field so his niece Petey staked it out, watching for suspect Sally Hofman who jogged in this forest of granite sarcophagi, obelisks, and mausoleums. In Mark Zubro's *The Only Good Priest,* Tom Mason and Scott Carpenter chased a murder suspect to Graceland Cemetery.

In *Death in Uptown,* Michael Raleigh, who teaches at Truman College and grew up in the shadow of Wrigley Field, described Uptown as home for drugs, winos and other kinds of homeless, gays, new immigrant groups, kids coming to the Big City, American Indians, and Asians. Its mean streets have sleaze and crime and filth, combined with exotic cuisine and odd shops in Chicago's version of Dickens's London, crossed with Nelson Algren's *A Walk on the Wild Side*.

In some mysteries the authors seem to combine Graceland and Rosehill Cemeteries. Visit both.

Rosehill Cemetery, 5800 N. Ravenswood Avenue (Western, Peterson, and Bryn Mawr Avenues.) Continue north on Clark Street to Edgewater and turn left on Rosehill Drive to the cemetery entrance. The nonsectarian cemetery was established in 1859. The castellated Gothic entrance gates are by William Boyington, who also designed the Chicago Water Tower. Distinguished tombs include those of First Ward heeler "Long John" Wentworth and eleven other mayors, Adam Schaaf, and a Civil War Soldiers Memorial. It dates from the same period as the south side's Oak Woods Cemetery and has much the same design.

In Craig Rice's *The Right Murder* John J. Malone, taking Jake and Helene Justus along as witnesses, went to "Rosedale" cemetery where they were greeted by Henry, a gnomelike custodian who owed Malone a favor. They went to the grave of Gerald Tuesday, who supposedly had died in 1921, but was also found murdered at the home of Mona McClane in 1941. They found that someone had been digging in the grave, but the grave was empty.

In Nash's *A Crime Story* the Governor-elect's wife visited the grave of her murdered stepson in Rosedale Cemetery by night. Earlier at the funeral, with state troopers keeping out curiosity seekers, a psychiatrist who claimed the murderer would come, and about a hundred black-clad mourners and limos, crime columnist Journey tipped the caretaker to tell him if anything strange happened near Day Ashmore's grave. The custodian, a little man who lived in the tiny blockhouse, called him. Mrs. Ashmore had come in and gone to Day's grave, passing the ornate and stately tombs of the patriarchal bones of the Midwest's super rich. This was the last bastion and refuge of social restriction where they had picked their company for eternity.

In Keeler's *Thieves' Nights* crooked tycoon John Atwood was buried there after his funeral was held in the front parlor of his mansion.

Evanston. This old city/suburb just north of Chicago on Lake Michigan has excellent train connections to the Loop. It is the home since 1851 of Methodist (dry) Northwestern University along Sheridan Road. Its boundary with Chicago is Calvary Cemetery and Howard Street. Evanston is one of the two "acceptable" suburbs in mysteries where good guys can live; the other is Oak Park. (See Walk 10.) Although an elm-lined, wealthy old town, Evanston is not one of the North Shore communities that house mystery's malefactors of great wealth.

Calvary Cemetery is on Sheridan Road at the boundary between Chicago's Rogers Park and the city of Evanston. To reach Calvary take the El or bus to Howard Street and then either walk west to Clark Street/Chicago Avenue and go north or walk east to Sheridan Road and go north two blocks.

In Harry Keeler's *The Washington Square Enigma,* Ford Harling and P.I. Red Saunders went to Calvary Cemetery to find the lost ruby belonging to Gold Coast socialite Trudel Vanderhuyden. The two went by boat at night from Lincoln Park to the cemetery where they found the ruby and a bundle of counterfeit money buried at Marker 67-N.

In Jonathan Latimer's *The Lady in the Morgue,* the gangster who invaded P.I. Bill Crane's room at the Sherman Hotel wanted to find his wife's body to bury it decently at Calvary Cemetery.

In Stuart Kaminsky's *When the Dark Man Calls,* talk-show commentator Jean Kaiser lived in Rogers Park but worked for radio station WSMK in Evanston. Kaiser got a series of on-air threatening calls, which turned out to be related to the long-ago murder of her parents. WSMK was a family-owned AM/FM station, something like WNIB. The owner often took Kaiser and her daughter to the Keg on Grove Street after Jean's show, but after the calls, Kaiser and Angie stayed at the Holiday Inn and ate at the McDonald's near Fountain Square. Stuart Kaminsky taught radio and film at Northwestern University, so Evanston was familiar stamping ground. He also arranged for MWA Midwest to hold its annual workshops called Dark and Stormy Nights on campus for several years during the '80s.

In Monica Quill's *Let Us Prey*, Sister Kimberly Moriarity of the diminishing Order of Martha and Mary was a grad student at Northwestern. Her brother was with the Chicago police and often asked for help from the Order's Mother Superior, Mary Theresa (Emtee).

In Kahn's *Grave Designs,* Professor Paul Mason was the Young Turk of American Literature who taught courses on detective fiction at Northwestern University. Rachel Gold met Mason when she rode her bike to the campus with her dog Ozzie and was reading a Robert Parker mystery. Mason picked her up by asking if she was a Spenser fan. Gold said she was a Hawk fan, while Mason liked Susan Silverman. Mason lived in a rented house just across Sheridan and he and Gold were quite friendly until she discovered he had "conferences" with all his female students, too.

In Michael A. Dymmoch's *The Man Who Understood Cats,* psychiatrist James Caleb drove to Evanston to consult Margaret Linsey, a fellow shrink, the day his client was found dead. She lived in a huge old house with a tree-shaded yard west of the Northwestern campus.

Edith Skom's *The Mark Twain Murders* were set on the lakefront campus of Midwestern University in Vinetown, a lovely tree-lined suburb north of Chicago. Midwestern's campus geography matches Northwestern closely, and Beth Austin teaches at Midwestern just as Skom teaches at Northwestern. The mystery and murder of a graduate student center around the theft of rare books from the university library. The hunt brought in FBI Special Agent Gil Bailey, an attractive authority on old books and good living who took a strong interest in Professor Austin, too.

In Sam Reaves's *A Long Cold Fall,* the mother of murdered Vivian Horstmann, who had been married to a Northwestern professor, lived in Evanston on Forest Avenue in a pleasant Victorian house. She took in her orphaned grandson, Dominic, after his mother's death and she also talked openly to Cooper MacLeish about her dead daughter.

In spite of the tree-lined streets and big old houses, Evanston has its share of homeless. In R. D. Zimmerman's *Blood Trance,* in which siblings Maddy and Alex Phillips used her skills at forensic hypnosis to solve a murder, one of the suspects was tracked to Evanston. Alex Phillips found Billy Long, an alcoholic, dining at a soup kitchen in the basement of an Evanston church.

The North Shore. The most recent "newsworthy" Chicago murder was a triple one in the comfortable and classy suburb of Winnetka, just north of Evanston. It has resulted in a true crime book by Gera-Lind Kolarik and Wayne Klatt called *I Am Cain.* The dead were Nancy and Richard Langert and their unborn child, all murdered "in cold blood" by New Trier High School student David Biro, aged 16.

Still farther along the North Shore are suburbs like Kenilworth, Glencoe, Highland Park, and Lake Forest, filled with the mansions of the rich, who often turn out to be malefactors of great wealth in Chicagoland mysteries. Since their homes are private—and well-guarded—the best you can do is drive along Sheridan Road, or Green Bay Road, and admire their gateposts.

Places to Eat on Side Trips

Ann Sather's Restaurant, 5207 N. Clark Street. Old Country Swedish cooking with herring, meatballs, and lingonberries. (Also in Hyde Park. See Walk 9.)

In Mark Zubro's mysteries his characters often go to Ann Sather's both here and in Hyde Park to eat and do a little informal interrogation.

The Green Mill, 4802 N. Broadway (Uptown). Gangster hangout cum nightclub popular with Al Capone, where Joe E. Lewis had his throat cut for kidding the wrong people. The movie *The Joker is Wild,* starring Frank Sinatra as Joe E. Lewis, was based on that episode. True jazz-lovers come here, especially for Saturday night jam sessions.

Since it is often mentioned in Chicago mysteries in connection with Al Capone's known hangouts, in D. J. H. Jones's *Murder at the MLA,* English professor Nancy Cook wheedled Chicago detective Boaz Dixon into taking her there after they solved the series of academic murders.

The Swedish Bakery, 5348 N. Clark Street. Swedish goodies like limpa bread, marzipan, pepperkakor made on premises.

In D. J. H. Jones's *Murder at the MLA,* detective Timmy Halleran brought some mandelbrot and ginger snaps there which he offered to murder suspect Deborah Rames as she was being interrogated at 11th and State.

8

NEAR SOUTH SIDE WALK

BACKGROUND

This walk includes Chicago's old First Ward, historically the scene of sleazy political shenanigans since the colorful Lords of the Levee, "Bathhouse John" Coughlin and Michael "Hinky Dink" Kenna took over as aldermen in the 1890s. Their annual First Ward Ball reputedly entertained every crook and hooker in town, together with most of the politicians. Mobster Big Jim Colosimo was one of their most powerful protégés but after his death in 1921 their power gradually waned. The aura of corruption, however, lingers on in the ward as ongoing indictments indicate.

The area began to be settled by 1836 when Henry Clarke built his handsome Georgian Revival house and opened a general store. Clarke was followed by other Chicago merchants who settled along south Van Buren near the Loop, and when the city was incorporated in 1837 its southern boundary was Cermak Road.

After the Chicago Fire in 1871 Chicago's major movers and shakers moved south to build mansions along Prairie Avenue. But a few blocks away from Polk to 16th Street was the Levee, or red light district, while four of Chicago's major railroad stations were built in the area with their sprawling yards and tracks.

Politics and gangsters took over again when the wealthy fled north, with Al Capone ruling his citywide empire from the Lexington Hotel (later the New Michigan Hotel) at Michigan and

Cermak, but the Burnham Plan of 1909 also led to the creation of the extensive lakefront area east of Prairie Avenue—much of it landfill—where the city's major museums were built and the World's Fair of 1933–34 was held. Today major gentrification and restoration is going on from Congress to Cermak, Lake Michigan to the Chicago River, making use of the miles of abandoned railroad tracks. The South Loop/Near South Side is on the rise again.

You may feel more comfortable having a companion along on this walk, but there are police all over the neighborhood all the time because of the Central Police Headquarters. Add to that the fact that there is a considerable amount of new mixed-use and residential building on your route and many tourists and conventioneers hanging out at the growing McCormick Place complex, and you will find "Old" Chicago a pleasant and fascinating place to explore. Perhaps the best way to explain Chicago's rough and ready charm is to point out that Capone's headquarters and the Fort Dearborn massacre site are less than four blocks apart and that Prairie Avenue's Millionaires' Row was next door to the Levee's red light district.

LENGTH OF WALK: About 2 miles

See the map on page 241 for the boundaries of this walk and page 356 for a list of the books and detectives mentioned.

PLACES OF INTEREST

American Police Center and Museum, 1705 S. State Street. Open Mon.–Fri. 9:30 A.M.–4:30 P.M. Donation requested. Tours available. Call 431-0005.

Central Station, Lake Shore Drive to Indiana/Michigan Avenues, Roosevelt Road to 21st Street. Expensive mixed-use development project begun in 1992 on air rights over railroad. In 1993 Mayor Richard M. Daley moved here from Bridgeport.

Chicago Coliseum, 14th and Wabash Avenue. Remaining walls of Civil War's Libby Prison, brought here from Richmond,

Virginia to be a Civil War Museum, then rebuilt as a convention hall. Almost entirely demolished in 1983.

Chicago Police Department Headquarters, 1121 S. State Street. Only the lobby is open to the public. No tours.

Dearborn Park, Polk Street at Dearborn. Development built in the late 1970s on old railroad yards with highrises, townhouses and garden apartments.

Dearborn Street Station, Polk Street at Dearborn Street. The oldest surviving Chicago railroad terminal, built in Romanesque Revival style in 1885. Converted to a mall.

McCormick Place-on-the-Lake, 2301 S. Lake Shore Drive. Chicago's Convention Complex.

New Michigan Hotel (formerly ***Lexington Hotel***), 1825 S. Michigan Avenue.

Prairie Avenue Historic District, 18th Street to Cermak Road. 1870s Post-Chicago Fire "Gold Coast." Tours: Chicago Architecture Foundation–Prairie Avenue Tour Center, Glessner House, E. 18th Street. Fee. Wed., Fri. noon, 1:00, 2:00 P.M. Sat.–Sun. 1:00, 2:00, 3:00 P.M. Call 922-3432.

Printing House Row District, Dearborn between Congress Parkway and Polk Street. Group of 1890s lofts and warehouses being preserved and gentrified. The ***Printers Row Book Fair*** is held the third weekend in June along Dearborn Street.

R. R. Donnelley Company, Lakeside Press Building, 731 S. Plymouth Court. Originally a printing plant designed by Howard Van Doren Shaw in 1897. Now a Columbia College residence hall.

R. R. Donnelley Company, the Lakeside Press, Calumet Plant, 350 E. Cermak Road. Industrial Gothic, designed by Howard Van Doren Shaw in 1912–24.

Second Presbyterian Church, 1936 S. Michigan (at Cullerton). Designed by James Renwick in 1874, restored by Howard Van Doren Shaw with the help of Frederic Clay Bartlett. Open Mon.–Fri. 9:00 A.M.–4:00 P.M., Sat.–Sun. 8:00 A.M.–noon. Sunday worship 11 A.M. Call 225-4951.

Tommy Gun's Garage, 1237 S. State (entrance behind State beneath the El). Roaring Twenties Comedy Musical Review, dinner or cover charge. Open Thur., Sat. 6:30 P.M. dinner, 8:15 P.M. show; Fri. 7:30 P.M. dinner, 9:15 P.M. show. Call RAT-A-TAT.

PLACES TO EAT

Burger King, Congress Parkway and State Street.

Dearborn Station/Printers Row, Dearborn and Polk Streets. Variety of places for coffee, snacks, or meals.

First National Frank of Chicago, 333 E. Cermak Road. Hot dogs and other Chicago delicacies.

Chinatown, Wentworth at Cermak. (See Possible Side Trips.) Many excellent restaurants.

McCormick Place, Several fast food places.

Sauer's, 311 E. 23rd Street. Dance academy cum warehouse, now serves charbroiled hamburgers on rye. Close to McCormick Place.

NEAR SOUTH SIDE WALK

Begin your walk on Congress Parkway at State Street next to the Burger King. Walk south on State Street past a block of parking lots to Harrison Street. Cross Harrison on State and continue to walk south. You pass the concrete highrise Jones Commercial High School, a modern, businesslike structure, to come to the world-famous Pacific Garden Mission at 646 S. State Street. You may also find a few panhandlers in its vicinity or see Chicago police escorting people in and out.

Founded in 1877, it was known as the Old Lighthouse. Everyone still is welcome and there are church services and guest speakers because it's still an old-fashioned mission with soup and sermons for the down-and-outers. This neighborhood has been the kind of urban slum graphically described by James Michael Ullman in *The Neon Haystack* and gives you a taste of what North Clark Street and Skid Row were like, with flophouses and Single Room Occupancy hotels and bars.

In Michael Cormany's *Lost Daughter*, skinny, drug-taking P.I. Dan Kruger, hired to find runaway suburban teenager Asia Dawson, called a buddy at the Pacific Garden Mission to get some names of detox places near Rockford where her brother might be.

In Michael Raleigh's *Death in Uptown*, P.I. Paul Whelan, who also had a soft spot for strays, helped a young man called Donny working at an Uptown mission like the Pacific Gardens decide to go home to his small town.

In Mark Zubro's *Political Poison*, police detectives Paul Turner and Buck Fenwick reversed your walk. They were chasing a suspect called Frank Ricken, implicated in the death of Fifth Ward Alderman *and* University of Chicago Professor Gideon Giles. Ricken lived in Dearborn Park, where they went to get him. But Ricken got away from them and dashed up State past the Pacific Garden Mission and Jones Commercial High School to take a left on Harrison and double back to the Dearborn Street Station.

Walk to Polk Street. Across the street is the new Burnham Market. Five blocks west on Polk at Wells is the trendy-looking River City complex, designed in 1984 by Bertrand Goldberg who also built Marina City, with which it shares a futuristic curvy look. (See Possible Side Trips.)

Turn right at Polk to walk one block west to Plymouth Court. You are across from the Dearborn (Polk Street) Station, now rehabbed into a mall. One block west on Polk at Dearborn is the area known as Printers Row. From 1880 to 1950 there were many railroad yards coming into this part of the city, so this became a major printing center. The two block area from Congress to Polk Street is filled with many landmark buildings which give you a good idea of what Chicago looked like in the late nineteenth century. Printers Row is also gentrifying with restaurants, loft apartments, bookstores, offices, and coffeehouses.

There is a handsome example of Chicago architecture at the corner of Plymouth Court and Polk. It is the Lakeside Loft Apartments (Lakeside Press Building), designed by Howard Van Doren Shaw in 1897 and originally a printing plant of R. R. Donnelley Company. It is now a residence hall for Columbia College. Until recently, the Lakeside Press printed the telephone redbooks, *Time*, and the *Sears Roebuck Catalog* at its more recent (1912) Calumet Plant.

If you have time, take a detour west to Dearborn to see some of the other landmarks, like the fourteen-story skyscraper Pontiac

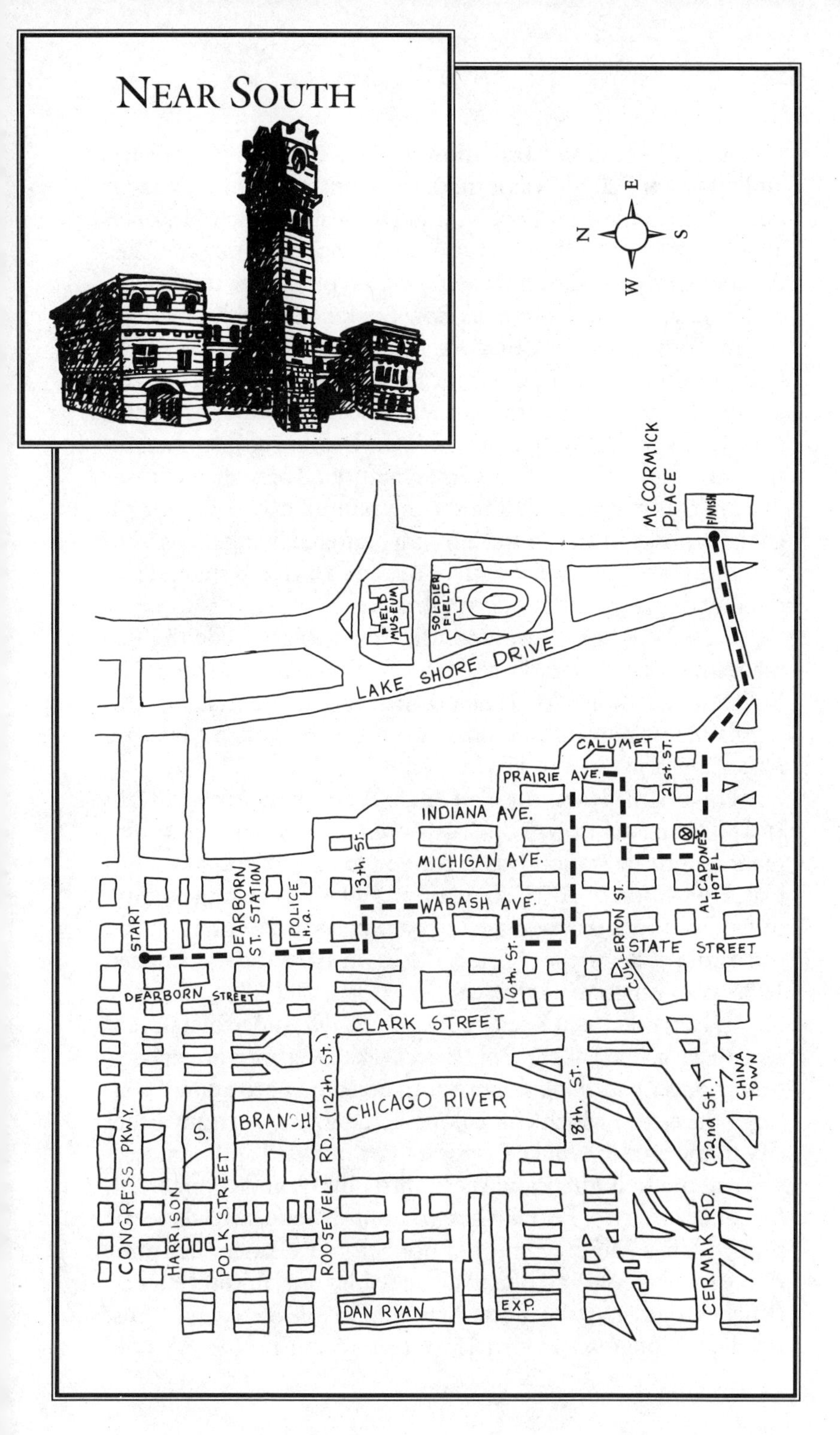
NEAR SOUTH
N
E
S
W
McCORMICK PLACE
FINISH
FIELD MUSEUM
SOLDIER FIELD
LAKE SHORE DRIVE
CALUMET
PRAIRIE AVE.
21st. ST.
INDIANA AVE.
13th. ST.
MICHIGAN AVE.
AL CAPONES HOTEL
CULLERTON ST.
WABASH AVE.
DEARBORN ST. STATION
POLICE H.Q.
START
16th. ST.
STATE STREET
DEARBORN STREET
CLARK STREET
CHINA TOWN
(22nd St.)
CHICAGO RIVER
18th. ST.
S. BRANCH
CONGRESS PKWY.
HARRISON
POLK STREET
ROOSEVELT RD. (12th St.)
CERMAK RD.
DAN RYAN
EXP.

Building at 542 S. Dearborn, the terra-cotta trimmed 1912 Franklin Building at 720 S. Dearborn, or the Transportation Building at 608 S. Dearborn where Eliot Ness and the real Untouchables operated out of Room 308 as they stalked Al Capone during the '20s. An especially good time to take this walk is during the third weekend in June, when the Printers Row Book Fair is held.

In Cormany's *Lost Daughter*, P.I. Kruger found Asia's alcoholic brother, Terrance Dawson, Jr., by trailing Rich Boccinelli, a confederate of Dawson's father. Boccinelli brought Junior back to his South Loop apartment on Dearborn, just north of the "abandoned" Dearborn Street Station. The apartment was in a multistory brick building above a plumbing company. Kruger later broke in and found a trendy, raftered living room with mahogany shelves stuffed with books and a stereo system, decorated with plants and modern furniture.

Cross Polk Street at Plymouth Court to go inside the Romanesque Revival Dearborn Street Station (also known as the Polk Street Station). Made of red brick and terra-cotta, it is Chicago's oldest remaining train station, but its Italian tower replaced an earlier Flemish tower that burned in 1922.

This originally was the Chicago & Western Railroad Station. In 1887 the Atchison, Topeka and Santa Fe Railroad became a tenant, and the station was expanded for the World's Columbian Exposition of 1893, so that by 1899 it was serving twenty-five railway lines. It was closed to passengers in 1971 but put on the National Register of Historic Places in 1976 and reopened in 1986 as an urban marketplace.

In Harry Stephen Keeler's *Thieves' Nights*, superthief Bayard DeLancey arrived at the Polk Street (aka Dearborn Street) Station and went strolling down South State Street to admire Chicago, the city in which crime flourished more than in any other city in the world. Unlike London in its outward appearance, it was still the London of the West, dirty, lively, and commercial. DeLancey let a hooker take him to a South State pub where she slipped him a Mickey Finn, but not before DeLancey had gone to the men's room and put all his valuables in a janitor's bucket. (Mickey Finn ran the Lone Star Saloon on State Street just north of Congress. His tricks were featured in *The Sting*, in which Paul Newman and Robert Redford staged an elaborate revenge on a big Chicago gangster.)

In Michael Cormany's *Red Winter*, during the 1983 primary fight between Jane Byrne, Richard M. Daley, and Harold Washington—who had a debate at Jones Commercial High School for which Mayor Byrne did not show—P.I. Dan Kruger had been hired by rich city contractor Nicholas Cheyney to deal with a group of "Reds" who were blackmailing him. Kruger agreed to meet the blackmailer's rep at Dearborn Station, a century-old redbrick train depot in an area of ancient warehouses, small service shops and multistory nineteenth-century buildings. At 11 P.M. Kruger met a tall, heavy-set black man in Bogie-like trench coat and dark fedora, but as they talked, another young black junkie came up and shot the other man, then rapidly headed north to the Loop.

In Mark Zubro's *Political Poison*, partners Turner and Fenwick chased suspect Frank Ricken into the station. A guy at the deli said someone went up the tower stairs, so Turner drew his gun and went all the way to the top. When Turner came down, Ricken got past him at the entrance but was caught by Turner's partner.

Go inside the station. It is now a mall that leads to Dearborn Park. You can see the logos of all the railroads that once came into Chicago's South Loop, get something to eat, or patronize the stores, but the security guard assured us that nobody can go up in the tower. To use the restrooms in the basement you must purchase something and get the combination for the locks.

Look the place over, then walk out the south door into Dearborn Park. Go through the parking lot (customer parking which you can use) and take Plymouth Court through Dearborn Park to 9th Street.

Dearborn Park is an upscale housing development, with highrises, townhouses and garden apartments. It was built in 1970 on the old railroad yards that went from State to Clark Street, planned as an integrated suburb in the city with parks and a public school of its own. It proved highly successful, and the more expensive Dearborn Park II is now going up south of Roosevelt Road (12th Street) to 15th Street.

In Zubro's *Political Poison*, suspect Frank Ricken got away from the cops the first time by jumping out the second-story window of his condo into a dumpster, so keep a lookout for some likely garbage cans.

Turn left at 9th Street to walk east to State Street and south to 11th Street. There are parking lots along here as well as cabs, public transportation (buses, subway and El), and many squad cars cruising by.

In Richard Whittingham's police procedural *State Street*, the six blocks to the Loop were described by detective Joe Morrison as a swath of penny arcades, strip shows, dingy bars, flophouses, pawnshops, and peep shows.

Try and find any today. But State Street was once junky going south from Jackson Street. In Jonathan Latimer's *Heading for a Hearse*, P.I. Bill Crane and his chum Doc Williams walked about a mile and a half down State Street to Police Headquarters after lunching at the Sherman House on Randolph Street. First, they passed great department stores, then came to the honkytonk area south of Van Buren with penny arcades, burlesque, and pawnshops. (Today much of this is DePaul University's Loop Campus. See Walk 2.) Near 11th and State they passed junk yards and coal yards with dirty fences and rows of brown tenement houses. Suddenly Williams yelled and pushed Crane over as a touring car with black curtains went past them. A man was leaning out of the front seat firing a submachine gun.

Cross State Street at 11th Street and walk to Police Headquarters, located in a large cream-colored building on the east side of the street. This is Chicago's Scotland Yard, but like that venerated London center of police activity, it is about to be decommissioned. Mayor Daley has promised to replace the 70-year-old building by 1996 with a new, state-of-the-art establishment on the west side near the Police Academy, new Crime Lab, and new morgue (aka Medical Examiner's Office. See Walk 10.) (The mayor added that there will always be a police station here, which is probably true since he has just left his Bridgeport roots to move into nearby Burnham Park. See Walk 1.)

The Police Headquarters does not give tours, although the

lucky members of MWA Midwest did get to see everything but the cells themselves. But you can walk into the lobby where the stars (badges) of police officers killed in the line of duty are displayed and there is an old green police call box like the ones that used to stand beside the red fire boxes on Chicago's street corners. The building itself is called the James J. Riordan Chicago Police Headquarters in memory of the highest-ranking police officer ever killed in action.

The one thing that is no longer in the lobby is the statue of the frock-coated policeman put up in memory of the Haymarket Riot on May 4, 1886, when a bomb killed seven or eight policemen (authorities disagree). The anarchists arrested (none of whom had actually thrown the bomb) were tried and convicted of murder, but Governor John Altgeld later pardoned three of them, destroying his chances of becoming a senator. The statue originally stood at Haymarket on west Randolph. It was moved to Police Headquarters after being blown off its base by the Weathermen in 1970. Finally, it was moved to the Police Academy on the west side where it has twenty-four-hour police protection. But you can see a replica in the American Police Museum down the street at 1717 S. State.

In Bill Granger's *The Priestly Murders*, Lieutenant Matt Schmidt held a council of war in his tiny sixth floor office here to plan a stakeout at St. Alma's Church. Police Headquarters was under heavy guard that day because someone had called to threaten to bomb the statue of the policeman in the lobby, keeping alive the old Socialist tradition of celebrating May Day.

From the standpoint of mystery buffs, this building, put up in 1929 and renovated in 1963, is the main "scene of the crime," where mysteries' cops and robbers all come, the nitty-gritty real-life setting for confronting and incarcerating murder suspects. But remember, too, that in the classic Chicago mystery the cops may be more venal—or dumber—than the crooks.

Known as the Big Cop Shop, it also houses the First District Police Station (there are twenty-five districts in the city). The only other district police stations mentioned often in mysteries are Area Six Headquarters, located on the northwest side at Belmont and Western on the site of the Riverview Amusement

Park, and the South Side's Area One at 5101 S. Wentworth off the Dan Ryan Expressway near the White Sox's Comiskey Park.

In Fredric Brown's *The Screaming Mimi* reporter William Sweeney, recuperating from a bender in Bughouse Square, saw a show girl called Yolanda rescued from murder by her dog and got himself assigned to the story. Police Captain Bline was more or less friendly to Sweeney—who in true reporter fashion held out on him—but he did save Sweeney's life when he was about to be carved up like the other victims of the Fiend.

Barbara D'Amato's freelancer Cat Marsala had a real friend and source in Captain Harold McCoo, a fanatic about coffee-making, who was often annoyed with Cat for going in harm's way. (In real life D'Amato is a good friend of Chicago cop Hugh Holton, whose mystery *Presumed Dead* includes a writer called Barbara Zoran who is very much like D'Amato.) In *Hard Women*, doing a TV piece on Chicago's prostitutes, Cat went to Branch 40 (Women's Court, familiarly known as hooker court) at 11th and State to find some hookers to interview.

In D. J. H. Jones's *Murder at the MLA*, the author acknowledged her debt to Chicagoan Connie Fletcher's nonfiction *What Cops Know* and *Pure Cop*. (Fletcher's sister is a cop.) In Jones's mystery detective Boaz Dixon came from the Violent Crimes unit at 11th and State. Bemused by the arcane academic jargon and mores surrounding the academic murders, he recruited Professor Nancy Cook to "translate" for him.

In Harry Keeler's *Behind That Mask,* the head of the Chicago Police Department was Sir John MacKenzie—known as Chief—who had a thick Scottish burr.

In Marc Davis's *Dirty Money*, P.I. Fred Wolf was pulled in by Police Lieutenant Patrick J. Duffy from Area One Homicide. Duffy, born "Back of the Yards," wanted to find out what Wolf knew about broker Abel Nockerman's murder. He told Wolf to call if he got any information or he'd yank his license. Wolf, en route to a Cubs game, offered instead to take Duffy along.

In Stuart Kaminsky's *You Bet Your Life*, P.I. Toby Peters, hired by Louis Mayer of Metro-Goldwyn-Mayer to get the mob off Chico Marx's back for a gambling debt, was met at the 12th Street Station by Sergeant Chuck Kleinhans of Maxwell Street

Station. (See Walk 10.) When Peters found a body in his hotel closet, Kleinhans took Peters to 11th and State to interrogate him. Then Kleinhans told Peters to go see Frank Nitti, Capone's second in command, and let him go. Outside Police HQ Peters was picked up by a cabby called Raymond Narducy, a little guy with glasses and a woolly blue scarf over his face, whose heater was not working. They drove south on State Street past Big Jim Colosimo's nightclub to the New Michigan Hotel. Narducy later helped Peters dispose of a body in Lincoln Park. (See Walk 7.)

In *The Public Murders*, Bill Granger's Sergeant Terry Flynn of Granger's mythical "Special Squad of Area One Homicide" also worked out of 11th and State. Flynn held interviews there in a dirty green office that echoed from the El that ran past the windows on Wabash Avenue. In Granger's *The Priestly Murders*, his author's note tells the mystery reader about the police department's long-time "special relationship" to city government (aka the Democratic organization).

In Eugene Izzi's *The Take*, Lieutenant Jimmy Capone, who was the head of Narcotics and a childhood chum of burglar Fabe Falletti, got a call about the body of Lucille Ortiz. She was the sister of one of the biggest drug suppliers in the Chicagoland area, and Homicide was trying to shove the problem off on Narcotics.

In Barbara Gregorich's *Dirty Proof*, Police Lieutenant Dragon Brdar, a childhood chum of P.I. Frank Dragovic from South Chicago, grilled Dragovic's client Suzanne Quering at headquarters after her ex-lover was pushed into his newspaper's presses. Brdar then put Quering in County Jail, but she escaped.

In Sara Paretsky's *Indemnity Only*, V.I. Warshawski's dead father Tony was a cop, so family friend Lieutenant Bobby Mallory acted like a Dutch uncle. Mallory bailed her out and bawled her out, repeating his basic theme that being a P.I. is an "Unsuitable Job for a Woman." (See the P. D. James mystery of that title.)

In *Bitter Medicine*, when V.I.'s old neighbor Mr. Contreras and his union buddies tried to keep Dr. Lotty Herschel's clinic open and got arrested, Contreras was brought to night court at

11th and State. Both V.I. and his public defender tried to persuade the old man to plead self-defense. V.I. noticed that parking was no problem at the deserted south end of the Loop with ramshackle businesses run out of warehouses by day and antiquated coffee shops at night. (This is not as true today.)

Craig Rice's Captain Daniel Von Flanagan was one of criminal lawyer John J. Malone's best friends. (Von Flanagan had changed his name to "Von" Flanagan so he wouldn't be just one more dumb Irish cop.) In every Rice mystery Von Flanagan dreamed of a new career like chicken farming or editing a country newspaper, while he either let Malone pull the wool over his eyes or helped him solve the crime so the good guys won. The Justuses often came to Von Flanagan's tiny office, too. Jake Justus annoyed Von Flanagan but he thought Helene was the cat's meow. The only time he ever locked her up, no matter how madly she drove, was on her wedding night in *The Wrong Murder*, as a joke on Jake.

Come out of the lobby of Police Headquarters and turn left to go south on State Street past the police parking lot to 12th Street (Roosevelt Road). Cross Roosevelt Road and continue south. Across State Street you can see the Dearborn Park II development.

In the next block on State Street you pass Tommy Gun's Garage Dinner Theater. To get inside the restaurant-theater you go through their parking lot to the back door under the El where they have a speakeasy-style entrance.

Turn left to take 13th Street east under the El to Wabash Avenue. Then turn right on Wabash to walk one block to 14th Street. For nearly fifty years this area was known as "Film Row," an exchange (or marketplace) where Chicago's eleven hundred movie theater owners came to get their feature films, cartoons, projectors, you name it, from film companies like Warner, Universal, Twentieth Century-Fox, and Paramount. Many of the films that gave Chicago its gangster image, beginning with *Little Caesar* starring Edward G. Robinson, were handled here. Now it is being rehabbed as condos.

Walk south on Wabash to 16th Street. Across Wabash at 1513 S. Wabash you can see the crumbling stone walls of the old

Coliseum, with a remaining tower and bits of the gate. The castle-like limestone wall originally surrounded the warehouse that had been the Confederates' infamous Libby Prison at Richmond, Virginia. A bunch of enterprising Chicagoans bought it and brought it to Chicago in 1888 to open as a Civil War Museum.

During the Columbian Exposition of 1893, Buffalo Bill Cody's Wild West Show, starring Annie Oakley and Chief Sitting Bull, performed here. But by 1899 public interest in the Civil War had died. The prison warehouse was torn down and the limestone wall was used for the Coliseum, a stadium built in 1900. When it was converted to a stadium, an annual horse show was held here with visitors like J. P. Morgan and Alice Longworth Roosevelt, while the Republican National Convention met here from 1904 to 1920. It was here that William Jennings Bryan made his famous "Cross of Gold" campaign pitch for cheap money.

Its most memorable use was for the wide open First Ward balls, held here under the sponsorship of the Lords of the Levee, "Bathhouse John" Coughlin and Michael "Hinky Dink" Kenna, the First Ward aldermen. They were typical Irish pols who supported (and lived off of) organized vice, saying "Chicago ain't no sissy town." According to Chicago reporters (and editors) Herman Kogan and Lloyd Wendt in *Lords of the Levee*, in 1908 every hooker and burglar in town came to the party to get drunk, all fifteen thousand of them. Most of the building except for the wall fragments was demolished in 1983, and what's left is on borrowed time.

According to Kenan Heise in *Is There Only One Chicago?*, here you are just north of the Levee (red light) district, whose 1910 boundaries went from 19th Street to Cermak Road (22nd Street), State to Clark. It was part of the notorious First Ward, which is still home to crooked Chicago politics today if criminal indictments mean anything.

The boundaries of Chicago's fifty wards change nearly every election, with gerrymandering still a popular political exercise, but redrawing boundaries to ensure your reelection is not quite as simple as Robert J. Campbell made it sound in *Hipdeep in Alli-*

gators. Campbell had old Sanitation Chief Donleavy sit at City Hall with a red pen and a map of Chicago, redrawing the boundaries to suit himself.

In Robert Bloch's *American Gothic*, set at the time of the World's Columbian Exposition of 1893, insurance salesman Jim Frazer bought his intrepid fiancee Crystal a ring downtown, then took her to the Coliseum to see Buffalo Bill's Wild West Show. They both enjoyed the famous Indian attack on the Deadwood Coach led by Chief Sitting Bull.

Roslynn Griffith's *Pretty Birds of Passage* was about Prairie Avenue, woman's rights and the 1893 Columbian Exposition. Aurelia Kincaid's Aunt Phaedra knew Buffalo Bill Cody, so Cody invited the entire family to see his Wild West Show. Later when Aurelia was in danger of being made into a mummy, Buffalo Bill rode his troop of cowboys and Indians down Prairie Avenue to the rescue.

In the 1950s in Frank Gruber's *The Scarlet Feather* the Auditorium (really the Coliseum because it is described as a big amphitheater south of the Loop) was the site of the Midwest Poultry Breeders' Exhibition. Two charming con men, Johnny Fletcher and Sam Cragg—the brains and the brawn—were in town to sell body-building books. They talked their way inside the convention and found the huge building filled with five thousand chickens of all sorts, shapes, and sizes in wire coops. Undaunted, the pair found an open space and Johnny went into his spiel. As Johnny talked, Sam clenched his fists so muscles leaped out in bunches on his arms and he broke a chain around his chest. They were down to three books when stopped. When a body was found under some chicken coops they ducked out by the back alley to Michigan Boulevard. (There still is an alley behind the Coliseum leading to the empty corner at 15th and Michigan where the old First Armory used to stand.)

Cross 16th Street at Wabash and turn right to walk back to State Street. Walk south on State Street to 17th Street and cross 17th Street to the Police Museum at 1705–17 S. State Street. There is a visitors' parking lot and a mural of different kinds of police personnel on the wall by the side entrance.

The American Police Center Museum was founded in 1974 to respect the work of law enforcement officers around the world after a decade of escalating tension with antiwar and inner-city riots. It is in one big room, with a wide variety of displays and exhibits which include uniforms, badges, weapons like sawed-off shot guns, and a copy of the often-bombed Haymarket Memorial Statue of a frock-coated policeman. There is a Gangsters Alley with mug shots of Chicago's famous crooks, several real electric chairs, drug paraphernalia, and a receiver broadcasting real police calls.

Come out of the Police Museum and walk to 18th Street. Cross 18th Street and go east to Wabash Avenue. Cross Wabash Avenue, then Michigan Avenue, to reach Indiana. You are now in the Prairie Avenue Historic District which runs from East 18th to Cullerton, Indiana to Calumet. This was Chicago's post-Fire "Gold Coast" where the city's leading citizens like Potter Palmer, Marshall Field, William Kimball, George Pullman, Philip Armour, and John Glessner (who joined the McCormicks to form International Harvester) built their mansions.

Arthur Meeker, the son of a Marshall Field executive who grew up here wrote about it in *Prairie Avenue*. There were no murders in his novel, but he knew Marshall Field, Jr., who shot himself in his mansion on Prairie. According to Ed Baumann, rumors persisted that Field was shot elsewhere and taken home to avoid a scandal, but the story was probably a hoax.

The area remained classy until 1900 when the expanding railroads brought more and more industry, manufacturing, and dirt, and Society followed Potter Palmer north to his swamp along Lake Shore Drive now called the Gold Coast. (See Walk 6.) Although there were some recluses still living on Prairie Avenue a generation ago, only a few of the houses are left. The Chicago Architecture Foundation maintains the Glessner House and the Henry Clarke House, and offers tours of both.

Cross Indiana. To your right is the shining white Widow Clarke House in Greek Revival style, thought to be Chicago's oldest surviving wooden structure. Built in 1836 on South Michigan when it was open country, in 1977 the house was moved back near its original site, crossing the Jackson Park El line one freezing night on jacks while all traffic stopped. It has been totally refurnished by the Colonial Dames of America.

Walk one more block east to Prairie Avenue to stare at the northeast corner. Tradition has it that this is the actual site of the Fort Dearborn Massacre, but the memorial statue, after a spell in the front hall of the Chicago Historical Society, is now on the lawn south of the Glessner House to your right. The statue portrays the heroic Potawatomi Chief Black Partridge keeping another Indian from scalping Margaret Heald, wife of the fort commander, while a child looks on. (Mrs. Heald was later ransomed; her husband's sword is in the Fort Dearborn exhibit at the CHS.) The reluctant garrison of soldiers and civilians, including women and children, had marched out of the fort at 9:00 A.M. on August 15, 1812, to the "Dead March." They were led by Indian Scout Captain William Wells who blackened his face because he knew he was as good as dead. Near 18th Street five hundred Potawatomi allies of the British attacked them in the sand dunes, losing only fifteen braves. But it was their last great victory because the government bought (or took?) their Chicago land rights in 1835 and banished them to Iowa.

In British John Malcolm's *Mortal Ruin* art expert Tim Simpson, in Chicago to investigate the connection, if any, between Winston Churchill's (American) uncle and a 1980s murder, had read up on the Fort Dearborn massacre. Simpson leaned out a window at the LaSalle Bank to see the site of the fort at Michigan Avenue, remembering Wells and his blackened face. (See Walk 4.) His interest makes a nice change from most visitors who want to see Al Capone's headquarters or the St. Valentine's Day Garage.

Over a century after the massacre, George Pullman, inventor of the railroad sleeping coach (chosen to carry President Lincoln's body in state from Washington to Springfield) and creator of the ultimate company town, Pullman, built his mansion on the site. But the 1894 Pullman Strike of his workers, put down by federal troops, permanently tarnished Pullman's memory, while concern for the poor and downtrodden was said to be a redeeming feature of Al "Robin Hood" Capone.

Turn right on Prairie Avenue and go by the Glessner House, a fortresslike, almost windowless building which is Chicago's only remaining example of H. H. Richardson's massive Romanesque style. It was built facing south around a walled courtyard and filled with the brightly colored arts and crafts decor and furniture which the Glessners liked. Glessner himself left it to the Chicago Architecture Society. It is now a museum and the headquarters of the Chicago Architecture Foundation. If you want to take their tour, this is the place to come.

Across Prairie Avenue on the opposite corner is the piano maker Kimball's French chateau, now U.S. Soccer's headquarters, and the massive sandstone Romanesque Coleman-Ames mansion next door. Farther down the west side is the Keith House and across the street at 1905 is the Marshall Field, Jr., house, neither in good repair. The sites of lost houses are shown on a map with photographs on the wrought iron fence south of the Glessner House.

For a description of the neighborhood in the 1890s, when you could stroll to the beach, read Roslynn Griffth's *Pretty Birds of Passage*. Several members of Aurelia Kincaid's family lived on Prairie Avenue and she was raised there by her Aunt Phaedra. One of Aurelia's suitors was a very conventional wet blanket named DeWitt Carlton who was clearly meant to be a son and heir of the Carson Pirie Scott department store families, or possibly, of the Marshall Fields.

In Barbara Michaels's *Search The Shadows*, Haskell Maloney came to the University of Chicago to discover the true identity of her father. Her dead mother had a Ph.D. in Egyptology, so Haskell became entangled with a wealthy family called Nazarian. The Nazarians were patrons of the U of C's Oriental Institute but still lived in their Prairie Avenue mansion. (The Nazarian mansion looked like Potter Palmer's north-side castle.) The Nazarian Collection was housed in a separate building, connected to the house by a tunnel, and there was also a yard with three small guest cottages where Haskell stayed. The scene of the crime was in the Nazarian museum. (Michaels is also Elizabeth Peters, creator of Amelia Peabody, the liberated nineteenth-century archeologist.)

Nineteenth Street does not go through, so walk south to Cullerton, a street named after a Back-of-the-Yards Irish alderman named Edward F. Cullerton. Cullerton, born in 1842, held city office from 1871 to 1920. There are still political Cullertons in Chicago.

Stand at the corner of Cullerton and Prairie and look southeast toward Calumet Avenue. Among the buildings of R. R. Donnelly's Lakeside Press, you can see the mansard roof of the Wheeler House, an 1860s mansion at one time a restaurant. In John M. Ashenhurst's mystery, *The World's Fair Murders*, star police reporter Allison (Al) Bennett was trying to solve the murder of Professor Arturo del Grafko of Almania at the 1933 World's Fair. Fellow reporter Helen Maynard originally was given the assignment, but was pulled off by their editor, so she and Bennett formed a team to solve the murder. They planned to snoop about the fair itself, but first Bennett took Helen to Ardito's Place. To get there, they drove down Michigan, catching a glimpse of the fantastic fairgrounds' brightly colored towers glistening in golden late afternoon sunshine, and drew up before a dilapidated old brownstone residence near Prairie Avenue.

Turn right on Cullerton to walk back to Indiana, passing more remnants of old mansions. Cross Indiana and walk to Michigan Avenue. On the northwest corner of Michigan and Cullerton is the Second Presbyterian Church. Designed in 1874 by James Renwick, the famous architect of St. Patrick's Cathedral on New York's Fifth Avenue, the original limestone building with its horizontal bands of black rock, steep roof, and rose window, was greatly altered after a fire in 1900 when the church was redone by Howard Van Doren Shaw, an admirer of the Arts and Crafts movement and the Pre-Raphaelites, with the help of Frederick Clay Bartlett. The result is a riot of color and design that shows off a spectacular collection of Tiffany windows, a huge gilded screen with herald angels, and a strap ceiling, shining against a background of dark oak pews and buff walls.

Go in to admire the church if you like, then go south on Michigan Avenue. Michigan Avenue from Roosevelt Road (12th Street) to 29th Street was once known as Automobile

Row, but the Stevenson Expressway and the growth of McCormick Place have meant most of its gleaming showrooms were torn down or converted to other uses.

Cross 21st Street and walk towards 22nd Street. One block west on Wabash Avenue there used to be a very famous nightclub called Colosimo's Cafe. Colosimo's was known nationally and frequented by VIPs like Enrico Caruso. Big Jim Colosimo, the first important Chicago bootlegger, who glittered with diamonds, had a number of threats from the Sicilian Black Hand, so he imported his nephew Johnny Torrio as a bodyguard. Torrio in turn brought a New York pal of his named Alphonse ("Scarface") Capone to help out.

When Big Jim fell in love with one of his singers, Dale Winter, and began to neglect business, his nephew Torrio had him shot on May 11, 1920—probably by Capone, who boasted he had done the deed. Colosimo had a fabulously flowery gangland-style funeral, attended by over five thousand people, many of them judges and politicians. In the movie *Little Caesar* starring Edward G. Robinson as "Rico" (aka Al Capone), this shooting was set up in the opening scene between "Rico" and his pal, played by Douglas Fairbanks, Jr.

Colosimo's three-story brick building, which stood between two taller ones, was torn down about 1955. A March 25, 1955 *Sun-Times* photo showed it had a tall cross-shaped neon sign very like the one in front of celebrity-heaven Sardi's in New York. (See *MRWG:NY*.)

A recent Bible exhibit at the University of Chicago included the "Gangster's Bible," which had been sold to the University's Divinity School by the last manager of Colosimo's. He said that the Bible had been used by his clients (customers) to swear oaths. When the Divinity School bought it, it was the oldest Greek testament in their collection, dating from the 9th or 10th century A.D. Known as the Argos Lectionary, it is leather bound, not quite as big as a pulpit Bible, with beautifully shaded uncial double columns, but certainly not a Bible the Mafia could read! But its great age and mysterious language would give it great charisma (or *amorta*), and during the Middle Ages, there was great trafficking between the Middle East and the Crusaders' Kingdom of the Two Sicilies—Naples and Sicily. Sicily still keeps its venerable tradition of gangs and vengeance.

In Jonathan Latimer's *The Lady in the Morgue*, P.I. Crane and his sidekicks Doc Williams and Tom O'Malley were trying to determine if the body in the morgue was the missing New York socialite who had followed a married band leader to Chicago. The morgue had several bodies of young women, which kept disappearing. One body was the wife of gangster Mike Paletta, whose wife Verona Vincent had gone off with another mobster called Frankie French. Paletta had met his wife when he was a player and she was a singer at Colosimo's.

In Mark Zubro's *The Principal Cause of Death,* high school teacher Tom Mason and his lover, star pitcher Scott Carpenter came here to investigate the Paradise Agency for Young Actors and Actresses. It was on Michigan Avenue about half a block north of Al Capone's headquarters in a 1910 building with industrial-strength rats. After the murder of the principal at Mason's school, one suspect was the high school drama coach because drama students at the high school got referrals and went abroad, never to reappear. Scott and Tom found the brains of the outfit, Blane Farnsworth, in an office where Miss Haversham of Dickens's *Great Expectations* would have felt at home. Farnsworth wanted Scott as a client but instead they had a major fight.

Walk to 22nd Street. On the northeast corner is the New Michigan Hotel, formerly the Lexington. This was the second Chicago hotel where Al Capone had his headquarters, a once handsome luxury hotel, built for the 1893 Columbian Exposition, with brick and terra-cotta walls, bay windows, and an internal atrium. Ideally, the hotel should be rehabbed to its original glory and used to house tourists who would adore staying in Capone's own place. More likely, between Italian-Americans' hyper-sensitivity to Chicago's most famous citizen and McCormick Place expansion plans, it will shortly be torn down.

In his 1986 TV special Geraldo Rivera found nothing buried in "Capone's vault" except old bottles because the vault was really the hotel's coal bin, beneath one of Chicago's old vaulted sidewalks. (There are tunnels under the Loop, too, as was dramatically demonstrated by the 1992 Great Chicago Flood.)

In Kenan Heise and Ed Bauman's *Chicago Originals* they suggest Capone's chief claim to fame was not taking over the entire city's mobdom, but the fact that he perfected the use of the Thompson submachine gun or "Tommy gun." Somewhat like our Uzis today, they were developed for World War I, then advertised as handy for protecting your estate. They were easily bought at local hardware stores, but the gun's kick sprayed bullets all over. Capone had the foresight to practice holding the gun steady *before* he shot, which made him a successful enforcer.

On the other hand, in *True Detective* Max Allan Collins suggests that Capone's importance was that he "created" the Democratic Machine by organizing the entire city for his own businesses, making a model which Democratic Mayor Anton Cermak (a Capone crony like his predecessor Big Bill Thompson) used when he was elected. Collins further hints that it was the mob that ordered Cermak's assassination and that Cermak, not President-elect FDR, was the real target.

When Capone moved his headquarters into the city from Cicero in 1925 (after he had shot O'Banion and reigned in peace) he first used the Metropole Hotel a block south of the New Michigan Hotel as his headquarters. Once a glittering establishment where Mayor "Big Bill" Thompson kept a suite, it had gotten seedy, but it was close to Capone's old nightclub, the Four Deuces at 2222 S. Michigan. In 1927 Capone moved into the Lexington. (Both the Metropole Hotel and the Four Deuces have been torn down.)

In both hotels Capone had gunmen patrolling the halls and lobby, open bars, an unending crowd of politicians and other supplicants visiting, and a suite of rooms where he lived like a king. At the Lexington he lived over the sign on the fifth floor until some stray bullets came his way, when he moved to the top floor where you can see the terra-cotta columns. His lavish parties, true to the Levee tradition, were orgies, but he also became a household name and associated socially with Chicago VIPs who enjoyed this '20s version of the '60s "radical chic." Chicago historians often write as though the awkward bully who spoiled the "fun" was the Untouchables' leader, Eliot Ness, not "the Big Fellow." They even suggest that Capone's showmanship, luxurious living, "loyalty," and "standards" were okay, but that Ness was a showoff who sought publicity!

But most Chicago mystery writers do not deify Scarface. In Whittingham's *State Street*, for example, when top mobster Rudy Facia refused to admit that his daughter had been raped, detective Joe Morrison said sarcastically "I understand, and Al Capone was just a good beer salesman." On the other hand, a Capone type was the hero of Richard Connell's amusing story "Brother Orchid," where a reformed gangster who became an Ellis Peters's Brother Cadfael-type, was killed for going straight.

Many mysteries include scenes at Capone's hotel. Most of them take place at the Lexington Hotel if they involve the mob—run by Frank Nitti and Capone's brother Ralph—after Capone was indicted and sent off to Atlanta and Alcatraz.

In Stuart Kaminsky's *You Bet Your Life*, P.I. Toby Peters went there twice to talk to Frank Nitti. Peters tried to convince Nitti that it was not Chico Marx who owed the mob a $120,000 gambling debt but a look-alike small-time crook. The second time Peters took the three Marx Brothers with him.

British mystery doyen Edgar Wallace produced a play and then a novelization of Capone's career called *On the Spot* the year Capone went to jail. (The title is gang slang for the more familiar phrase "taken for a ride.") Like Eugene Izzi many years later, Wallace based part of his plot on the fact that Capone and succeeding mob elders did not deal drugs because they destroyed you and made you squeal easily.

In Wallace's version, Tony Perelli, the Big Shot, who was taking over Chicago had a Capone-like retinue of bodyguards, elegant clothes, expensive tastes, loved opera, and got his start in "Cosmolino's" orchestra. From his Michigan Avenue penthouse he looked down on the city he planned to rule. Perelli's drawing room was a replica of the Doge's palace at Venice, where the final betrayal was played out between Perelli, the honest but ineffective police chief and a rival North Side gangster (aka O'Banion).

After meditating upon Capone's image and reputation,

turn left to walk along Cermak Road to Indiana Avenue past some sleazy buildings to the Metropole Restaurant at the corner of Indiana. They are among the few left of the South Loop's SRO (Single Room Occupancy) hotels for society's strays. The others are being torn down as part of the gentrification process.

In Sara Paretsky's *Burn Marks*, V.I. Warshawski's alcoholic trick-turning Aunt Elena appeared on her doorstep after her SRO burned down. Back there looking for clues, V.I. discovered it was arson. She also discovered that pols and "connected" contractors were buying up all the land around McCormick Place for a new stadium-retail-housing complex. This is much the same plot as Brian Michaels's mystery about a new stadium complex, called *Illegal Procedure*. (Chicago mystery writers know how their town really works.)

When V.I. combed this area looking for another transients' hotel her aunt could afford, she thought about the fact that a century ago the near south side had housed the Fields, the Searses, and the Armours. Today it consisted of vacant lots, auto dealers, public housing and the occasional SRO, while the block of mansions stood like a macabre ghost town. V.I. was forgetting the extensive development plans for McCormick Place, which according to city boosters will transform the entire "south Loop" or "near south" side all the way to 35th Street. Later V.I. got another call from Elena who was hiding in another deserted hotel, the Prairie Shores, near the Indiana Arms. When V.I. went there to rescue Elena, the arsonist burned the SRO hotel down around them.

Cross Indiana and walk to Prairie, cross Prairie and continue toward Calumet. On your left is the landmark building of the R. R. Donnelley Company's Calumet Plant. Designed in 1914 by Howard Van Doren Shaw, it is the city's best example of industrial Gothic, but it no longer prints the Sears, Roebuck catalogs.

Cermak Road, named for Mayor Anton Cermak who was shot in Florida standing next to President-elect Franklin D. Roosevelt, ends here. In Max Allan Collin's *True Detective* the mob sent P.I. Nate Heller to Florida to prevent Cermak's assassination because as a city cop working Michigan Avenue, Heller had seen Jake Lingle's blond killer, who had been hired to hit Cermak.

Turn left at Calumet to walk toward the bridge (and a covered walkway) over the railroad tracks and the Outer Drive that connects the various buildings of the McCormick Place complex. Before you reach the bridge you can turn right and go south on Calumet to walk to 23rd Street to get some lunch at Sauer's, an old dance hall cum warehouse famous for its charbroiled hamburgers on black bread. Or you can stop at the First National Frank on Cermak to have Chicago-style hot dogs. After eating at either place, walk back to McCormick Place where, despite the endless construction, you can get a cab or bus or take Metra back to the Loop from the 23rd Street Station.

You can also go into McCormick Place North on your left and get a snack on the lower level. There are a number of places to eat at the main convention hall on the lake, but they are not always open.

The first McCormick Place burned in 1969, and this stark Mies van der Rohe building replaced it. Both buildings broke the commandment handed down by Daniel Burnham and enforced by Montgomery Ward that nothing be allowed to destroy the lakefront which was to be kept "forever open, clear, and free." This area is now Chicago's chief convention spot and hopes to install a speedy transit system to the Loop soon, too.

Cross the roadway to McCormick Place. If it's a nice day, turn right at the entrance to walk to the end of the outdoor balcony overlooking the city and the Outer Drive. To the south and west of the Drive are the buildings of Michael Reese Hospital and just west of it along the Stevenson Expressway, the new tower of Mercy Hospital.

In Sam Reaves's *A Long Cold Fall*, cabbie Cooper MacLeish dropped a rude customer at the huge black monolith. The customer had gotten into his cab bellowing "You speak English?" Cooper, a Vietnam vet, sarcastically replied "You number one GI—chop chop—?" On another occasion Cooper drove a suspicious fare to the south side via Michigan Avenue. They drove past Chinatown, then Mercy Hospital, the lakefront projects and past Michael Reese Hospital into the "urban renewal" land of highrises built for doctors and professionals. You can see these highrise buildings, the public housing is farther south beyond Stephen A. Douglas's old estate of Oakenwald (site of Camp Douglas).

The new Mercy Hospital at 26th and Cottage Grove was established by the Sisters of Mercy in 1863. In Eugene Izzi's *The Take*, high-living Dr. Javier Chacona had lost his visiting rights at Mercy because of drinking and doping too much, but he continued to horse around with the sister of big dope dealer Ortiz.

South of Mercy at Lake Shore Drive and 31st Street is Michael Reese Hospital. In Paretsky's *Burn Marks*, V.I. went there to talk with Aunt Elena's friend from the Indiana Arms, Zerlina Ramsey, the mother of druggie Cerise who was found dead at a Streeterville construction site.

In Fredric Brown's *The Screaming Mimi*, burlesque stripper Yolanda Lang was taken there when an attacker slashed her. She had a police guard, but reporter William Sweeney talked his way in to see her.

Turn back to go inside McCormick Place to end this walk.

POSSIBLE SIDE TRIPS

The Raymond M. Hilliard Center, Chicago Housing Authority, 2030 S. State Street. Walk or drive west on Cermak Road to State Street, two blocks west of the New Michigan Hotel, to admire the Raymond Hilliard Center. It is a group of circular highrises designed in 1966 by Bertrand Goldberg, architect of Marina City and River City. Public housing for the elderly, the complex is built on the site of the notorious Everleigh Club at 2131–33 S. Dearborn, which housed the most elegant and expensive whorehouse in the Levee from 1900 to 1911. According to Heise and Baumann in *Chicago Originals*, the sisters Ada and Minna charged $50 per night—roughly $500 today. The ambiance was Prairie Avenue at its best, and the girls were expected to be genteel and ladylike. The sisters closed up shop when they heard they were going to be shut down, leaving with over a million in assets.

This area north to Polk Street was the red-light district. In Robert Bloch's historical mystery, *American Gothic*, intrepid girl reporter Crystal stood on the street near a church to see which city fathers went into 441 Clark Street, the fabulous Carrie Wilson's brothel.

Chinatown, Cermak Road and Wentworth Avenue. Walk or drive west on Cermak Road to Wentworth (or park at McCormick Place and get a cab from there). If you walk it is about eight blocks (one mile). At Wentworth you see the ceremonial red arched gateway and the On Leong Merchants' Association Building. There are many shops and restaurants trimmed with dragons and Chinese lions and painted red and gold, the most famous of which is undoubtedly Won Kow at 2233 S. Wentworth. Hemmed in for decades by railroad tracks, Chinatown has now expanded north and west with Chinatown Square at Archer and Cermak, built by Harry Weese.

In Edgar Wallace's *On the Spot* Minn Lee (a Columbia University graduate) lived in a Chinatown apartment where Tony Perelli visited an old Sicilian musician called Peter Melachini, who had played in Cosmolino's orchestra with him. Perelli was smitten with Minn, whom he made his mistress.

In Harry Stephen Keller's *Behind That Mask* the brilliant young Chinese Yin Yi who made wax masks for museums and stores had a studio on the narrowest street in Chinatown. The windows were painted halfway down with red paint, with green letters in English "Yin Yi, Wax Worker" and the three Chinese characters for his name.

In Marc Davis's *Dirty Money*, P.I. Frank Wolf and Tina Nockerman drove from her art gallery at 618 N. Michigan to Chinatown. (See Walk 4.) They parked near the On Leong building, an ornate three-story pagoda with red-tile roof, where crowds of tourists ambled up and down sidewalks and went to a storefront Szechwan restaurant to eat Kung Bao shrimp and shredded beef with peppers and scallions.

As you went west to Chinatown you passed under an extension of the Dan Ryan Expressway which goes by Wentworth Avenue to 26th Street. In Paretsky's *Burn Marks*, trying to prove the SRO arson was tied into big-time graft on construction sites in Streeterville and the Dan Ryan, V.I. put on a hard hat and climbed up to the Ryan construction site off Cermak, nearly becoming a construction casualty.

In Robert Bloch's story "Yours Truly, Jack the Ripper," Sir Guy Hollis, a thin tweedy Englishman with a moustache, was taken to an African-American bar in the ghetto at Halsted and 29th Street by Chicago psychiatrist John (Jack) Carmody. Sir Guy was on the trail of Jack the Ripper, whom he insisted was alive and well, living off the blood of his hooker victims, and due to murder any day. The foggy ambiance of this part of town, where the streets were tangled alleys and twisted streets like London's East End, seemed the right place and sure enough, Sir Guy met Jack the Ripper there.

River City, 800 S. Wells. Designed by Bertrand Goldberg in 1986, this is a pair of S-shaped buildings that contain a highrise atrium, three-level penthouses, a health club, and shops on the South Branch of the Chicago River. You can drive west on Polk Street from the south Loop and park to look around.

In Mark Zubro's *Sorry Now*, detective partners Paul Turner and Buck Fenwick worked out of Area Ten police headquarters just south of River City. The police building was as old and crummy as River City was new and shining. This odd couple was assigned to investigate the murder of TV evangelist Reverend Bruce Mucklewrath's daughter on the Oak Street Beach. (See Walk 5.)

Cook County Criminal Court House and Jail, 2600 S. California (three blocks south and about four miles west of McCormick Place). To get there, take a cab or drive. There is a parking lot across California. CTA rapid transit goes there from the Loop, but don't take it unless you have company. Cook County Jail is directly behind the Courts and you can see the guard towers as you drive west on 26th Street into Little Village.

Built in 1927 with classical columns and SPQC carved under the eagles to remind Chicagoans that their city is the New Rome, this building replaced the handsome old Criminal Courts on Hubbard. (See Walk 4.) When the courts moved, the powers-that-be brought along the gallows being kept for cop murderer Terrible Tommy O'Connor who had escaped from the old Illinois Street jail. Since the law said he must hang, not die in the electric chair, the authorities took the gibbet along to the new building and stored it. According to Kenan Heise and Ed Baumann, in *Chicago Originals*, in the mid-1970s Chief Justice Richard J. Fitzgerald ordered that the gallows be thrown out, but took a look at it first himself. Then Larry Donley, owner of the Seven Acres Museum in Union, drove into Chicago, loaded up the gallows, and took them home.

The Criminal Courts (often referred to simply as "26th and California") appear in many Chicago mysteries. In Jonathan Latimer's *Heading for a Hearse* the opening scene took place there on Death Row with a broker, a union official, and a Pole who murdered his girlfriend. Well bribed, the warden let the broker, Richard Westland, confer with his partners, a new shyster lawyer, and two detectives on how to solve the murder of his wife in the one week remaining before he was to die in the electric chair.

In Paretsky's *Blood Shot*, V. I. Warshawski had been a public defender. She was searched by a bailiff and went to the third floor to talk to Assistant States' Attorney Steve Dresberg. In *Killing Orders*, when arrested in Skokie, V. I. was locked up here with a group of prostitutes until she was sprung by her lawyer on an I-bond (individual recognizance). She had found Lotty Herschel's Uncle Stefan beaten up but was accused of doing it herself.

In *The Public Murders*, Bill Granger described how they bring prisoners across by an underground tunnel to the lockups behind the courtrooms. Overcrowding means prisoners can change cells or even skip, which was just what southern white murder suspect Norman Frank did. In Granger's *The El Murders* a conference was held there with Jack Donovan, the chief of the Criminal Division, and Homicide detectives. In *The Newspaper Murders*, Granger wrote that the building was gray like the day and the slum neighborhood around it with a classic front of pillars and tall gloomy windows. Brotherhood of Allah member Marcus Elijah had spent six weeks in Cook County Jail for the brutal holdup of Pap's Liquors on East 47th Street, but Sergeant Terry Flynn still wanted to question him about the murder of reporter Francis X. Sweeney.

In Barbara Gregorich's *Dirty Proof*, P.I. Dragovic's client Suzanne Quering was put in County Jail (aka Cook County Department of Corrections) accused of murdering "Madam" Ruby Good. Dragovic conned his brother-in-law into acting as her lawyer and they met in a small room empty except for a table and two chairs. Suzanne, wearing an orange jail uniform, told them she was never at Ruby's modern-day bordello. Later Quering, with the help of friends who brought her a rope, climbed out of County Jail and escaped to Frank Dragovic's apartment.

In Eugene Izzi's *The Bad Guys*, Jimbo Marino, an undercover cop, was arrested in a Loop bar owned by a mobster and ended up spending the night at 26th and California. He found out the stories were true: you get no sleep because others try to steal your stuff or attack you.

In Sherlockian Vincent Starrett's famous 1937 story "The Eleventh Juror," the narrator was serving on a Chicago criminal jury here. The jury was hung by the narrator, who convinced his fellows to let off the prisoner, who had shot his girl's husband. (Women did not serve on Cook County juries until 1939.)

In Craig Rice's *The Lucky Stiff*, Death Row inmate Anna Marie St. Clair was about to be executed when the true murderer confessed and she was freed. She then blackmailed the authorities into reporting her execution so she could snoop about (as a ghost) and find out who framed her.

In Harry Keeler's *Thieves' Nights* Big Tim O'Hartigan, Governor of Illinois, drove from his home on Cleveland in Lincoln Park to a large graystone building, the Criminal Courts, where he talked privately with condemned murderer Frank Porley. The governor, who had to keep Porley from telling the world he was married to a black woman locked up as insane, told Porley he would keep him from the chair by having the greatest alienist in America declare him insane.

Pilsen/Little Village, directly north and west of the Criminal Courts, both were originally the home of Polish, Czech and German immigrants. More recently they have become

Hispanic. The best time to visit is during the Independence Day Parade, held early in September along 26th Street or at the Fiesta en la Villita for the four days before the parade. Call 521-5387.

In Martin Blank's *Shadowcase*, the original suspects in the killing of two recent Irish immigrants were some Hispanic gang members. Detectives Hutch and Lamp went through Pilsen looking for a Hispanic murder suspect called Herrara, who turned out to be innocent.

In Michael Cormany's *Rich or Dead*, P.I. Kruger was working for an illegal Hispanic immigrant called Elvia Reyes. She had hired Kruger to find her brother Ricardo, who had stolen a brown paper bag with all her money. Kruger first found Ricardo dead in a flophouse without the bag, then took part in a shootout in a Little Village garage, which left a group of Hispanics dead, Kruger tied up, and Elvia on her way to Mexico with the money.

9

HYDE PARK/ UNIVERSITY OF CHICAGO WALK

BACKGROUND

Hyde Park began in 1853 when lawyer and developer Paul Cornell bought 300 acres of lakefront land between 51st and 55th Streets and deeded 60 acres to the Illinois Central Railroad in return for a train station. Hyde Park was incorporated as a village in 1861. A series of parks designed by Frederick Law Olmstead of Central Park fame helped bring settlers here, as did the development of Kenwood, north of Hyde Park at 47th Street. Both neighborhoods escaped the Chicago Fire, and remained pleasantly rural but convenient to the Loop until Chicago swallowed up the entire village in 1889. The city's object was to become as big as possible to lure the World's Columbian Exposition of 1893, which it won.

The fair was held in Hyde Park, which led not only to the development of Jackson Park, but to the founding in 1893 of a second University of Chicago with money provided by John D. Rockefeller. The first had failed about the time of the Civil War for lack of money. The fair's White City and the University's Gray City began together on the Midway and still define Hyde Park today. The Museum of Science and Industry in Jackson Park at 57th Street and Lake Michigan is the only remaining fair building, while the University's Gothic campus spreads from 55th to 61st Street from Dorchester to Cottage Grove. Both are known world-wide and attract visitors year-round.

At the same time, ever since the great southern black migrations of World War I, there has been a tendency in mysteries to equate the South Side, including Hyde Park, with crime and African-Americans. In fact, in the mid-'50s the neighborhood organized itself and began the first big national urban renewal project, with the result that today Hyde Park is known as "an integrated community of high standards, or "Lincoln Park South." In addition, the University of Chicago has its own Campus Police force which patrols the community.

University of Chicago graduate Barbara Mertz, aka Barbara Michaels and Elizabeth Peters, in *Search the Shadows* noted that "in their heyday Hyde Park and Kenwood were among the most affluent and elegant of Chicago's suburban areas . . . [and] the neighborhood had held its own, thanks in large part to the university and the museums and the professional schools that filled the area."

Present-day Hyde Parker Sara Paretsky took violent exception to the ghetto stereotype in *Indemnity Only.* When an Ajax Insurance employee assumed that Peter Thayer, a U of C student, was murdered by "one of those drug addicts who are always killing people in Hyde Park," V.I. Warshawski replied sarcastically, "You make Hyde Park sound like the Tong Wars. . . . Of the thirty-two murders in the twenty-first police district last year, only six were in Hyde Park—one every two months."

Hyde Parkers are a special breed, made up of all races, creeds, ethnic backgrounds, and degrees of education from street smarts to Ph.D.s. They have included many famous people as well as murderers like Richard Loeb, Nathan Leopold, and William Heirens, all three of whom attended the University of Chicago.

Hyde Park is also where I was born, went to school, and

now live in the Victorian house where I grew up. My family has worked to preserve and protect the community, especially my mother, Dr. Ursula B. Stone, a professor at George Williams College who was the only woman on the Committee of Five which set up the South East Chicago Commission, which brought about urban renewal, and my brother George B. Stone, First Deputy Commissioner of Housing under Hyde Park's own Mayor Harold Washington.

A special word, too, about my reader/checkers. For Hyde Park I had ten, most of them Hyde Parkers. Loving the neighborhood, they all added details, so that keeping the walk in bounds became a tremendous task. It has been ruthlessly pruned, but extras are included in Possible Side Trips.

Come join us for a delightful trip through a college town in the middle of a large city. To get to Hyde Park from the Loop, drive south on Lake Shore Drive and get off at 57th Street. You can park near the Museum of Science and Industry, or two blocks north on Lake Park Avenue by the Hyde Park Shopping Center. Or take the #6 Jeffrey Express Bus on State Street and get off at 57th Street, or take the Metra train from one of its Loop stations to 55th-56th-57th Street or the main 59th Street Station.

LENGTH OF WALK: About 5 miles

Part One: Hyde Park—2½ miles
Part Two: University of Chicago—2¾ miles

See the map on page 275 for the boundaries of this walk and page 359 for a list of the books and detectives mentioned.

You can do it in two parts, one day at a time, or make a day of it, stopping to refresh yourself in the middle. There are also three major (and several minor) Possible Side Trips listed.

PLACES OF INTEREST

Court Theater, 5535 S. Ellis Avenue. Designed by Harry Weese in 1981. Professional company presents classics and contemporary drama. Call 753-4472.

Hyde Park Shopping Center, 55th Street and Lake Park Avenue. Designed in 1960 by I. M. Pei and constructed by Harry Weese; home of Hyde Park's famous Co-op (grocery store).

William H. Ray Public Elementary School (old Hyde Park High School), 5631 S. Kimbark. Redbrick 1893 Queen Anne. Site of Annual 57th Street Art Fair (oldest one in Chicago), held the first weekend in June.

Robie House, 5757 S. Woodlawn Avenue. Frank Lloyd Wright's Prairie School design created in 1909 for bicycle manufacturer, now the University of Chicago Alumni Office. Tours given daily at noon. Fee. Call 684-1300.

Saint Thomas Apostle Roman Catholic Church, 5472 S. Kimbark Avenue. 1924 building with Prairie School colors and terra-cotta trim, combined with elegant verticals. Not open except for church services.

Jackson Park, 56th Street to 67th Street, Stony Island to Lake Michigan. (Connected to Washington Park by Midway Plaisance.) The site of the 1893 World's Columbian Exposition, planned by Daniel Burnham.

Midway Plaisance, 59th–60th Streets, from Washington Park to Jackson Park.

Linne Statue, Midway Plaisance between Ellis and University Avenues. Honors great Swedish scientist Linneas.

Masaryk Memorial, Midway Plaisance at Blackstone Avenue. In honor of Thomas Masaryk, president of Czechoslovakia.

Washington Park, 51st Street and Martin Luther King Drive to 60th Street and Cottage Grove Avenue. Designed in 1871 by Olmstead and Vaux but not completed until 1893 World's Columbian Exposition.

Fountain of Time, at entrance to Washington Park. Designed in 1922 by Hyde Parker Lorado Taft. Covered with plastic in winter because its concrete is crumbling. Taft himself appears wearing a smock.

Du Sable Museum of African-American History, Washington Park, 740 E. 56th Place at Cottage Grove Avenue. Named for Chicago's first settler. Exhibits on black history. Fee. Admission free on Thursdays. Open Mon.–Fri. 9:00 A.M.–5:00 P.M., Sat.–Sun. noon–5:00 P.M. Call 947-0600.

University of Chicago, Main Campus: University to Ellis Avenue, 57th to 59th Street. Financed by John D. Rockefeller, its Gothic quadrangles were designed by Henry Ives Cobb to create a unified campus for a world-class university. Free. Tours given Mon.–Sat. 10:00 A.M. Visitors Center, Ida Noyes Hall, 1212 E. 59th Street (metered parking available). Call 702-8374.

Nuclear Energy, Ellis Avenue between 56th and 57th Street, once the West Stands of University of Chicago's Stagg Field. Helmet-shaped cloud by Henry Moore on the site of the first self-sustaining controlled nuclear chain reaction.

Oriental Institute Museum, 1155 E. 58th Street. "The Bull Pen," showcase of history and art of ancient Near East. Open Tues., Thur.–Sat. 10:00 A.M.–4:00 P.M. Wed. 10:00 A.M.–8:30 P.M., Sun. noon–4:00 P.M. Free. Call 702-9522.

David and Alfred Smart Museum of Art, 5550 S. Greenwood Avenue. Houses university's art collection and has special exhibits. Free. Open Tues.–Fri. 10:00 A.M.–4:00 P.M., Sat.–Sun. noon–6:00 P.M. Call 702-0200.

BOOKSTORES

Hyde Park is a haven for book lovers, including mystery readers. Here are some stores well worth checking out in the course of your walk.

Fifty-Seventh Street Books, 1301 E. 57th Street (basement).

Louis Kiernan, Bookseller, 1342 E. 53rd Street.

Kroch's and Brentano's, 1530 E. 53rd Street.

O'Gara & Wilson's, Ltd., 1311 E. 57th Street.

Powell's, 1501 E. 57th Street.

Seminary Co-op Bookstore, 5757 S. University Avenue (basement of Chicago Theological Seminary).

University of Chicago Bookstore, 970 E. 58th Street.

PLACES TO EAT

There are many places to eat, offering everything from fast foods to bagels to shish kebob. The ones listed below appear in mystery stories or reflect special local color.

Ann Sather, 1329 E. 57th Street. Swedish diner with authentic menu.

Jimmy's Woodlawn Tap (aka University Tap), 1172 E. 55th Street. Beer and hamburgers and chess. *Encyclopaedia Britannica* kept on premises. Readings Sundays at 3:00 P.M. by Molly Daniel's Clothesline School of Writing.

The Medici on 57th Street, 1327 E. 57th Street. Collegiate coffee house. Hamburgers, deep-dish pizza.

The Medici on Harper, Harper Court. Thin-crust pizza.

Museum of Science and Industry, 57th Street at Lake Shore Drive: McDonald's.

University of Chicago:

- ***Hutchison Commons/C Shop***, inside Mandel Hall, 57th Street and University Avenue (delicatessen).
- ***Ida's Cafe, The Pub***, inside Ida Noyes Hall, 1212 E. 59th Street. (Membership [$15.00] required at the Pub.)
- ***Swift Hall***, student-run coffee shop in basement (Thai cuisine).
- ***University of Chicago Bookstore***, 970 E. 5th Street (delicatessen).

University Gardens, 1373 E. 53rd Street. Storefront restaurant serving Middle Eastern food.

Valois, 1518 E. 53rd Street. Cafeteria; subject of a best-selling book, *Slim's Table,* by U of C sociology student Mitchell Duneier.

HYDE PARK/ UNIVERSITY OF CHICAGO WALK

HYDE PARK

Begin your walk at 55th Street and Lake Park Avenue at the Hyde Park Shopping Center. Before urban renewal came about in the middle 1950s, Lake Park Avenue was a dingy commercial street lined with garages, gas stations, bars, a bowling alley, a movie house, and a funeral parlor. Its multicultural urban ambiance spread west along 55th Street to Cottage Grove.

The Hyde Park Police Station used to be two blocks north on the corner of 53rd Street, across from today's Kroch's & Brentano's Bookstore. In Jonathan Latimer's *The Lady in the Morgue,* P.I. William Crane drove to Hyde Park with Doc Williams and Tom O'Malley looking for a girl's body missing from the morgue. They drove under the I.C. (Metra) tracks at 53rd and turned right on Lake Street (old name) and went past the Hyde Park Police Station to the Star Mortuary at 5217 Lake Street (Charles Bilger's). Inside they found the body of the redheaded undertaker who had stolen the girl's body from the morgue, but no girl. They left a note for the police signed "Shirley Temple."

Farther north on Lake Park Avenue was the George Harding Museum, a very eccentric collection, housed in a mansion connected to a small castle. The Harding Museum was there when Barbara Michaels got her Ph.D. in Egyptology at the University of Chicago, and in *Search the Shadows* her Nazarian family lived in a family mansion with an attached museum. (See Walk 8.)

Across the street at Lake Park and 55th Street is a 1929 Art Deco terra-cotta office building that was once a garage. The Hyde Park Shopping Center, designed by I. M. Pei, is being rehabbed. It houses numerous stores, including the famous Hyde Park Co-op, founded in the '30s by former Alderman and future Senator Paul Douglas and NBC newscaster Clifton Utley, among others. It remains a neighborhood institution and the home of liberal causes.

Explore the Shopping Center, where you might see Sara Paretsky, then walk to Harper Avenue (the western side of the Shopping Center) and walk one half block north to the yellow apartment building just south of 54th Street.

In Sara Paretsky's *Indemnity Only,* V.I. Warshawski was hired by union boss McGraw to find his daughter Anita, who was living with Peter Thayer. She went to Thayer's student apartment in a dirty yellow brick building behind the Co-op Shopping Center and found Thayer dead, so she went back to the Shopping Center to phone an anonymous tip to the cops.

Return to 55th Street and keep walking west past the I. M.

Pei/Harry Weese townhouses built in the 1960s to replace the old multistory walk-up storefronts. Cross Blackstone Avenue and go right around University Park Condominium, Pei's twin highrises in the middle of 55th Street. Cross Dorchester, then Ridgewood Court to reach the University National Bank. Beyond the bank building are two bookstores: Louis Kiernan, Bookseller, who knows mysteries and has great bargains, and Ex Libris Theological Books at the corner of Kenwood Avenue.

Cross Kenwood and keep walking along the north side of 55th Street past the Hyde Park Neighborhood Club to Kimbark Avenue. Cross Kimbark to St. Thomas Apostle Roman Catholic Church, with its high walls surrounding the church, school, rectory, and convent. The church, designed in 1924 by a former employee of Frank Lloyd Wright, has the Prairie School's pale, sand-colored brick and terra-cotta trim, combined with steep verticals and a high decorated roof.

Although it is not gray '20s Gothic, St. Thomas Apostle Church makes a good substitute for Bill Granger's St. Alma's in *The Priestly Murders*, which was located farther north at 47th and Ellis on the site of the real St. Ambrose's Church. In Granger's mystery a policeman shot the young priest officiating at early mass. Later Sergeant Terry Flynn and the tactical homicide squad held a stakeout in the church to catch the murderer.

St. Thomas Apostle Church is not left open during the week. Daily masses are said in the chapel at 6:30, 8:30, and 5:30, at which times you might ask to look around.

Walk one more block west on 55th Street past St. Thomas's School to Woodlawn Avenue and cross Woodlawn. In Mark Zubro's *Political Poison,* Detectives Buck Fenwick and Paul Turner went to interview former Fifth Ward Committeeman Mike McGee at his home just north of 55th and Woodlawn. McGee's house covered three normal-sized lots and had driveways on both sides. Of the two houses on the block, the graystone house with a wide side yard is the best choice. McGee claimed that lakefront liberal Gideon Giles had really sold out to the Machine.

Then walk past the cleaner's to the dingy storefront that houses Jimmy's Woodlawn Tap, a famous university hangout

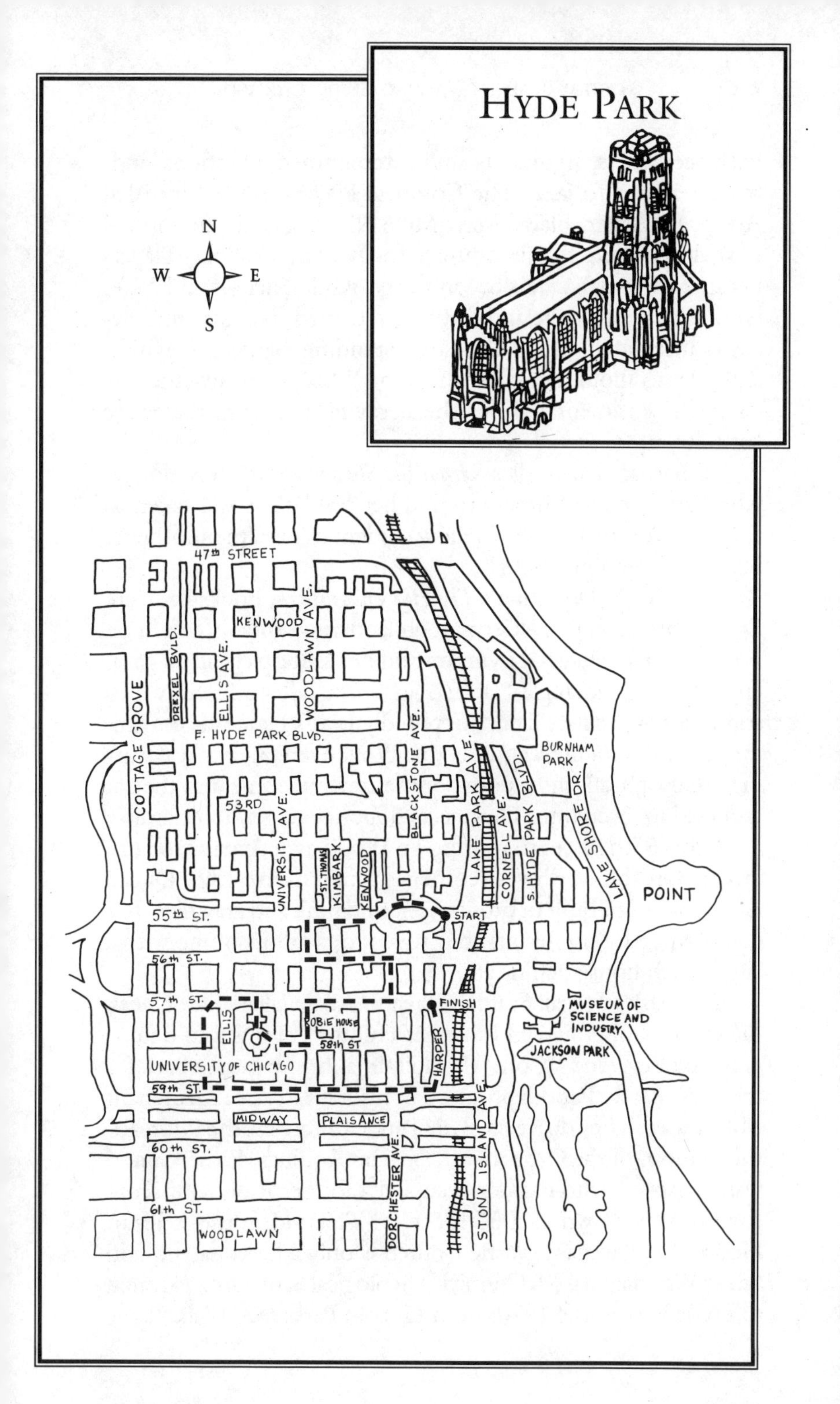

HYDE PARK
N
W
E
S
47th STREET
KENWOOD
DREXEL BLVD.
ELLIS AVE.
WOODLAWN AVE.
COTTAGE GROVE
E. HYDE PARK BLVD.
BURNHAM PARK
BLACKSTONE AVE.
LAKE PARK AVE.
CORNELL AVE.
S. HYDE PARK BLVD.
LAKE SHORE DR.
53RD
UNIVERSITY AVE.
ST. THOMAS
KIMBARK
KENWOOD
POINT
55th ST.
START
56th ST.
57th ST.
FINISH
MUSEUM OF SCIENCE AND INDUSTRY
ELLIS
ROBIE HOUSE
58th ST
HARPER
JACKSON PARK
UNIVERSITY OF CHICAGO
59th ST.
MIDWAY
PLAISANCE
60th ST.
DORCHESTER AVE.
STONY ISLAND AVE.
61th ST.
WOODLAWN

with beer, chess, arguments, and entertainment of various kinds from readings to jazz. The Compass Players, started by Alan Arkin, Ed Asner, Elaine May, Mike Nichols, et al., performed next door where the firehouse is today. The Compass Players became the north side's Second City, while Nichols and May, who went on to fame and fortune, returned to accuse middle-class, integrated Hyde Park of "standing black and white, shoulder to shoulder against the poor." Like many ex-students they felt sentimental about the decaying buildings that were torn down.

In Barbara Michaels's *Search the Shadows* Haskell Maloney, who had come to Chicago to find her real father, was taken to the "University Tap" by a fellow student of her dead mother's, who was now a professor.

In H. E. F. Donohue's *The Higher Animals,* bookstore clerk Dan Conn, several professors, a philandering student wife, a reporter, and a teen-aged nympho and her sailor pick-up all gathered at the Quadrangle Place (Lou's Place) after a fire in which some elderly recluses died. Supposedly Lou's Place was *not* Jimmy's, but it certainly seemed like it. While everyone else was waxing philosophical, three poor Southern whites came into the bar and held up everyone. They needed money to get home again.

Cross 55th Street to walk down Woodlawn Avenue to 56th Street. On the northwest corner is a handsome 1892 Queen Anne mansion, built of brownstone and pink and gray tiles. It is now owned by the Jesuits, but was once a family home with a large coach house behind it.

In Charles Merrill Smith's *Reverend Randollph and the Unholy Bible* an old miser named Johannes Humbrecht was found murdered by Reverend "Con" Randollph, a former quarterback for the L.A. Rams. Randollph called in his friend Police Lieutenant Mike Casey. They drove to Hyde Park to interview the Prior, Father Simon, of the Order of St. Thomas Aquinas. Father Simon was a suspect, whose order occupied a former Protestant seminary at Woodlawn and 56th Street. This old house is Jesuit House, St. Thomas Apostle Church is only a block north, and across Woodlawn is McCormick Theological Seminary, relocated to Hyde Park in the 1970s from Lincoln Park. (See Walk 7.)

Jesuit House is in the right location for the gloomy mansion in Mignon G. Eberhart's *Hasty Wedding,* which was large and ugly, built before the North Shore became fashionable, huge and solid, with plate-glass windows and a black slate roof and somber chimneys. Heiress Dorcas Whipple married a man she didn't love to please her mother, but the night before the ceremony Dorcas sneaked out to see her old boyfriend, who was found dead the next day. The wedding was held at the Gold Coast's Episcopal St. Chrystofer's (St. Chrysostom's), then everyone returned here for the reception.

Cross 56th Street to the sandstone Romanesque Hyde Park Union (Baptist) Church, associated with the founders of the University of Chicago and John D. Rockefeller, the university's chief benefactor. Then cross Woodlawn to a row of brick townhouses. Past the row houses you can see a large brick house with a high iron fence and driveway. This is probably the house that Thomas McCall was thinking of in *A Wide and Capable Revenge,* although he put it two blocks east (see below). When detective Nora Callum decided suspect Professor Georgi Glazunov was making a getaway she tailed him home from the University.

Go east on 56th Street to Kimbark Avenue. On either side are redbrick townhouses built for U of C faculty. Cross Kimbark to the Ray School block and walk past its annex to the alley. The Victorian William H. Ray Public School was built as Hyde Park High School. Thanks to urban renewal, whose plans called for opening up space around all public buildings, Ray School now occupies the entire block except for one highrise. Hyde Park's 57th Street Art Fair, the city's oldest, is held on the William H. Ray playground the first Saturday and Sunday in June.

At the alley look across 56th Street. To the north you will see a small red barn with a cupola. This is the spot where Studs Lonigan committed his first holdup in James T. Farrell's classic south-side Irish trilogy *Studs Lonigan.*

Continue walking east past the highrise apartment to Kenwood Avenue, which deadends in a cul-de-sac on your right. To your left in one of the six Victorian houses on the west side of Kenwood U of C English Professor Bill Veeder wrote his two scholarly books on Bram Stoker's *Dracula* and Mary Shelley's

Frankenstein. In McCall's *A Wide and Capable Revenge,* Detective Nora Callum followed murder suspect Dr. Georgi Glazunov home to this block. McCall said the block had "post-Victorian beauties with black wrought-iron fences . . . and huge ancient oaks and maples dappled the street and sidewalks." Most of the houses are Victorian, there never were any oaks, and the shady elms and cottonwoods died thirty years ago.

Cross Kenwood Avenue and turn right to walk past another group of brick townhouses, some frame houses, and a courtyard building to the Bixler Playground at 57th Street. In *Political Poison* Mark Zubro put the Fifth Ward office of murdered alderman Gideon Giles, a U of C English professor, in a storefront across from the children's playlot and the Ann Sather Restaurant, but there is no place for it.

Cross 57th Street to the Ann Sather Restaurant. It was once the Agora, a Greek restaurant, probably the place where Bill Granger's murderous cop, who shot the priest at early mass at St. Alma's, got a free meal in *The Priestly Murders.*

In Zubro's *Political Poison* gay Detective Paul Turner went to Ann Sather's while investigating the murder of Gideon Giles. Sitting in a booth by the lace-curtained windows Turner met with U of C student Clark Burke who was working in Giles's office and had been there when the alderman died of poison.

This is a good place to rest. You have gone about 1½ miles and are on the same block as two famous bookstores and about four blocks west of the 57th Street Metra Station. Have some coffee and a muffin or cinnamon bun.

Then come outside and walk to the corner of Kenwood and look right toward 58th Street. On the east side of the street just past a '20s highrise, you will see a row of big square stone houses. In Zubro's *Political Poison* murder victim Giles and his stockbroker wife Laura lived on Kenwood Avenue between 57th and 58th Street in one of the houses with a driveway. Turner and his partner interviewed the neighbors on either side. A woman in a beige Christian Dior suit said she didn't get involved with University people. Another in jeans and a Save the Whales T-shirt offered them tea and gossip in a room with polished wood floors, teak furniture, pillows, and stark white walls.

Walk west along 57th Street past the collegiate hangout, the Medici on 57th, and Edwardo's Pizza. Cross the alley to Kinko's and two more bookstores, first O'Gara's, then Fifty-Seventh Street Books in the basement at the corner of Kimbark Avenue. O'Gara's is the oldest used bookstore in the city and has second-hand mysteries, while Fifty-Seventh Street Books has all the new ones.

According to her cousin Damaris Hendry Day, mystery writer Craig Rice once lived in the apartment building above Fifty-Seventh Street Books. Members of Rice's family lived in Hyde Park and she always sent "my very dear Aunt Jess" (Day's grandmother) copies of her current mysteries. To them, she was–and still is–Georgiana. Her pen name, incidentally, did not come from her numerous husbands, but from her father's family. Her reporter dad, whom she adored, was Harry Craig, while his half-sister, who raised Georgiana, was Nan Rice.

In H. E. F. Donohue's *The Higher Animals,* Daniel Conn was minding a basement bookstore on 57th Street for its owner Gahagan. (Probably Stavers', which used to occupy Fifty-Seventh Street Books' space.) Conn's day was full of mythic significance, reminiscent of James Joyce's Bloomsday. (For more on that read Andrew Greeley's Father Blackie mystery, *Happy Are the Peacemakers,* set in Dublin, Ireland.)

Stop to browse or buy a book or two, then cross Kimbark Avenue and walk west to Woodlawn Avenue. Between Kimbark and Woodlawn on the north side of the street there is a row of old frame houses, with one new one in the middle. It was built on the site of another old frame house which burned up in the 1950s in a spectacular fire in which three elderly sisters lost their lives.

In Donohue's *The Higher Animals,* Conn heard the engines and came out of the bookstore to see a fire in a frame house occupied by a bizarre family where he had roomed as a student. (In fact, Compass Player/Hollywood star Mike Nichols roomed next door as a U of C student.) One of Conn's faculty drinking buddies went into the house and got one resident out, but she went in again and died.

In Greeley's first Father Blackie mystery, *Happy Are the*

Meek, Cardinal Sean Cronin told Father Blackie (Monsignor John Blackwood Ryan) to solve the murder of Wolf Quinlan. The Quinlan family had been going to the Church of the Angels of Light, which specialized in drugs, Babylonian prayers, and free sex. It was run by an unfrocked priest and was located in an old frame house about 57th and Dorchester. (There is no such house there.) When Father Armande kidnapped Laurel Quinlan, her mother Sue came after her. Father Armande had tied them both up naked on a marble altar and sprinkled them with kerosene just as Father Blackie roared to the rescue in a Coast Guard helicopter from Michigan City.

At the corner of Woodlawn Avenue and 57th Street is the gray limestone Meadville/Lombard Theological School, which trains Unitarian ministers. Across the street is the perpendicular Gothic First Unitarian Church of Chicago.

Meadville Seminary was the real-life model for Patricia Houck Sprinkle's Markham Institute, a University of Chicago affiliate that trained students for the diplomatic service, like Tufts's Fletcher School of Diplomacy. Sprinkle, a Unitarian minister, went to Meadville and the layout of her school of diplomacy is a perfect fit from stacks to parlor. For years Meadville, like Markham, also had a Japanese-American receptionist/secretary.

In *Murder at Markham,* Sheila Travis, widow of a career diplomat, got a secretarial job at Markham. The first day on the job Travis discovered the body of a missing Markham student in the library stacks, rolled up in a missing oriental rug.

Walk south on Woodlawn toward 58th Street. On either side of the street you are passing landmark houses built for University of Chicago faculty, many now university offices. They were built in red brick because it was more informal than limestone and made a good contrast to the University.

At 58th Street is one of Frank Lloyd Wright's most famous homes, the Robie House. Built in 1906, it is the quintessential Prairie House with strong horizontal lines and sweeping eaves and leaded casement windows. It is occupied by the University of Chicago's Alumni Association and its Alumni Magazine staff, and there are official tours at noon.

Cross Woodlawn and walk west on 58th Street towards the main University of Chicago campus. On the north side of the street you pass the Chicago Theological Seminary, a group of redbrick Gothic buildings. CTS houses both the tiny Hilton Chapel and larger Graham Taylor Chapel; in the basement on University is the Seminary Co-op Bookstore, famous for having every book you ever wanted.

Across 58th Street is the University of Chicago's Oriental Institute, affectionately known as the "Bull Pen" because of its gigantic Assyrian bull. The Oriental Institute was built in 1931 in Art Deco Gothic by the architects of Rockefeller Chapel. It replaced 1896 Haskell Hall on the main campus, which was also a museum. The Oriental Institute is the alma mater of best-selling mystery writer Dr. Barbara Mertz, who writes under *two* pen names, Barbara Michaels and Elizabeth Peters. One of her series stars nineteenth-century scholar/archaeologist Amelia Peabody. In *The Fine Art of Murder* Mertz explains that in the 1950s you never got to do field work unless you were your husband's assistant, so she wrote about it instead.

Writing as Barbara Michaels, she set *Search the Shadows* in Hyde Park. Haskell Maloney came to Chicago to find out who her real father had been because her dead mother had been a graduate student at the Oriental Institute and named her for Haskell Hall! On arriving, Haskell ignored the museum on the first floor to go up the staircase to the second-floor library. There you can see a Fabergé-style King Tut egg made by Rachel Marshall Goetz, a real life U of C grad. Haskell had a run-in with a female professor, then staked out the classroom of Professor David Wertheim, who had been her mother's classmate. When Wertheim appeared she bullied him into getting her a job at the Nazarian Museum on Prairie Avenue. (See Walk 8.)

In Andrew Greeley's *Happy Are the Meek,* the phony Father Armande found his Babylonian chants in the library of the Oriental Institute. Father Blackie wondered aloud why he thought Lucifer (the devil) would understand Babylonian any better than English. Cross 58th Street to explore the Oriental Institute to end the first part of this walk.

UNIVERSITY OF CHICAGO

Begin this half of the walk on the west side of University Avenue, where you are at the main entrance to the campus of the University of Chicago. Founded with money given by John D. Rockefeller, a Baptist like its bright young President William Rainey Harper, it opened in 1892 with 500 students and one building, Cobb Hall. One hundred years later the university has more than sixty Nobel Prizes to its credit.

The 175-acre Gothic campus set in six quadrangles represented an American Oxbridge. But also, as Jean F. Block wrote in *The Uses of Gothic,* "classic buildings were built by merchant princes, Gothic [by] humble workmen. Classicism referred to Europe's palaces, Gothic to Europe's great seats of learning and timeless religious values."

The university has its cultured despisers, and a perpetual battle rages in Hyde Park between town and gown over mutual civility. In 1952 the University *and* the community at a mass meeting in Mandel Hall chose to practice "urban renewal" rather than to cut and run, the choice of many other Chicago companies and institutions. But the fact that the university provided most of the clout and the cash did not make it easy to live with.

You pick up this ambivalence in mysteries. Bill Granger in *The Priestly Murders* wrote that the university was an imitation of ancient European universities nestled in a comfortable old neighborhood that floated in the black ghetto of the South Side like a cruise ship on a dangerous sea. On the other hand, in U of C grad Richard Himmel's thriller *The Twenty-Third Web,* Loop banker Livingston Stonehill declared that there was no South Side *except* the University of Chicago.

Many Andrew Greeley characters share a love-hate relationship with the university as Irish-Chicagoans. In *Angel Fire* Nobel prize-winning faculty member Sean Desmond, who studied angels scientifically, sent his daughters to St. Ignatius Prep instead of the University's Laboratory Schools. But according to Greeley in *Andrew Greeley's Chicago,* Father Blackie presides over a seminar at the Divinity School one quarter a year.

A subtler form of higher criticism appeared in Michael A. Kahn's *Grave Designs* where a very expensive call girl named Andi Hebner was also a University of Chicago grad student!

Former grad student Philip Roth took literary pot shots at both Hyde Park and the university in *Letting Go,* as did former faculty member Saul Bellow. English professors Robert Herrick and James Webber Linn wrote about campus life, unlike Norman McLean, who wrote *A River Runs Through It* about his pre-student days.

But it was English professor Walter Blair, a longtime colleague of McLean's, who wrote an academic mystery called *Candidate for Murder,* using the amusing pen name of Mortimer Post, or Post, Mortimer. His mystery took place at Chatham University in Chicago. The campus architecture was colonial rather than Gothic; but Chatham closely resembles the U of C.

As you walk into the main campus, to your left on University Avenue across from the Oriental Institute is the 1971 Albert Pick Hall for International Studies.

In Thomas McCall's *A Wide and Capable Revenge,* detective Nora Callum came there to interview murder suspect Russian émigré Georgi Glazunov. Callum casually parked on University Avenue, which is most unlikely since the campus streets get parked up by 8:00 A.M. Glazunov was Chairman of Russian Studies (there is no such department) and his office and classroom were in a tiny old Gothic building. The Linguistics Department, where my father's old friend, Russian émigré George V. Bobrinskoy taught Sanskrit, is in Classics, a small 1915 Gothic building all the way across campus at Ellis and 59th Street.

Walk into the campus between the tennis courts. As you walk towards the center circle drive, glance left into the first quadrangle where the women's dorms used to be. The Social Sciences Building on 59th Street houses the history, economics, and political science departments.

In Jane Langton's *The Dante Game,* filled with quotations from the Dante translation of British mystery writer Dorothy L. Sayers, there was a new and struggling American School for Florentine Studies. Among its rather strange staff was an instructor in Italian History who was a self-important and portly scholar from the University of Chicago called Himmelfahrt. When there were a number of messy murders, Himmelfahrt finked out for home.

Follow the circle to the left, passing two Gothic buildings beyond Pick, the Walker Museum and Rosenwald (geography and geology). Those departments have moved and the buildings are now occupied by the ever-expanding Graduate School of Business (GSOB).

One of the famous graduates of the School of Business in 1925 was Eliot Ness. Ness found business too tame, so he got himself employed by the Justice Department through the good offices of his brother-in-law, Alexander Jamie. Jamie was the chief investigator for the Secret Six, the powerful group dedicated to eradicating Al Capone. Ness, of course, then created his special team, known as the Untouchables, whose career he described in *The Untouchables: The Real Story*.

Beyond Rosenwald look into the main south quad. To your left is the old Law School building, designed like Cambridge University's King's College Chapel, also taken over by the GSOB. But in Jonathan Latimer's *The Lady in the Morgue* it would have been the alma mater of obnoxious Assistant State's Attorney Burman, whose family had wanted him to be a rabbi.

Chances are that Paretsky's V.I. Warshawski, whose Law School graduation picture hung in her cousin Boom Boom's fancy condo in *Deadlock,* had classes in this building. It was in her student days that she had a crush on demonstration organizer Jasper Heccomb, the blond messiah-type who was running the not-for-profit Home Free in *Tunnel Vision*. V.I. also studied here under Manfred Yeo, in whose honor law professor Fabian Messenger had a peculiar party at his mansion in Kenwood (See Possible Side Trips).

Straight ahead in the south quad is twin-towered Harper Memorial Library, where the College (undergraduate school) has classes and uses the elegant third floor reading room. It would have been at Harper or at Cobb Hall that the murderous undergraduate pair, Richard Loeb and Nathan Leopold, met on campus. A fellow student of theirs was Meyer Levin, who wrote about them in *Compulsion.* (The pair also lived near one another in Kenwood.)

Facing the old Law School is Haskell Hall, originally the Oriental Institute, but since 1931 it has been the home of the GSOB. Mystery writer William F. Love is a GSOB grad as well as a former Benedictine, and in *The Chartreuse Clue,* his murder suspect was a young fun-loving Chicago priest named William Fuller. Fuller had been sent to New York to do grad work at Fordham University, but woke up to find his girlfriend dead. (See *Mystery Reader's Walking Guide: New York.*)

Keep walking around the circle. The next building to your left is Swift Hall, home of the Divinity School, with a cloister that connects it with Bond Chapel, a wood-paneled beauty with angel rafters (shades of Dorothy L. Sayers' *The Nine Tailors*) and spectacular blue stained-glass windows.

Swift also has a handsome wainscotted commons room on the first floor. In Barbara D'Amato's *Hardball* freelancer Cat Marsala, who was doing a story on drugs, went to a meeting on the U of C campus. D'Amato's geography is vague, but the room described could well be Swift's commons. Cat was talking to the main speaker, Louise Sugarman, when Sugarman was blown to bits by a remote-control bomb.

In Mark Zubro's *Political Poison,* U of C English professor Gideon Giles, who was also the newly elected Fifth Ward Alderman, was poisoned in his third floor office in Swift. Zubro put the English Department in Swift Hall, but it is really in the next quadrangle in Gates-Blake Halls. At the same time, Zubro's description makes Swift Hall sound more like Cobb Hall, a much older building. Zubro's mystery has definite echoes of the real-life unsolved shooting of the Divinity School's Rumanian Professor Culianu, which occurred on Swift's third floor in 1991.

Detectives Fenwick and Turner investigated the scene of the Giles crime. A student offered to take the detectives to the student-run cafeteria in Swift's basement but they chose to go across campus instead. They later returned and went upstairs in Swift, where someone shot at them. In Sara Paretsky's *Indemnity Only,* V.I. Warshawski, a U of C grad like her creator, went into the Swift basement coffee shop. Sitting there V.I. heard other students gossiping about Peter Thayer's murder and decided to go to a meeting of the University Women's Union, to which Thayer's missing girlfriend belonged.

Walk inside Swift, go down the long corridor to look at the commons room, and feel free to run up the stairs to eye the third floor or go to the basement to visit the Swift coffee shop.

Then go past Swift to the western side of the main campus on Ellis Avenue. To your left is Cobb Hall, then the oldest quadrangle, made up of Blake, Gates, Snell, Classics, and Wieboldt Halls. In the archway between Classics and Wieboldt that leads to 59th Street there is a stone from the first University of Chicago which had been located near Camp Douglas but failed for lack of financial support and students.

Cobb Hall, Chicago's "Old Main," was built the year the university opened, and its steep roofs, gables, and oriel windows established the Gothic ambiance the trustees wanted. The building has been rebuilt several times since the days when it held all the University offices and classrooms, as well as the chapel. On the fourth floor is the Bergman Gallery of the Renaissance Society, which is open to the public. Across from Cobb is the C Bench, given by a graduating class of long ago.

In Mortimer Post's *Candidate for Murder,* Professor Gaylord taught Elizabethan drama in a lofty boxlike room lined with tall windows in Hanover Hall which sounds like Cobb. Appointed by the president to handle campus pro-Nazi problems involving tenure and ending in murder, Gaylord formed his own faculty committee to solve the crime.

To the right of Cobb Hall is the utilitarian Administration Building, put up just after World War II during the tag end of Robert M. Hutchins's presidency. Using the commanding site meant for a great library or hall, this nondescript building demonstrates Hutchins's attitude toward tradition.

The University of Chicago Press is located in the Ad Building. The Press published the life work of Dorothy Sayers' college friend, Muriel St. Clare Byrne, which was an annotated edition of the *Lisle Letters,* a collection dating from Tudor times. Byrne is mentioned as a mentor in Charles Nicholls's *The Reck-*

oning, a Crime Writers Association award-winning book on Elizabethan Christopher Marlowe, and both ladies would have been fascinated by Nicholls' attempt to solve the mystery of Marlowe's murder.

In Paretsky's *Indemnity Only,* V.I. went to the Registrar's Office in the Ad Building to get Peter Thayer's address. Then she went to the fourth floor of an older building to the left of the Ad Building (Cobb Hall), looking for Prof Harold Weinstein of the College political science department. But Professor Weinstein, an old '60s rebel, proudly refused to cooperate with the "pigs" (cops). Irked by Weinstein's pigheadedness, V.I. walked outside and sat on the C Bench to plan her next move, then went through the cloisters to the Swift coffee shop.

Explore Cobb Hall and the Renaissance Society, then continue walking around the main circle past the Ad Building and two Gothic science buildings, Jones and Kent. At the crossroad turn left to walk north to Hull Gate and the northern three quadrangles. Landscaped by Olmstead, these were the university's original scientific quadrangles with laboratories for anatomy, botany, physiology, and zoology.

As you come to the wrought-iron Hull Gate, to your left you can see the one remaining residential quad, where convicted murderer and U of C undergrad William Heirens roomed in Hitchcock Hall. It was in his dorm room there that the Chicago police found evidence that they claimed linked him to the lipstick murderer and the killing of Suzanne Degnan, whose dismembered body was dumped into city sewers. Max Allan Collins wrote up Heirens's story in his *Dying in the Postwar World,* changing the names but not the locales. But Delores Kennedy in *William Heirens: His Day in Court,* argues for Heirens's innocence and his "conviction" by the media and the justice system. Chicago mystery maven and veteran crime reporter Craig Rice, brought to town by Hearst to interview Heirens, also concluded he was not guilty.

Walk through Hull Gate to the stone gateway to 57th Street, with its cuddly gargoyles climbing about its peak like playful squirrels. Under the archway look for the word "Anatomy" carved above the door to your left.

In Harold L. Klawans's *Sins of Commission,* medical student John Adson said that as a med student in the '30s his dad used to hang out of the windows in Anatomy to watch Amos Alonzo Stagg's football team play. Across 57th Street there used to be a battlemented wall surrounding Stagg Field. The former playing field is now occupied by Regenstein Library. Opinions vary, but from a distance, slablike, concrete Regenstein resembles Stonehenge with its huge, uneven standing stones.

Return to walk across the Botany Pond Bridge by its famous ginkgo trees and go through the Botany building into the corner quadrangle with a circular fountain in center. The fountain is a replica of the Christ Church College fountain in Tom Quad called Mercury, where Lord Saint-George tossed Harriet Vane's damaged meringues to the carp after he had collided with her in Dorothy L. Sayers's *Gaudy Night.*

Known as Hutchinson Court (or the Tower Group) these buildings were directly based on Oxford University. Mitchell Tower is almost identical to Magdelen Tower, where in *Gaudy Night* Sayers's Harriet Vane heard the ancient May Day concert, and its bells are used for the change-ringing which Sayers described so vividly in *The Nine Tailors.* Mitchell Tower is the home of the university's radio station and the place where "The Round Table," an academic talk show, used to be broadcast live.

Walk across the quad and go into Mandel Hall. Straight ahead is a ticket booth for concerts and plays presented here, but the Court Theater on 56th and Ellis has its own box office. Down the corridor to your right is Mandel Hall with dramatic green Arts and Crafts wallpaper and black oak. It has been the scene of drama, music, and graduations since 1903, and the first performance of the Chicago Symphony was here under Theodore Thomas. Across the hall is the entrance to the Reynolds Club, a student center, originally for men only, with a massive black oak staircase.

To your left is the C Shop, a student snack shop with ice cream and bakery goods. You can stop there for something to eat, or walk farther into the tower and go in the doorway to Hutchinson Commons.

Hutchinson Commons was copied from the Dining Hall of

Christ Church College. It is a lofty handsomely paneled hall with a hammer-beam roof, a dais for high table, a minstrel gallery and gilt portraits of great benefactors like Rockefeller, Ryerson, and Hutchinson, together with University presidents, lining the walls. You can have a meal, catered cafeteria-style by Morry's Deli, and sit on the dais under the eye of Harper and Rockefeller. (There are restrooms for men in the Reynolds Club basement and for women up the stairs to the right as you go into Hutchinson's Commons.)

In Mark Zubro's *Political Poison,* after examining the scene of the crime in Swift Hall Fenwick and Turner walked across campus to the Commons, grabbed a couple of sandwiches and some coffee, and sat in the dark wood-paneled dining hall. Fenwick stared at the portraits staring down at them and asked, "Who are all the old farts?"

After refreshing yourself, go back to Mitchell Tower and walk out under the iron portcullis front door/archway to 57th Street. (If you want to read the campus papers they are usually left lying about here.)

Across University Avenue you can see the redbrick Quadrangle Club with tennis courts behind it. South of the Club are the 1904 Mason House, now the Hillel Foundation, and Calvert House, once the home of English professor and writer Robert Herrick, where Paretsky's V.I. went in *Indemnity Only* to a group called University Women United to get news about the missing Anita McGraw.

The Quadrangle Club is a private club, open to all faculty members. In Mortimer Post's *Candidate for Murder* it was called the Scholars' Club and housed in a colonial mansion left by a rich alum's widow. It was also the main scene of the crime, beginning with the stabbing death of a German refugee the night of a Club dance when Professor Gaylord was there playing bridge with his cronies, and ending at the Club's annual Halloween Masquerade Party. In Post's mystery, the faculty members who solved the murders lunched together every day at the Round Table in the bay window of the club's medieval dining hall.

Other world-class authors had University connections and

undoubtedly ate there, among them Thornton Wilder, whose brother Amos was on the Divinity School faculty, and T. S. Eliot. Wilder's *The Eighth Day* was the story of a convicted murderer who fled to South America, while poet Eliot was a Sherlock Holmes fan who quoted Conan Doyle in *Murder in the Cathedral*.

In *Letting Go,* his lengthy *bildungsroman* about writing and teaching at the University of Chicago, Philip Roth described the Quad Club as filled with hypocritical pseudointellectuals. Something of this populist attitude toward the "professors" crops up in mysteries. In Zubro's *Political Poison,* detectives Fenwick and Taylor went to the Quadrangle Club because English faculty members went there for lunch. They interviewed department chairman Atherton Sorenson, who had a fringe of white hair around a bald scalp and a mellifluous baritone. The chairman felt that the murdered Giles had had an "above us all '60s attitude."

In Andrew Greeley's *Angel Fire* University of Cook County [sic] scientist Sean Seamus Desmond, who won a Nobel Prize for his work on "guardian angels," liked to bait his fellow University of Cook County academics at the Faculty Club Round Table, a time-honored institution in the bay window of the second-floor Gothic dining room with medieval banners and a huge fireplace for roasting oxen. (This is pure Quad Club.)

Cross 57th Street to Bartlett Gym, a memorial to Frank Bartlett, the brother of famous Chicago muralist Frederick Clay Bartlett. (See also Walk 8.) Look at the gorgeous stained-glass window over the entrance and, if you have time, go inside to admire the dark oak staircase and Bartlett's mural of medieval manly sports. In the Trophy Room is the first Heisman Trophy for college football. It was awarded to halfback Jay Berwanger in 1935, about a year before President Hutchins ended U of C participation in Big Ten football, an action for which many alums would have liked to murder him.

Standing outside Bartlett, look north on University Avenue. This street is the closest the university comes to a "fraternity row." The colonial brick house at 5635 S. University was used to film TV's *Moment of Rage* about Richard Speck. Speck really murdered eight student nurses far south of here near Calumet Harbor, but in the TV show he murdered U of C sorority sisters (there are none).

Dennis Breo and William J. Martin gave a detailed account of Speck's murders in *The Crime of the Century,* while in Zubro's *Political Poison,* Turner remarked that fingerprinting as a method of solving a case was highly overrated. But once you had a suspect, they were excellent for confirming whether the criminal had been there or not. He added that Richard Speck had left one clear print at the scene of the crime, so they got him. (See also Walk 10.)

A block north at 56th Street there are several old apartment buildings occupied by grad students like poet lawyer Nick Silver and his wife in Charles Cohen's *Silver Linings.* They had lived in a basement apartment, but by the time the mystery takes place, had moved to the North Shore where Silver stayed home as house-husband to write while his wife worked as a CPA.

In Elizabeth Peters's *The Love Talker,* Laura Morton sublet an apartment in Hyde Park near the University of Chicago libraries to work on her dissertation. But in midwinter, fed up with her boyfriend and the weather, she went to Maryland where her Great Aunt Lizzie was heard talking to fairies in the woods.

On the corner of 56th Street and University is the Crown Field House. Past it on Greenwood Avenue you can see the Smart Gallery, with Court Theater behind it between 55th and 56th Streets on Ellis.

Turn left and walk west on 57th Street to Regenstein Library. You can go inside to see the Special Collections exhibit without having a card. Special Collections not only has a copy of Mortimer Post's mystery *Candidate for Murder,* but it also has the Argos Lectionary, a leather-bound Bible purchased in 1955 from the manager of Colosimo's. (See Walk 8.) He told the University the Bible was used by his "clients" to swear oaths, hence its nickname "the Gangster's Bible." Dating from the ninth or tenth century A.D., written in beautiful uncial script in Greek, it is not a book Al Capone could read, but one he would have regarded with superstitious dread. Its Sicilian origins conjure up the Norman Kingdom of the Two Sicilies, Naples, the Cosa Nostra, and the Black Hand.

Continue walking west to Ellis Avenue. To your right on Ellis in midblock is Henry Moore's *Nuclear Energy*. It resembles an ancient Greek helmet (and a mushroom-shaped cloud), and sits on the site of the old West Stands of Stagg Field where the Manhattan Project scientists under Enrico Fermi created the first self-sustaining, controlled nuclear reaction.

Cross 57th Street and Ellis to walk to the new Science Quadrangle. Take the diagonal path to the new Crerar Library and go inside to look at *Crystara,* a hanging sculpture. In Greeley's *Angel Fire* Professor Desmond walked over to look at this new sculpture; later, when his guardian angel had nonhuman manifestations, she resembled it.

Take the sidewalk from Crerar Library past the old neoclassical building on 58th Street (once the Quad Club, as Mortimer Post knew). Go left to the taller redbrick building with Gothic gables on the corner of Ellis. It was once the home of the University of Chicago Press and is now the University of Chicago Bookstore. Go inside to browse among the first floor's travel and mystery sections; textbooks and campus souvenirs are upstairs. Many Chicago mystery writers sign books here. In nice weather you can buy a soft drink inside and go sit on the patio.

From Ellis Avenue to Cottage Grove, 58th to 59th Street is the huge habitat of the University of Chicago Hospitals. In Sara Paretsky's *Deadlock,* V.I. ended up here after her car was hit on the Dan Ryan Expressway. In Paretsky's "Settled Score," after Chaim Lemke, a clarinetist with the Aeolus Woodwind Quintet, loused up a concert and lost his clarinet, he was locked up in the Psychiatric Wing of Mitchell Hospital, where V.I. visited him.

In Harold Klawans's *Sins of Commission* the scene of the crime was Billings Hospital, where a virus spread by medication killed some patients of Dr. Paul Richardson. In Martin Blank's *Shadowchase* Valerie Anderson, an IRA terrorist given a new identity, was accepted at the University of Chicago Medical School.

Take Ellis Avenue to 59th Street. Ahead of you is the Midway Plaisance, with a sunken center—once filled with water—left over from the carnival of the 1893 World's Columbian Exposition. The fairgrounds began at the lakefront in Jackson Park and ended at Washington Park. Olmstead and Vaux of New York's Central Park had prepared a plan for the South Parks as early as 1871, but nothing much was done about the swamp until Chicago annexed Hyde Park and chose the site for its 1893 Fair. During the Fair there were restaurants, hotels, and a racetrack in Washington Park as well.

There were a number of mysteries written at the time of the Fair, like *Fairground Fiction,* as well as reconstructions like *Pretty Birds of Passage* and Robert Bloch's *American Gothic,* a fictionalized account of the actual Fair murderer Herman W. Mudgett aka Henry H. Holmes, who lured female lodgers to his wooden castle and, seizing their assets, disposed of them. Reporter Crystal decided there was something fishy about the whole castle scene and deliberately pretended to be an innocent in town.

Two blocks to the right at Cottage Grove Avenue you can see Lorado Taft's *Fountain of Time* at the entrance to Washington Park. If it is winter, the whole thing will be covered in blue plastic. A block west of Ellis across the Midway are the Midway Studios, where Taft had his home and worked.

Cross 59th Street at Ellis to walk to the north plaisance (take the sidewalk). Turn to walk east along the Midway, now University playing fields and park.

In Robert J. Campbell's *Hipdeep in Alligators,* precinct captain Jimmy Flannery was banished to the sewers and supposedly waded through the sewer tunnel from Washington Park, along the Midway, through Jackson Park to Lake Michigan, where he found a body that had been chewed by an alligator and was clogging the drain into Lake Michigan. These tunnels are too narrow for such activities, however, and Chicago does *not* dump its sewage in the lake.

As you walk east, on your right across the Midway at 60th Street is a group of modern University of Chicago buildings, whose architects are a roll call of twentieth-century greats. At Ellis is the stark black and glass Mies van der Rohe Social Service Administration. On the other side of Ellis Avenue are the '20s

Gothic Burton-Judson dorms which connect with the Eero Saarinen Law Quadrangle from Ellis to University Avenue.

Cross University and look right. NORC, the National Opinion Research Center with which Andrew Greeley is associated, is in the complex that goes from Ellis to University. In Bill Granger's *The Priestly Murders,* trendy criminology professor Father Bill Conklin taught at the "Institute of Criminology Research."

Across University on your left is the President's House with massive Rockefeller Chapel next to it. Donated by John D. Rockefeller in 1928, it was renamed in his honor when he died in 1937. It is the grandest Gothic church in Chicago, 265 feet long and 207 feet tall. Its woodwork and tiled ceiling was recently restored and it has a splendid carillon given in memory of Rockefeller's mother. In Sprinkle's *Murder at Markham,* Sheila Travis commented that you could hear the Rockefeller chimes every hour on campus. Former Senator Charles Percy's daughter Sharon was married at Rockefeller Chapel to (Senator) John D. "Jay" Rockefeller IV shortly after her twin sister, Valerie, was murdered in the family home in Kenilworth. Jay Rockefeller's uncle, David Rockefeller, is a graduate of the U of C's GSOB.

Cross Woodlawn and return to 59th Street to walk past the Elizabethan Tudor manor house called Ida Noyes Hall. It was built in 1916 to provide women on campus with social and recreational facilities. Today it is coed and the official Visitors Center. You can go inside the front door into the elegant raftered hallway and get something to eat at either Ida's Cafe or the Pub in the basement, where there are also restrooms. William Heirens, while an undergraduate, took modern dance here with some friends of mine. He also politely escorted one of them back to campus from the 59th Street I.C. (Metra) Station one dark night.

In Granger's *The Priestly Murders,* Father Conklin was crossing the main campus at dusk when he felt followed. He ran past Ida Noyes Hall to the Midway, walked down the incline, saw someone in a police uniform behind him, panicked and ran between parked cars on Midway Plaisance. He was nearly hit by a

CTA bus, and dashed up the steps of the Institute of Criminology Research where he was saved by a University security guard.

Go past Ida Noyes to cross Kimbark Avenue. You have reached the University of Chicago Laboratory Schools, begun by John Dewey in 1903. Murderer Richard Loeb went to Lab, where my mother's best friend, Rachel Marshall Goetz, had him as a cooking parter. (Dewey was big on learning by doing!) Rachel reports that Loeb was a beautiful boy whose mother gave wonderful children's parties at their Kenwood mansion. Another Lab graduate, Juliette Myers Rosenblum, in whose memory a small garden at Lab is named, was at Vassar College when the two were arrested. Her father cabled her not to admit she knew either Leopold or Loeb, but she gleefully cabled him back "Too late."

In *Tunnel Vision,* Paretsky's V.I. went to talk with Lab School teacher Alice Cottingham about Emily Messenger, the disturbed daughter of a prominent U of C law professor. After Emily's mother Deirdre turned up dead in V.I.'s Loop office, Emily ran away from home, taking her two small brothers with her.

Walk past the Lab School to Kenwood Avenue (which dead-ends with a playground). The major entrance to the World's Columbian Exposition's midway was at the Kenwood Entrance, and mystery characters came here to see Little Egypt or other exotic delights like Swiss cows.

Walk one more block east to Dorchester Avenue past Lab's Jackman Field. To the left at Dorchester you can see the tall, massive redbrick apartment building called the Cloisters, where many U of C faculty live. Among the famous tenants have been Nobel Prize winners Milton Friedman and Saul Bellow, whose novel *Herzog* is descriptive of his views on Hyde Park. In Andrew Greeley's *Angel Fire,* scientist Sean Desmond lived there with his two teenage daughters after his wife left him to fulfill herself.

Cross Dorchester Avenue to International House, built in Art Deco Gothic to house the University's foreign students. You can go inside, use the restrooms, and visit the cafeteria to get something to eat or drink.

Then walk east to Blackstone Avenue. To your right in the center of the Midway near the Metra (I.C.) elevated tracks is a mounted knight in memory of Thomas Masaryk, president of Czechoslovakia. Continue one more block to Harper Avenue, and turn left to walk north to 57th Street.

The quiet residential street now called Harper originally was Rosalie Villas, a two-block stretch that was the area's first planned community. It was designed about 1883 by Solon S. Beman, Pullman's architect, for Rosalie Buckingham. Since the I.C. tracks then ran at grade level, her houses had views of the open parkland and Lake Michigan.

One of the most elegant Queen Anne houses is the much gabled painted lady known as the Armour House at 5736 S. Harper, currently occupied by Fifth Ward Alderman Larry Bloom. In Andrew Greeley's *Death in April,* his famous expatriate Chicago-Irish author James O'Neill was taken to visit the Fifth Ward alderman Emil Stern at his Hyde Park house to enlist his support in defeating a crooked criminal charge. The local Great Novelist (Saul Bellow?) was also invited, but he was a no-show, not liking to meet real competition.

Keep walking north to 57th Street. The block between Blackstone and Harper on 57th Street has some storefront buildings more suitable for Zubro's Fifth Ward office of murdered Gideon Giles in *Political Poison* than any at Kenwood Avenue. The Christian Science Reading Room would do nicely. Giles had a group of typical Hyde Park activists working there and it was plastered with cause-oriented posters. According to Zubro, Giles's staff did little about potholes or garbage pickup, but they were big on Central America and wetlands. This block between Blackstone and Harper was also the location of the old frame house in Andrew Greeley's *Happy Are the Meek,* but there are none here.

You are at the corner where Powell's Bookstore is located, filled with books galore including many mysteries. Just beyond Powell's is the elevated Metra (I.C.) 57th Street Railroad Station, very near the site of the 1893 Columbian Exposition's train station.

End your walk here after exploring Powell's Bookstore. You

can catch a train back to the Loop or walk under the viaduct one block east to Stony Island to catch a Jeffrey Express bus. If you parked your car at 55th Street, walk two blocks north beside the Metra embankment to reclaim it.

POSSIBLE SIDE TRIPS

Neighboring Kenwood and Jackson Park can be done on foot, but it would be better to drive through Woodlawn. The expressway sites also require a car.

Kenwood. You can walk here from Hyde Park, ending up at 55th and Woodlawn near Jimmy's University Tap to get a bus back to Lake Park Avenue.

Begin either at 55th Street or at 57th Street and walk north to 53rd Street. Directly north of Hyde Park, Kenwood was founded in 1856 by dentist John A. Kennicott and named for his mother's Scottish home. An easy commute to the Loop or the Union Stockyards, by the 1870s Kenwood had become the home of the Chicago's merchant princes like the Ryersons, Armours, Swifts, Fields, and Wilsons, who built large mansions and churches here. Today Kenwood has regentrified and its huge mansions have become the address of choice for prominent or affluent university professors like the Law School's Fabian Messenger in Sara Paretsky's *Tunnel Vision.*

Harper Court is on Harper Avenue from 51st to 53rd Street. This square housing small shops, workshops, and restaurants was built for businesses relocated by urban renewal as well as the artists from the old 57th Street Art Colony at 57th and Stony Island.

The Medici on Harper restaurant is located in Harper Court. In Mark Zubro's *Political Poison,* Fifth Ward alderman and English Professor Gideon Giles and his wife Laura lunched there the day he died of poison. Across the courtyard is Health Foods where the dead alderman had shopped for the vegetables and juices to make his own health drink (which was poisoned).

Madison Park is between 51st and 50th Streets, Dorchester to Woodlawn. Built in the 1880s as a subdivision, it is one of

123 private streets listed in the Chicago street guide. In Zubro's *Political Poison* English department secretary Gwendolen Harleth lived in Madison Park, where detectives Buck Fenwick and Paul Turner interviewed her. At Dorchester there are some modernist atrium houses designed by W. C. Wong.

At Kenwood and 49th Street there are two early Frank Lloyd Wright houses, the George Blossom house, 4858 S. Kenwood Avenue and the Warren McArthur House, 4852 S. Kenwood. Wright "bootlegged" them while he was still working for Louis Sullivan. (The two architects' poor relationship is described in Roslynn Griffith's historical mystery *Pretty Birds of Passage*.)

The yellow Mediterranean/Modernist home at 4855 S. Woodlawn was built for Elijah Muhammad of the Nation of Islam (Black Muslims). It is now the home of Louis Farrakhan. The smaller houses across Woodlawn were built for Muhammad's four sons.

Mosque 1, 47th Street and Woodlawn Avenue, was recently completed by a son of Elijah Muhammad. You can walk up the steps and go inside the lobby, where you can see the mosque interior through a glass wall.

In Bill Granger's *The Newspaper Murders* the Brothers of Mecca are a black street gang with an Islamic ambiance who operated out of Shrine Number 1 on Drexel Boulevard three blocks west of here. Their gang symbol was found painted on the wall of the north side alley where a reporter was found dead. (See Walk 4.)

In Percy Spurlark Parker's *Good Girls Don't Get Murdered,* a similar black gang called the Renegades operated out of a storefront on the West Side. Big Bull Benson went there to get information about a murder that occurred outside his Woodlawn bar at Cottage Grove and 63rd Street.

St. Ambrose Roman Catholic Church at Ellis and 47th Street is locked during the day. To get in you will have to attend mass. In Bill Granger's *The Priestly Murders* a policeman at early weekday mass at St. Alma's (placed at this location) shot the young priest who was filling in for trendy priest cum professor Bill Conklin. Later, Sergeant Terry Flynn set up a stakeout in the church, using Conklin as a Judas goat, or decoy.

The Rosenwald Mansion is at 4901 S. Ellis. A 42-room mansion of Sears Roebuck's Julius Rosenwald who contributed $5 million to the Museum of Science and Industry. In Hugh Holton's mystery *Presumed Dead* the Space Museum was founded and funded by a Jewish philanthropist named Emil Rotheimer.

Rosenwald was also the grandfather of Bobby Franks who was murdered by the neighborhood's "supermen," Richard Loeb and Nathan Leopold. Meyer Levin, a fellow U of C student of both murderers, wrote a novel about them called *Compulsion,* which was made into a movie starring Orson Welles as Hyde Parker Clarence Darrow, the lawyer for the defense. In Levin's book the compulsion was their need to show off. Read Darrow's account in *Chicago Stories* or Nathan Leopold's *Life Plus Ninety-Nine Years.* The site of the Loeb mansion at 5019 S. Ellis is a vacant lot.

Drexel Square at Drexel Avenue and 51st Street has an old fountain cum horse watering trough. In Richard Wright's 1940 *Native Son,* the Dalton family who hired Bigger Thomas as a chauffeur lived on Drexel Boulevard, and the film in which Oprah Winfrey played Bigger's mother was filmed here. Lorraine Hansberry, author of *Raisin in the Sun,* grew up just north of here and her family owned a number of buildings in Kenwood. Poet Laureate Gwendolyn Brooks also lived on the South Side, which she described in her poems about Bronzeville–the name given to the area north of 47th Street and west of Drexel Boulevard where Chicago jazz flourished.

In real life Dr. John Branion, tried and convicted of murdering his wife Donna, lived on Drexel Square. Later on Barbara D'Amato and her husband Northwestern law professor Tony D'Amato entered the case at the request of Branion's second wife, working on his behalf until he died of heart failure. In Barbara D'Amato's double award-winning *The Doctor, the Murder, the Mystery,* she showed that it was nearly impossible for Dr. Branion to have had time to murder his wife.

The Heller House, 5132 S. Woodlawn Avenue, is another early Frank Lloyd Wright classic with a handsome frieze along the third floor. Go five blocks south of the Heller House on

Woodlawn and you will be back at Jimmy 's University Tap on 55th Street.

North of Hyde Park Along the Dan Ryan Expressway. Comiskey Park, 37th and Dan Ryan. The new White Sox stadium is only a few years old and has a huge parking lot. In Harold Klawans' *Sins of Commission* the White Sox were a major enthusiasm of Dr. Paul Richardson, beginning when he went to a game in 1950 with Mrs. Comiskey in the next box. She had the ball boy give him a baseball used in the game. Richardson grew up with the team of Minnie Minoso, Nellie Fox, and Billy Pierce, and remembered 1959 when South Siders Mayor Daley and Fire Commissioner Quinn set off the air raid sirens to celebrate winning the pennant. Richardson felt that Mayor Daley I would never let it snow on Sox Opening Day.

Chicago Police Area Two Headquarters, 5101 Wentworth near Comiskey Park. In Michael Cormany's *Lost Daughter,* P.I. Dan Kruger had worked out of there as a cop until he shot a 15-year-old black kid. Then Cormany quit and would no longer carry a gun. In Cormany's *Red Winter* when Kruger was a rookie cop his partner was Dave Buhrmann who later worked on the Red Squad. Kruger called Buhrmann to get some info on local Chicago Leftists still around from the '60s and '70s.

Jackson Park and the Museum of Science and Industry. 56th Street to 67th Street, Stony Island to Lake Michigan. This was the site of the 1893 World's Columbian Exposition, planned by Daniel Burnham and landscaped by NYC's Frederick Law Olmstead. It contains a model of *The Republic,* by Daniel Chester French, aka the Golden Lady, and the Wooded Island with its Japanese Garden.

Walk east (right) on 57th Street under the I.C. viaduct to Stony Island Avenue. You pass the site of the famous 57th Street Art Colony where so many of Chicago's writers and artists lived before World War I in quaint but derelict storefronts left over from the 1893 World's Fair. Among them were Sherwood Anderson, Vachel Lindsay, Edgar Lee Masters, and Carl Sandburg.

Cross Stony Island and go through Jackson Park to Cornell Drive, cross Cornell Drive and turn right to the Museum of Science and Industry's main entrance.

Across from the Museum's parking lot on 56th Street is a large 1920s residential hotel called Windemere House. In Hugh Holton's *Presumed Dead,* African-American Police Commander Larry Cole had his command headquarters to watch the movements of the gang leaders' cars at the Leamington Hotel on 56th Street overlooking the Space Museum. There was a high-level gang meeting scheduled for Seagull Island behind the museum. Across Hyde Park Boulevard from the Windemere is 1700 E. 56th Street, a contemporary highrise like the one where Space Museum Curator Eurydice Vaughan lived.

The Museum of Science and Industry (Palace of Fine Arts Building) is the second most visited U.S.A. museum; designed by Charles B. Atwood, it is the only building left from the 1893 World's Columbian Exposition. Until 1920 it housed the Field Museum, then it was rebuilt with funds donated by Julius Rosenwald to house science and technology exhibits. The most popular are the coal mine, the U-505 German submarine and Colleen Moore's Fairy Castle. (Fee. Open daily Memorial Day to Labor Day 9:30 A.M.–5:30 P.M.; rest of the year 9:30 A.M.–4:00 P.M. Closed Christmas Day. Call 684-1414.)

Turn right and go up the steps. Along with its submarine and old automobiles and airplanes, there are a number of medical exhibits. In Les Roberts's *Seeing the Elephant,* P.I. Saxon, home in Chicago for the funeral of his old chum and mentor, ex-cop Gavin Cassidy, was told that his pal's liver should have ben put in the Museum of Science and Industry as a medical exhibit.

In Craig Rice's *Knocked for a Loop* John J. Malone had Alberta Commandy, murdered Estapool's 9-year-old stepdaughter dumped on him, but she escaped with Helene Justus who took her to the Museum of Science and Industry. A gangster named Tony who had followed them gave Alberta the high sign in the Coal Mine and she got away from Helene, too.

Police Lieutenant Hugh Holton set *Presumed Dead* here in the "National Science and Space Museum." In his mystery, in 1901 Katherine Rotheimer, the daughter of millionaire Emil Rotheimer was doing some secret experiments on embryos in a lab behind the old History Museum. When the Space Museum was built in 1906 with Rotheimer money, although the museum had a twenty-four-hour police guard, odd spooks began to roam at will. Police files listed over 183 people as "missing, presumed dead." (In David Mamet's '70s play *The Museum of Science and Industry Story,* the homeless camped out in the Museum of Science and Industry and came out at night.)

Katherine Rotheimer's black lover Jim Cross had installed some missiles on Seagull Island (aka the Wooded Island) behind the museum. Many years later in the 1990s instead of a gang summit meeting there, the police had to deal with a massacre of gang leaders. At the same time the DeWitt Corporation, a city-connected development outfit, was negotiating to turn the museum and lakefront into another Disneyland.

Fifty-seventh Street is a major entrance/exit from Lake Shore Drive (the Outer Drive). In Zubro's *Political Poison* detectives Turner and Fenwick sent to investigate Professor/Alderman Giles's murder got off Lake Shore Drive at the Museum of Science and Industry and took 59th Street west to Woodlawn and the University. The same route was taken by Lieutenant Casey and Reverend Randollph when they come south to talk to the Prior of the Order of St. Thomas Aquinas in *Reverend Randollph and the Unholy Bible.*

Watch out for the 57th Street Beach. In Patricia Houck Sprinkle's *Murder at Markham,* widowed Sheila Travis, a secretary at the U of C's Markham Institute, met Professor David MacLean on a wintry day at the bench nearest the Museum. Suddenly the two ends of her scarf were yanked tight and her purse torn off her shoulder.

In Brian Michaels's *Illegal Procedure,* Police Lieutenant Frank Lesniak and his partner chased a jogging suspect down the Drive to the 57th Street Beach. They parked at the Museum, then chased their guy through the Museum's marble-sided vestibule, under the antique planes hanging from the ceiling and into the rotunda. The suspect took the escalator overlooking the Santa Fe RR, so Lesniak dashed through the Medical Exhibit with its row of bottled fetuses into the giant heart, then down to the basement restrooms and cafeteria, into the kitchen and out the back door into Jackson Park, but lost the suspect.

Explore the museum and have something to eat in the Museum cafeteria, then walk behind the museum to explore Jackson Park. The 1893 World's Columbian Exposition stretched along the lake from 57th Street to Marquette Road.

You come first to the Columbian Basin. At its south end is the Clarence Darrow Bridge to the Wooded Island. The bridge was named for Hyde Park's most famous lawyer, who defended Eugene Debs, Leopold and Loeb, and Evolution, but failed to win the audience over in a Biblical debate with Father Brown's creator G. K. Chesterton. Darrow's ashes were thrown into the lagoon and he promised to return there after death. Every year on his birthday, March 13, Darrow's admirers throw a wreath over and memorialize him.

South of the Wooded Island is the statue of *The Republic,* known as the *Golden Lady,* a replica of the statue by Daniel Chester French that was three times as big and stood in the Fair's Court of Honor.

In Robert J. Campbell's *Nibbled to Death by Ducks,* precinct captain Jimmy Flannery, investigating the nursing home where his old Chinaman Donovan was, heard that a staffer had taken an old lady to ride in the paddle boats operated on Jackson Park's lagoon. He arrived just as the staffer tipped the old lady out to hold her under.

In Emma Murdoch Van Deventer's 1894 *Against the Odds* Secret Service agent Carl Masters, at the Fair to catch some international jewel thieves, rescued a handsome Columbian Guard who was attacked on the Wooded Island. During the same period, U of C English Professor Robert Herrick wrote *The Web of Life,* contrasting the glitter of the Fair with the grim Depression of 1893, during which an army of unemployed camped out in the fairgrounds after it closed.

In a far zanier mood in Craig Rice's *8 Faces at 3,* Jake Justus and Helene Brand "sprang" Maple Park (Lake Forest) heiress Holly Inglehart from the Blake (Lake) County jail and drove around Jackson Park until they drank up all the champagne Helene's chauffeur Butch had brought along.

Woodlawn, 61st Street to 67th Street, Stony Island to Cottage Grove. Drive through this area if you want to explore it. Go south at 57th Street and Stony Island to the Midway, then keep going past Hyde Park Career Academy (High School) to 63rd Street. Go west to Cottage Grove, then turn right (north) and return to the Midway Plaisance at 60th Street.

When Housing Restrictive Covenants were declared illegal in 1947, the so-called Black Belt, which began at Cottage Grove and went west to Ashland, exploded into other neighborhoods like Woodlawn. By the 1960s, it was considered a slum.

In Ross Thomas's *The Porkchoppers* Indigo Boone, a black man who knew how to steal an election "Chicago style" lived in Woodlawn across from the U of C. Boone had worked his way up the Democratic ladder and helped steal the election for Jack Kennedy, whose autographed photo hung on his wall. Black union VP Marvin Harmes was sent to him to take lessons in election stealing for a $3,250.00 fee.

In Sam Greenlee's *The Spook Who Sat by the Door,* Freeman, a former "token" black for the CIA, left Washington to go to work for the liberal South Side Youth Foundation. Freeman also trained a black street gang called the Cobras in guerrila warfare. When a Chicago cop shot a 15-year-old boy and a riot started, Freeman's gang sniped, keeping the violence going until the South Side was in ruins. Much of this story echoes the real riots of 1968 which occurred on the West Side when Martin Luther King was shot and the National Guard camped in Jackson Park.

In O. G. Benson's *Cain's Wife,* a blackmailer told Naomi Cain (a Kim Novak look-alike who had married old money) to meet him on 63rd Street at the Lido Lounge, a black and tan musician's hangout, with the dough. She hired P.I. Max Raven (aka Maxim Ravensky) to come, too. Raven sat at the bar with the few customers until Naomi Cain came in at 2:30, followed by a small time drifter whom Raven then followed north to the Loop.

Big Bull Benson's Benson's Hotel, Transients Welcome, was at 63rd and Cottage Grove in Percy Spurlark Parker's *Good Girls Don't Get Murdered.* The first floor was taken up by the restaurant-lounge whose red neon sign said "The Bullpen." Benson, raised in the neighborhood, had won the hotel in a poker game.

Just west of Woodlawn in Washington Park is the DuSable Museum. In Eleanor Taylor Bland's *Slow Burn* on the anniversary of the day her Chicago policeman husband Johnny shot himself, black Detective Marti MacAlister came south to visit his grave and passed the DuSable Museum. Her purse was eyed by a black teenager on roller blades until she flashed her badge at him and he gave her a military salute and took off.

Oak Woods Cemetery has its main entrance at 67th and Cottage Grove on the southern border of Woodlawn. This cemetery's charter predates the city. It is a major burial place for the Civil War's Confederate and Union dead, as well as having the mausoleum of Mayor Harold Washington, graves of Jesse Owens, Ida B. Wells, and many other city notables of all races. It is *not* the burial place of Al Capone.

In Hugh Holton's *Presumed Dead,* the philanthropist who built the Space Museum had also started a tunnel project to link the South Side museum to a nearby cemetery called Havenhurst. Commander Cole and his driver Detective Edna Gray went there to consult the old caretaker Luke Eddings, who knew something about the tunnel where people went missing.

In Thomas McCall's *A Wide and Capable Revenge* Professor Georgi Glazunov was buried in a cemetery near the University of Chicago. Detective Nora Callum took the morning off to go with her babysitter Anna and Glazunov's wife Sophie. The three Russian émigrés had known each other in World War II Leningrad.

Far South Side. There are a number of locations south of Hyde Park that are connected with real-life and/or fictional mysteries. Most lie between the Chicago Skyway (I-90) and the Calumet Expressway (I-94). To reach them, drive south on Stony Island Avenue from Hyde Park. At 69th Street you can enter the Chicago Skyway, which will take you to the eastern part of Chicago's far south side. Or you can remain on Stony Island to the Calumet Expressway entrance at 107th Street.

If you take the Skyway, on your left you will see South Chicago and the old Tenth Ward steel mill area, which stretches from Rainbow Beach at 79th Street past Calumet Harbor at 106th Street.

In *Indemnity Only* V.I. Warshawski mentioned having grown up at 90th and Commercial, a neighborhood to which she often returned on cases. In Paretsky's *Blood Shot,* SCRAP's offices were at 92nd Street near Commercial Avenue in a storefront office between a beauty parlor and a florist. The Tenth Ward Offices of Art Jurshak, Senior, were on the East Side on Avenue M. V.I. went there and saw young Art with his Michelangelo profile, who had been the murdered Nancy Cleghorn's lover.

In Robert Campbell's *Hipdeep in Alligators* Jimmy Flannery's grandfather had worked at a steel mill at 109th and lived in an apartment on Manistee Street, but his father was a city fireman and lived north around Bridgeport Back of the Yards.

In Bill Granger's *The Newspaper Murders* Sergeant Terry Flynn and Managing Editor Michael Queeney ended up in a small bar on the Southeast Side not far from the shuttered South Works of U.S. Steel (about 95th Street).

In Barbara Gregorich's *Dirty Proof* both P.I. Dragovic and his police chum, Lieutenant Dragon Brdar, grew up in South Chicago.

Harry Mark Petrakis, one of Chicago's most famous ethnic writers, wrote about the Greek community around the steel mills in *Lion at My Heart.*

The Chicago Skyway runs into Indiana at 106th Street. It then crosses Wolf Lake heading east to Gary. Wolf Lake is part of the local wetlands and a big migratory bird area. In Harry Keeler's *Thieves' Nights* Van Slyke, the disguised secretary of the dead John Atwood, was sent by Atwood's heir Calvin to Wolf Lake late at night on a made-up errand, so young Atwood could figure out what Van Slyke was hiding. All he found was a secret manuscript of the adventures of superthief Bayard DeLancey.

The other route south from Chicago is the Calumet Expressway (I-94). This begins at 107th and Stony Island and runs west of the Skyway on the other side of Lake Calumet and the Port of Chicago. This is the area that Mayor Richard M. Daley wanted to fill in to build a third major airport. (His father, Richard J. Daley, had wanted to build an airport in Lake Michigan.)

Pullman, George Pullman's famous company town that

generated the Pullman strike begins at 111th west of the Calumet Expressway. In Paretsky's *Blood Shot* Ron Kappelman, Nancy Cleghorn's ex-lover, had an office at 113th and Langley. Kappelman was the attorney for SCRAP who grew up in Highland Park but moved as far away as he reasonably could get. He lived in one of Pullman's neat brick row houses with a totally renovated interior, decorated with perfect Victoriana.

The Port of Chicago is on Lake Calumet from about 115th Street to 130th Street. It was in this area that seaman Richard Speck shipped out on a ore ship for Inland Steel, from which he was fired for getting drunk and assaulting an officer. He then returned to the neighborhood, living in a series of flophouses, and murdered eight student nurses who lived in a townhouse dorm at 2319 East 100th Street. For the gory details read Dennis L. Breo and William J. Martin's *The Crime of the Century*.

In Paretsky's *Deadlock* V.I. Warshawski's's cousin Boom Boom, the Black Hawk's star wing, went to work here for Eudora Grain Company and was shoved off a dock under a ship's screw. Going to investigate his death, V.I. took the 130th St. exit east to Eudora Grain Company's modern single-story offices next to a giant (grain) elevator on the river. She met the Viking-like Niels Grafalk, whose family owned the Grafalk Steamship Company, the oldest company on the lakes. The Grafalks were very like the Minary Family in Mignon G. Eberhart's *Dead Men's Plans*.

Near the south end of Lake Calumet, east of the Calumet Expressway, is Dead Stick Pond, famous as the place where Nathan Leopold dropped his glasses when he and Richard Loeb dumped the body of Bobby Franks there. Leopold was known to be an avid bird watcher, so the glasses and location led to their arrest. Their crime and its locales tend to resonate in mysteries. In Barbara Gregorich's *Dirty Proof* P.I. Frank Dragovic sarcastically mentioned the "two geniuses" who had left their glasses at the scene of the crime.

In Sara Paretsky's *Blood Shot* V.I. Warshawski, who boated and swam in that area as a kid, got dumped there and left for dead. She was rescued by her neighbor Mr. Contreras and her dog Peppy.

Hegewisch is located just south and east of the Port of Chicago at 126th Street between the Calumet Expressway and the Chicago Skyway. This is the tidy ethnic neighborhood that Mayor Daley wanted to turn into an airport runway.

In Eugene Izzi's *The Booster* Vincent Martin, who agreed—for a price—to help his old mentor Bolo climb the Sears Tower to retrieve some Mafia tapes, had grown up there.

In Barbara D'Amato's *Hard Women* Cat Marsala—who was researching prostitutes—went to Hegewisch, which she found an ethnic enclave where time seemed frozen in the late 1940s. Hooker Sandra Lupica, whom Cat interviewed before she was murdered had grown up there in an abusive family where her father beat her mother to death. They lived on Avenue F "almost as far south as you can go and still be in Chicago in a house just blocks from the Indiana border and Wolf Lake."

Beyond Hegewisch you come to Indiana, the place where, according to Edgar Wallace in *On the Spot,* Tony Perelli's mob and his competitors regularly dumped bodies in cornfields.

10

NEAR WEST SIDE WALK

BACKGROUND

The Near West Side has remained a multi-ethnic neighborhood, mixed with pockets of blight and urban renewal. Even today, with major changes underway, this walk will show you why Chicago is known as a "city of neighborhoods."

Cut off from the Loop by the Dan Ryan Expressway on the east and stretching to Western Avenue on the west, the Near West Side was split in half by the Eisenhower Expressway, which Sara Paretsky in *Killing Orders* called a "fenced-in prison yard." This walk will be south of the Eisenhower, but the major sights to the north are included under Possible Side Trips (see p. 330).

The original settlement spread west from the Chicago River's factories, shipyards and lumberyards. In 1837 the city limits were at Ashland Avenue, but by 1851 they were at Western Avenue. From the 1850s on, this was the "port of entry" for many immigrant groups. First came the Germans, Bohemians, French and Irish, then the Jews, Italians and Greeks, and finally, Hispanics and African-Americans. But far from being one big melting pot, the area was always divided geographically along ethnic, economic, and racial lines, with no love lost among them.

At the same time, from the Civil War until about 1900, there were exclusive residential enclaves, like the west side's

"Gold Coast" where Mayor Carter H. Harrison I lived at Ashland and Jackson Boulevard. You can take a look back in time by going across the Eisenhower Expressway to see the Jackson Boulevard Historic District in the 1500 block near Whitney Young Magnet High School at 211 S. Laflin.

In 1870 the Jesuits founded St. Ignatius College next to Holy Family Church on Roosevelt Road, and in 1871 the Chicago Fire began in the O'Leary barn at DeKoven just east of the present location of the Dan Ryan Expressway. (Most authorities insist the cow was not to blame.) The fire burned east and north in what might be called Chicago's first major "urban renewal" project, but left the Near West Side unscathed.

But by the 1880s tenements and slum conditions had developed south of Taylor Street and gradually those groups who could, like the German Jewish community, moved south and west, selling Ashland Avenue's Temple Anshe Sholom to the Greeks, who christened it St. Basil's Orthodox Church.

North of the Eisenhower Ashland Avenue became Union Row, i.e., headquarters, and the old Garment District bounded by Monroe, Halsted, and Racine is full of commercial lofts now becoming condos. Halsted Street was named for two Philadelphia brothers who financed the real estate ventures of Chicago's first mayor William B. Ogden. Halsted runs north and south from about 4000 North to 13000 South, showing incredible diversity along the way.

On May 4, 1886 the Haymarket Riot occurred in the open-air market at Randolph and Des Plaines at a workers' rally for an eight-hour day. Seven (some sources say eight) policemen were killed by a bomb, with the result that eight anarchists were arrested, four were hanged, one committed suicide in jail, and three were pardoned by Governor John P. Altgeld ten years later. (See Walk 4.) The Haymarket Memorial Statue which has been attacked a number of times since is currently under twenty-four-hour guard in the courtyard of the Chicago Police Training Academy at 1300 W. Jackson. There are plans to build a new Central Police Station nearby soon.

One major result of the Haymarket Riot was the establishment in 1889 by Jane Addams and her friend Ellen Gates Starr of the settlement house called Hull House, modeled upon Toynbee Hall in London's East End. It was established at 800 S. Halsted in the 1856 country house of Charles Hull, but by 1907 they had a block-square complex, where they achieved all kinds of social work "firsts," supporting labor, children's rights, and the peace movement.

All but Hull House, preserved as a museum, were torn down in the 1960s when the city won the federal backing and funding needed for its Harrison-Halsted Urban Renewal project from a grateful President John F. Kennedy. Fifty-five acres were cleared, despite major protests led by Florence Scala which included sit-ins in Mayor Daley's office. Florence Scala recently closed Florence's Restaurant at 1030 W. Taylor in the graystone three-flat where her parents moved before World War I and her father had a tailor shop.

Circle Campus was originally meant to be an undergraduate commuter college replacing the one at Navy Pier, but today known as the University of Illinois at Chicago, it is a booming graduate school with residential halls. Growing like Topsy, UIC is now reaching out to take more of the neighborhood, including what's left of the historic Maxwell Street Market. Closed August 15, 1994, it will be re-located between Clinton and Canal.

By 1900 the area around Maxwell Street had become an Eastern Jewish ghetto with an open-air pushcart and stalls market which went from Polk Street to 16th Street, Canal to Blue Island. Today's merchants, however, are mostly black and Hispanic, much like the Lower East Side in New York City. (See *Mystery Reader's Walking Guide: New York.*)

The Greeks had arrived in the 1890s and lived and worked in the Delta, bounded by Harrison, Halsted, Polk, and Blue Island. They went into the restaurant, ice cream, and entertainment businesses, but today only the Greektown restaurants along Halsted are left.

The Italian immigrants have stayed the longest in "Little Italy," centered around Taylor Street. The most numerous ethnic group with the largest Catholic population, their neighborhood had—and still has—gangster connotations, dating back to Prohibition and the Roaring Twenties, when booze was king and 12th Street and Halsted was Bootleggers' Square. Then the Italians began moving out to Oak Park, Cicero, and River Forest, while Hispanics and blacks moved in.

The other major Near West Side industry has been medicine. The first hospital was built there in 1874 and the area from Ashland to Western is now known as the West Side Medical Center, a huge complex along Harrison west of Ashland. Also known as the UIC's West Campus it is composed of Cook County, Rush-Presbyterian-St. Luke's, the University of Illinois, a veterans' hospital, as well as Rush Medical School and the University of Illinois College of Medicine.

This walk will begin at Cook County Hospital, which you can reach from the Loop either by taking the O'Hare/Congress El, which stops at Cook County Hospital, or taking the O'Hare/Douglas El to the Polk Street stop and walking four blocks west. Or you can drive, parking across the street from the Rush-Presbyterian-St. Luke's Atrium Center at Harrison and Paulina, or farther west in the lots along Congress west of Damen. By day there are always crowds of people coming and going from the Medical Center and students galore at the East Campus. The area in between along Polk and Taylor Street has many people on the streets, too, especially at lunch or dinner time.

LENGTH OF WALK: About 2 miles

See the map on page 316 for the boundaries of this walk and page 361 for a list of the books and detectives mentioned.

PLACES OF INTEREST

Chicago (West Side) Medical Center, Ashland Avenue to Ogden, Eisenhower Expressway to Roosevelt Road. Cook County Hospital, Rush-Presbyterian-St. Luke's Hospital, University of Illinois Hospital, and Veterans' Hospital.

Holy Family Church, 1080 W. Roosevelt Road. Barnlike 1857 Gothic painted brick church with a large green sheet metal tower. Once the largest English-speaking Roman Catholic parish in the city.

Jane Addams's Hull House Museum, Polk and Halsted Streets (surrounded by UIC East Campus). 1856 Italianate mansion. UIC opened it as a museum in 1963. Open Mon.–Fri. 10:00 A.M.–4:00 P.M. Sun. noon–5:00 P.M. Free. Call 413-5353.

Little Italy, Taylor Street from Ashland to Morgan. Much of it was torn down to build UIC.

Maxwell Street Market: Historic flea market/open-air vendors. Closed August 15, 1994 and moved east to Canal and Clinton. Open (officially) Sunday 6:00 A.M.–noon; closed for Jewish Sabbath.

Maxwell Street Police Station, 943 W. Morgan at Maxwell Street. 1870s redbrick Police Station—the oldest in Chicago.

Medical Examiner's Office (the new one), 2121 W. Harrison (at Oakley). Not open to the public.

St. Ignatius College Preparatory School, 1076 W. Roosevelt Road. Roman Catholic prep school (originally for boys only) founded in 1870 by Jesuit Father Arnold Damen as St. Ignatius College.

University of Illinois at Chicago (UIC), East Campus, Eisenhower Expressway to Roosevelt Road, Halsted Street to Racine Avenue. Opened in 1965 to strong local opposition. Called Fortress Illini, it is being modified in the 1990s.

UIC West Campus, Polk, Walcott, Taylor, and Wood Streets. 1920s redbrick Gothic campus of the University of Illinois College of Medicine & Dentistry, which combined with UIC in 1982.

PLACES TO EAT

Greektown, Halsted Street from Monroe Street to Van Buren. Mystery characters like Paretsky's V.I. Warshawski often treat themselves to meals in "Greektown" without being specific, as she did in *Guardian Angel*, returning from a grim hospital visit to her elderly neighbor, Mrs. Frizell. These are among the famous places:

Courtyards of Plaka, 350 S. Halsted Street (between Jackson and Van Buren).

Greek Islands, 200 S. Halsted Street (at Adams).

The Parthenon, 314 S. Halsted Street. The granddaddy of the group.

Santorini, 138 S. Halsted Street. Seafood specialties.

Little Italy, Taylor Street from Morgan Street to Ashland Avenue. As many places to choose from as Greektown. These are mentioned in mysteries:

Mategrano's, 1321 W. Taylor Street. Once popular with Al Capone's bodyguard.

New Rosebud Cafe, 1500 W. Taylor Street.

Rush-Presbyterian-St. Luke's Medical Center Atrium Building, 1653 W. Congress Parkway. Second-floor cafeteria open to the public.

University of Illinois at Chicago East Campus. Chicago Circle Center, 710 S. Halsted Street (behind Hull House). Students cafeteria open to the public. Restrooms up one floor.

Maxwell Street Market (see Possible Side Trips), Canal and Clinton. Vendors/pushcarts.

NEAR WEST SIDE WALK

Begin your walk in front of the 1913 Cook County Hospital at 1835 W. Harrison overlooking the Eisenhower Expressway. The first Chicago hospital was built here in 1874, in the area now called the Chicago Medical Center, or the West Side Medical Center, which contains half a dozen major hospitals and medical schools.

Walk inside the lobby to look about. Cook County is the hospital of last resort for county residents, especially victims of violence who end up in the emergency room. In Stuart Kaminsky's *You Bet Your Life*, P.I. Toby Peters, in Chicago to resolve a gambling debt Chico Marx owed the mob, got shot and ended up here. His "child" doctor called State Senator Richard J. Daley for him and Daley said he would "inform" the right people but advised Peters to leave town. When Peters was released, he found his medical bill had been paid by Dr. Hugo C. Hackenbush (Groucho Marx).

In Sara Paretsky's *Guardian Angel* one of V.I. Warshawski's neighbors, elderly, eccentric Mrs. Frizell, broke her hip and was brought to County. While she was there, some neighbors had all her dogs put to sleep. V.I. came to visit the old lady, noting that the public poured money into jails and courts, but left the hospital in terrible shape.

In Richard Whittingham's *State Street,* a retarded Mafia princess attacked on Taylor Street was taken to County's Emergency Room. Later detectives Joe Morrison and Norbert Castor interviewed Nurse Fralick. Nurse Fralick, a graduate of the UIC School of Nursing, told the cops she saw more blood, guts and human carnage at County than most Vietnam field doctors did.

In the *Crime of the Century,* Dennis L. Breo and William J. Martin described how nurse murderer Richard Speck was rushed to Cook County emergency room from a West Side flophouse when he cut his wrists. His life was saved before Dr. Leroy Smith recognized him from his "Born to raise hell" tattoo and called police—allowing him to stand trial and die in jail.

Go back outside Cook County Hospital and look north (straight ahead) across the Eisenhower Expressway. Directly across from Cook County Hospital is Malcolm X College at 1900 W. Van Buren. Several blocks north of Malcolm X on Madison was the old Chicago Stadium, which is being replaced by the new United Center across the street. To the east of the Stadium along between Adams and Jackson are the Whitney Young Magnet High School, the Jackson Historic District and the Police Academy. (See Possible Side Trips.)

South and west at Damen and Roosevelt will be a new state-of-the-art Illinois State Police Forensic laboratory (Crime Lab). Chicago's crime lab was a direct result of Al Capone's St. Valentine's Day massacre because the hit men were dressed like police and carried police-style Thompson submachine guns. The authorities needed to know if any police officers were actually involved in the multiple hit, so Northwestern University established a crime lab which the Chicago Police bought in 1940 and moved to 11th and State. (See Walk 8.)

Walk east on Harrison to Wood. The morgue was located at Wood and Harrison until 1958. In Max Allan Collins's *True*

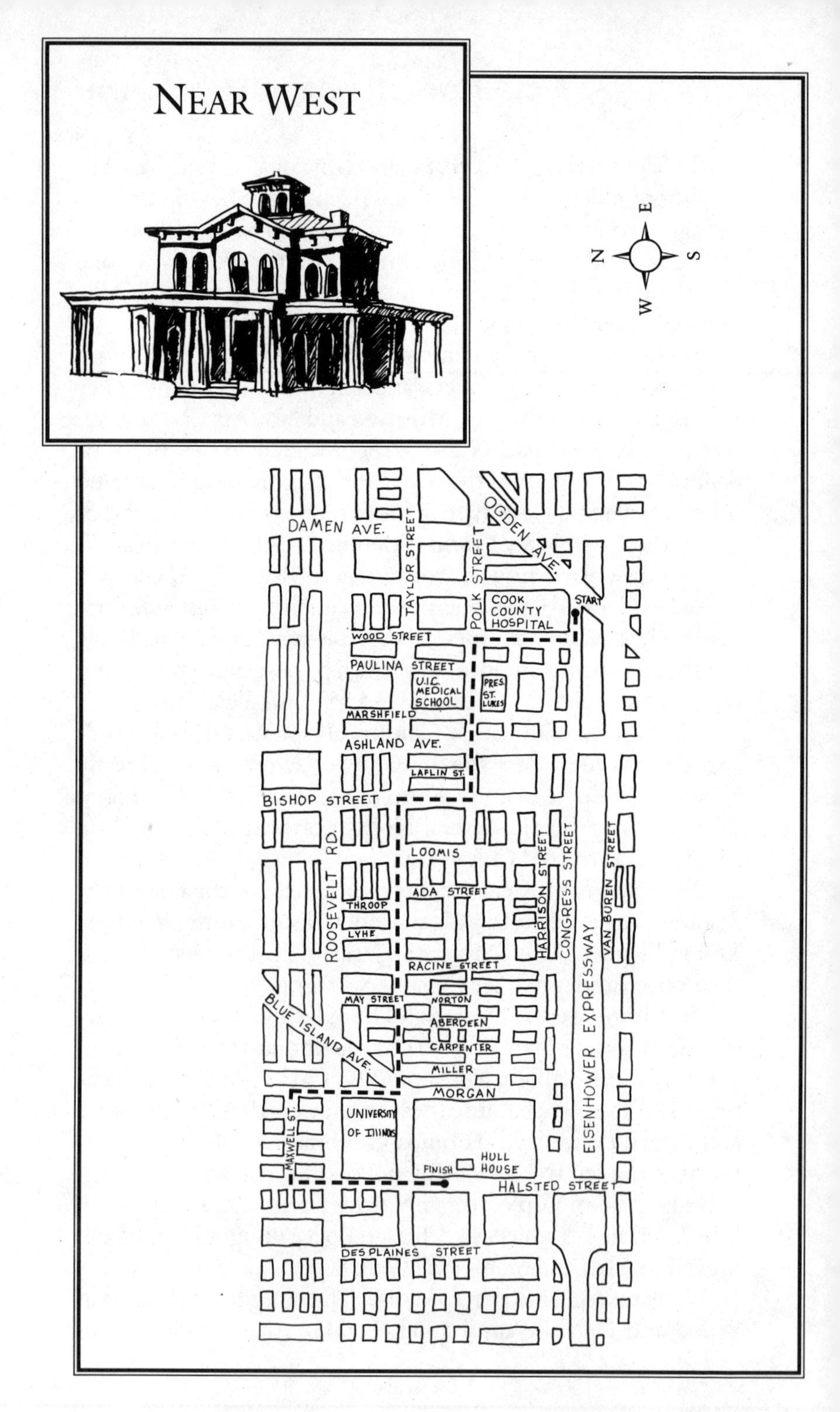
NEAR WEST
N
E
S
W
DAMEN AVE.
TAYLOR STREET
POLK STREET
OGDEN AVE.
COOK COUNTY HOSPITAL
START
WOOD STREET
PAULINA STREET
U.I.C. MEDICAL SCHOOL
PRES. ST. LUKES
MARSHFIELD
ASHLAND AVE.
LAFLIN ST.
BISHOP STREET
ROOSEVELT RD.
LOOMIS
ADA STREET
HARRISON STREET
CONGRESS STREET
VAN BUREN STREET
THROOP
LYHE
RACINE STREET
EISENHOWER EXPRESSWAY
MAY STREET
NORTON
ABERDEEN
CARPENTER
MILLER
BLUE ISLAND AVE.
MORGAN
MAXWELL ST.
UNIVERSITY OF ILLINOIS
HULL HOUSE
FINISH
HALSTED STREET
DES PLAINES STREET

Crime, he described how John Dillinger's body lay in state while hundreds of people lined up to see it and bought souvenirs. P.I. Nate Heller tipped a cop ten dollars to get inside the place, where the body was propped up at a 45-degree angle and the face covered with a damp white mass because a group was making a death mask. (The Chicago Historical Society still has Dillinger's death mask. See Walk 7.)

In Craig Rice's *The Right Murder,* John J. Malone's police chum Von Flanagan made Malone go view a body in the morgue. It turned out to be the tall, handsome stranger who had stumbled into Joe the Angel's City Bar on New Year's Eve, shouted "Malone," and dropped dead, slipping a key into Malone's hand as he died.

In Leslie Charteris's *Call for the Saint,* Detective Lieutenant Kearney asked the Saint (Simon Templar) to identify a body that turned out to be Junior, the mobster the Saint had left (alive) with Sammy de Leg in *Wheaton*. The Saint had come to Chicago to get rid of the King of the Beggars, a mobster who preyed on the homeless and disabled.

In Jonathan Latimer's *The Lady in the Morgue,* a wealthy young socialite followed a married band leader to Chicago. His wife also died, but there was a big mix-up because the authorities were not sure if the body of a dead girl in their possession was the socialite or the wife. P.I. William Crane was sent from New York to sort it out. Latimer described the morgue in loving detail, from the marble-floored waiting room with mahogany benches, men's room, and drinking fountain, to the basement where the bodies were kept in two long rows of metal cabinets. The reporters were playing a gruesome game called "Black or White." They guessed a color, then pulled out a drawer. You won if the corpse was the correct shade. Later the attendant was hit over the head and a girl's corpse stolen.

Walk one block south on Wood to Polk Street where there is a parking lot. In 1958 a new Coroner's building was put up here at 1828 W. Polk, replacing the one at Wood and Harrison; this is the place mentioned in mysteries set between 1960 and 1970. It had an underground tunnel to Cook County Hospital and you also went to the basement to view the bodies.

Since the mid-1970s, however, the Medical Examiner's Office has been five blocks west at 2121 W. Harrison, and the county's Chief Medical Examiner is now an appointed medical doctor, not an elected Coroner without medical experience. (According to English common law, the Coroner had to impanel a jury to determine the cause of death when anyone died a violent or unexpected death. He also had jurisdiction over buried treasure and beached whales.)

Ordinary visitors still cannot get inside the "morgue." In 1993, British mystery writer H. R. F. Keating, his wife Sheila Mitchell, and Catherine Kenney, author of *The Remarkable Case of Dorothy L. Sayers,* and the Dales went there as guests of Catherine's husband, Dr. Jack Kenney. Kenney is a dental forensic pathologist who is an authority on bite-marks. We walked around the outer core of rooms in the one-story structure, which included the waiting rooms for families where the furniture is nailed down, the viewing room offering either closed-circuit TV or the actual body, then the labs. Through interior windows into the central core we glimpsed the storage area with black bags on steel racks.

In Robert J. Campbell's *The Junkyard Dog,* sewer worker and precinct captain Jimmy Flannery's old childhood chum Eddie Fergusen let him in to see the girl killed when an abortion clinic was bombed. Eddie also told Flannery the girl was shot. In *Hipdeep in Alligators,* Eddie let Flannery look at the body chewed by an alligator.

In Paretsky's *Guardian Angel,* V.I. and her neighbor Mr. Contreras went to the morgue to see if the body found in the Sanitary Canal was his old pal Mitch Kruger. Contreras fainted when he saw the corpse was missing part of a finger.

In D. J. H. Jones's *Murder at the MLA,* the body of Wellesley College English Chair Susan Engleton was brought here. The cause of death turned out to be juniper berries, available locally at city cemeteries like Graceland and Rosehill.

In Michael Cormany's *Rich or Dead,* his scrawny P.I. Dan Kruger told a man looking for Ricardo Reyes to look at the morgue. (Kruger had found Reyes dead while trying to locate him for his sister Elvia, from whom Reyes had stolen money.)

To your right at Polk and Wood Street is the redbrick collegiate Gothic campus of the University of Illinois College of Medicine. Cross Wood to the UIC's West Campus Administration Building, a modern red brick, and go east along Polk to Marshfield, where there is a CTA stop. Cross Marshfield and go under the El to Ashland. To the left there is a small park and on your right are UIC buildings with restrooms and a coffee shop called On the Mall.

At Polk and Marshfield you are directly behind Rush-Presbyterian-St. Luke's Hospitals, which were combined in 1956 at the site of Presbyterian Hospital, founded in 1883. Rush Medical College, founded in 1837, was reestablished in 1969. The city's Poison Control Center is also located here. The public parking lot is one block left on Paulina. Most mysterious episodes about St. Luke's refer to the old highrise on Indiana Avenue. (See Walk 8.)

In *Sins of Commission* Harold L. Klawans, Professor of Neurology and Pharmacology at Rush Medical College, wrote about Dr. Paul Richardson, who taught neurology at the Austin-Flint Medical Center. But most of the action happened on the South Side in the University of Chicago Hospitals, where an elderly lady patient died after minor surgery. (See also Walk 9.)

Across the Eisenhower Expressway Ashland Avenue is Union Hall territory with many union headquarters. In Jonathan Latimer's *Heading for a Hearse,* Dave Connors, the head of Coal Wagon Chauffeurs, Local 241, was on Death Row with stockbroker Richard Westland, who was convicted of killing his wife. In a jailhouse talk, Connors suggested Westland hire his lawyer, Charley Finklestein, to save his neck, so Westland did. (He had only one week before his execution.)

Cross Ashland Avenue to the huge domed St. Basil's Greek Orthodox Church, a Greek Revival temple built in 1910 as Temple Anshe Sholom but sold in 1927 after the congregation had moved south. To your left along Harrison is a group of new townhouses and condominiums called Garibaldi Square and to your right another called Campus Green.

In spite of all the gentrification going on here, this is where Robert J. Campbell put the Twenty-seventh Ward of Jimmy

Flannery. Campbell's sense of Chicago geography is flimsy, accentuating the reader's conviction he or she is reading about times gone by or a different place (maybe Newark, where Campbell grew up?). Flannery lived on Polk Street in a six flat with humble neighbors like the family of Stanley Recore, and Joe and Pearl Pakula who ran a deli downstairs. In *The Junkyard Dog,* Flannery walked six blocks through Skid Row to get home, another time he took the El from Polk to Madison. How? Madison runs parallel to Polk several blocks north of the Eisenhower.

In Campbell's mysteries, Flannery's "Chinaman" Devlin at City Hall who gave him a job walking sewers was warlord of the Twenty-seventh (i.e., Ward Committeeman), but lived outside the ward in Bridgeport! All in all, Campbell's Chicago mysteries deserve the comment by the late Mary Craig, President of MWA. When Campbell won an Edgar for *The Junkyard Dog,* Craig asked Campbell if he had ever been to Chicago. He told her that he never had been there, and Craig responded tartly, "it shows."

Skid Row has been torn down for some little time; it is now the site of Presidential Towers, built in 1986. (See Walk 3.) For an impressive description of the real thing, read Willard Motley's *Let No Man Write My Epitaph,* which described Skid Row as "a crazy, numbing, neon-lighted world bounded on the north by Nelson Algren, on the west by Saul Bellow and on the south by James T. Farrell." In spite of his insistence that the mystery was centered on North Clark Street, I would add James Michael Ullman's *The Neon Haystack.*

Straight ahead of you on Polk between Ashland and Laflin is tiny Garibaldi Park surrounded by more housing developments and some old mansions that are being rehabbed. Two blocks south of you at Fillmore is the 1884 Thomas Jefferson Public School, one of Chicago's old school buildings.

Cross Laflin Street. To your right one block south on Taylor Street is the New Rosebud Cafe with its handsome Roman-colored striped awning of gold and red and green. If you are hungry, detour there now. If you don't detour, keep walking east on Polk to Bishop.

To your right at Bishop there is a double gate with four stone chess bishops, where two rows of old houses face one another across a parkway. To the east of Bishop are streets with names like Cabrini, because you are now in Little Italy. Turn right and walk south along Bishop to Taylor Street past a fascinating block, many of whose old houses still are owned by Italian families. At Taylor Street the streetlights are hung with banners saying "Welcome to Taylor Street/A touch of Italy."

Cross Bishop and walk east on Taylor. You pass Leona's and then at the northwest corner of Taylor and Loomis you come to the Taylor Street Bistro, at 1400 W. Taylor, with the mandatory red-checked tablecloths. They make good substitutes for older places no longer here.

Look left at the corner of Loomis and Taylor. You can see a row of yellow brick houses with red awnings. Street gossip says Al Capone's lawyer once lived there. But, contrary to Hollywood, Alphonse Capone was not a native of Little Italy. He was not even a native of Sicily, because his father Gabriel immigrated from there in 1893. Born in Brooklyn, the Big Guy's origins were New York's gang-ridden Five Points near Centre Street (NYC police headquarters). (See *MRWG: NY.*) Brought to Chicago by Johnny Torrio, a nephew of Big Jim Colosimo's, Capone worked at the trade of mobster at Colosimo's and the Four Deuces. By 1925 when he had enforced "peace" citywide, Capone moved his headquarters back into the city's Near South Side, first at the Metropole, later the Lexington Hotel. (See Walk 8.) But thanks to the media and the movies made about Scarface, and the fact that moonshining and bootlegging went on in Little Italy, it remains "Capone territory" to many.

In Clarence A. Andrews's *Chicago in Story; A Literary History,* he agrees that the major source of the myth was W. R. Burnett's 1929 novel *Little Caesar.* Made into a film starring Edward G. Robinson—and, more improbably, Douglas Fairbanks, Jr., it led to Robinson's career as a bad guy. It is the story of young Italian thug Cesare Bandello, nicknamed Rico—or Little Caesar—who has Capone's tastes: fancy clothes, women, fast cars, and guns and an Irish cop named Flaherty who was "out to get Rico." He set up a dragnet for Rico and chased him through Little Italy alleys to a hideaway at Ma Magdelana's, a mom and pop store. Rico escaped to Hammond, was kicked out of there for pulling a gun, went to Toledo, and ended up shot in an alley. In 1929 this was wishful thinking—a morality play—not what actually happened to Capone. The impact of Burnett's book was added to by the character "Scarface" in Chester Gould's *Tribune* comic strip "Dick Tracy," later written by Max Allan Collins, as well as many other "Capone" mysteries like Edgar Wallace's *On the Spot*.

In *Mr. Capone,* Robert J. Schoenberg pointed out that in real life Capone saw himself as a kind of Marshall Field who gave the public what it wanted. As he said, "When I sell liquor, it's called bootlegging. When my patrons serve it on silver trays on Lake Shore Drive, it's called hospitality." British mystery writer G. K. Chesterton was also against Prohibition because the rich got their liquor while the poor man lost out.

Richard Connell's short story "Brother Orchid," filmed in 1940 with Humphrey Bogart and Edward G. Robinson, was a more amusing version of the legend. Little John Sarto, released from prison, headed back to Chicago via the Wisconsin woods (Capone had a vacation place there). He hid out in a monastery of the Floratines—the Little Brothers of the Flowers, where Little John was called Brother Orchid. When the Chicago flower market was taken over by gangsters, who demanded that the monastery join the Floral Protection Association, Brother Orchid went to Chicago and "persuaded" the flower sellers to "talk." Their testimony let the District Attorney convict some gangsters, but the rest of them wanted Brother Orchid to run the mob again. When he refused they took him "for a ride."

Cross to the south side of Taylor at Loomis and continue to walk east. On the north side of the street are some tacky public housing units, while on your side of the street there are shops like Scafuri Bakery at 1337 Taylor and Gianna's Italian Deli at 1335 W. Taylor.

In Richard Whittingham's *State Street,* Detective Norbert Castor told his partner Joe Morrison that the old-line Italian neighborhood along Taylor Street was an ethnic island surrounded by a sea called the projects. The two factions coexisted, neither bothering the other, so long as the project people did not bother the Italian women, kids, or cars. Under the circumstances, the detectives were surprised that anyone had dared to rape the daughter of major Mafioso Rudy Facia there.

Walk past a tiny alley with an iron fence to Mategrano's on the corner of Ada and Taylor, at 1321 Taylor. In Whittingham's *State Street* Lynn and Bert, a trendy couple who lived in a north-side loft, were headed to Mategrano's when they found the crying Mafia Princess and called the cops. This act of kindness was not appreciated by her Mafioso daddy, who yanked his daughter out of Cook County Hospital's Emergency Room without filing any charges.

In Bill Granger's *The Newspaper Murders*, Sergeant Terry Flynn went to the Vernon Park Tap on Taylor Street to talk to a juice collector named Michael Vincent Teatettero. Known as Mr. Theodore, he weighed 300 pounds and was 6 feet 4 inches tall, had gray hair and eyes and a large nose, smelled of lavender, and wore gold chains and a cashmere sports coat. Murdered newspaper reporter Francis X. Sweeney owed Mr. Theodore money, but when Flynn and his partner Karen Kovacs hauled him in, Theodore wouldn't talk.

As you walk along, notice that some of the stores are in old cast-iron buildings (look for pillars and iron steps). Cross Ada and continue east to Throop, Lytle and then Racine.

To your left between Throop and Racine there are some landmark buildings like the 1889 James Foley Building at 626 S. Racine, a Queen Anne "flats above the storefront" with pressed-metal bays, terra-cotta panels, and a cast-iron storefront and cornice. This could be an appropriate six-flat for Campbell's Jimmy Flannery. On Lexington, a short street two blocks north of Taylor, there are an 1871 house and the 1870 Onahan Row, Italianate houses made of yellow brick with English basements, built when this was an Irish stronghold called Macalister Place. Detour north to look at these Victorian gems if you like.

Racine is a major north/south thoroughfare and an exit from the Eisenhower Expressway. At the south corner is a big modern building that houses the Daniel and Ada Rice Boys and Girls

Club. Across Racine along the Eisenhower in Vernon Park Place there is more gentrification going on. You are now on the outskirts of UIC's East Campus expansion and development.

Cross Racine and walk one block east to May Street. You pass a Chinese restaurant and other older houses with English basements and high front steps. At the corner of May Street are the House of Vittori and Chicago Busy Burger. To the south across some vacant lots you can see the green dome and cross of Holy Family Roman Catholic Church at Roosevelt Road. Holy Family Church has had a great deal of publicity lately as the rector mounted a campaign to save the painted brick 1857 German Gothic church building. The most recent plan of the Archdiocese is to merge its tiny parish with the booming Hispanic parish of St. Francis of Assisi two blocks east.

The founder of Holy Family Parish was Jesuit Father Arnold J. Damen (whom you see on street banners along Taylor). Next door to the church is the tall, 1866 French-style St. Ignatius College Prep at 1076 S. Roosevelt Road. Like many tall, high-windowed 19th-century schools, St. Ignatius has an assembly hall on its top floor as well as a two-story natural history museum. Today St. Ignatius is probably the premier Roman Catholic parochial school in the city. Its only real rival is Quigley Seminary on the near north side.

In Andrew Greeley's mysteries St. Ignatius is the high school of choice for his characters' children. In *Angel Fire* professor Sean Desmond had gone there, as did his daughters, Fiona and Deirdre, known as Fee and Dee.

Cross May and walk east on Taylor through another restaurant and shopping block to Aberdeen. Cross Aberdeen and go on to Carpenter. You can see the storefront offices of the Near West Side Community Committee at 1044 W. Taylor. It is a lone reminder of the community's loud protests, led by local resident Florence Scala, about the Harrison-Halsted Urban Renewal Project that built the University of Illinois Chicago campus. For years Florence Scala also ran the Florence Restaurant at 1030 W. Taylor. Under her leadership, the community engaged in massive protexts, including sit-ins at the office of Mayor Richard J. Daley, but the Supreme Court refused to intervene. As a result of Daley's help with the 1960 election that won Jack Kennedy the Presidency, the city got the money it needed, too.

But the issue never dies. It came up again when the powers that be insisted on building a new Stadium and again when the UIC proposed to uproot the famous Maxwell Street Market. Former First Deputy Housing Commissioner George B. Stone who worked on the original Harrison-Halsted urban renewal project told me that the worst "removals" had always occurred as a result of major road-building (expressways) which the public wanted, and that if you put a fence around any area and refused to let anyone new move in, within five years it would be empty.

"Harrison-Halsted's" neighborhood is home base for many Italian childhoods. In Michael Cormany's *Red Winter,* P.I. Kruger was working for a "connected" contractor called Nicholas Cheyney, whose "chinaman" was Alderman Frankie Nilardo. Nilardo's old man ran a mom-and-pop grocery store where Circle Campus (UIC) is now and the alderman, who came over in diapers, was a great flag waver.

In Martin Blank's *Shadowchase,* Paul Lazzeri and his big brother Tom lived at Taylor and Halsted. Paul grew up to be the student of a transplanted IRA terrorist, now the respected Professor Odin Anderson, and lived in his suburban basement apartment.

Cross Carpenter and continue to Morgan. This is the western corner of UIC's East Campus. Several blocks straight north of you across the Eisenhower on Washington Boulevard near Morgan is the Museum of Holography. In Campbell's *Thinning the Turkey Herd,* Alderwoman Janet Canaris's lover, model Joyce Lombardi, had a loft apartment in a renovated building next door. When Joyce disappeared, Canaris asked her precinct captain, Jimmy Flannery to investigate. Flannery visited the Museum of Holography, then found Joyce's body. He also got to know Willy Dink, the exterminator who used organic methods like snakes for catching rats and gave Flannery his dog, Alfie.

Cross Morgan at Taylor and turn right to walk south past the UIC Police Headquarters to Roosevelt Road. Cross Roosevelt Road, which is also 12th Street, and walk two more blocks to Maxwell Street, which is between 13th and 14th Streets and dead ends at Blue Island. You are walking past UIC athletic fields all the way.

To your left at Roosevelt Road you pass architect Harry Weese's Physical Education Building where the UIC swimming pool is located. In Sara Paretsky's story "At the Old Swimming Hole," in *Murder and Mystery in Chicago,* V.I. Warshawski got shanghaied into sponsoring her high school chum Alicia Alonzo Dauphine in a swimathon for cancer. She was also forced to attend the actual event at UIC. Once there V.I. was the first to realize a swimmer had been shot and dived in to pull her out.

Cross Maxwell Street to the southeast corner where you will find the Chicago Police Department's Maxwell Street Station. The oldest station left in Chicago, it is the redbrick building with an arched doorway made famous by the TV cop series *Hill Street Blues.* It is still the Seventh District police station, with barred windows in the basement. A sign on the double front door says that the public is not admitted, but that is illegal, so try your luck if you wish.

In Stuart Kaminsky's *You Bet Your Life,* when P.I. Toby Peters came from Miami he was met by Sergeant Chuck Kleinhans from the Maxwell Street Station who kept an eye on him during his stay in the city. In fact, Sergeant Kleinhans made it tough for Peters to prove that Chico Marx didn't owe the mob a big gambling debt.

Look the police station over, then turn left to walk east toward the old site of the Maxwell Street Market. (The land has been sold to UIC and Maxwell Street Market moved east to Canal and Clinton.)

The sidewalks are broken and covered with lots of leftover junk, so it's best to walk down the middle of the street. Except for police cars, Maxwell Street is quiet on a weekday. The neighborhood now is predominantly black, so most merchants were either black or Hispanic. But in mysteries, the original Jewish ambiance lingers on, and real life VIPs like Supreme Court Justice Arthur Goldberg and "king of swing" Benny Goodman proudly claimed Maxwell Street childhoods.

In Marc Davis's *Dirty Money,* P.I. Frank Wolf had grown up with dead broker Abel Nockerman near Harrison-Halsted, where Nocky had been Wolf's hero because of his knack for making money and for attracting beautiful women.

In Kaminsky's *You Bet Your Life,* Peters went with Sergeant Kleinhans to see Maxwell Street on a quiet day. The street was crammed with pushcarts and had shops and stores and signs all over the place, many in Yiddish. The air smelled as if everything on sale had been grilled in onions. They bought hot dogs from a pushcart and Peters told Kleinhans he knew who the killers were.

In Cormany's *Rich or Dead* P.I. Dan Kruger was working for illegal alien Elena, whose brother had stolen money from her. They went to Maxwell Street Market and parked Kruger's old Skylark under the Dan Ryan Expressway. Elvia told Kruger she had worked a table here selling paintings on black velvet. The two ran into a black band called the Stony Island Hawks with a poor white player at lead guitar. The band leader let Kruger play, then told him he had a lifetime invitation to sit in.

In Max Allan Collins's *True Detective,* ex-cop Nate Heller's union organizer Pa had a stall on Maxwell Street where he sold books and school supplies, but when Nate's mother died, they moved out to Lawndale on the west side.

In Michael Raleigh's *The Maxwell Street Blues,* Uptown's P.I. Paul Whelan searched the Maxwell Street Market after the murder of old black vendor Sam Burwell. Whelan had been hired to find the old blues player.

Walk three blocks along Maxwell Street until you reach Halsted. In Harry Stephen Keeler's *Thieves' Nights,* the fleabag Paris Hotel was at the corner of Halsted and Maxwell Street and Ward Sharlow stayed there, looking out at a scene that resembled London's Petticoat Lane. Sharlow was reading the *Chicago Evening Dispatch,* where three separate ads asked someone looking like him to come talk about a job. It turned out the ad was run by millionaire John Atwood who hired Sharlow to pretend to be his drowned son Calvin for $10,000.

In Latimer's *Heading for a Hearse,* P.I. Bill Crane and his sidekick Doc Williams took Emily Lou Martin (death-row inmate Westland's financee) and Margot Brentano (Westland's secretary at the brokerage office) to Maxwell Street to find a Mr. G. The four took a cab from the Cook County Criminal Courts at 26th and California to Joe Petro's Italian restaurant on Halsted. They had an elegant Italian lunch, complete with martinis, then asked for the boss, who told them that Manny Grant would be at Cafe Montmartre tonight. They went there but Grant was shot dead at a table in front of them.

After exploring Maxwell Street, turn left on Halsted to walk north. Regular establishments like drugstores are not many, but in Whittingham's *State Street,* a Warner's Discount Drugs located on Halsted not far from Little Italy was hit by drug thieves who then murdered the owner, Theo Warner, by drowning him in a drum of water.

Walk north to Roosevelt Road. To your left is the redbrick St. Francis of Assisi church, which the Cardinal wants to merge with Holy Family next to St. Ignatius Prep. If you want to detour to visit the Fire Academy, located where the Chicago Fire began in 1871, walk east on Roosevelt Road under the Expressway to Jefferson and go left one block to DeKoven. (See Possible Side Trips, p. 330.) Cross Roosevelt Road and return to UIC's main East Campus. Originally it was known as Harrison/Halsted, then as Circle Campus. (West Campus is the medical center you just came from.) The two were combined in 1982 to become the University of Illinois at Chicago. Planned to be only a four-year college to replace the temporary facility at Navy Pier, UIC now has full-fledged graduate programs, dorms, and over 25,000 students.

The sandblasted, stark gray exposed-concrete buildings were designed in 1965 around a lecture center that connected six buildings with a highrise administration building under a shared roof. Its chief architect, Walter M. Netsch, Jr., meant to create an environment harmonious with its urban setting, but the result has been called "Fortress Illini." (It has a lot in common with Netsch's Stonehenge-like Regenstein Library at the University of Chicago. See Walk 9.) The demolition of a considerable amount of the original walkways and the amphitheater—always too hot or too cold—began in 1992.

In Sara Paretsky's short story "Strung Out" in *Deadly Allies,* Monica Larush and Gary Oberst were high school classmates of V.I. Warshawski. Monica got pregnant so they had to get married, which ruined Larush's chance to play on the girls' championship basketball team. V.I. assumed they'd have lots of kids in a small house, but instead they put one another through UIC, got good jobs and produced a daughter Lily, a top notch tennis player who turned pro at fifteen.

In Mark Zubro's *Sorry Now,* detective Paul Turner's neighbor Mrs. Talucci, who helped him care for his two sons, had started taking courses at UIC after her husband died. She ended up with degrees from three universities.

Cross Taylor and walk to another great Chicago social experiment, the redbrick Hull House at 800 South Halsted. Built for Charles Hull in 1856 in Italianate cube-and-cupola design, it was converted to a settlement house in 1889 by Jane Addams and Ellen Gates Starr. Using Toynbee Hall in London's East End as a model, they offered the urban poor of the area social, cultural, and educational facilities. The Hull House Theater has long been one of the leading lights of Chicago's little theater, but probably the greatest accomplishment was to create an environment where the different ethnic groups met in peace.

The two women greatly impressed British reformer William T. Stead, who visited Chicago during the Panic of 1893 and wrote the classic *If Christ came to Chicago* in 1894. During its heyday Hull House added thirteen more buildings and was a model for similar places across the world. Addams wrote *Twenty Years at Hull House* and shared the Nobel Peace Prize in 1931. The original Hull House was bought by the university in 1963; it has been renovated and its Victorian furnishings restored or replaced to make it a museum dedicated to Jane Addams. End your walk by visiting Hull House if you have time. It makes a nice change from murder.

Overshadowing Hull House is the UIC Student Center. There are restrooms on the second floor and three separate cafeterias on the ground floor. Or you can walk one block north to Polk Street and catch the El back to the Loop, or walk across the Eisenhower Expressway on Halsted to eat in Greektown.

POSSIBLE SIDE TRIPS

Greektown, across the Eisenhower Expressway at Halsted from Monroe to Van Buren. Heavy Greek immigration began about the 1880s, with many working as peddlers, then going into the restaurant, candy, and ice cream business. The original Greek settlement was in the Delta, formed by Halsted, Harrison, Blue Island, and Polk Street. Today it is only represented by the string of restaurants on Halsted because the Greek community has dispersed. Its most famous author is Harry Mark Petrakis, who wrote about the Washington Park Greek neighborhood where he grew up. (See also Walk 9.)

Chicago Police Training Center, 1300 W. Jackson Boulevard. The original statue of a policeman put up in memory of the Haymarket Riot is here in the courtyard with a twenty-four-hour police guard. Plans are in the works to create an entire Police Campus nearby with a new 911 Emergency Center at Madison and Loomis and a new Police Headquarters next door, replacing the present one at 11th and State.

In Hugh Holton's *Presumed Dead,* Commander Larry Cole was sent to the Police Training Academy for a checkup after being hospitalized as a result of a nighttime raid on Seagull Island behind the Space Museum in Hyde Park. (See also Walk 9.)

Chicago Fire Academy, 558 W. DeKoven. (Between Jefferson and Clinton east of the Dan Ryan Expressway. About five blocks from Hull House.) Built on the very spot where the 1871 Chicago Fire began in the O'Leary barn on Sunday October 8. Legend says that the O'Leary cow knocked over a lantern and started the conflagration, but the Chicago Historical Society says that is a myth fostered by the ever-eager media to sell papers.

Mary Craig, former president of MWA, wrote a historical thriller about the fire called *Dust to Diamonds.* Visitors to the

academy are welcome any time. If you call ahead you can see the recruits doing drills on ropes, fire escapes, etc. (Open Mon.–Fri. 8:30 A.M.–4:00 P.M. Call 747-7239.)
Maxwell Street Market (new), Canal to Clinton. Vendors and pushcarts. Sundays 6:00 A.M.–noon.
Jackson Boulevard Historic District, 1500 West Jackson Boulevard (from Laflin to Oakland). Designated an historic district in 1976, it consists of thirty-one Victorian row houses restored to their former grandeur. Worth a look if you cross the Eisenhower Expressway.

United Center (Chicago Stadium), Wood and Madison. This replaces the boxlike Art Deco building built in 1929 that was home to both the Chicago Bulls (basketball) and Blackhawks (ice hockey). Site of the 1996 Democratic Convention.

In Elliott Roosevelt's *The President's Man* the 1932 Democratic Convention was held at the Chicago Stadium. After his schoolmate "Blackjack" Endicott had convinced gangsters like Dutch Schultz and Frank Nitti that it would not be worthwhile to assassinate Franklin Delano Roosevelt, FDR broke with precedent both by flying in and by accepting the nomination in person.

In Paretsky's *Deadlock,* V.I.'s cousin Bernard Warshawski, or Boom Boom, was a star wing with the Blackhawks. But Boom Boom fractured an ankle, so he went to work for the Eudora Grain Company, where he slipped on deck and fell or was pushed under a ship's screw.

In Michael J. Katz's *Murder off the Glass,* sportscaster Andy Sussman did the Chicago Flames basketball play-by-play for WCGO radio. Sussman rated the old Stadium one of the worst in the civilized world, and never drove anywhere near it at night if there was no game. But during a game all the lights went out and "color" man Lester Beldon, an old Flames player, was shot dead.

In Robert J. Campbell's *The 600 Pound Gorilla,* Simmy Dugan and Princess Grace owned a bathhouse/health club called the Paradise near the Chicago Stadium. The mayor, worried about keeping Baby, the city's pet gorilla warm, made Jimmy Flannery find a warm nest for her and he chose the Paradise.

Cicero is straight west on Roosevelt Road at the city limits, about a mile south of the Eisenhower Expressway. This became Al Capone's headquarters, which has given it a bad name ever since. In Campbell's *The Junkyard Dog,* Flannery said that Capone was pushed into Cicero where, even today, anything goes. (See Robert J. Schoenberg's *Mr. Capone* for more authentic details about Capone's operations.) On January 17, 1994 in the midst of a terrible cold spell a savings and loan took the wrecking ball to Capone's old Alton Hotel at 4835 W. 22nd Street. An eyesore, it will become a parking lot because Cicero isn't partial to mementos of "Scarface." The Hawthorne Hotel next door was another Capone hotel, where Capone's room was protected with steel shutters. He was eating lunch there when rival northside gangsters drove by and used tommy guns to pump a thousand rounds into the hotel, but missed him. Capone also owned the 4811 Club, a nightclub, across the street, and the three supposedly were connected by tunnels, like Capone's buildings in the South Loop. (See Walk 8.) The Hawthorne burned down in 1970 and there is an auto parts shop where the nightclub was.

In Stuart Kaminsky's *You Bet Your Life,* trying to establish contact with the mob, P.I. Toby Peters went to The Fireside in Cicero, where he found a large, softly lit room with sixty people gambling and a pillar in the center with a man inside with a gun. Peters played roulette beside a tall, lean guy in his early thirties, perfectly groomed, who talked in upper-crust English. It turned out to be British spy Ian Fleming (before he wrote the James Bond thrillers), and he helped Peters escape.

In the Gordons's *Case File: FBI* (Gordon Gordon was a former FBI agent), Special Agent John (Rip) Ripley, whose partner had been shot, took over three cases that were interrelated in Zach's files. During Ripley's FBI investigation, the body of one victim was found in a garbage dumpster at The Round-up in Cicero by a cook's assistant.

Oak Park is just west and north of Cicero on the Eisenhower Expressway at Austin. A suburban village, which grew at the end of the railroad line, Oak Park was incorporated in 1902 because its middle-class residents did not want to be swallowed up by Chicago. It was the home of Frank Lloyd Wright who invented the Prairie School of Architecture and left twenty-five examples of it here, including the famous Unity Temple. It was also the home of Edgar Rice Burroughs, creator of Tarzan the Ape Man, and adventurer/writer Ernest Hemingway. The Oak Park Visitors Center, in Wright's Home and Studio at 158 Forest, sponsors walking tours. Call 1-708-848-1500. Mystery buffs should also visit *Centuries and Sleuths,* a mystery-history bookstore at 743 Garfield Blvd. (1-708-848-PAGE; August Aleksy, bookseller.)

In mysteries Oak Park is one of two "okay" suburbs to live in. The other is Evanston. Neither of them is described as full of the rich or murderous like the North Shore.

In Stuart Kaminsky's *When the Dark Man Calls* Lloyd, Jean Kaiser's minister brother lived there with his wife and kids in the typical Oak Park Victorian house, with a lot of varnished wood. The family came to Jean's rescue, taking in her daughter and supporting her career as a talk show psychologist.

In the Gordons's *Case File: FBI*, special agent Ripley followed a lead to Oak Park, taking the El to Ridgeland Avenue where he captured a suspect.

In Barbara Michaels's (aka Elizabeth Peters) *Search the Shadows,* Haskell Maloney's old aunt and grandmother lived in Oak Park on Kenilworth Avenue. When Haskell came to Chicago to find out who her real father was, she visited them but found they lived a strange, strict life, based on her dead grandfather's rules. Their house was broken into later by someone searching for Haskell's personal records. While Haskell worked at the Nazarian Museum on Prairie Avenue, her ex-fiance appeared. He suggested she take her prim grandmother to see the Oak Park Frank Lloyd Wright houses.

In Roslynn Griffith's historical mystery *Sweet Birds of Passage* Aurelia Kincaid, an architect who worked for an architectural firm like Adler and Sullivan, met a young and very prepossessing Frank Lloyd Wright. Later Kincaid went to Oak Park to inspect a building her firm was putting up and was attacked.

In Gerald DiPego's *Keeper of the City,* Detective Jim Dela saw himself as a G. K. Chesterton urban knight, responsible for keeping the city streets safe. Chasing a serial killer—of mafia overlords—took him to Oak Park where a gangster named McCauley had been shot in his own backyard. The murderer always sent word of the murder ahead of time to a self-important Chicago columnist, who thought the vendetta was clever, until he was threatened himself.

River Forest is just north and west of Oak Park on Harlem Avenue. This is the area where the big-time Mafia bosses like the late Tony Accardo, popularly known as the Big Tuna, lived to give their families the benefit of a nice suburban upbringing. In Eugene Izzi's *The Take,* the head of the Outfit was a willy old man called the Swordfish who followed Al Capone's rule: no drug dealing.

River Forest also has some lovely Frank Lloyd Wright houses and is the home of the highly respected Rosary College. In Martin Blank's *Shadowchase* there is a suburban college much like Rosary College called Ardmore College, where former IRA informer Professor Owen Anderson taught. Paul Lazzeri was taking a degree in there in religion and became a kind of Anderson protege, living for a time in the basement of the Anderson house. It was a Georgian red brick with white shutters and some strange lumps in the lawn.

A number of characters who regularly appear in Andrew Greeley's mysteries moved to River Forest's St. Luke's Parish from St. Ursula's (aka St. Angela's) on the western edge of the city after World War II. (See *Andrew Greeley's Chicago.*) In Greeley's *Ascent into Hell* his priest turned stockbroker Hugh Donlon moved to River Forest, and former Deputy Police Superintendent Mike Casey, related to Father Blackie's Ryan clan, lived here and went to school with Anne Reilly, who ran a gallery off Michigan in *Angels of September.* See also *Happy Are Those Who Thirst for Justice.*

Morton Arboretum, about 9 miles farther west at 53 and Lisle, is a 1,500 acre year-round oasis of trees, plants, shrubs, and flowers. In Bill Granger's *The Priestly Murders,* Sergeant Terry Flynn took Policewoman Karen Kovacs there on their day off for a mid-winter picnic, just to get away from crime.

SPECIAL HELPS

Authors, Books, and Sleuths by Walk

LAKEFRONT/MUSEUMS WALK: Authors and Books

Ashenhurst, John M., *The World's Fair Murders* (1934)
Asimov, Isaac, *Murder at the ABA* (1976)
Bland, Eleanor Taylor, *Slow Burn* (1993)
Browne, Howard, *Pork City* (1988)
Campbell, Robert J., *The 600 Pound Gorilla* (1987)
Caspary, Vera, *Evvie* (1960)
Clason, Clyde B., *The Man from Tibet* (1938)
Collins, Max Allan, *Dying in the Postwar World* (1991); *Kill Your Darlings* (1984); *True Crime* (1984); *True Detective* (1983)
Collins, Wilkie, *The Moonstone*
Cormany, Michael, *Red Winter* (1989)
Craig, Mary —
Cross, Amanda *In The Last Analysis* (1964)
Donohue, H. E. F., *The Higher Animals* (1965)
D'Amato, Barbara, *Hardball* (1991); *Hard Tack* (1992); "The Lower Wacker Hilton" in *Cat Crimes* (1991)
Eberhart, Mignon G., *Dead Men's Plans* (1952); *The Glass Slipper* (1938)
Engleman, Paul, *Catch a Fallen Angel* (1986)
Engling, Richard, *Body Mortgage* (1989)
Fink, John, *The Leaf Boats* (1991)
Granger, Bill, *The Newspaper Murders* (1985); *The Priestly Murders* (1984); *The Public Murders* (1980)
Greeley, Andrew, *Happy Are the Peacemakers* (1993); *Happy Are Those Who Thirst for Justice* (1987); *The Patience of a Saint* (1987)
Griffith, Roslynn, *Pretty Birds of Passage* (1993; set in 1893)

Haddad, Carolyn, *Caught in the Shadows* (1992)
Himmel, Richard, *The Twenty-Third Web* (1977)
Jones, D. J. H., *Murder at the MLA* (1993)
Kahn, Michael A., *Grave Designs (The Canaan Legacy)* (1988)
Kaminsky, Stuart, *When the Dark Man Calls* (1983); *You Bet Your Life* (1978)
Keeler, Harry Stephen, *Behind That Mask* (1930); *Thieves' Nights* (1929)
Kenney, Catherine, *The Remarkable Case of Dorothy L. Sayers* (1990)
MacDonald, John D., *One Fearful Yellow Eye* (1966)
Maling, Arthur, *Dingdong* (1974); *The Snowman* (1973)
McCall, Thomas, *A Wide and Capable Revenge* (1993)
McGivern, William P., *Very Cold for May* (1950)
Michaels, Brian, *Illegal Procedure* (1988)
Ness, Eliot, *The Untouchables* (1957)
Paretsky, Sara, *Blood Shot* (1988); *Deadlock* (1984); *Guardian Angel* (1992); *Indemnity Only* (1982)
Poe, Edgar Allan, *Tamerlane* (1827)
Post, Mortimer, *Candidate for Murder* (1936)
Raleigh, Michael, *A Body in Belmont Harbor* (1993); *Death in Uptown* (1991)
Reaves, Sam, *A Long Cold Fall* (1991); *Fear Will Do It* (1993)
Rice, Craig, *Having a Wonderful Crime* (1943); *Knocked for a Loop* (1957); *The Wrong Murder* (1940)
Roosevelt, Elliott, *The President's Man* (1991; set in 1932)
Sherer, Michael W., *An Option on Death* (1988)
Smith, Charles Merrill, *Reverend Randollph and the Unholy Bible* (1983)
Starrett, Vincent, *The Private Life of Sherlock Holmes* (1966)
Targ, William, *The Case of Mr. Cassidy* (1939)
Thomas, Ross, *The Porkchoppers* (1972)
Wallace, Edgar, *On the Spot* (1931)
Whitney, Phyllis, *The Red Carnelian (Red Is for Murder)* (1943)
Yastrow, Shelby, *Undue Influence* (1990)
Zubro, Mark, *Sorry Now* (1991)

LAKEFRONT/MUSEUMS WALK: Sleuths

Becky Belski Haddad
Allison Bennett Ashenhurst

Officer Norm Bennis D'Amato
Gregory Blake Engling
Detective Nora Callum McCall
Professor Nancy Cook Jones
Bayard DeLancey Keeler
Detective Boaz Dixon Jones
"Blackjack" John Endicott Roosevelt
Professor Kate Fansler Cross
Officer Susannah Maria Figuroa D'Amato
Jimmy Flannery Campbell
Sergeant Terry Flynn Granger
Professor Lowell E. Gaylord Post
Frank Gillespie Fink
Rachel Gold Kahn
Jake Harrison McGivern
Rue Hatterick Eberhart
Nathan (Nate) Heller Collins
Sherlock Holmes Conan Doyle
Chief Kelly Wallace
Aurelia Kincaid Griffith
Dan Kruger Cormany
Lieutenant Frank Lesniak Michaels
Abe Lieberman Kaminsky
Cooper MacLeish Reaves
Mallory Collins
John J. Malone Rice
Catherine (Cat) Marsala D'Amato
Detective Marti MacAlister Bland
Travis McGee MacDonald
Hugh Morris Targ
Ches Novak Maling
Phil Ogden Yastrow
Toby Peters Kaminsky
Reverend C. P. Randollph Smith
Mark Renzler Engleman
Father "Blackie" Ryan Greeley
Livingston Stonehill Himmel
Paul Turner Zubro
Emerson Ward Sherer

V.I. Warshawski Paretsky
Theocritus Lucium Westborough Clason
Paul Whelan Raleigh
Mike Wiley Maling
Linell Wynn Whitney

EAST LOOP WALK: Authors and Books

Bloch, Robert, *American Gothic* (1974; set in 1893); "Yours Truly, Jack the Ripper" in *The Dark Descent* (1987)
Browne, Howard, *Pork City* (1988)
Brod, D. C., *Murder in Store* (1989)
Caspary, Vera, *Evvie* (1960; set in 1920s)
Charteris, Leslie, "The King of the Beggars" in *Call for the Saint* (1948)
Clason, Clyde B., *The Man from Tibet* (1938)
Collins, Max Allan, *True Detective* (1983); *True Crime* (1984); *Dying in the Postwar World* (1991)
Conan Doyle, Sir Arthur, "The Valley of Fear" (1915) in *Adventures of Sherlock Holmes* (1930)
Cormany, Michael, *Red Winter* (1989)
Craig, Mary (Shura), *The Chicagoans: Dust to Diamonds* (1981; set in 1871)
Crawford, Dan, "Father's Day Special" in *Ellery Queen's Mystery Magazine* (March 1991)
D'Amato, Barbara, *Hardball* (1990)
Davis, Marc, *Dirty Money* (1992)
Eberhart, Mignon G., *The Glass Slipper* (1938)
Evers, Crabbe, *Murder in Wrigley Field* (1991)
Gordons, The, *Case File: FBI* (1954)
Granger, Bill, *Drover* (1991); *Infant of Prague* (1987); *The El Murders* (1987); *The Newspaper Murders* (1985)
Griffith, Roslynn, *Pretty Birds of Passage* (1993; set in 1893)
Greeley, Andrew, *Happy Are the Clean of Heart* (1986); *The Patience of a Saint* (1987); *War in Heaven* (1992)
Haddad, Carolyn, *Caught in the Shadows* (1992)

Hammett, Dashiell, *The Maltese Falcon* (1930); *The Thin Man* (1932)

Himmel, Richard, *The Twenty-Third Web* (1977)

Hoch, Edward D., "The Theft of the Overdue Library Book" in *Murder and Mystery in Chicago* (1991)

Hoffman, Dennis E., *Scarface Al and the Crime Crusaders* (1994)

Hughes, Dorothy B., *The Fallen Sparrow* (1942); "The Spotted Pup" in *Murder and Mystery in Chicago* (1991)

Jones, D. J. H., *Murder at the MLA* (1993)

Kahn, Michael A., *Grave Designs (The Canaan Legacy)* (1992)

Keeler, Harry Stephen, *Behind That Mask* (1930)

Kennedy, Delores, *William Heirens: His Day in Court* (1991)

Latimer, Jonathan, *Heading for a Hearse* (1935); *The Lady in the Morgue* (1936)

Levitsky, Ronald, *The Innocence That Kills*

Liebow, Eli, *Dr. Joe Bell, Model for Sherlock Holmes* (1992)

Love, William F., *The Chartreuse Clue* (1990)

Malcolm, John, *Mortal Ruin* (1988)

Maling, Arthur, *Dingdong* (1974); *Go-Between* (1970); *The Snowman* (1973)

MacDonald, John D., *One Fearful Yellow Eye* (1966)

McGivern, William P., *Very Cold for May* (1950)

Queen, Ellery, ed., *101 Years of Entertainment: The Great Detective Stories 1841–1941* (1942)

Paretsky, Sara, *Bitter Medicine* (1987); *Blood Shot* (1988); *Burn Marks* (1990); *Guardian Angel* (1992); *Killing Orders* (1985); *Indemnity Only* (1982); "The Maltese Cat" (1991); *Tunnel Vision* (1994)

Pickard, Nancy, *Bum Steer* (1990)

Pinkerton, Allan, *The Burglar's Fate and the Detectives* (1883)

Poe, Edgar Allan, *Tamerlane* (1827)

Reaves, Sam, *Fear Will Do It* (1993)

Rice, Craig, *Knocked for a Loop* (1957); *The Wrong Murder* (1940)

Roosevelt, Elliott, *The President's Man* (1991; set in 1932)

Sherer, Michael W., *Death Came Dressed in White* (1992)

Smith, Charles Merrill, *Reverend Randollph and the Unholy Bible* (1983); *Reverend Randollph and the Wages of Sin* (1974)

Starrett, Vincent, "The Eleventh Juror" in *Ellery Queen's 101 Years of Entertainment 1841–1941* (1942); *The Private Life of Sherlock Holmes* (1960)
Stuart, Ian, *Stab in the Back* (1986)
Targ, William, *The Case of Mr. Cassidy* (1939)
Wallace, Edgar, *On the Spot* (1931)
Williams, Kirby, *The C.V.C. Murders* (1929)
Whitney, Phyllis, *The Red Carnelian (Red Is for Murder)* (1943)
Yastrow, Shelby, *Undue Influence* (1990)

EAST LOOP WALK: Sleuths

Becky Belski Haddad
Jenny Cain Pickard
Nick Charles Hammett
Professor Nancy Cook Jones
William Crane Latimer
Crystal Bloch
Devereux (the November Man) Granger
Detective Boaz Dixon Jones
Jimmy Drover Granger
"Blackjack" John Endicott Roosevelt
Sergeant Terry Flynn Granger
Rachel Gold Kahn
Jake Harrison McGivern
Nathan (Nate) Heller Collins
Charlie Hogan Bloch
Sherlock Holmes Conan Doyle
Duffy House Evers
Chief Kelly Wallace
Aurelia Kincaid Griffith
Dan Kruger Cormany
Cooper MacLeish Reaves
John J. Malone Rice
Cat Marsala D'Amato
Quint McCauley Brod
Travis McGee MacDonald

Kit McKittrick Hughes
Hugh Morris Targ
Ches Novak Maling
Phil Ogden Yastrow
Detective Terrence (Terry) O'Rourke Keeler
Phil Ogden Yastrow
Allan Pinkerton Pinkerton
Dr. Thackeray Place Williams
Reverend C. P. Randollph Smith
Bishop Regan Lover
Special Agent John Ripley The Gordons
Nathan (Nate) Rosen Levitsky
Father "Blackie" Ryan Greeley
The Saint (Simon Templar) Charteris
Kip Scott Hughes
Tim Simpson Malcolm
Sam Spade Hammett
Emerson Ward Sherer
V.I. Warshawski Paretsky
Theocritus Lucius Westborough Clason
Mike Wiley Maling
Frank Wolf Davis
Linell Wynn Whitney

WEST LOOP WALK: Authors and Books

Allingham, Margery, *The Tiger in the Smoke* (1952)
Ashenhurst, John M., *The World's Fair Murders* (1934)
Ballinger, Bill S., *Portrait in Smoke* (1950)
Benson, O. C., *Cain's Wife (Cain's Woman)* (1960)
Bland, Eleanor Taylor, *Dead Time* (1992)
Blank, Martin, *Shadowchase* (1989)
Bloch, Robert, "The Play's the Thing" in *Murder and Mystery in Chicago* (1991)
Brown, Fredric, *The Fabulous Clipjoint* (1947)
Brashler, William, *Traders* (1991)
Campbell, Robert, *The Junkyard Dog* (1986); *Hipdeep in Alligators* (1987); *The 600 Pound Gorilla* (1987)

Clason, Clyde B., *The Man from Tibet* (1938)
Collins, Max Allan, *Dying in the Postwar World* (1991); *Kill Your Darlings* (1984); *True Crime* (1984)
Cormany, Michael, *Red Winter* (1989)
Craig, Mary, *The Third Blond* (1985)
D'Amato, *Hardball* (1990); *Hard Luck* (1992)
Davis, Marc, *Dirty Money* (1992)
Dewey, Thomas B., *A Sad Song Singing* (1963)
Eberhart, Mignon G., *The Glass Slipper* (1938)
Elkins, Aaron and Charlotte, "Nice Gorilla" in *Malice Domestic I* (1992)
Gordons, The, *Case File: FBI* (1954)
Granger, Bill, *The Priestly Murders* (1984); *The El Murders* (1987); *The Public Murders* (1980); *The Newspaper Murders* (1985)
Greeley, Andrew, *Ascent into Hell* (1983); *Lord of the Dance* (1984); *The Patience of a Saint* (1987); *Wages of Sin* (1992)
Gruber, Frank, *The Scarlet Feather (The Gamecock Murders)* (1949)
Haddad, Carolyn, *Caught in the Shadows* (1992)
Himmel, Richard, *The Twenty-Third Web* (1977)
Hughes, Dorothy B., "The Spotted Pup," in *Murder and Mystery in Chicago* (1991)
Izzi, Eugene, *The Booster* (1989)
Jones, D. J. H., *Murder at the MLA* (1993)
Kahn, Michael A., *Grave Designs (The Canaan Legacy)* (1988)
Kaminsky, Stuart, *When the Dark Man Calls* (1983); *You Bet Your Life* (1978)
Keeler, Harry Stephen, *The Face of the Man from Saturn* (1933); *Behind That Mask* (1930); *Thieves' Nights* (1929)
Kennedy, Delores, *William Heirens: His Day in Court* (1991)
Lathen, Emma, *Death Shall Overcome* (1966)
Latimer, Jonathan, *The Lady in the Morgue* (1936)
MacDonald, John D., *One Fearful Yellow Eye* (1966)
Malcolm, John, *Mortal Ruin* (1988)
Maling, Arthur, *Go-Between* (1970); *The Snowman* (1973)
Mayer, Mary, *The Devil's Card* (1992)
Michaels, Brian, *Illegal Procedure* (1988)
Nash, Jay Robert, *A Crime Story* (1981)
Ness, Eliot, *The Untouchables* (1957)

Paretsky, Sara, *Bitter Medicine* (1987); *Burn Marks* (1990); *Deadlock* (1984); *Indemnity Only* (1982); *Killing Orders* (1985)

Raleigh, Michael, *Death in Uptown* (1991)

Reaves, Sam, *A Long Cold Fall* (1991)

Rice, Craig, *Knocked for a Loop* (1957); *The Fourth Postman* (1948); *Trial by Fury* (1941)

Smith, Charles Merrill, *Reverend Randollph and the Avenging Angel* (1977); *Reverend Randollph and the Holy Terror* (1980); *Reverend Randollph and the Unholy Bible* (1983); *Reverend Randollph and the Wages of Sin* (1974)

Stuart, Ian, *Stab in the Back* (1986)

Thomas, Ross, *The Porkchoppers* (1972)

Turow, Scott, *Burden of Proof* (1990)

Ullman, James Michael, *The Neon Haystack* (1965); *The Venus Trap* (1966); *Lady on Fire* (1968)

Whitney, Phyllis, *The Red Carnelian (Red Is for Murder)* (1943)

Yastrow, Shelby, *Undue Influence* (1990)

Zubro, Mark, *Political Poison* (1993)

WEST LOOP WALK: Sleuths

Danny April Ballinger

Becky Belski Haddad

Allison Bennett Ashenhurst

Angie Bromley Craig

Albert Campion Allingham

Jon Chakorian Ullman

Professor Nancy Cook Jones

Sam Cragg Gruber

William Crane Latimer

Bayard DeLancey Keeler

Detective Boaz Dixon Jones

"Blackjack" John Endicott Roosevelt

Jimmy Flannery Campbell

Johnny Fletcher Gruber

Sergeant Terry Flynn Granger

Julian Forbes Ullman
Rachel Gold Kahn
Rue Hatterick Eberhart
Nathan (Nate) Heller Collins
Ed Hunter Brown
Jack Journey Nash
Jimmie Kentland Keeler
Dan Kruger Cormany
Lieutenant John Lamp Blank
Lieutenant Frank Lesniak Michaels
Detective Abe Lieberman Kaminsky
Mac Dewey
Detective Marti MacAlister Bland
Cooper MacLeish Reaves
Mallory Collins
John J. Malone Rice
Cat Marsala D'Amato
Vincent Martin Izzi
Tom Martin Mayer
Travis McGee MacDonald
Ches Novak Maling
Phil Ogden Yastrow
Toby Peters Kaminsky
Reverend C.P. Randollph Smith
Max Raven Benson
FBI Agent Jack Ripley The Gordons
Father "Blackie" Ryan Greeley
Kip Scott Hughes
Nick Silver Hoch
Tim Simpson Malcolm
Sandy Stern Turow
Livingston Stonehill Himmel
William Sweeney Brown
John Putnam Thatcher Lathen
Detective Paul Turner Zubro
V.I. Warshawski Paretsky
Theocritus Lucius Westborough Clason
Paul Whelan Raleigh

Frank Wolf Davis
Linell Wynn Whitney

NEAR NORTH WALK: Authors and Books

Ashenhurst, John M., *The World's Fair Murders* (1933)
Behn, Noel, *Lindbergh, the Crime* (1993)
Bloch, Robert, "Yours Truly, Jack the Ripper" in *The Dark Descent* (1987)
Breen, Jon L., "Malice at the Mike," in *Murder and Mystery in Chicago* (1991)
Brod, D. C., *Murder in Store* (1989)
Brown, Fredric, *The Fabulous Clipjoint* (1947)
Brown, Fredric, *The Screaming Mimi* (1949)
Browne, Howard, *Pork City* (1988)
Collins, Max Allan, *Stolen Away* (1991); *True Crime* (1984)
Cormany, Michael, *Red Winter* (1989)
Craig, Mary (M.S.), *The Chicagoans: Dust to Diamonds* (1981)
Crawford, Dan, "The Dark, Shining Street" in Alfred Hitchcock's *Mystery Magazine* (Nov. 1988)
Davis, Marc, *Dirty Money* (1992)
Dymmoch, Michael A., *The Man Who Understood Cats* (1993)
D'Amato, Barbara, *The Hands of Healing Murder* (1980); "The Lower Wacker Hilton" in *Cat Crimes* (1991); *Hard Women* (1993)
Eberhart, Mignon G., *The Glass Slipper* (1938)
Engleman, Paul, *Catch a Fallen Angel* (1986)
Engling, Richard, *Body Mortgage* (1989)
Evers, Crabbe, *Murder in Wrigley Field* (1991)
Granger, Bill, *The Newspaper Murders* (1985); *The Public Murders* (1980); *The Priestly Murders* (1984)
Greeley, Andrew M., *Happy Are the Clean of Heart* (1986); *Angels of September* (1986); *The Patience of a Saint* (1987)
Gregorich, Barbara, *Dirty Proof* (1988)
Haddad, Carolyn, *Caught in the Shadows* (1992)
Hecht, Ben and Charles MacArthur, *The Front Page* (1928)
Holton, Hugh, *Presumed Dead* (1994)

Izzi, Eugene, *The Booster* (1989); *The Take* (1987); *The Bad Guys* (1988)
Kahn, Michael A., *Grave Designs (The Canaan Legacy)* (1992)
Kaminsky, Stuart, *When the Dark Man Calls* (1983)
Keating, H. R. F., *Crime & Mystery; The 100 Best Books* (1987)
Keeler, Harry Stephen, *Behind That Mask* (1930); *The Washington Square Enigma* (1933); *Thieves' Nights* (1929)
Latimer, Jonathan, *Heading for a Hearse* (1935); *The Lady in the Morgue* (1953)
Love, William F. —
Malcolm, John, *Mortal Ruin* (1988)
Maling, Arthur, *The Snowman* (1973); *Bent Man* (1975); *Go-Between* (1970); *The Koberg Link* (1979)
Mayer, Mary, *The Devil's Card* (1992)
McCall, Thomas, *A Wide and Capable Revenge* (1993)
McInerny, Ralph, *Bishop as Pawn* (1978)
Nash, Jay Robert, *A Crime Story* (1981)
Paretsky, Sara, *Deadlock* (1984); "The Case of the Pietro Andromache" in *Sisters in Crime* (1989); *Tunnel Vision* (1994)
Poe, Edgar Allan, *Tamerlane* (1827)
Quill, Monica, *Let Us Prey* (1982)
Raleigh, Michael, *Death in Uptown* (1991); *A Body in Belmont Harbor* (1993)
Reaves, Sam, *A Long Cold Fall* (1991); *Fear Will Do It* (1993)
Rice, Craig, *The Corpse Steps Out* (1940); *My Kingdom for a Hearse* (1957); *The Lucky Stiff* (1945)
Roberts, Les, *Seeing the Elephant* (1992)
Skom, Edith, *The Mark Twain Murders* (1989)
Smith, Charles Merrill, *Reverend Randollph and the Holy Terror* (1980); *Reverend Randollph and the Unholy Bible* (1983)
Targ, William, *The Case of Mr. Cassidy* (1939)
Ullman, James Michael, *The Neon Haystack* (1965); *Lady on Fire* (1968); "Dead Ringer" in *Murder and Mystery in Chicago* (1991)
Van Dine, S. S., *The Canary Murder Case* (1927)
Wallace, Edgar, *On the Spot* (1931)
Williams, Kirby, *The C.V.C. Murders* (1929)
Yastrow, Shelby, *Undue Influence* (1990)

Zubro, Mark, *A Simple Suburban Murder* (1989); *Why Isn't Becky Twitchell Dead?* (1990)

NEAR NORTH WALK: Sleuths

FBI Agent Gil Bailey Skom
Becky Belski Haddad
Allison Bennett Ashenhurst
Officer Norm Bennis D'Amato
Gregory Blake Engling
Detective Nora Callum McCall
Scott Carpenter Zubro
William Crane Latimer
Dr. Gerritt De Graff D'Amato
Bayard DeLancey Keeler
Sister Mary Theresa Dempsey (Emtee) Quill
Father Roger Dowling McInerny
Frank Dragovic Gregorich
Fabe Falletti Izzi
Officer Susannah Maria Figuroa D'Amato
Sergeant Terry Flynn Granger
Julian Forbes Ullman
The Go-Between Maling
Rachel Gold Kahn
Ford Harling Keeler
Nathan (Nate) Heller Collins
Duffy House Evers
Ed Hunter Brown
Walter Jackson Maling
Jack Journey Nash
Chief Kelly Wallace
Dan Kruger Cormany
Barney Lear Ullman
Detective Abe Lieberman Kaminsky
Cooper MacLeish Reaves
John J. Malone Rice

Jimbo Marino Izzi
Cat Marsala D'Amato
Tom Martin Mayer
Vincent Martin Izzi
Tom Mason Zubro
Quint McCauley Brod
Gordon McGregor Crawford
Hugh Morris Targ
Ches Novak Maling
Phil Ogden Yastrow
Dr. Thackeray Place Williams
Brock Potter Maling
Reverend C. P. Randollph Smith
Mark Renzler Engleman
Father "Blackie" Ryan Greeley
Saxon Roberts
Tim Simpson Malcolm
William Sweeney Brown
Detective John Thinnes Dymmoch
Philo Vance Van Dine
V. I. Warshawski Paretsky
Paul Whelan Raleigh
Frank Wolf Davis

STREETERVILLE WALK: Authors and Books

Ashenhurst, John M., *The World's Fair Murders* (1934)
Blank, Martin, *Shadowchase* (1989)
Campbell, Robert J., *The Junkyard Dog* (1986)
Collins, Max Allan, *True Crime* (1984)
Cormany, Michael, *Red Winter* (1989)
D'Amato, Barbara, *Hard Case* (1994); *The Hands of Healing Murder* (1980); *The Doctor, the Murder, the Mystery* (1992)
Davis, Marc, *Dirty Money* (1992)
Dymmoch, Michael A., *The Man Who Understood Cats* (1993)
Engleman, Paul, *Catch a Fallen Angel* (1986)
Granger, Bill, *Drover* (1991)

Greeley, Andrew, *Happy Are the Clean of Heart* (1986); *Happy Are the Meek* (1985); *Angels of September* (1986)
Gregorich, Barbara, *Dirty Proof* (1988)
Izzi, Eugene, *The Booster* (1989)
Jance, J. A., *Dismissed with Prejudice* (1989)
Kahn, Michael A., *Grave Designs (The Canaan Legacy)* (1988)
Kaminsky, Stuart, *When the Dark Man Calls* (1983); *You Bet Your Life* (1978)
Keeler, Harry Stephen, *Thieves' Nights* (1929); *The Face of the Man from Saturn* (1930); *Behind That Mask* (1930)
Latimer, Jonathan, *The Lady in the Morgue* (1953)
MacDonald, John D., *One Fearful Yellow Eye* (1966)
Maling, Arthur, *Dingdong* (1977); *The Koberg Link* (1979); *The Snowman* (1973); *Go-Between* (1970)
McCall, Thomas, *A Wide and Capable Revenge* (1993)
Paretsky, Sara, *Deadlock* (1984); *Burn Marks* (1990); *Blood Shot* (1988)
Raleigh, Michael, *Death in Uptown* (1991)
Rice, Craig, *Having a Wonderful Crime* (1986); *My Kingdom for a Hearse* (1957); *Knocked for a Loop* (1957); *The Corpse Steps Out* (1940); *The Fourth Postman* (1948); *The Lucky Stiff* (1945); *The Right Murder* (1941); *The Wrong Murder* (1940)
Ross, Sam, *He Ran All the Way* (1947)
Smith, Charles Merrill, *Reverend Randollph and the Unholy Bible* (1983)
Targ, William, *The Case of Mr. Cassidy* (1939)
Wallace, Edgar, *On the Spot* (1931)
Whittingham, Richard, *State Street* (1993)
Yastrow, Shelby, *Undue Influence* (1990)
Zubro, Mark, *Sorry Now* (1991); *Why Isn't Becky Twitchell Dead?* (1990)

STREETERVILLE WALK: Sleuths

J. B. (Beau) Beaumont Jance
Allison Bennett Ashenhurst
Detective Nora Callum McCall

Scott Carpenter Zubro
William Crane Latimer
Dr. Gerritt De Graff D'Amato
Bayard DeLancey Keeler
Frank Dragovic Gregorich
Jimmy Drover Granger
Jimmy Flannery Campbell
Rachel Gold Kahn
Nathan (Nate) Heller Collins
Chief Kelly Wallace
Jimmie Kentland Keeler
Dan Kruger Cormany
Lieutenant John Lamp Blank
Detective Abe Lieberman Kaminsky
John J. Malone Rice
Cat Marsala D'Amato
Vincent Martin Izzi
Tom Mason Zubro
Travis McGee MacDonald
Hugh Morris Targ
Detective Joe Morrison Whittingham
Ches Novak Maling
Phil Ogden Yastrow
Toby Peters Kaminsky
Brock Potter Maling
Reverend C. P. Randollph Smith
Mark Renzler Engleman
Father "Blackie" Ryan Greeley
Detective John Thinnes Dymmoch
Detective Paul Turner Zubro
V.I. Warshawski Paretsky
Paul Whelan Raleigh
Mike Wiley Maling
Frank Wolf Davis

GOLD COAST WALK: Authors and Books

Algren, Nelson, *The Man with the Golden Arm* (1949)
Ballinger, Bill S., *Portrait in Smoke* (1950)

Bard-Collins, Joan, "The Fowler Solution" (1993)
Bloch, Robert, *American Gothic* (1974; set in 1893)
Breo, Dennis L. and William J. Martin, *The Crime of the Century* (1993)
Brown, Fredric, *The Fabulous Clipjoint* (1947); "I'll Cut Your Throat Again, Kathleen" in *Murder and Mystery in Chicago* (1991); *The Screaming Mimi* (1949)
Caspary, Vera, *Evvie* (1960)
Charteris, Leslie, "King of the Beggars" in *Call for the Saint* (1948)
Cormany, Michael, *Lost Daughter* (1988)
Craig, Mary, *The Chicagoans: Dust to Diamonds* (1981)
D'Amato, Barbara, *Hardball* (1990); *Hard Women* (1993)
Davis, Marc, *Dirty Money* (1992)
Dymmoch, Michael A., *The Man Who Understood Cats* (1993)
Eberhart, Mignon G., *The Dark Garden* (1933); *Hasty Wedding* (1937); *Dead Men's Plans* (1952); *The Cases of Susan Dare* (1934); *The Glass Slipper* (1938)
Engleman, Paul, *Catch a Fallen Angel* (1986)
Engling, Richard, *Body Mortgage* (1989)
Evers, Crabbe, *Murder in Wrigley Field* (1991)
Granger, Bill, *The Newspaper Murders* (1985); *The Infant of Prague* (1987); *The Priestly Murders* (1984)
Greeley, Andrew, *Happy Are the Clean of Heart* (1986)
Griffith, Roslynn, *Pretty Birds of Passage* (1993; set in 1893)
Gruber, Frank, *The Scarlet Feather* (1949)
Hecht, Ben and Charles MacArthur, *The Front Page* (1928)
Izzi, Eugene, *The Take* (1987); *The Booster* (1989)
Kaminsky, Stuart, *You Bet Your Life* (1978)
Keeler, Harry Stephen, *Thieves' Nights* (1929); *The Washington Park Enigma* (1933)
MacDonald, John D., *One Fearful Yellow Eye* (1966)
Maling, Arthur, *Dingdong* (1974); *Lover and Thief* (1988)
McGivern, William P., *Very Cold for May* (1950)
McInerny, Ralph, *Bishop as Pawn* (1978)
Nash, Jay Robert, *A Crime Story* (1981)
Paretsky, Sara, *Indemnity Only* (1982); "The Case of the Pietro Andromache" (1989)
Poe, Edgar Allan, *Tamerlane* (1927)
Quill, Monica, *Let Us Prey* (1982)

Reaves, Sam, *Fear Will Do It* (1993)
Rice, Craig, *The Wrong Murder* (1940); *The Corpse Steps Out* (1940); *The Right Murder* (1941); *The Fourth Postman* (1948)
Sherer, Michael W., *An Option on Death* (1992)
Smith, Charles Merrill, *Reverend Randollph and the Unholy Bible* (1983)
Starrett, Vincent, "The Eleventh Juror" in Ellery Queen's *101 Years of Entertainment: The Great Detective Stories, 1841–1941* (1942); *The Secret Life of Sherlock Homes* (1960)
Targ, William, *The Case of Mr. Cassidy* (1939)
Terkel, Studs, *Division Street: America* (1967)
Ullman, James Michael, *The Venus Trap* (1966)

GOLD COAST WALK: Sleuths

Danny April Ballinger
Calvin Bix Maling
Gregory Blake Engling
Marge Blake Bard-Collins
Jon Chakorian Ullman
Sam Cragg Gruber
Crystal Bloch
Susan Dare Eberhart
Bayard DeLancey Keeler
Sister Mary Theresa Dempsey (Emtee) Quill
Devereux (the November Man) Granger
Father Roger Dowling McInerny
Fabe Falletti Izzi
Johnny Fletcher Gruber
Sergeant Terry Flynn Granger
Ford Harling Keeler
Jake Harrison McGivern
Rue Hatterick Eberhart
Duffy House Evers
Ed Hunter Brown
Jack Journey Nash
Aurelia Kincaid Griffith
Dan Kruger Cormany

Cooper MacLeish Reaves
John J. Malone Rice
Cat Marsala D'Amato
Vincent Martin Izzi
Travis McGee MacDonald
Hugh Morris Targ
Toby Peters Kaminsky
Reverend C. P. Randollph Smith
Mark Renzler Engleman
Father "Blackie" Ryan Greeley
The Saint (Simon Templar) Charteris
William Sweeney Brown
Detective John Thinnes Dymmoch
Emerson Ward Sherer
V.I. Warshawski Paretsky
Mike Wiley Maling
Frank Wolf Davis

LINCOLN PARK/DEPAUL WALK: Authors and Books

Algren, Nelson, *A Walk on the Wild Side* (1956)
Ballinger, Bill S., *Portrait in Smoke* (1950)
Bloch, Robert, *American Gothic* (1974; set in 1893)
Brod, D. C., *Murder in Store* (1989)
Browne, Howard, *Halo in Brass* (1949)
Campbell, Robert J., *Hipdeep in Alligators* (1987); *The 600 Pound Gorilla* (1987)
Caspary, Vera, *Laura* (1942)
Collins, Max Allan, *Kill Your Darlings* (1984); *True Crime* (1984)
Cormany, Michael, *Lost Daughter* (1988); *Rich or Dead* (1990); *Red Winter* (1989)
Davis, Marc, *Dirty Money* (1992)
Dymmoch, Michael A., *The Man Who Understood Cats* (1993)
Eberhart, Mignon G., *The Glass Slipper* (1938); *The Cases of Susan Dare* (1934)
Elkins, Aaron and Charlotte, "Nice Gorilla" in *Malice Domestic* (1992)
Engleman, Paul, *Catch a Fallen Angel* (1986)

Evers, Crabbe, *Murder in Wrigley Field* (1991)
Goldsborough, Robert, "A Wolfe on Our Doorstep"
Granger, Bill, *The El Murders* (1987); *The Newspaper Murders* (1985)
Greeley, Andrew, *The Patience of a Saint* (1987)
Gregorich, Barbara, *Dirty Proof* (1988)
Gruber, Frank, *The Scarlet Feather* (1949)
Haddad, Carolyn, *Caught in the Shadows* (1992)
Hillerman, Tony, *Sacred Clowns* (1993)
Hoch, Ed, "The Theft of the Overdue Library Book" in *Murder and Mystery in Chicago* (1991)
Hyer, Richard, *Riceburner* (1986)
Izzi, Eugene, *The Bad Guys* (1988); *The Take* (1987)
Jones, D. J. H., *Murder at the MLA* (1993)
Kahn, Michael A., *Grave Designs (The Canaan Legacy)* (1988)
Kaminsky, Stuart, *When the Dark Man Calls* (1983); *You Bet Your Life* (1978)
Katz, Michael J., *Murder Off the Glass* (1987)
Keeler, Harry Stephen, *The Face of the Man from Saturn* (1933); *Behind That Mask* (1930); *Thieves' Nights* (1929); *The Washington Square Enigma* (1933)
Kolarik, Gera-Lind and Wayne Klatt, *I Am Cain* (1994)
Latimer, Jonathan, *The Lady in the Morgue* (1953)
Maling, Arthur, *Bent Man* (1975); *Lover and Thief* (1988)
McCall, Thomas, *A Wide and Capable Revenge* (1993)
McInerny, Ralph, *Bishop As Pawn* (1978)
Nash, Jay Robert, *A Crime Story* (1981)
Paretsky, Sara, *Killing Orders* (1985); *Bitter Medicine* (1987); *Blood Shot* (1988)
Pulver, Mary Monica, *Murder at the War* (1984)
Quill, Monica, *Let Us Prey* (1982)
Raleigh, Michael, *A Body in Belmont Harbor* (1993); *Death in Uptown* (1991)
Reaves, Sam, *A Long Cold Fall* (1991); *Fear Will Do It* (1993)
Rice, Craig, *The Lucky Stiff* (1945); *My Kingdom for a Hearse* (1957); *The Corpse Steps Out* (1940); *The Right Murder* (1941)
Sherer, Michael W., *Option on Death* (1992)

Skom, Edith, *The Mark Twain Murders* (1989)
Ullman, James Michael, *The Venus Trap* (1966); *Lady on Fire* (1968)
Williams, Kirby, *The C.V.C. Murders* (1929)
Zimmerman, R. D., *Blood Trance* (1993)
Zubro, Mark, *Sorry Now* (1991); *A Simple Suburban Murder* (1989); *The Principal Cause of Death* (1991); *The Only Good Priest* (1991)

LINCOLN PARK/DEPAUL WALK: Sleuths

Danny April Ballinger
FBI Agent Gil Bailey Skom
Becky Belski Haddad
Calvin Bix Maling
Peter and Kori Brichter Pulver
Detective Nora Callum McCall
Scott Carpenter Zubro
Jon Chakorian Ullman
Professor Nancy Cook Jones
Sam Cragg Gruber
William Crane Latimer
Crystal Bloch
Harry Dane Hyer
Susan Dare Eberhart
Bayard DeLancey Keeler
Sister Mary Theresa Dempsey (Emtee) Quill
Detective Boaz Dixon Jones
Father Roger Dowling McInerny
Frank Dragovic Gregorich
Fabe Falletti Izzi
Jimmy Flannery Campbell
Johnny Fletcher Gruber
Sergeant Terry Flynn Granger
Julian Forbes Ullman
Rachel Gold Kahn
Ford Harling Keeler
Rue Hatterick Eberhart

Nathan (Nate) Heller Collins
Duffy House Evers
Walter Jackson Maling
Jack Journey Nash
Jimmie Kentland Keeler
Dan Kruger Cormany
Joe Leaphorn Hillerman
Detective Abe Lieberman Kaminsky
Cooper MacLeish Reaves
Mallory Collins
John J. Malone Rice
Jimbo Marino Izzi
Detective Mark McPherson Caspary
Tom Mason Zubro
Quint McCauley Brod
Toby Peters Kaminsky
Maddy and Alex Phillips Zimmerman
Paul Pine Browne
Dr. Thackeray Place Williams
Mark Renzler Engleman
Father "Blackie" Ryan Greeley
Nick Silver Hoch
Andy Sussman Katz
Detective John Thinnes Dymmoch
Detective Paul Turner Zubro
Emerson Ward Sherer
V. I. Warshawski Paretsky
Paul Whelan Raleigh
Frank Wolf Davis

NEAR SOUTH SIDE WALK: Authors and Books

Ashenhurst, John M., *The World's Fair Murders* (1934)
Blank, Martin, *Shadowchase* (1989)
Bloch, Robert, *American Gothic* (1974; set in 1893) "Yours Truly, Jack the Ripper" in *The Dark Descent* (1987)

Brown, Fredric, *The Screaming Mimi* (1949)
Campbell, Robert J., *Hipdeep in Alligators* (1987)
Collins, Max Allan, *True Detective* (1983)
Connell, Richard, "Brother Orchid" in *Murder and Mystery in Chicago* (1991)
Cormany, Michael, *Rich or Dead* (1990); *Lost Daughter* (1988); *Red Winter* (1989)
Davis, Marc, *Dirty Money* (1992)
D'Amato, Barbara, *Hard Women* (1993)
Fletcher, Connie, *What Cops Know* (1990)
Granger, Bill, *The El Murders* (1987); *The Newspaper Murders* (1985); *The Priestly Murders* (1984); *The Public Murders* (1980)
Gregorich, Barbara, *Dirty Proof* (1988)
Griffith, Roslynn, *Pretty Birds of Passage* (1993; set in 1893)
Gruber, Frank, *The Scarlet Feather* (1949)
Holton, Hugh, *Presumed Dead* (1994)
Izzi, Eugene, *The Take* (1987); *The Bad Guys* (1988)
Jones, D. J. H., *Murder at the MLA* (1993)
Kaminsky, Stuart, *You Bet Your Life* (1978)
Keeler, Harry Stephen, *Thieves' Nights* (1929); *Behind That Mask* (1930)
Kogan, Herman and Lloyd Wendt, *Lords of the Levee: The Story of Bathhouse John and Hinky Dink* (1943)
Latimer, Jonathan, *The Lady in the Morgue* (1936); *Heading for a Hearse* (1935)
Malcolm, John, *Mortal Ruin* (1988)
Michaels, Barbara (aka Elizabeth Peters), *Search the Shadows* (1988)
Michaels, Brian, *Illegal Procedure* (1988)
Paretsky, Sara, *Bitter Medicine* (1987); *Bloodshot* (1988); *Burn Marks* (1990); *Indemnity Only* (1982); *Killing Orders* (1985)
Raleigh, Michael, *Death in Uptown* (1991)
Reaves, Sam, *A Long Cold Fall* (1991)
Rice, Craig, *The Right Murder* (1941); *The Lucky Stiff* (1945)
Starrett, Vincent, "The Eleventh Juror" in Ellery Queen's *101 Years of Entertainment 1841–1941* (1942)
Ullman, James Michael, *The Neon Haystack* (1965)
Wallace, Edgar, *On the Spot* (1931)

Whittingham, Richard, *State Street* (1993)
Zubro, Mark, *Sorry Now* (1991); *Political Poison* (1993); *The Principal Cause of Death* (1991)

NEAR SOUTH SIDE WALK: Sleuths

Allison Bennett Ashenhurst
Commander Larry Cole Holton
Professor Nancy Cook Jones
Sam Cragg Gruber
William Crane Latimer
Crystal Bloch
Bayard DeLancey Keeler
Detective Boaz Dixon Jones
Frank Dragovic Gregorich
Fabe Falletti Izzi
Jimmy Flannery Campbell
Johnny Fletcher Gruber
Sergeant Terry Flynn Granger
Nathan (Nate) Heller Collins
Aurelia Kincaid Griffith
Dan Kruger Cormany
Lieutenant John Lamp Blank
Lieutenant Frank Lesniak Michaels, Brian
Cooper MacLeish Reaves
John J. Malone Rice
Haskell Maloney Michaels, Barbara
Jimbo Marino Izzi
Cat Marsala D'Amato
Detective Joe Morrison Whittingham
Toby Peters Kaminsky
Tim Simpson Malcolm
Detective Paul Turner Zubro
V.I. Warshawski Paretsky
Paul Whelan Raleigh
Frank Wolf Davis

HYDE PARK/UNIVERSITY OF CHICAGO WALK: Authors and Books

Bellow, Saul, *Herzog* (1964)
Benson, O. G., *Cain's Wife* (1960)
Bland, Eleanor Taylor, *Slow Burn* (1993)
Blank, Martin, *Shadowchase* (1989)
Bloch, Robert, *American Gothic* (1974; set in 1893)
Breo, Dennis and William J. Martin, *The Crime of the Century* (1993)
Brooks, Gwendolyn, *Bronzeville Boys and Girls* (1956)
Byrne, Muriel St. Clare, *The Lisle Letters* (1981)
Campbell, Robert J., *Nibbled to Death by Ducks* (1989); *Hipdeep in Alligators* (1987)
Cohen, Charles, *Silver Linings* (1989)
Collins, Max Allan, *Dying in the Postwar World* (1991)
Cormany, Michael, *Lost Daughter* (1988); *Red Winter* (1989)
D'Amato, Barbara, *Hard Women* (1993); *The Doctor, the Murder, the Mystery* (1992); *Hardball* (1990)
Donohue, H. E. F., *The Higher Animals* (1965)
Eberhart, Mignon G., *Hasty Wedding* (1937)
Eliot, T. S., *Murder in the Cathedral* (1935)
Farrell, James T., *Studs Lonigan* (1934)
Granger, Bill, *The Newspaper Murders* (1985); *The Priestly Murders* (1984)
Greeley, Andrew, *Death in April* (1980); *Angel Fire* (1988); *Happy Are the Peacemakers* (1993); *Andrew Greeley's Chicago* (1989); *Happy Are the Meek* (1985)
Greenlee, Sam, *The Spook Who Sat by the Door* (1969)
Griffith, Roslynn, *Pretty Birds of Passage* (1993; set in 1893)
Hansberry, Lorraine, *Raisin in the Sun* (1959)
Herrick, Robert, *The Web of Life* (1900)
Himmel, Richard, *The Twenty-Third Web* (1977)
Holton, Hugh, *Presumed Dead* (1994)
Izzi, Eugene, *The Booster* (1989)
Kahn, Michael A., *Grave Designs (The Canaan Legacy)* (1988)
Keeler, Harry Stephen, *Thieves' Nights* (1929)
Kennedy, Delores, *William Heirens: His Day in Court* (1991)

Klawans, Harold L., *Sins of Commission* (1982)
Langton, Jane, *The Dante Game* (1991)
Latimer, Jonathan, *The Lady in the Morgue* (1936)
Levin, Meyer, *Compulsion* (1956)
Love, William F., *The Chartreuse Clue* (1990)
Mamet, David (play), "The Museum of Science and Industry" in *Chicago Stories* (1993)
McCall, Thomas, *A Wide and Capable Revenge* (1993)
Michaels, Barbara (aka Elizabeth Peters), *Search the Shadows* (1987)
Michaels, Brian, *Illegal Procedure* (1988)
Ness, Eliot, *The Untouchables* (1957)
Paretsky, Sara, *Blood Shot* (1988); *Deadlock* (1984); *Indemnity Only* (1982); "Settled Score" in *A Woman's Eye* (1991); *Tunnel Vision* (1994)
Parker, Percy Spurlark, *Good Girls Don't Get Murdered* (1974)
Post, Mortimer, *Candidate for Murder* (1936)
Rice, Craig, *Knocked for a Loop* (1957); *8 Faces at 3* (1939)
Roberts, Les, *Seeing the Elephant* (1992)
Roth, Philip, *Letting Go* (1962)
Sayers, Dorothy L., *Gaudy Night* (1935); *The Nine Tailors* (1934)
Smith, Charles Merrill, *Reverend Randollph and the Unholy Bible* (1983)
Sprinkle, Patricia Houck, *Murder at Markham* (1988)
Thomas, Ross, *The Porkchoppers* (1947)
Van Deventer, Emma Murdoch, *Against the Odds* (1984) in *Fairground Fiction* (1992)
Veeder, William, *Mary Shelley and Frankenstein* (1986); and Gordon Hirsch, eds. *Dr. Jekyll and Mr. Hyde After 100 Years* (1988)
Wallace, Edgar, *On the Spot* (1931)
Wilder, Thornton, *The Eighth Day* (1967)
Wright, Richard, *Native Son* (1940)
Zubro, Mark, *Political Poison* (1993)

HYDE PARK/UNIVERSITY OF CHICAGO WALK: Sleuths

Detective Nora Callum McCall
William Crane Latimer

Commander Larry Cole Holton
Crystal Bloch
Bayard DeLancey Keeler
Jimmy Flannery Campbell
Sergeant Terry Flynn Granger
Rachel Gold Kahn
Nathan (Nate) Heller Collins
Homer Kelly Langton
Aurelia Kincaid Griffith
Dan Kruger Cormany
Lieutenant John Lamp Blank
Lieutenant Frank Lesniak Michaels, Brian
Professor Lowell E. Gaylord Post
Detective Marti MacAlister Bland
John J. Malone Rice
Haskell Maloney Michaels, Barbara
Cat Marsala D'Amato
Vincent Martin Izzi
Detective Carl Masters Van Deventer
Dr. Paul Richardson Klawans
Reverend C. P. Randollph Smith
Max Raven Benson
Bishop Regan Love
Father "Blackie" Ryan Greeley
Saxon Roberts
Nick Silver Hoch
Livingston Stonehill Himmel
Shelia Travis Sprinkle
Detective Paul Turner Zubro
V.I. Warshawski Paretsky
Dorcas Whipple Eberhart
Lord Peter Wimsey Sayers

NEAR WEST SIDE WALK: Authors and Books

Addams, Jane, *Twenty Years at Hull House* (1910)
Andrews, Clarence A., *Chicago in Story; A Literary History* (1982)
Blank, Martin, *Shadowchase* (1989)

Breo, Dennis L. and William J. Martin, *The Crime of the Century* (1993)
Burnett, W. R., *Little Caesar* (1931)
Campbell, Robert J., *Hipdeep in Alligators* (1987); *The 600 Pound Gorilla* (1987); *The Junkyard Dog* (1986); *Thinning the Turkey Herd* (1988)
Charteris, Leslie, "King of the Beggars" in *Call for the Saint* (1948)
Collins, Max Allan, *True Crime* (1984)
Connell, Richard, "Brother Orchid" in *Murder and Mystery in Chicago* (1991)
Cormany, Michael, *Red Winter* (1989); *Rich or Dead* (1990)
Craig, Mary, *The Chicagoans: Dust to Diamonds* (1981; set in 1871)
Davis, Marc, *Dirty Money* (1992)
DiPego, Gerald, *Keeper of the City* (1987)
Gordons, The, *Case File: FBI* (1954)
Granger, Bill, *The Newspaper Murders* (1985); *The Priestly Murders* (1984)
Greeley, Andrew, *Ascent into Hell* (1983); *Angel Fire* (1988); *Happy Are Those Who Thirst for Justice* (1987); *Angels of September* (1986)
Griffith, Roslynn, *Pretty Birds of Passage* (1993; set in 1893)
Holton, Hugh, *Presumed Dead* (1994)
Izzi, Eugene, *The Take* (1987)
Jones, D. J. H., *Murder at the MLA* (1993)
Kaminsky, Stuart, *When the Dark Man Calls* (1983); *You Bet Your Life* (1978)
Katz, Michael J., *Murder off the Glass* (1987)
Keeler, Harry Stephens, *Thieves' Nights* (1929)
Kenney, Catherine, *The Remarkable Case of Dorothy L. Sayers* (1990)
Klawans, Harold, *Sins of Commission* (1982)
Kogan, Herman and Kenan Heise, *Is There Only One Chicago?*
Latimer, Jonathan, *Heading for a Hearse* (1935); *The Lady in the Morgue* (1936)
Michaels, Barbara (aka Elizabeth Peters) *Search the Shadows* (1987)
Motley, Willard, *Let No Man Write My Epitaph* (1958)
Paretsky, Sara, *Guardian Angel* (1992); *Deadlock* (1984); "At the Old Swimming Hole" in *Murder and Mystery in Chicago* (1991); "Strung Out" in *Deadly Allies* (1992)
Peters, Elizabeth (aka Barbara Michaels), *The Love Talker*

Raleigh, Michael, *The Maxwell Street Blues* (1994)
Rice, Craig, *The Right Murder* (1941)
Roosevelt, Elliott, *The President's Man* (1991; set in 1932)
Schoenberg, Robert J., *Mr. Capone* (1992)
Whittingham, Richard, *State Street* (1993)
Zubro, Mark, *Sorry Now* (1991)

NEAR WEST SIDE WALK: Sleuths

Commander Larry Cole Holton
Professor Nancy Cook Jones
William Crane Latimer
Bayard DeLancey Keeler
Detective Jim Deno DiPego
Detective Boaz Dixon Jones
"Blackjack" John Endicott Roosevelt
Fabe Falletti Izzi
Jimmy Flannery Campbell
Sergeant Terry Flynn Granger
Nathan (Nate) Heller Collins
Aurelia Kincaid Griffith
Dan Kruger Cormany
Lieutenant John Lamp Blank
Detective Abe Lieberman Kaminsky
John J. Malone Rice
Haskell Maloney Michaels
Detective Joe Morrison Whittingham
William Crane Latimer
Dr. Paul Richardson Klawans
Toby Peters Kaminsky
FBI Agent Jack Ripley The Gordons
Father "Blackie" Ryan Greeley
The Saint (Simon Templar) Charteris
Andy Sussman Katz
Detective Paul Turner Zubro
V.I. Warshawski Paretsky
Paul Whelan Raleigh
Frank Wolf Davis

BIBLIOGRAPHY

These are the books that were especially helpful in writing this guide. At the end I also have included a short list of past and present mystery writers who used Chicago as a setting but whose action either took place "offstage" where these walks do not go, or had a location too vague to use. Many authors like to appeal to the "Chicago" ambiance without being too specific. Also mentioned here are Chicago authors who write about other places.

AIA Guide To Chicago: New York: Harcourt Brace & Company, 1993.

Andrews, Clarence A. *Chicago in Story: A Literary History*. Iowa City, Iowa: Midwest Heritage Publishing Company, 1982.

Ashenhurst, John, and Ruth L. Ashenhurst, *All About Chicago*. Boston: Houghton Mifflin Company, 1933.

Bach, Ira J. *Chicago's Famous Buildings*, 3rd ed. Chicago: University of Chicago Press, 1980.

Baumann, Ed. *May God Have Mercy on Your Soul*. Chicago: Bonus Books, 1993.

Baumann, Ed, and John O'Brien. *Polish Robbin' Hoods*. Chicago: Bonus Books, Inc., 1992.

Beadle, Muriel and the Centennial Committee. *The Fortnightly of Chicago, The City and Its Women: 1873–1973*. Chicago: Henry Regnery Company, 1973.

Block, Jean F. *Hyde Park Homes*. Chicago: University of Chicago Press, 1978.

______. *The Uses of Gothic*. Chicago: University of Chicago Press, 1983.

Dedmon, Emmett, *Fabulous Chicago*. New York: Random House, 1953.

Goldsborough, Robert. "Chicago Voices: the Loop (circa 1950)," *Chicago Tribune Magazine*, Nov. 1, 1992.

Gorman, Ed, Martin H. Greenberg, and Larry Segriff with Jon I. Breen, eds. *The Fine Art of Murder*. New York: Carroll & Graf, Pub. Inc., 1993. See especially Barbara D'Amato, "Chicago as a Mystery Setting."

Hayner, Don and Tom McNamee. *Streetwise Chicago*. Chicago: Loyola University Press, 1988.

Hecht, Ben. *1001 Afternoons in Chicago*. 1922. Reprint, Chicago: University of Chicago Press, 1992.

Heise, Kenan, and Mark Frazel. *Hands on Chicago*: Chicago: Bonus Books, 1987.

Heise, Kenan, and Ed Baumann. *Chicago Originals*. Chicago: Bonus Books, 1990.

Leopold, Nathan F., Jr. *Life Plus 99 Years*. New York: Doubleday & Co., 1958.

Lindberg, Richard. *Ethnic Chicago*. Chicago: Passport Books, 1993.

Marks, Norman. *Norman Marks's Chicago*. Chicago: Chicago Review Press, 1987.

O'Brien, John, and Ed Baumann. *Teresita, The Voice from the Grave*. Chicago: Bonus Books, 1992.

Mayer, Harold M., and Richard C. Wade. *Chicago: Growth of a Metropolis*. Chicago: University of Chicago Press, 1969.

Pacyga, Donald A., and Ellen Skerrett. *Chicago, City of Neighborhoods*. Chicago: Loyola University Press, 1986.

WPA Federal Winters Project. *Chicago and Suburbs, 1939*. Reprint, Evanston, Ill.: Chicago Historical Bookworks, 1991.

Wurman, Richard Saul. *Chicago Access*. New York: HarperCollins Publishers, 1993.

OTHER MYSTERY STORIES WITH A CHICAGO AREA AUTHOR OR LOCATION

Anderson, Paul Dale. *Claw Hammer*. New York: Pinnacle Books, 1989.

Archer, Jeffrey. *Kane and Abel*. New York: Fawcett Crest, 1979.

Ardai, Charles. "The Case." *Alfred Hitchcock Magazine*, December 1992.

Bard-Collins, Joan. "Road Test." *Tyro*, no. 16, April 1988.

______. "Play Your Hunches." *Detective Story Magazine*, no. 2, September 1988.

______. "Deadbolt." *Tyro*, no. 7, December 1990.

Black, Malacai [Barbara D'Amato]. *On My Honor*. New York: Pinnacle Books, 1988.

Brashler, William. *City Dogs*. New York: Harper and Row, 1976.

Dams, Jeanne M. "The Windfall." *Woman's World*, Nov. 3, 1987.

Everson, David. *Suicide Squeeze*. New York: Ballantine Books, 1990.

Goldsborough, Robert. *Death on Deadline*. New York: Bantam Books, 1987.

Gorman, Edward. *Murder Straight Up*. New York: Ballantine Books, 1986.

Hillerman, Tony. *Sacred Cows*. New York: HarperCollins Publishers, 1993.

Hunter, Fred. *Presence of Mind*. New York: Walker & Co., 1994.

Irelan, Patrick. "Top Secrets." *Ellery Queen Magazine*, July 1990.

Love, William F. *The Chartreuse Clue*. New York: Donald I. Fine, 1990.

Oppenheim, E. Phillips. *The Million Dollar Deposit*. Boston: Little, Brown & Co., 1930.

Pulver, Mary Monica. *Original Sin*. New York: Walker & Co., 1991.

Turow, Scott. *Presumed Innocent*. New York: Warnerbooks, 1987.

Waugh, Carol-Lynn Rossel, Frank D. McSherry, Jr., and Martin H. Greenberg, *Murder and Mystery in Chicago*, New York: Dembner Books, 1987.

INDEX